American Culture in the 1940s

Twentieth-Century American Culture
Series editor: Martin Halliwell, University of Leicester

This series provides accessible but challenging studies of American culture in the twentieth century. Each title covers a specific decade and offers a clear overview of its dominant cultural forms and influential texts, discussing their historical impact and cultural legacy. Collectively the series reframes the notion of 'decade studies' through the prism of cultural production and rethinks the ways in which decades are usually periodized. Broad contextual approaches to the particular decade are combined with focused case studies, dealing with themes of modernity, commerce, freedom, power, resistance, community, race, class, gender, sexuality, internationalism, technology, war and popular culture.

American Culture in the 1910s
Mark Whalan

American Culture in the 1920s
Susan Currell

American Culture in the 1930s
David Eldridge

American Culture in the 1940s
Jacqueline Foertsch

American Culture in the 1950s
Martin Halliwell

American Culture in the 1960s
Sharon Monteith

American Culture in the 1970s
Will Kaufman

American Culture in the 1980s
Graham Thompson

American Culture in the 1990s
Colin Harrison

American Culture in the 1940s

Jacqueline Foertsch

Edinburgh University Press

© Jacqueline Foertsch, 2008

Edinburgh University Press Ltd
22 George Square, Edinburgh

Typeset in 11/13 pt Stempel Garamond by
Servis Filmsetting Ltd, Manchester, and
printed and bound in Great Britain by
Antony Rowe Ltd, Chippenham, Wilts

A CIP record for this book is available from the British Library

ISBN 978 0 7486 2412 6 (hardback)
ISBN 978 0 7486 2413 3 (paperback)

The right of Jacqueline Foertsch to be identified as author of this work
has been asserted in accordance with the Copyright, Designs and Patents Act 1988.

Contents

List of Figures	vi
List of Case Studies	vii
Acknowledgements	ix
Chronology of 1940s American Culture	xi
Introduction: The Intellectual Context	1
1. Fiction and Journalism	33
2. Radio and Music	63
3. Theatre and Film	97
4. Visual Art, Serious and Popular	135
5. The Arts of Sacrifice and Consumption	169
Conclusion: The 1940s in the Contemporary American Imagination	201
Notes	227
Bibliography	257
Index	269

Figures

I.1   'Share the Meat' poster (1942)   11
I.2   'It's Okay – We're Hunting Communists!' (1947)   27
1.1   Richard Wright   42
1.2   Bill Mauldin's 'Willy and Joe' (1944)   60
2.1   Edward R. Murrow   72
2.2   Fred Allen   75
2.3   Duke Ellington   84
3.1   *A Streetcar Named Desire* (1947)   111
3.2   *Citizen Kane* (1941)   117
3.3   *The Lost Weekend* (1945)   130
3.4   *Double Indemnity* (1944)   132
4.1   Mark Rothko, *Untitled No. 10* (1949)   141
4.2   Horace Pippin, *Interior* (1944)   157
5.1   Salvage in Yard   176
5.2   Salvage Worker   177
5.3   Russel Wright's *American Modern*   192
C.1   Marines on Mount Suribachi   203
C.2   *Saving Private Ryan* (1998)   217
C.3. World War II Memorial, Washington DC   224

Case Studies

Introduction
The Anti-isolationist Cartoons of Dr Seuss   8
John Hersey's *Hiroshima* (1946)   23
Modern Woman: The Lost Sex (1947)   30

1. Fiction and Journalism
William Faulkner's Banquet Speech, 1949 Nobel Prize
    in Literature   36
Richard Wright's *Native Son* (1940)   40
Life Magazine and 'The American Century'   51

2. Radio and Music
Eddie 'Rochester' Anderson   78
The International Sweethearts of Rhythm   82
Bob Hope's USO Tours   89

3. Theatre and Film
Anna Lucasta and the American Negro Theatre   106
Orson Welles and *Citizen Kane*   114
HUAC in Hollywood   121

4. Visual Art, Serious and Popular
Peggy Guggenheim and Art of This Century   143
Horace Pippin, Self-taught Master of the 1940s   155
The 'Critical Internationalism' of *Johnny Everyman*   166

5. The Arts of Sacrifice and Consumption
I Am an American Day (1940–52)   180
The 1939–40 New York World's Fair   185
Russel Wright's *American Modern*   189

Conclusion: The 1940s in the Contemporary
    American Imagination
Andy Rooney's *My War* (1995)   208
HBO's *Band of Brothers* (2001)   211
The Atomic Café (1982)   221

Acknowledgements

I wish to thank those who have helped me construct this project, especially its image collection: Kathryn Blackwell and Erica Kelly at the Library of Congress; Jim Gerberich and Marcia Schiff at Associated Press; Edward Gottlieb; Peter Huestis at the National Gallery of Art; Lori Moss at Manitoga / The Russel Wright Design Center; Jennifer Phillips, Laura Uglean, and the staff in Digital Collections and Archives, Tisch Library, Tufts University; Jennifer Stepp at *Stars and Stripes*; and the staffs of the University of Wisconsin Archive and the Auburn Public Library (Auburn, Alabama). Special thanks to Steve Craig, Department of Radio, Television, and Film at the University of North Texas; to Charlotte Wixom at *Studies in the Novel*, University of North Texas; and to David Peterson, Department of English at the University of Nebraska, Omaha, who was instrumental in the completion of Chapter 5.

Thanks also to Martin Halliwell, Series Editor, and to Nicola Ramsey, Senior Commissioning Editor at Edinburgh University Press, for their invaluable assistance.

Chronology of
1940s American Culture

Date	Events	Criticism	Literature	Performance
1940	1940 Olympics cancelled. Nylons sold as substitute for silk stockings. Germans enter Paris Battle of Britain (July–October). Forty-hour work week implemented, under the Fair Labor Standards Act of 1938. Roosevelt wins third term in office, defeating Wendell Willkie. Roosevelt in radio discussion proclaims US 'arsenal of democracy'.	Lewis Mumford, *Faith for Living* W. E. B. Du Bois, *Dusk of Dawn* Alaine Locke, *The Negro in Art*	Richard Wright, *Native Son* Ernest Hemingway, *For Whom the Bell Tolls* Raymond Chandler, *Farewell, My Lovely* Walter Clark, *The Ox-Bow Incident* Carson McCullers, *The Heart is a Lonely Hunter* John Steinbeck wins Pulitzer Prize for *Grapes of Wrath* F. Scott Fitzgerald dies of a heart attack at forty-four	Richard Rodgers and Lorenz Hart, *Higher and Higher* (musical) Vernon Duke and John Latouche, *Cabin in the Sky* (musical) Cole Porter, *Panama Hattie* (musical) Richard Rodgers and Lorenz Hart, *Pal Joey* (musical)

Film	Radio	Music	Art
1939 Oscars awarded – *Gone with the Wind*, wins eight awards, including Best Picture, Best Actress (Vivian Leigh) and Best Supporting Actress (Hattie McDaniel) *The Grapes of Wrath* (John Ford) *Foreign Correspondent* and *Rebecca* (Alfred Hitchcock) *The Philadelphia Story* (George Cukor) *His Girl Friday* (Howard Hawks) Charles Chaplin's *The Great Dictator* opens at two cinemas in New York; Chaplin and his wife, co-star Paulette Goddard, make appearances at both *Pinocchio* and *Fantasia* (Walt Disney) *Tom and Jerry* (Hanna-Barbera) Weekly cinema attendance: eighty million	*The Adventures of Superman* (1940–51) *Truth or Consequences* (1940–57) *Take It or Leave It*, later *The $64,000 Question* (1940–52) *The Bell Telephone Hour*, concert series (1940–58) Edward R. Murrow's London Broadcasts	Glenn Miller Orchestra's 'In The Mood' number one Woody Guthrie writes 'This Land Is Your Land' Artie Shaw Orchestra records Hoagy Carmichael's 'Stardust' for RCA Victor Frank Sinatra joins Tommy Dorsey's Orchestra Thelonius Monk begins performing	American Negro Exhibition Edward Hopper, *Gas* *Brenda Starr*, first comic strip by a woman In *Batman* (comic strip) mobsters do away with a circus family known as the Flying Graysons, leaving their son Dick (Robin) an orphan

Date	Events	Criticism	Literature	Performance
1941	Tuskegee Airmen (all-black flying unit) commissioned; will fly their first mission in June 1943. FDR delivers 'Four Freedoms' speech in State of the Union address. Congress approves the Lend-Lease Act. Cheerios introduced. FDR signs Executive Order 8803, barring racial discrimination in the war-industry workplace. Mount Rushmore completed. Japanese attack Pearl Harbor (7 December, 7.50 a.m.). Alexander Fleming discovers penicillin. Manhattan Project begins.	Henry R. Luce, 'The American Century' Erich Fromm, *Escape from Freedom* John Crowe Ransom, *The New Criticism*	James Agee, *Let Us Now Praise Famous Men* (non-fiction) William Shirer, *Berlin Diary* Eudora Welty, *A Curtain of Green* (short fiction) F. Scott Fitzgerald, *The Last Tycoon* James M. Cain, *Mildred Pierce* H. A. Rey and Margaret Rey, *Curious George* (children's story)	Lillian Hellman, *Watch on the Rhine* Joseph Kesselring, *Arsenic and Old Lace* Kurt Weill, Ira Gershwin, Moss Hart, *Lady in the Dark* Eugene O'Neill completes *Long Day's Journey into Night* (first performed 1956)

Film	Radio	Music	Art
1940 Oscars awarded – Best Picture: Alfred Hitchcock's *Rebecca*; Best Director: John Ford (*The Grapes of Wrath*) *Citizen Kane* (Orson Welles) *The Maltese Falcon* (John Huston) *How Green was My Valley* (John Ford) *The Lady Eve* (Preston Sturges) *Meet John Doe* (Frank Capra) *The Little Foxes* (William Wyler) *Sergeant York* (Howard Hawks)	*Inner Sanctum*, mystery series (1941–52) *Duffy's Tavern*, situation comedy (1941–52) *The Great Gildersleeve* (1941–57) *A Date with Judy* (1941–49) *The Life of Riley* (1941–51) Dave Garroway hosts his first jazz programme for troops serving in US Navy Bob Hope's first performance for troops takes place as a *Pepsodent Show* broadcast live from Riverside California's March Field Fireside Chat, FDR discusses declaration of war on Japan (9 December)	Ethno-musicologist Alan Lomax meets blues artists Muddy Waters and Son House Duke Ellington, 'Take the A Train' The Andrew Sisters, 'Boogie Woogie Bugle Boy' Benny Goodman integrates his big band	National Gallery of Art opens in Washington, DC Adolph Gottlieb begins *Pictograph* series (1941–50) Robert Motherwell moves to Greenwich Village and decides to paint full-time *Wonder Woman* (comic book) is first published *Captain America* (comic book) is first published

Date	Events	Criticism	Literature	Performance
1942	Roosevelt signs Executive Order 9066, to relocate Japanese Americans from the West Coast to the US interior. US government launches 'Salvage for Victory' campaign. General Douglas MacArthur leaves Corregidor in the Philippines for Australia, vowing: 'I shall return'. Battle of Bataán (9 April). Bataán Death March to prison camp near Cabanatuan: prisoners forced to march 85 miles in six days with only one meal of rice during the entire journey; some 10–15,000 soldiers perished. US air attack on Tokyo (14 April). Battle of Midway (4–7 June) Anne Frank receives diary as a birthday present in Amsterdam (12 June). Office of War Information instituted (13 June). Battle of Guadalcanal (7 August–7 February 1943). US Department of Labor's Bracero Program sends Mexican workers to the US to help the labour shortage; 10 per cent of their salaries mishandled and never repaid	Earl Brown, 'American Negroes and the War' Philip Wylie, *A Generation of Vipers*	Marion Hargrove, *See Here, Private Hargrove* (comic non-fiction) John Steinbeck, *The Moon is Down* (novel) *The New York Times* inaugurates its Bestseller List Marjorie Kinnan Rawlings, *Cross Creek*	Thornton Wilder, *The Skin of Our Teeth* (comedy) Richard Rodgers and Lorenz Hart, *By Jupiter* Cole Porter, *Du Barry was a Lady* Irving Berlin, *This is the Army* Eugene O'Neill, *A Touch of the Poet* (first performed 1958)

Film	Radio	Music	Art
Actress Carol Lombard (wife of Clark Gable) killed with twenty others in an aeroplane crash on a war bond-selling tour 1941 Oscars awarded – Best Picture and Best Director: *How Green Was My Valley* (beating *Citizen Kane*) *The Pride of the Yankees* (Sam Wood) *Casablanca* (Mchael Curtiz) *Mrs. Miniver* (William Wyler) *The Road to Morocco* stars Bing Crosby, Bob Hope and Dorothy Lamour	Voice of America begins broadcasting *Suspense* (1942–62) *The Cisco Kid* (1942–56) *It Pays to Be Ignorant* (1942–51) *Mr. and Mrs. North* (1942–54) *The March of Time* switches from dramatisations of current events to actual news reporting	Count Basie Orchestra, 'One O'Clock Jump' – Basie Orchestra the first African American swing band to play at New York's Hotel Lincoln Glenn Miller Orchestra, '(I've Got a Gal in) Kalamazoo' Benny Goodman, 'Jersey Bounce' American Federation of Musicians' strike (1942–43) Aaron Copeland/Agnes de Mille, *Rodeo*, New York Metropolitan Opera House Aaron Copeland, *Fanfare for the Common Man*	Edward Hopper, *Nighthawks* Norman Rockwell, *Four Freedoms* Peggy Guggenheim opens Art of This Century Gallery (1942–47) *First Papers of Surrealism* exhibition at Whitelaw Reid Mansion in New York *VVV*, a journal devoted to surrealism, opens (1942–44) *Archie* (comic book) begins

Date	Events	Criticism	Literature	Performance
1943	Frankfurters replaced by Victory Sausage, a mixture of meat and soya meal. To cut down on the need for metal replacement parts at bakeries, government bans sliced bread. Battle of Anzio, Italy (22 January). US begins food-rationing programme. Riot, Mobile, Alabama shipyard over upgrading twelve black workers (25 May). Race riot, Detroit, resulting in thirty-four deaths and six hundred injured. Allied invasion of Italy, Patton crosses Sicily (July–August) Race riot, Harlem, resulting in several deaths (1 August). Patton slaps a private, a shell-shocked soldier in Sicily, accusing him of cowardice. Italian surrender (8 September). Battle of Salerno, Italy, against Germans (9–14 September).	Wendell Willkie, *One World* Cleanth Brooks and Robert Penn Warren, *Understanding Fiction* James A. Porter's *Modern Negro Art*	Isaac Bashevis Singer becomes naturalised US citizen Ayn Rand, *The Fountainhead* William Saroyan, *The Human Comedy*	Richard Rodgers and Oscar Hammerstein II, *Oklahoma!* (musical) Oscar Hammerstein, *Carmen Jones* (musical) Kurt Weill and Ogden Nash, *One Touch of Venus* (comedy) George Gershwin, *Porgy and Bess* (musical) Thornton Wilder, *The Skin of Our Teeth*

Film	Radio	Music	Art
1942 Oscars awarded – *Mrs. Miniver* wins Best Picture, Best Director (William Wyler), and Best Actress (Greer Garson) *Cabin in the Sky* (Vincente Minnelli) *Heaven Can Wait* (Ernst Lubitsch) *Shadow of a Doubt* (Alfred Hitchcock)	*The Adventures of Nero Wolfe* (1943–44) *The Billie Burke Show* (1943–46) *The Judy Canova Show* (1943–55) Edward R. Murrow's 'Orchestrated Hell' broadcast	Duke Ellington, *Black, Brown and Beige*, (jazz composition) Carnegie Hall, for Russian War Relief Band-leader/trumpet-player Harry James weds Betty Grable Frank Sinatra on *Your Hit Parade* (radio programme); his 1 January performance at the Paramount Theatre caused hysterical bobby-soxers to tie up New York traffic for hours Miles Davis's career begins	Norman Rockwell's *Rosie the Riveter* on the cover of *The Saturday Evening Post* Jacob Lawrence, *Ironers* Paul Cadmus, *The Shower* In Washington DC, the Jefferson Memorial and Pentagon are completed (architecture)

Date	Events	Criticism	Literature	Performance
1944	Congress passes Servicemen's Readjustment Act (aka the GI Bill of Rights). D-Day – one million Allied troops land at the beaches of Normandy, France (6 June). Liberation of Paris (29 August). African American petty officer Robert Jones, USS *Intrepid*, shoots down kamikaze pilot, awarded the Medal of Honor in 1997 (29 October). Battle of the Bulge (16 December–16 January 1945). Eisenhower invites African Americans into combat units; 2,221 signed up, giving up military rank to replace white casualties. Lieutenant Jackie Robinson, US Army, refuses to give his seat to a white man, court-marshalled and acquitted. Roosevelt wins fourth term, defeats Thomas E. Dewey. US Army announces the end of Japanese American internment. Silicone and polyethylene invented.	Gunnar Myrdal, *An American Dilemma* (non-fiction) Reinhold Niebuhr, *The Children of Light and the Children of Darkness* Lewis Mumford, *Condition of Man*	Saul Bellow, *Dangling Man* Lillian Smith, *Strange Fruit* Betty Smith, *A Tree Grows in Brooklyn*	Lillian Hellman *The Searching Wind* (drama) Harold Arlen and E. Y. Harburg, *Bloomer Girl* Cole Porter, *Mexican Hayride* Leonard Bernstein, Betty Comden and Adolph Green, *On the Town* American Negro Theater's *Anna Lucasta* (musical) opens on Broadway

Film	Radio	Music	Art
1943 Oscars awarded – *Casablanca* wins Best Picture and Best Director (Michael Curtiz) *Double Indemnity* (Billy Wilder) *Gaslight* (George Cukor) *Arsenic and Old Lace* (Frank Capra) *Hail the Conquering Hero* (Preston Sturges) *Laura* (Otto Preminger) *Lifeboat* (Alfred Hitchcock) *Since You Went Away* (John Cromwell) *To Have and Have Not* (Howard Hawks)	*The Adventures of Ozzie and Harriet* (1944–54) The black maid character Beulah (played by white male actor Marlin Hunt) first appears on *Fibber McGee and Molly* (1935–59)	Leonard Bernstein, *Jeremiah* (classical composition) Leadbelly, 'Goodnight Irene' Aaron Copeland and Martha Graham, *Appalachian Spring* Big band leader Glenn Mitchell killed in military service, aeroplane crash over English Channel (15 December)	Georgia O'Keeffe, *Pelvis IV* Horace Pippin, *Interior* *Johnny Everyman* (educational comics series) launches a four-year run

Date	Events	Criticism	Literature	Performance
1945	Allied air raid on Berlin (3 February). Yalta summit attended by Big Three (Roosevelt, Churchill and Stalin) dividing European territories post-war (4–11 February). General MacArthur leads US troops into Manila (5 February). Allied bombing of Dresden (14 February). Battle of Iwo Jima (18 February–26 March). Marines plant flag on Mount Suribachi (23 February). Battle of Okinawa (1 April–22 June). Americans liberate Buchenwald (11 April). FDR dies of cerebral haemorrhage; Harry S. Truman becomes thirty-third president (12 April). Delegates from fifty countries meet in San Francisco to establish the UN (25 April). US and Russian troops link up at Elbe River, dividing Germany (25 April). Mussolini executed (28 April). Hitler commits suicide (30 April). VE (Victory in Europe) Day (8 May). Trinity atomic bomb test, Alamogordo, New Mexico (16 July). US drops atomic bomb on Hiroshima (6 August) and Nagasaki (9 August). VJ (Victory in Japan) Day (15 August).	Norman Cousins, *Modern Man is Obsolete* Hannah Arendt, 'German Guilt' St Clair Drake and Horace R. Cayton, *Black Metropolis: A Study of Negro Life in a Northern City* Walter White, *A Rising Wind* W. E. B. Du Bois, *Color and Democracy*	John Hersey wins Pulitzer Prize for *A Bell for Adano* Chester Himes, *If He Hollers, Let Him Go* John Steinbeck, *Cannery Row* E. B. White, *Stuart Little* (children's story) Richard Wright, *Black Boy*	Tennessee Williams, *The Glass Menagerie* (drama) Richard Rodgers and Oscar Hammerstein II, *Carousel* (musical) Sigmund Romberg, *Up in Central Park* (musical) Arthur Laurents, *Home of the Brave* (drama) Mary Chase, *Harvey* (comedy)

Film	Radio	Music	Art
1944 Oscars awarded – *Going My Way* wins Best Picture, Best Director (Leo McCarey), and Best Actor (Bing Crosby) *Mildred Pierce* (Michael Curtiz) *The Lost Weekend* (Billy Wilder) *Spellbound* (Alfred Hitchcock) *They Were Expendable* (John Ford) *The Bells of St. Mary's* (Leo McCarey)	*Beulah* (1945–54) *Queen for a Day* (1945–57) Lionel Barrymore replaces Cecil B. DeMille as host of *Lux Radio Theatre* Academy Awards are radio broadcast in their entirety for the first time	Bing Crosby, *Merry Christmas* (album) Nat King Cole, *Nat King Cole Trio* (album) Dizzy Gillespie, 'Salt Peanuts' Bill Monroe, 'Blue Moon of Kentucky' Fred Kirby, 'Atomic Power'	Willem de Kooning, *Study for Pink Angels* and *Still Life* Jackson Pollock and Lee Krasner purchase home and studio in East Hampton, New York

Date	Events	Criticism	Literature	Performance
1946	Truman establishes the Central Intelligence Agency (CIA). First issue of Roosevelt dime (10-cent piece), on Roosevelt's birthday (30 January). ENIAC (first large-scale computer) performs first function. George Kennan sends 'long telegram' from Moscow to US State Department (22 February). Winston Churchill's 'Iron Curtain' speech at Westminster College, Fulton, Missouri (5 March). 'Operation Crossroads' atomic bomb test at Bikini Atoll, Marshall Islands (1 July). Bikini bathing suit introduced.	John Hersey, *Hiroshima* Benjamin Spock, *The Common Book of Baby and Child Care* Malcolm Cowley, *The Portable Faulkner* Clement Greenberg, 'Avant Garde and Kitsch'	William Carlos Williams, *Patterson* (long poem) Robert Penn Warren, *All the King's Men* Eudora Welty, *Delta Wedding*	Garson Kanin, *Born Yesterday* (comedy) Irving Berlin, *Annie Get Your Gun* (musical) Duke Ellington and John LaTouche, *Beggar's Holiday* (musical) Cole Porter and Orson Welles, *Around the World* (musical) Eugene O'Neill, *The Iceman Cometh* (drama) Harold Arlen and Johnny Mercer, *St. Louis Woman* (musical) First Tony Awards

Film	Radio	Music	Art
1945 Oscars awarded – *The Lost Weekend* wins Best Picture, Best Director (Billy Wilder) and Best Actor (Ray Milland) *It's a Wonderful Life* (Frank Capra) *The Big Sleep* (Howard Hawks) *The Best Years of Our Lives* (William Wyler) *Duel in the Sun* (King Vidor) *The Killers* (Robert Siodmak) *Notorious* (Alfred Hitchcock) *My Darling Clementine* (John Ford)	*Twenty Questions* (1946–54) *Arthur Godfrey's Talent Scouts* (1946–56) *The Bickersons* (1946–51)	Louis Jordan and his Tympani Five, 'Choo Choo Ch' Boogie' Nat King Cole Trio, 'The Christmas Song' Duke Ellington, 'Take the A Train' Stan Kenton, 'Shoo Fly Pie and Apple Pan Dowdy' (vocals by June Christy) Charlie 'Yardbird' Parker and Dizzy Gillespie play Carnegie Hall	Jacob Lawrence, *Seamstress* Architect Mies van der Rohe begins *Farnsworth House* (1946–51) Art critic Robert Coates coins the term 'Abstract Expressionism' Peggy Guggenheim publishes memoirs, *Out of this Century* Romare Bearden criticises Harmon Foundation for supporting 'mediocre' art

Date	Events	Criticism	Literature	Performance
1947	Arabs and Jews reject a British offer to split Palestine. Truman promulgates Truman Doctrine, to halt the growth of communism in Europe (12 March). Truman issues Executive Order 9835, requiring federal employees to swear a loyalty oath. At the Big Four meeting in Moscow, Secretary of State George C. Marshall inaugurates the Marshall Plan, to aid reconstruction of Europe with western support. Jackie Robinson signed to play for Brooklyn Dodgers, first African American to play for a major-league baseball team (12 April); named 'Rookie of the Year' (19 September). Jewish refugees aboard the *Exodus* turned back by British (18 July). After labour strikes throughout the preceding two years, Senate approves Taft–Hartley Act, limiting the power of unions.	Henry L. Stimson, 'The Decision to Use the Atom Bomb' Walter Lippmann, *The Cold War: A Study in US Foreign Policy* Erich Fromm, *Man for Himself: An Inquiry into the Psychology of Ethics* Ferdinand Lundberg and Marynia F. Farnham, *Modern Woman: The Lost Sex* Anne Frank, *The Diary of Anne Frank* Cleanth Brooks, *The Well Wrought Urn*	James A. Michener, *Tales of the South Pacific* Margaret Wise Brown, *Goodnight Moon* (children's story) Truman Capote's *Others Voices, Other Rooms* Mickey Spillane, *I, the Jury*	Arthur Miller, *All My Sons* Tennessee Williams, *A Streetcar Named Desire* Alan Jay Lerner and Frederick Lowe, *Brigadoon* (musical) Burton Lane and E. Y. Harburg, *Finian's Rainbow* (musical) Kurt Weill, Langston Hughes, and Elmer Rice, *Street Scene* (musical)

Film	Radio	Music	Art
1946 Oscars awarded – *The Best Years of Our Lives* wins Best Picture, Best Director (William Wyler), Best Actor (Fredric March), and Best Supporting Actor (Harold Russell) House Un-American Activities Committee convenes to investigate communist activity in Hollywood *Crossfire* (Edward Dmytryk) *A Double Life* (George Cukor) *Gentleman's Agreement* (Elia Kazan)	*You Bet Your Life* (1947–50) *My Friend Irma* (1947–54) Margaret Truman (daughter of Harry Truman) has vocal debut for national radio audience	Frankie Laine, 'All of Me' Dick Haymes, 'How are Things in Glocca Morra?' The Weavers (folk group) begin performing	Jackson Pollock produces his first 'drip paintings', paints *Cathedral* Norman Rockwell begins *Four Seasons* calendars for Brown and Bigelow

Date	Events	Criticism	Literature	Performance
1948	Berlin Airlift begins, bringing food and supplies by air into blockaded West Berlin, sustaining residents until blockades were lifted. (26 June–12 May 1949). Truman signs Executive Order 9981, desegregating armed forces (26 July). Whitaker Chambers admits to 1930s-era communist espionage activity to HUAC, implicates Algier Hiss. After intense conflict in Palestine, leading to entrenchment of Israeli state, flag of Israel adopted. In election-night upset, Truman wins second term; 'Dewey Defeats Truman' incorrectly printed in the next morning's *Chicago Daily Tribune* (2 November).	Alfred Kinsey's *Sexual Behavior in the Human Male* Francis E Merrill, *Social Problems and the Homefront: A Study of War-time Influences*	T. S. Eliot wins Nobel Prize in Literature Irwin Shaw, *The Young Lions* William Faulkner, *Intruder in the Dust* Zora Neale Hurston, *Seraph on the Sewanee* Norman Mailer, *The Naked and the Dead* Shirley Jackson, 'The Lottery' (short story)	Second Annual Tony Awards – Best Play: *Mr. Roberts* (beating *A Streetcar Named Desire*) Milton Berle debuts as host of NBC TV's *Texaco Star Theater* Tennessee Williams, *Summer and Smoke* (drama) Frank Loesser, *Where's Charley?* (musical comedy) Cole Porter, *Kiss Me, Kate* (musical) Jule Styne and Sammy Cahn, *High Button Shoes*

Film	Radio	Music	Art
1947 Oscars awarded – *Gentleman's Agreement* wins Best Picture and Best Director (Elia Kazan) *Force of Evil* (Abraham Polonsky) *Johnny Belinda* (Jean Negulesco) *The Lady from Shanghai* (Orson Welles) *Red River* (Howard Hawks) *The Snake Pit* and *Sorry, Wrong Number* (Anatole Litvak)	*Life with Luigi* (1948–52) *Our Miss Brooks* (1948–57)	Dinah Shore, 'Buttons and Bows' Vaughn Monroe and the Sons of the Pioneers, 'Cool Water' (western) Moses Asch founds Folkways Records John Cage, *Suite for Toy Piano* Aaron Copeland, *Red Pony Suite*	Walt Kelly, *Pogo* (comic strip) Andrew Wyeth, *Christina's World* Jackson Pollock, *No. 5, 1948* Anne Redpath, *Window in Menton* After a year filled with tragedy, Arshile Gorky commits suicide

Date	Events	Criticism	Literature	Performance
1949	North Atlantic Treaty enacted (24 August). Riot prevents Paul Robeson from singing in Peekskill, New York (28 August). Soviet Union detonates its first atomic bomb (28 August). Television sales hit 60,000 per week. First Emmy Awards – Most Outstanding Television Personality: Shirley Dinsdale Layburn and her puppet Judy Splinters. *Look* magazine proclaims radio 'doomed' to takeover by television within three years. Board games: Candyland and Clue.	Margaret Mead, *Male and Female* Joseph Campbell, *The Hero With a Thousand Faces*	William Faulkner wins Nobel Prize for literature Nelson Algren, *The Man with the Golden Arm* Paul Bowles, *The Sheltering Sky*	Third Annual Tony Awards – Best Play: *Death of a Salesman*; Best Musical: *Kiss Me, Kate* Arthur Miller wins Pulitzer Prize for drama Kurt Weill and Maxwell Anderson, *Lost in the Stars* (musical drama) Arthur Miller, *Death of a Salesman* T. S. Eliot, *The Cocktail Party* Richard Rodgers and Oscar Hammerstein II, *South Pacific* (musical) Jule Styne and Leo Robin, *Gentlemen Prefer Blondes* (comedy)

Film	Radio	Music	Art
1948 Oscars awarded – *Hamlet* wins Best Picture and Best Actor (Laurence Olivier) *All the King's Men* (Robert Rossen) *Pinky* (Elia Kazan and John Ford) *Intruder in the Dust* (Clarence Brown) *The Heiress* (William Wyler) *She Wore a Yellow Ribbon* (John Ford) *The Third Man* (Carol Reed) *White Heat* (Raoul Walsh) *Adam's Rib* (George Cukor) *Cinderella* (Walt Disney)	*Yours Truly, Johnny Dollar* (1949–62) *Crime Does Not Pay* (1949–52) *Dr. Kildare* (1949–51) *Father Knows Best* (1949–53)	Ray Charles's first recording, 'Confession Blues' Birdland (jazz club) opens in New York Anthony Benedetto changes stage name to Tony Bennett at the suggestion of Bob Hope 'You're Breaking my Heart' recorded by Buddy Clark (who dies in an aeroplane crash, 1 October), Vic Damone, and The Inkspots Hank Williams, 'Lovesick Blues'	Willem de Kooning, *Woman* Barnett Newman, *Abraham* Robert Motherwell, *Five in the Afternoon* Philip Johnson, *Glass House* (architecture)

The Intellectual Context

For the United States, as for the world, the 1940s may be said to have begun on 1 September 1939, when Hitler crossed the eastern border of Germany and invaded Poland, violating a non-aggression pact made between the two nations five years earlier. This act triggered an armed conflict that would eventually involve not only all of Europe but the United States and most nations of the world until its cataclysmic conclusion – the United States's atom bombing of Hiroshima and Nagasaki in Japan in 1945. While historians read the bomb as a decisive break by which the two halves of this decade must be viewed as separate entities ('hot' war versus cold war, the Soviets as first western ally then arch enemy), in fact the bomb did as much to ensure continuity – of a dangerously armed ideological conflict, of a universally held siege mentality – as it did to separate the early and late 1940s. Popular editor and essayist Norman Cousins observed, just as the war ended, that 'victory has given us no real "respite" . . . but has created instead an emergency' as intense as 'Dunkirk or Stalingrad or Pearl Harbor'.[1] Out of victors' quarrels over division of spoils in the immediate postwar period came the alliances and oppositions that would constitute the cold war enshadowing most of the second half of the twentieth century. The momentous events of the mid-1940s are thus pivotal in multiple respects, dividing as they join early and later parts of a decade and a century.

While it is as futile as it is dishonest to attempt to interpret the chaos of human history in discrete ten-year periods (much less in arbitrary but insistent 'decades' beginning with year '0' and ending with year '9'), it has nevertheless proven helpful, and even essential, to the enterprises of personal and collective memory to do exactly that. Often, events themselves seem almost compliant in the scheme – the stock market crash of 1929, the Korean War of 1950, the World Trade Center bombing of 11 September 2001 – though more often, the periodisation of world events (and in this case the American cultural response to these) is a necessary crutch to faulty memories and small minds otherwise unable to comprehend the enormity and significance of it all. Hence the impulse to look back upon a decade such as 'the 1940s', with an eye towards the numerous historical cultural phenomena occurring just at the turn of the decade which, indeed, shaped fundamentally the experience of the next ten years. If almost as many important developments occurred at the mid-point, then hence the secondary impulse to read the 1940s as a decade that is as neatly bisected as it neatly hangs together. The study commencing here will establish the decade's important continuities – of conflict, fear, prosperity, and patriotism – that generated a well-integrated and cumulatively meaningful cultural product. At the same time, it will observe the many historical and cultural realities that changed irrevocably with the 'noiseless flash' at Hiroshima that inaugurated the postmodern era.[2]

One key event from the dawn of the decade was the appearance of silent-film mogul Charlie Chaplin's *The Great Dictator* (1940), a famous scene from which is captured on this book's cover. To the strains of Richard Wagner's *Lohengrin Overture*, the mad dictator Adenoid Hynkel does a dance of erotic conquest with a lightweight, inflatable globe. Lofting it into the air, embracing it sensuously, Hynkel (a parody of Hitler, played by Chaplin, who bore him a disturbing resemblance) dreams of world takeover, but is clapped into a concentration camp by his own storm troopers who mistake him for a humble Jewish barber (also played by Chaplin). Admirably, the film depicted Jewish persecution in a period of US neutrality towards (and wilful ignorance about) the Nazi agenda; it thus joins an illustrious company of early 1940s cultural texts, including Edward R. Murrow's London broadcasts (see Chapter 1) and Marvel Comics' Hitler-hitting Captain America (see Chapter 4), that pushed the United States towards recognising and acting upon its ethical imperative to enter the war. At the same time, the film is read by some modern viewers as dated, even morally questionable, for its essentially comic estimation of the threat Hitler posed and for its sentimentalised, comic (that is, happy) ending, when the Jewish barber assumes Hynkel's post and in a maudlin speech declares Nazism permanently defunct. Yet the film was embraced by its original audience (it was Chaplin's most commercially successful film) and is regarded today as a national treasure. It was preserved in the US Library of Congress's National Film Registry in 1997.

Given the momentous events that marked the start of the 1940s in the United States, it is not surprising that this decade's history of ideas is almost indistinguishable from its politics and its undertakings – the momentous events themselves. The leading thinkers of the decade were less often philosophers and college professors and more often journalists, senators, and presidential advisers; the debates were joined in local papers and on ordinary street corners by average citizens of all social classes and racial or ethnic backgrounds, each of whom felt s/he had a stake in the vital decisions being made on a daily basis through-out the war and at the start of the cold war in the late 1940s. Since many of the major 'isms' of this decade – isolationism, interventionism, patriotism, nationalism – verged often into impassioned opinion and even irrational jingoism and paranoia, it is difficult to speak in terms of a calm and well-reasoned 'intellectual' history in this period; the bomb's debut on the world stage elicited a similarly strong and diverse response – from patriotic support for atomic weaponry and energy, to existential cynicism, to anti-communist hysteria, to newly articulated fears of global destruction and urgent pleas for disarmament from the pacifist Left.

From Isolation to War

Having annexed Austria in 1938 and Czechoslovakia in 1939, on 1 September of that year Hitler was well on his way to a full dismantling of the Treaty of Versailles, whose terms had stripped Germany of many of its traditionally held and newly gained territories and enabled the end of World War I (still known as the Great War in 1939). Yet, as opposed to the almost friendly takeover or *Anschlüss* of Austria and Czechoslovakia (the latter given to Hitler by the British in a morally fraught gesture of appeasement), Poland had special arrangements with France and Great Britain – the United States' two closest allies – who proceeded to declare war on Germany on 3 September.

Their declaration intensified a debate in the United States that had divided the nation bitterly since the end of the Great War in 1918: whether to maintain an isolationist stance in all future European wars or to rejoin the fray so as to attempt once more to quash the mania for ter-ritorial expansion that had never relinquished its hold upon the German people and especially their iconoclastic leaders. Our tendency today is to read the isolationist stance as the conservative one; we may know of the notoriously anti-Semitic 'radio priest', Father Coughlin, who spoke approvingly of Hitler and Mussolini to his vast listening audience in the late 1930s and early 1940s. Or we may remember Charles Lindbergh, the aviator and fascist sympathiser, prominent within the arrogantly named America First movement, who spoke emphatically against American entry into a second Great War. True to their rightist roots, Lindbergh and his committee were avidly inclined towards military build-up – for maximum defence of home shores – despite their pacifist rhetoric.[3] As early as 1933, leftist Americans protested against Nazi persecution of the Jews,[4] and the interventionist counter-argument was espoused by everyone from Henry R. Luce (see Chapter 1) to the future Dr Seuss (see the following case study). But it would be well into the war before German atrocities became so plainly evident that almost every US citizen felt proud to have intervened. In the late 1930s, a sizeable contingent of average Americans questioned the sacrifice being asked of them for a second time in a twenty-year time span.

In fact, in its early days, the war for many appeared less a campaign of genocide than an excuse to advance – as University of Chicago chancellor Robert M. Hutchins argued in early 1941 – the British empire[5] or as a bonanza for war profiteers, as the eminent Columbia historian Charles Beard saw it.[6] The Swedish sociologist, Gunnar Myrdal, reported in 1943 that 'many isolationists to the left put the Negro cause to the forefront. A Georgia senator who had made a lengthy talk about the danger to democracy abroad was challenged by an isolationist co-senator with the question whether the fight for democracy should not begin in Georgia.'[7] Americans across the political spectrum thought twice about US involvement. Indeed, in the late 1930s, American munitions-makers sought to do business with both defenders and aggressors in the new European conflict, while the wealthy and prominent wished to maintain their schedule of transatlantic crossings uninterrupted by embargoes, inspections, or, worse, commandeering or attack by hostile entities. In his brief but penetrating study from some thirty years ago, Paul Sothe Holbo illuminates the inverse relationship between economics and politics at this juncture, between neutral, free trade and the various political/military interventions weighed and worried over by national leaders.[8] To sell arms to or book passage with nations on either side of a conflict was deemed an exercise of 'neutral rights' by those who wished to augment business relations by remaining politically circumspect. But since United States neutrality – doing business with both sides – could easily be read by one or both sides as an act of betrayal (for also supporting the other side), Americans across the political spectrum realised the elusive nature of true neutrality and considered instead their best options for intervention.

Suppliers to the conflict may have preferred at least one customer base if not access to belligerents on both sides but, for the great majority of Americans, embargo against *all* war participants was deemed the more neutral stance, and this was the policy undertaken in the late 1930s. Yet economic withdrawal included the same hazards as economic involvement: cutting off defender-nations did greater harm than cutting off powerful aggressors – as Roosevelt noted in the case of the Spanish Civil War – and yet again one or both factions might take issue with the limitations set in place and therefore turn upon the United States.[9] And what specifically would be embargoed? Only munitions and warships? Everything but 'ostrich feathers', since all supplies must be seen to enable the war effort in some way?[10] A further step along the path to outright military intervention was embargo against the aggressor(s), who might again take offence; defending nation(s) might read it as a promise of continuing support. When material supply to a beleaguered faction was no longer a business arrangement between private parties but a matter of national policy – as with Roosevelt's cash-and-carry and lend-lease arrangements, which allowed the Allies at first to buy and then to receive on credit essential rations and materiel – total engagement was an even more likely possibility. Embargoes carried the added moral taint, which military engagement did not, of hitting civilian populations harder than their well-padded armed forces. We see that, despite the vast array of isolationist positions held by average and prominent Americans, isolationism was less a sand patch in which to bury heads than an ever-eroding shore; whatever the United States would do or not do affected the conflict across the Atlantic, positioned it as one country's antagonist and thus the other's defender; there was no sure footing economically, politically or morally until one reached the front lines of war.

Illuminating this reality in specifically moral terms were prominent and prolific American thinkers such as urban historian, Lewis Mumford, and psychologist, Erich Fromm, whose interventionist position was plainly, persuasively articulated in their works from the early 1940s. In *Faith for Living* (1940), Mumford identified the rapaciousness of the Nazi agenda, criticising 'the denial by the fascists of the positive values by which civilised men have always sought to live'.[11] For Mumford, Hitler capitalised on the 'modern cult of the machine',[12] specifically the military machine, to produce legions of robotic 'sub-men'[13] whereby his autocratic powers could be exponentially disseminated. As would Fromm, Mumford explored the psychological aspects of Nazism and, like Fromm, indicated that charismatic, autocratic leaders offered a weakened populace power, identity (though, ironically, this was primarily a group identity) and intoxicating (though ultimately false) freedom.[14] Mumford and Fromm provided similarly disparaging opinions of the strategy of appeasement, most famously demonstrated in the Munich Agreement of 1938, by which British Prime Minister Neville Chamberlain, in an effort to maintain 'peace in our time', signed over to Hitler the strategic territory of the Czech Sudetenland. Mumford discerned this gesture not as the bribe it was meant to be but as 'an insult that needed to be avenged. One might as well offer the carcass of a dead deer in a butcher store to a hunter who values it only as a symbol of his personal prowess in hunting.'[15]

Fromm observed that, ironically, 'as long as [Hitler] felt Britain to be powerful, he loved and admired her . . . When he recognised the weakness of the British position before and after Munich his love changed into hatred and the wish to destroy it.' From this viewpoint, 'appeasement' was a policy which for a personality like Hitler was bound to arouse hatred, not friendship.[16] Mumford considered both appeasers (Britain) and isolationists (the United States) to be 'passive barbarians' who 'no less than the more active ones . . . have produced fascism . . . deny[ing] the values of mind and spirit, and renounc[ing] the discipline and sacrifice that make men truly human.'[17]

Fromm observed that modern life had given humans too much freedom – a sense of responsibility and aloneness that frightened the weak-minded:

> We have seen that man cannot endure this negative freedom; that he tries to escape into new bondage which is to be a substitute for the primary bonds which he has given up. But these new bonds [in this case, the 'volk' ideology of Hitler] do not constitute real union with the world. He pays for the new security by giving up the integrity of his self.[18]

Two years later, across the ocean in occupied France, the philosopher Jean Paul Sartre would publish *Being and Nothingness* (1943), whose thesis on existentialism accorded well with Fromm's formulation here. For Sartre, whose theories would prove so influential to American intellectuals (and earnest pseudo-intellectuals) in the postwar period, freedom is a traumatic state, indicating solitude, responsibility and culpability – likely a response to the rationalising undertaken by Vichy collaborationists during the war. As Eric Matthews puts it, the inescapability of freedom is not to be seen as a joyful liberation so much as a source of anguish: we are, as Sartre puts it, *'condemned* to be free'. It would be much more comfortable for us if we were determined, since then the external determinants of our actions could always be made the scapegoats or the excuses . . . Accepting that freedom is inescapable and total removes all possibility of such excuses: no human or individual nature makes me act greedily – if I do so, it is because I choose to do so, and the responsibility is therefore all mine.[19]

It is the cynical, nihilistic version of existentialism espoused by the French novelist (and Sartre protégé) Albert Camus that has always attracted angry young Americans, specifically the implication that our unbreachable aloneness confines us to a sort of permanent, pointless paralysis. Yet for Sartre, existentialism is a call to responsible human action that should guide human behaviour during ordinary moments and – even more so – upon the world-historical occasions of persecution, occupation, and armed conflict.

Towards the end of the war, the German-born Jewish intellectual, Hannah Arendt, who fled occupied France for the United States in 1941, published an essay on 'German Guilt' that complicates as it reinforces this vital issue of responsibility. Developing arguments – regarding the 'banality of evil' – that would play a central role in her controversial book, *Eichmann in Jerusalem* (1963), Arendt in this essay sees Heinrich Himmler as a 'bourgeois . . . functionary', devoted to family and security, the consummate order-follower and order-creator within his branch of the organisation.[20] Finally, 'those who actively organise an anti-Nazi underground movement in Germany today would meet a speedy death if they failed to act and talk precisely like Nazis. In a country where a person attracts immediate attention by failing either to murder upon command or to be a ready accomplice of murders, this is no light task.'[21] In 'Concentration Camps', an essay-review published in *Partisan Review* in 1948, Arendt explored the jarring juxtaposition of unspeakable monstrousness and the indifferent bystander: 'Without concentration camps, without the undefined fear they inspire and the very well-defined training they offer in totalitarian domination, . . . a totalitarian state can neither inspire its nuclear troops with fanaticism nor maintain a whole people in complete apathy'. Assessing the political stakes in Germany thus, Arendt draws the conclusion that as all 'ordinary citizens' in Germany were guilty to some degree, so none of them was guilty, since 'suicide' was the only viable form of rebellion in this period.[22]

The Anti-isolationist Cartoons of Dr Seuss

The renowned children's author, Theodor Geisel (aka Dr Seuss) began his career in journalism, drawing political cartoons for the leftist New York daily, *PM*. Historian Richard H. Minear observes that Geisel drew for *PM* throughout 1941 and 1942; in the first eleven months of 1941, Geisel attacked isolationism per se; once the United States entered the war, he criticised the isolationist offshoots of complacency, over-optimism, and self-interest, all of which hampered maximum war effort. His cartoon images anticipate clearly the beaked, hunched, generically indeterminate creatures that for children and for adult readers have always rested provocatively on the threshold between the endearing and the grotesque. One recurrent *PM* character, the American eagle, sported a striped top hat à la Uncle Sam, an obvious precursor to the Cat in the Hat.

Though Seuss's drawings sharply criticised anti-Semitism at home and abroad, as well as workplace discrimination against African Americans, Minear laments the artist's 'blind spot'[26] with respect to anti-Japanese American sentiment: in a 'scurrilous' drawing from February 1942 a horde of caricatured Japanese lines up along the California coast to receive their allotment of TNT and point a telescope westwards to await 'the signal from home'. Such renderings indicate the failure of both Geisel and *PM* to challenge the anti-Japanese sentiment that led to mass deportation. Not surprisingly, depictions of the actual Japanese enemy are equally racist, in keeping with (though hardly justified through) widely adopted political cartoon styles of the era. While Geisel searingly caricatures Hitler and Mussolini, the Japanese figure (often simply marked 'Japan') resembles less an actual personage than a composite of the classic stereotypes – slanted, squinting eyes, round glasses, buck teeth, foolish (or insidious) grin. Since the racial designation was unmistakable, Geisel's frequent labelling of this figure with 'Japan' seems unnecessary; yet it conveyed the sense that Japan as a whole was his target, that all Japanese are alike, that every Japanese American is an enemy – all sentiments that enabled not only the deportations during the war but the atomic bombings that ended it. Perhaps referring to the Japanese caricatures that appeared in his cartoons of this period, Geisel once remarked, 'When I look at them now, they're hurriedly and embarrassingly badly drawn. And they're full of many snap judgments that every political cartoonist has to make between the time he hears the news at nine AM and sends his drawings to press at five PM.'[27]

Geisel's penchant for the lanky, stubbly bird-creatures manifested not only as the ailing American eagle but also as the ostrich of isolationism in many of his war-era cartoons. In one, the Eagle/Uncle Sam rests complacently on the last standing tree, while an angry-looking woodpecker bearing a swastika chops down the tree of England, having already felled trees named Greece, Norway, Holland, and France. In April 1941, Geisel lampooned Charles Lindbergh as an ostrich buried to his neck in the sand on the 'the Lindbergh Quarter'. The caption asks, 'since when did we swap our ego [punning on eagle] for an ostrich?' Lindbergh (in human form) is skewered in a later sketch, petting the head of a swastika-marked dragon that has just crossed the Atlantic to reach the east coast of the United States. Another Lindberghian figure – dressed like a capitalist and labelled 'America First' – places corks on the spines of the cactus of 'stiffening U.S. Foreign Policy', lest anyone get hurt. In August 1941, Geisel depicted 'The Appeaser' perched on a small rock in a vast ocean, doling out lollipops to the ring of menacing dragon-like figures (again, marked by the swastika) surrounding him. The caption here is 'Remember . . . . One More Lollypop and Then you All Go Home'. Said Geisel of his polemical prewar stance, 'I believed the USA would go down the drain if we listened to the America-first-isms of Charles Lindbergh and Senators Wheeler and Nye. And the rotten rot that the Fascist priest Father Coughlin was spewing out on radio. I, probably, was intemperate in my attacks on them. But they almost disarmed this country at the time it was obviously about to be destroyed.'[28]

Once war had begun, Geisel continued to goad the advocates of isolationism, reborn as the big talkers and small thinkers who minimised the threat posed by war, and thus rationalised their attempt to evade the sacrifices required of them. In a series of 'War Monuments', Geisel poked fun at 'John F. Hindsight', 'Walter Weeper' (who cried crocodile tears while others bled), and the 'Wishful Listeners' (who 'spent the war listening for the sudden cracking of German morale') among others. Geisel decried the congressional windbags who held up aid to Great Britain and direct action by the United States, as well as the red-tape bureaucrats and industrial foot-draggers who also slowed the war's progress. He criticised early-victory sentiments, in-fighting, attacks against Roosevelt (even from the press), shirkers who never bothered to recycle their scrap metal, and hoarders of household goods. His tone shifted from sardonic to solicitation when reminding his audience to buy war bonds, but his sharpest satire was just as inspiring, indeed galvanising as his gentle pleas: in August 1942, Geisel envisioned a 'Parade in[to] Berlin' that celebrated the 'few of us going full blast': a tiny male figure and two struggling felines labouring to propel and play an enormous tuba – as it lambasted 'most of us doing too little' – an oversized, well-dressed man smugly smoking and 'tinkling' ineffectually on a puny triangle as he brings up the rear.

Many of Geisel's children's books adopt a similar leftist slant: 'Anti-isolationism is espoused in *Horton Hears a Who* (an allegory about the need for the US to help Japan after the war), racial equality in *The Sneetches*, anti-authoritarianism in *Yertle the Turtle*, . . . and environmentalism in *The Lorax* . . . The [nuclear] arms race is criticised in *The Butter Battle Book*, . . . Geisel's most controversial work.' It is 'criticised widely for being too frightening for children and for not using the typical happy ending format'.[29] Geisel argued that even the light-hearted *Cat in the Hat* is a 'revolt against authority' and that throughout his career he has regarded himself as 'subversive as hell'.[30] Philip Nel observes that many of Seuss's best-known children's books confronted its readership with ethical imperatives similar to those posed by his cartoons: 'Most of Seuss's books . . . conclude by inviting the reader to contemplate further the book's message. His cartoons do the same, addressing YOU [the reader] directly, asking YOU to intervene.'[31]

As complex and pointed as were opinions on these question for western thinkers throughout the war, the debate in the United States was extinguished in an instant in the early morning of 7 December 1941. A surprise attack on Pearl Harbor, a naval installation off the coast of Oahu in the Hawaiian islands, sank twenty-one US ships and took the lives of 2,400 service personnel. Theories circulated as to Roosevelt's schemes to provoke Japan, so as to force the United States from hesitation into action.[23] Yet when the smoke had cleared, the US was left with a clear mandate: set aside internal disputes and mobilise totally, instantly, and as one against the Axis threat. The once-vociferous isolationist, Senator Arthur Vandenberg, recorded in his diary on 7 December that 'my convictions regarding international cooperation and collective security for peace took form on the afternoon of the Pearl Harbor attack. That day ended isolationism for any realist.'[24] As Richard H. Pells astutely observes, 'the bombs at Pearl Harbor completed the unification of the nation. On the day the United States joined the war, Americans were finally at peace with themselves for the first (and possibly the last) time in the twentieth century.'[25]

Wartime America

In the four years that followed Pearl Harbor, the questions that preoccupied average citizens and leading intellectuals focused entirely on how to win the war, when there was time to think at all, so time consuming were the campaigns to conserve, construct, train, and execute that employed almost every American during this period. Supporting the sixteen million troops eventually deployed were millions of workers and volunteers in the defence industries – weapons, transport, material comfort, even entertainment. Even those retired, unemployed, or of school age did their part through rubber, metal, and newspaper drives and, of course, through sacrifice of their loved ones – almost half a million Americans killed and 670,000 wounded – to the voracious military machine. The traditionally 'unemployable' sectors – white middle-class women, poor whites, Americans of colour, and the physically impaired – had opportunities for meaningful, lucrative work.

As Arthur Verge observed, '[white] women and minorities particularly benefited during the war, as previously closed factory doors were swung open to them both by need and by President Franklin Roosevelt's 25 June 1941 Executive Order 8802, which barred discrimination in federal defense industry work'.[32] K. Scott Wong notes that California's Chinese communities were 'finally able to leave jobs

Figure I.1 'Share the Meat' poster – Government Printing Office, 1942. The war united Americans in willingness to contribute and sacrifice. Library of Congress, Prints and Photographs Division, US Government Printing Office Collection (LC-USZ62-91147).

that were dictated by the Chinatown economy or other limited choices such as laundries and restaurants' to 'join other Americans, many for the first time, in shipyards, aircraft factories, offices, and white-collar professions'.[33] Americans of ethnic and non-white racial backgrounds distinguished themselves on the battlefield as well, despite their often segregated status, leaving behind insular identities formed in pre-war enclaves and gaining the respect of white counterparts. The remarkable record left by servicemen of colour caused President Truman to des-egregate the troops in 1948 – a final positive outcome of the mass mobilisation necessitated by war and an early milestone in American civil rights history. Kevin Allen Leonard documents the rhetoric of 'Unity' that shaped the relationship between African Americans and Mexican Americans in this period but, in fact, unity was a goal shared by almost all Americans during the war, which encouraged them to set aside prejudice and partisan debate.[34] Even an individual's psychic disorders were alleviated or postponed on the occasion of national emergency, as noted by sociologist Francis E. Merrill just after the war:

> citizens find it comparatively easy 'to act together toward a goal' and thus purge the attitudes which cause men to work at cross purposes. Under these conditions, the individual tends to be diverted from his own problems, whose unsuccessful solution in peacetime may disorganise him. The neophyte neurotic, the potential psychotic, and the would-be suicide become so enveloped in the national euphoria that they thereby solve their own personal problems.[35]

Yet Executive Order 8802 and the Fair Employment Practices Committee created by it came into being only when African American labour leader A. Philip Randolph, President of the Brotherhood of Sleeping Car Porters, threatened Roosevelt with an embarrassing March on Washington if he did not enact legislation 'with teeth in it'.[36] Writing for *Harper's* in 1942, Earl Brown documented opposition by both FDR and first lady, Eleanor Roosevelt, who 'feared the conse-quences' for protesters and other black citizens if racist whites became angered.[37] And resistance to integrated assembly lines remained intense; Brown criticised the disappointing pay-off of 'token' employ-ment, lip service from industrialists, and a do-nothing investigative committee.[38] Massive race riots erupted in Harlem, Detroit, and Los Angeles in 1943 when white locals resented the influx of black, Latino, and Asian war-workers into shipyards and factories. In Detroit, the

Sojourner Truth Housing Project caused violent controversy when homes were set aside for black families; in Harlem, rioters protested against abuse of black servicemen and war-workers.[39] In Los Angeles, thousands of white residents attacked and stripped young Mexican and Mexican American 'zoot-suiters' whose excessive, heavily draped clothing style was thought to mark them as subversive and even unpatriotic in their flouting of fabric-rationing policies then in place.

Likewise, it was primarily the lobbying efforts and forthright reporting of NAACP executive secretary, Walter White, that inspired Truman to desegregate United States armed forces. White's detailed and persuasive *A Rising Wind* (1945) documented the frustrations of willing, well-trained black soldiers sent to Europe and North Africa on combat missions, only to find themselves demoted to the status of port battalions and quartermasters – charged with unloading ships, transporting equipment and personnel, and moving supplies – upon arrival at the front. White observes this institutional discrimination and records numerous incidents of black soldiers attacked by white counterparts for dancing with, or accepting invitations from, European women in the villages they occupied. Augmented by reports from the States, especially in the Deep South, of pathological fear and resentment leading to the assault and lynching of black soldiers in uniform, White described frustration with eloquence and force. He returned to the subject in greater detail in the autobiography he published in 1948, *A Man Called White*. In both texts, White refers to wounded African American support troops on Anzio Beach, whose willingness to run supplies under heavy fire, while unarmed themselves, proved their mettle and encouraged their commanders – all the way up to Truman – to integrate their abilities into the larger military effort.

In his massive and influential study of black life in the United States, *An American Dilemma* (1943), Gunnar Myrdal outlines the potential at this historical juncture, even as he indicates the entrenched injustice threatening every hope:

> As he ['the Negro'] finds himself discriminated against in the war effort, he fights with new determination. He cannot allow his grievances to be postponed until after the War, for he knows that the War is his chance. If he fails now to get into new lines of work when labor is scarce, it means that he has missed the best opportunity he is going to have for years.[40]

In almost fifteen hundred well-worded, closely documented pages, Myrdal dissected the pathologies of white racism and the inequities of

black life in exhaustive detail. He examined stereotypes, jokes, mis-
conceptions; disparities in African American living standards and violence against African Americans; and African American cultural life,
including schools, churches, journalism, and leadership. Throughout,
he interrogated the schizoid experience of blacks and whites in the
United States: the hypocrisy of so-called Christian whites extolling so-
called democracy and the double consciousness of black Americans
who led lives in always-conflicting spheres.

Two years later, the similarly lengthy *Black Metropolis* (1945) by
African American sociologists St Clair Drake and Horace R. Cayton
studied the racial strife of Chicago from its origins as a settlement
founded by a 'French-speaking Negro' in 1790,[41] to its role as a haven
for escaped slaves, to its current-day status as a rapidly industri-
alised, overbuilt metropolis of cheek-by-jowl slums and stockyards.
Throughout, Drake and Cayton observed Chicago's diverse populations, most of which moved eventually from stringently marked ethnic
neighbourhoods into the melting-pot mainstream, and questioned why
the city's black residents remained physically cordoned off and socially
limited. Like Myrdal, Drake and Cayton considered the importance
of the war to, in their phrase, 'advancing the race'. They documented
multiple efforts of Chicago's Black Belt (or Bronzeville) residents to
'prove their patriotism' by selling war bonds and performing bravely in
the armed forces.[42] With sentiments close to Myrdal's, Drake and
Cayton observed that 'when the country needs men to work and fight,
Negroes have a chance to prove – in a fashion they do not always have
in times of peace – that they, too, are Americans.'[43] It is significant that
both Myrdal's and Drake and Cayton's enormous studies came into
print in the heart of the war years. While some may have wished that
such controversial works had been kept under wraps until after the war,
the domestic crises described therein persisted despite international
conflict or the need to present to the world a united, democratic front;
as both texts point out, the war did not exist on a separate plane from
such internal affairs but profoundly affected, and was affected by, race
relations in the United States.

Looking ahead, Myrdal noted that 'there looms a "Negro aspect"
over all post-war problems. There may be radical changes ahead – both
in the Negro's actual status and in ideologies affecting him. America
has lost the protection of the oceans, and there will be many more
international implications to national policies.'[44] But the United States
did not need to think in terms of the post-war environment to realise
that its isolationist days were over, that its dirty racial secrets were no

longer a strictly private matter. As White observed on his way overseas to study the problem of discrimination for the first time, 'In the old days, when time and space were material obstacles, the world could afford separate racial and national compartments . . . Now England was less than a score of hours from New York; . . . and here I was on my way to probe the transplanting of racial emotions and patterns from Mississippi to the Midlands.'[45] The internationalising achieved by the war had multiple effects: not only were racist Americans broadcasting and even transmitting their unjust practices around the world, but the eyes of black soldiers – encountering for the first time hospitality in white homes and neighbourhoods in Europe, working compatibly with white counterparts who chose temporarily to set aside their bigotries, and feeling 'a sense of kinship with coloured, and also oppressed, peoples of the world'[46] – were opened. Both Myrdal and White quote Pearl S. Buck, who warned her white audience that 'every lynching, every race riot gives joy to Japan . . . . "Look at America", Japan is saying to millions of listening ears [in the contested Pacific islands]. "Will white Americans give you equality?"'[47]

The prolific sociologist and humanitarian W. E. B. Du Bois also saw race and the war – as he saw so much of life – in incisive internationalist terms. In his autobiographical *Dusk of Dawn* (1940), Du Bois, already over seventy, though he would live to ninety-five, looked back on the events of his life as these intersected with momentous race-related landmarks nationally and internationally. 'My discussions of the concept of race', he noted there, 'and of the white and colored worlds, are not to be regarded as digressions from the history of my life; rather my autobiography is a digressive illustration and exemplification of what race has meant in the world in the nineteenth and twentieth centuries.'[48] In his journalism, academic writing and social commentary, Du Bois compared the records of colonial oppression and racial discrimination of Americans to other democracies, such as Second World War allies Great Britain and France, and even to autocracies such as Russia and China. In *Color and Democracy* (1945) Du Bois daringly identified democracy within the socialist system of Stalin's Soviet Union and hoped it would not fall to capitalism in the post-war period, as many speculated it might. He noted that socialism had brought literacy, health care, and equal opportunity to the ethnically diverse masses of the Soviet Union while the United States 'had lynched 3,047 Negroes in thirty-five years, and in 1917 [the year of the Bolshevik Revolution] was still lynching over 50 a year and refusing to take effective legal steps to block this lawlessness.'[49]

Yet another egregious exception to the pose of national unity during this period regarded the plight of Japanese Americans, who were prevented from demonstrating their patriotism (and gleaning rewards for this demonstration) by a hostile, paranoid white mainstream. Attacked verbally and physically in the days following Pearl Harbor, and rumoured to be plotting with compatriots in their ancestral homeland to launch an invasion of California, 112,000 Japanese Americans from the West Coast were evacuated and interned in detention camps located in 'barren and forbidding parts' of several western states and Arkansas in the spring of 1942.[50] While President Roosevelt claimed this drastic measure was 'for their protection',[51] this extremely un-American gesture was made primarily to assuage the groundless fears (and thirst for revenge) of the white mainstream. So heedless, finally, was the intention to maintain a united front that perceived threats to American solidarity, no matter how false the perceptions generating them, were ousted with universal approval.

While race was (as it remains) the most significant divisive issue during the war, a host of skirmishes and controversies related to party politics also marked the period. Between the 1940 and 1944 presidential elections, the latter was especially controversial: Roosevelt bested his 1940 opponent Wendell Willkie fairly straightforwardly, while the 1944 election elicited a split between the 'liberal' Willkie and his rightward-leaning fellow Republicans, while Democrats argued over 'the dominant issue for liberals',[52] the vice-presidential nomination. Sharing Roosevelt's ticket in 1941, Henry Wallace was an old-style New Deal progressive with pronounced leftist, even socialist, ties and inclinations who, by the mid-1940s, had proved too extreme for a patriotic, increasingly conservative mainstream. Though he would run for president for the Progressive Party in 1948, Wallace was demoted to Secretary of Agriculture in 1945. His replacement by the more moderate Harry S. Truman as Roosevelt's last running mate marked another milestone in the decline – that began with the demoralising alliance between Stalin and Hitler initiated by the Molotov–Ribbentrop Pact of 1939 – of the radical American Left. Yet, despite the increasingly conservative mood of the country, Roosevelt, having guided the United States out of its Depression and with growing success through the heart of the war years, managed to beat the identifiably conservative Thomas Dewey that year.

Dewey would be defeated again, by Harry Truman, in 1948, despite polls indicating a Republican victory up until election day. The press leapt upon the pollsters' bandwagon, and a famous photograph from this episode features Truman, smiling with an odd mixture of smugness, surprise and relief, and holding aloft a morning-after *Chicago Tribune* whose headline trumpets 'Dewey Defeats Truman'. Pells observes that 'Truman may well have triumphed because the electorate perceived him as the most *conservative* of the candidates . . . In 1948, Truman appeared safer than Dewey, more familiar, less likely to overturn the economic gains of the postwar years.'[53] Pells notes that Truman's 'Fair Deal' programme, launched in 1949 and again probably inspired by the persuasive arguments of social activists such as White and Du Bois, was stalemated in Congress for seeming to threaten these 'economic gains', however unequally distributed they continued to be.

A Crisis of Conscience

Even as the United States imprisoned its own citizens of Japanese ancestry, final attacks on its Japanese enemy threw many Americans into a crisis of conscience.[54] We might say that, following four years of unified total action, the nation was thrust back into modes of opinion, dissent, and debate as the war ended with the dropping of the atom bomb on Hiroshima on 6 August 1945, and on Nagasaki three days later (see the following case study). If we read these attacks as the mirror of Pearl Harbor, completing the Japanese-United States conflict as it started, with early-morning, surprise, successful attacks, it is a mirror held to the sun: against the conventional warfare deployed by the Japanese, compare the 13-kiloton 'Little Boy', which left a 4-square-mile crater where Hiroshima had been. Against Pearl Harbor's status as an active military base, compare the mix of military and civilian activity in Hiroshima. Against Pearl Harbor's 2,400 military casualties compare the 100,000 lives lost at the atomic ground zero and the tens of thousands more who succumbed in the months and years following, owing to radiation burns, radiation poisoning, and radiation-induced cancers and blood disorders. Even among the bomb's most vigorous defenders, many came to regret the human toll that was taken.

It was argued that the bomb spared the United States having to invade Japan, saving the lives of thousands of American and Japanese troops by bringing an immediate end to war. It eased tension between the United States and its European allies (especially the Soviet Union) who faced the prospect of joining the US in the Pacific theatre with extreme reluctance, and it demonstrated to the world (again, especially

to the Soviets) the awesome might of America's new weapon.[55] It positioned the United States as the undisputed leader of the free world
(and, for a brief interval the entire world) with respect to scientific
achievement, political prowess, and by some circuitous path, moral
rectitude. In a speech taped for broadcast on 10 August, Truman called
the bomb 'an awful responsibility which has come to us. We thank
God it has come to us, instead of to our enemies. And we pray that he
may guide us to use it in His ways and for His purposes.'[56] Millions of
Americans felt this same euphoric gratitude; they massed in Times
Square in New York and in city centres across the nation celebrating
and welcoming returning soldiers. Had they considered it more
deeply, Americans may have felt less as though God were on their side
than that they had now, Prometheus-like, managed to steal divine force
and bend it to their own purposes.

Why was the city of Hiroshima bombed instead of (for demonstration purposes) some uninhabited island in the Pacific? Why this city
and not one with more military significance? Why this city *and*
Nagasaki, when surely one such attack would have secured Japanese
surrender had the United States given Japan enough time to find its
voice? Physicist and 'father of the atom bomb', J. Robert Oppenheimer,
who directed bomb production in Los Alamos, New Mexico (known
by its code name as The Manhattan Project), argued against attempting
a demonstration on uninhabited land, because to foil the plans, the
Japanese had only to move American prisoners of war to the site.
Secretary of War, Henry L. Stimson, in a detailed account in *Harper's*
in 1947, argued that neither demonstration nor advance warning was
regarded as 'likely to be effective in compelling a surrender of Japan'.[57]
Further, 'nothing would have been more damaging to our effort to
obtain surrender than a warning or a demonstration followed by a
dud'.[58] Yet earlier in the essay, Stimson calls 'rather silly' the concerns
of an unnamed official that the Manhattan Project would produce a
'lemon'.[59] Finally, a dud would have been primarily very embarrassing,
and United States leaders were as intent to save face as they constantly
accused their Japanese counterparts of being. And while Stimson
pointed out that both Hiroshima and Nagasaki had military significance, the implication elsewhere is clearer: pointing out both that 'we
had no bombs to waste' and 'the two atomic bombs which we had
dropped were the only two bombs we had ready',[60] Stimson indicates
that two cities were bombed in part because the United States had gone
through the trouble and expense of manufacturing two bombs to drop.
Instead of the 'last-chance warning' Stimson reads Hiroshima as being,

others have argued that this city was selected as the one urban centre not holding American PoWs and as a city, still in pristine condition, that would provide the best means by which to demonstrate to the world the bomb's devastating might.

As various persons among the 'fanatical military' in Washington DC shunned the embarrassment entailed in anything less than total success with the atom bomb, many on the intellectual Left articulated the shame felt (or that should have been felt) expressly because of this so-called success. Ironically, the very scientists who gave the bomb life – J. Robert Oppenheimer, Edward Teller and Albert Einstein – were disturbed by the damage they had wrought and spent much of the remainder of their lives speaking in favour of internationalising atomic science and preventing its ever being used as a weapon again. On an NBC television documentary broadcast in 1956, Oppenheimer recalled that at a test launch, called Trinity, at Alamagordo on 16 July 1945, a passage from the Bhagavadgita had leapt to mind: ' "I am become death, the destroyer of worlds." I suppose we all thought that one way or another.' Alice Kimball Smith notes that, among Oppenheimer's fellow Project scientists, 'many who accepted Hiroshima were deeply shocked by the second bomb dropped on Nagasaki three days later'.[61] Smith quotes Project consultant I. I. Rabi:

> I would say that we are frankly pleased, terrified, and to an even greater extent embarrassed when we contemplate our wartime efforts. Our terror comes from the realisation – which is nowhere more strongly felt than among us – of the tremendous forces of destruction now existing in an all too practical form.[62]

Eventually adding to this sense of embarrassment, two other Project scientists with deep leftist sympathies, Klaus Fuchs and Theodore Hall, managed to internationalise atomic knowledge by turning Soviet informant during the bomb's construction phase in the mid-1940s. Both thought it wrong that the United States and Great Britain shared atomic secrets while refusing to include their Soviet allies in the discussion. They feared a Western empire based upon atomic intimidation, and shared what they knew with Stalin's operatives by way of balancing the field. Fuchs was convicted to a fourteen-year prison term in 1950; Hall was never tried, owing to lack of evidence.

The role of science in this era is complex. In a new-found, empowering partnership with the federal government, and especially with the US military, scientists became the darlings of the American intellectual and cultural scene. People turned towards physicists (who developed the atom bomb), chemists (who developed a wide spectrum of synthetic materials useful during the war with just as much promise for the post-war marketplace), and technologists of all kinds for information and wisdom, for the keys to the American future. While some researchers in the post-war era continued to comply with military demands, others took the opportunity to speak against nuclear arms build-up, to establish a civilian oversight committee that became known as the Atomic Energy Commission, and to push for the information sharing that would internationalise atomic technology. As Jessica Wang observes, Project scientists were 'pushed out of their complacency by images of nuclear devastation'. They felt that 'without drastic, intelligent, and informed action, the former Manhattan Project scientists feared, global disaster would result'.[63] In 1945, a group of these scientists, led by Eugene Rabinowitch and Hyman Goldsmith, founded the still-in-print *Bulletin of the Atomic Scientists*, a bimonthly, non-technical magazine that assesses the global threat posed by nuclear arms and other weapons of mass destruction. The *Bulletin*'s iconic 'Doomsday Clock' was conceived in 1947, originally depicted as a clock's left-upper quadrant with the minute hand set somewhere between 9 and 12, the midnight hour. In 1947, the *Bulletin* scientists deemed the world poised at seven minutes to midnight; the hand was moved to four minutes to midnight in 1949 when the Soviet Union detonated its first atomic bomb. The closest to midnight the hand ever came was two minutes in 1953, when the United States and the Soviet Union detonated nuclear test weapons within nine months of each other.

Despite the scientists' best efforts, the allure of atomic energy (and the many new fields of industry it promised to open) was strong, as was the fear of communism and the Soviet Union's own technological achievements with atomic weapons. Both tended to encourage nuclear arms build-up, as well as deep suspicion of left-leaning sentiments issued from the scientific community. As Wang reports, scientists were subjected to loyalty oaths and House Un-American Activities Committee (HUAC) investigations; when the espionage scandals were exposed, the government inclined towards even tighter control of the scientific enterprise.

Military historian Gar Alperovitz has well documented the near-universal opinion among military leaders and presidential advisers that the atom bomb was largely gratuitous to the ending of World War II. These various officials had ample evidence that Japan was already near collapse, that the much-dreaded invasion would never be necessary, and that any Russian overtures towards joining the battle would surely have sufficed to bring Japan to terms. In the sentiments of General Dwight D. Eisenhower (later thirty-fourth president of the United States), 'it wasn't necessary to hit them with that awful thing'; Chief of Staff Admiral William D. Leahy protested, 'I was not taught to make war in that fashion, and wars cannot be won by destroying women and children'.[64] More damning is Alperovitz's contention that Truman knew that Japanese surrender was imminent, as conveyed repeatedly by his many advisers, and ordered the bombings anyway, so as to communicate with the Soviet Union in the manner discussed above.[65]

Considering the bombings in these terms – Japanese civilians set up as test dummies in a violent communiqué intended not for Japanese leaders (over whose heads this conversation was taking place) but for Russian ones – we see the wisdom in the editorialising of W. E. B. Du Bois, who saw the bombings in incisive racial terms and lamented the resulting human tragedy. Theorising that the United States atom bombed a racial other though it never would have done the same to its racial ancestors in Europe, Du Bois asked in the *Chicago Defender* shortly after the attacks,

> . . . is it possible to keep the secret of the loosing of atomic energy as a monopoly of white folk? Can we hope that Japanese and Chinese brains, the intelligence of India and the rising intelligence of Pan-Africa all over the world, will never be able to unlock the atom? And if these Colored people ever do, even in small and limited degree, master this language of force, it will be the peoples with massed cities, with sky-scrapers and factories, with piled material wealth, which will suffer all the more easily before desperate men in forest and on steppe, with nothing to lose but their chains.[66]

Elsewhere in the popular press, the Catholic weekly *Commonweal* immediately condemned the bombings in an editorial entitled 'Horror and Shame'. 'Our victory . . . is defiled', the editors wrote: 'The name Hiroshima, the name Nagasaki are names for American guilt and shame.'[67] Alperovitz also notes the protestations of the protestant *Christian Century*[68] and that Pope Paul the VI 'called Hiroshima an act of "butchery of untold magnitude" '.[69]

Well-known journalist Norman Cousins published an editorial in the *Saturday Review* (which he edited from 1942 until 1972) entitled 'Modern Man is Obsolete' months after the bomb, published shortly thereafter in book form. Like the Manhattan Project leaders in their scientific context, Cousins urged an internationalising of the bomb through the effective adoption of a policy of world government of all nations' foreign affairs. Cousins described the compression of both time and space created by the bomb: 'in the glare brighter than sunlight produced by the assault on the atom, we have all the light we need with which to examine this new world that has come into being with such clicking abruptness. Thus examined, the old sovereignties are seen for what they are – vestigial obstructions in the circulatory system of the world.'[70] Cousins argued that internationalising the bomb would force a focal shift from weapons to technology. Theorising that soon, thanks to the bomb, 'no more than half a week will be spent earning a living', Cousins urged those already in possession of atomic secrets to share these with the rest of the world.[71] Not surprisingly, he placed great faith in the potential of the United Nations Organization, which had been formed in April 1945, noting that the charter drawn up at that time was already hopelessly unsuited to the new atomic reality, but that it could be re-adapted to set the world on its only viable course – united and life affirming.

Cousins's populist appeal updated for an atomic era the mid-war sentiments of two very different proponents of world governance. One of these was former presidential hopeful Willkie, whose *One World* (1943), quickly a multi-million seller, urged the codification of international relations, and stressed the vital significance of China following the war. Geoffrey Perrett regards this book as 'an epochal point in America's education in internationalism'[72] and quotes a review in the *Herald Tribune* that considered it 'probably the most influential book published in America during the war'.[73] The other world-governance proponent was the renowned protestant theologian, Reinhold Niebuhr, who cautioned against idealistic notions of naturally occurring post-war peace but saw instead the need for coercion – within nations and among nations – by the forces of democracy.[74] Like Cousins, Niebuhr observed a 'technical civilisation' seized together by its own distance-shattering inventions but knew that, even while certain technologies (the telephone, the aeroplane) brought peoples together, others (especially the weapons of war) threatened to tear them apart. For Niebuhr 'balance of power' politics 'is a kind of managed anarchy. But it is a system in which anarchy invariably overcomes the management in the end.'[75] Therefore, 'the first task of a [world] community is to subdue chaos and create order; but the second task is . . . to prevent the power, by which initial unity is achieved, from becoming tyrannical.'[76]

John Hersey's *Hiroshima* (1946)

In 1946, *The New Yorker* devoted its entire 31 August issue to publication of John Hersey's non-fiction account, *Hiroshima*. Having interviewed at length six survivors of the 6 August atomic bombing, Hersey related their stories in dispassionate prose, setting a vivid scene as he did. His objective approach did not obscure the horror of his subject; the *New Yorker* issue sold out within hours, was published in book form shortly thereafter, and has been in print ever since.[77]

The narrative follows six survivors – two doctors, two churchmen, a clerical worker, and a housewife selected by Hersey primarily for being 'good interview subjects'[78] – from the moment of the blast into the days and months of the early recovery period. Dr Fujii was enjoying a peaceful morning on the deck of his private hospital; Dr Sasaki walked along a hospital corridor, and Father Kleinsorge read the paper as he reclined in his underwear when the bomb struck. (It was a hot morning and many Hiroshima inhabitants were caught half-dressed and exhausted by the long summer spell.) Reverend Tanimoto was helping a neighbour to move his possessions to an outlying area, Ms Sasaki was just beginning work; and Mrs Nakamura was awake but worn out by a night disturbed by multiple air raids. Each subject's distance from ground zero, in yards, is recorded, such straightforward data jarring with the devastation unfolding around them and the terror and confusion experienced within: Dr Sasaki working three days without stopping; Father Kleinsorge bleeding and disoriented, moving through the streets in his underwear; Ms Sasaki suffering a compound leg fracture and being left under an awning among the dying and dead for several days; Mrs Nakamura and her children vomiting after their first drink of (likely contaminated) water after hours of panicked search for refuge.

Worse yet is the devastation witnessed by these survivors, or *hibakusha*. Reverend Tanimoto reaches for a woman by the hands, but 'her skin slipped off in huge glovelike pieces'. With typical Japanese stoicism, the reverend reports that 'he was so sickened by this that he had to sit down for a moment';[79] later he remarks upon the dignified silence with which the wounded and dying suffered on that day,[80] while Father Kleinsorge finds 'the silence in the grove by the river, where hundreds of gruesomely wounded suffered together, one of the most dreadful and awesome phenomena of the whole experience'.[81] Near this same river, the priest encounters a soldier lying prostrate beneath a bush, but

[w]hen he penetrated the bushes, he saw that there were about twenty men, and they were all in exactly the same nightmarish state: their faces wholly burned, their eyesockets were hollow, and fluid from their melted eyes had run down their cheeks. (They must have had their faces upturned when the bomb went off; perhaps they were anti-aircraft personnel.) Their mouths were mere swollen pus-covered wounds, which they could not bear to stretch enough to admit the spout of the teapot. So Father Kleinsorge got a large

piece of grass and drew out the stem to make a straw, and gave them all a drink that way.[82]

In the fourth and final part of the work, Hersey takes up the longer-term effects of radiation sickness – hair loss, un-healing wounds, fever, and fatigue – that affected all six subject-survivors.

Throughout, Hersey describes the devastated setting, referring to Hiroshima after the bomb as a 'reddish-brown scar, where nearly everything had been buffeted down and burned . . . [The] naked trees and canted telephone poles; the few standing, gutted buildings only accentuat[ed] the horizontality of everything else.'[83] Immediately following the blast, raging fires everywhere and a 'whirlwind' that seems to be more of a tornado – 'a wild array of flat things revolved in the twisting funnel'[84] – indicate the ways in which the very atmosphere at ground zero convulsed in reaction to an atomic blast. Upon publication, many criticised Hersey's understated style on this heart-rending narrative occasion; a reviewer for the *Times Literary Supplement* argued that it 'spoke too quietly',[85] while another 'complained that the author's "antiseptic" naturalism evoked so little pity, horror, or indignation that the victims described "might just as well be white mice" '.[86] But in fact, Hersey's calm, observant treatment not only may be read as a respectful, subdued, even awestruck tone but may also constitute for many the most informative, 'scientific' report of the effects of atomic war that we will, with luck, ever have.

Albert Einstein reportedly ordered a thousand copies of *Hiroshima*, while the Book of the Month Club distributed it free to its membership. *Hiroshima* was translated into dozens of languages and enjoyed almost worldwide distribution only months after its *New Yorker* debut. Ironically, Japan was prevented from reading the work as long as the American Occupation Authority in Japan, headed by General Douglas MacArthur, imposed its ban.[87] Hersey's writing inspired the anti-war research and writing of psychologist Robert J. Lifton, whose several statements against the build-up of atomic weapons often sprang from a narrative of traumatised Hiroshima *hibakusha*. In *Death in Life: Survivors of Hiroshima* (1967), Lifton records the healing, instructive impact Hersey's 'humanitarian' narrative eventually had on Japanese bomb survivors.[88] As American foreign correspondents in Europe during the war brought England's plight 'home' in ways that were instrumental in involving the United States in the conflict (see Chapter 1), so Hersey vivified the incomprehensible experience of a US 'enemy', transformed in flash into a sympathy-deserving victim of massive atomic destruction.

A Post-war Nation

Du Bois was certainly correct that, even as Americans celebrated the cataclysmic defeat of their Japanese adversaries, they rushed to the aid of ruined European nations – even their former enemies Germany and Italy – in the months and years following the war. Americans supported not only the establishment of a Jewish state in Palestine but also the Berlin Airlift of 1948, which defied Stalin's attempt to blockade the beleaguered, partitioned capital, and especially the Marshall Plan to finance the reconstruction of Europe. Decades later, in his most influential work, *The Myth of the Machine: Technics and Human Development* (1966), Lewis Mumford pathologised the Marshall Plan and other such reconstructive efforts as examples of humans' perverse tendency to reconstruct immediately that which they have just destroyed.[89] The successful implementation of these initiatives marked the United States's new embrace of its role as partner and leader in world affairs, permanently jettisoning the isolationist option that had lured its constituency throughout the first decades of the twentieth century. The Marshall Plan and the Berlin Airlift also informed the United States's growing resolve to establish a firm presence in Western Europe, in response to what many soon perceived as the overwhelming threat posed by their former ally, the Soviet Union. As John C. Chalberg observes, 'The United States, vaulted from its relative isolationism to international preeminence by World War II, now chose to remain intimately involved in world affairs as the leader of the fight against global communism.'[90] On 4 April 1949, various nations in Western Europe formed with the United States a military alliance known as the North Atlantic Treaty Organization (NATO), through which each pledged to defend each other on the occasion of outsider aggression, especially that coming from the Soviet Union.

The Soviets and the West both recognised the ideological divide that would characterise relations in the post-war era. On both sides, each attempt to secure its own position by laying claim to territories in western and eastern Europe was read by the other side as an unfair land-grab, worthy of diplomatic rebuke, or perhaps the parry of yet another strategic annexation. Three rhetorical events – US foreign policy adviser George F. Kennan's 'long telegram' from the American embassy in Moscow in February 1946, Churchill's Westminster College (or 'Iron Curtain') speech three weeks later, and the issue of the 'Truman Doctrine', a foreign policy speech to a congressional joint session in March 1947 – exacerbated national concerns about an uncontrollable Soviet menace that should be stemmed at any cost. Each of these texts did the work of setting the West–East opposition in sharp relief. What had been, for many in the United States and worldwide, a shifting, multidimensional arrangement of European, Asian, and Middle Eastern nations in various states of post-war recovery, became a clear and hostile opposition between the forces of freedom (or, if you asked the Soviets, imperialism) in the West and of repression (or, conversely, classless equality) in the eastern bloc.

In his long telegram and in an article (signed by 'X') for *Foreign Affairs* that he later claimed to have authored, Kennan stressed the rapidly organising threat Stalin represented. As Fraser and Murray observe, 'In combating Soviet aims, Kennan argued for "a policy of firm containment, designed to confront the Russians with unalterable counter-force at every point where they show signs of encroaching upon the interests of a peaceful and stable world"'.[91] At a speaking opportunity provided (and attended) by Truman at Westminster College in Truman's home state of Missouri, Churchill, in even more vivid terms, warned of an 'iron curtain' that had descended 'from Stettin in the Baltic to Trieste in the Adriatic'. In his speech to Congress in 1947, Truman pressed for American commitment to finance the struggle against communism wherever it cropped up in the world. His immediate request was for $400 million to assist Greece and Turkey, but his 'doctrine', within which he again drew a sharp line between a free, democratic West and an oppressed, suppressed East, would influence the foreign policy of the United States for much of the rest of the twentieth century.[92] These and other widely influential political statements led to a nationwide hysteria regarding foreign-born or home-grown communist infiltration that would ruin the careers of many in government, education and entertainment. The Red Scare reached its height, under the instigation of Senator Joseph McCarthy, in the 1950s but was already creating a distinctly unintel-lectual context of heedless overreaction in the late 1940s.

In 1947, the prolific journalist and founding editor of the *New Republic*, Walter Lippmann, dissected Kennan's arguments in a slim but searing polemic entitled *The Cold War*, bringing that phrase into common currency. Lippmann called into question the logistics of con-tainment – pointing out the vastness of the Eurasian territory at stake and the ways in which following Stalin step for step at conceivably dozens of unrelated, unpredicted points of contact would be expensive beyond imagination, would require the State Department to comman-deer the legislative and budgetary powers of Congress, would require the United States to do business with the most unsavoury of agent-dictators, and would mean that foreign policy was in effect being con-trolled by Stalin himself. Instead, Lippmann argued, the participants in the Yalta Conference shortly before VE (Victory in Europe) Day – 8 May 1945 – should have shifted away from the business of dividing spoils to pressing for the unmitigated withdrawal of all non-European

Figure I.2 'It's Okay – We're Hunting Communists!' This Herblock cartoon from 1947 pokes fun at the anti-communist hysteria that divided post-war Americans and led to their rights being trampled by an overzealous Congress. © by The Herblock foundation.

armies (American, British and Russian) from European soil. With the Red Army firmly tucked within Soviet territory, Lippmann theorised, central European nations teetering between western and eastern-bloc ideologies would have greater hope to organise themselves into viable democracies, and any step outside its home territory by the Red Army could be read straightforwardly as an act of aggression, more easily because more directly countered by western forces. It is difficult to think back upon the military and political briar patches stumbled into by the United States throughout the 1960s, 1970s and 1980s and not assent to the wisdom of Lippmann's prescription. While he argued that his proposed strategy was not new isolationism,[93] it is interesting that his argument begins – in defence of law-makers' and private citizens' right to conduct independent business – exactly where the isolationist/ interventionist debate centred before the war.

As he theorised on the pathology of Nazism so persuasively during the United States's isolationist days, so Erich Fromm in 1947 not only confirmed America's growing sense of the evils of communism but presented the eastern bloc as a mirror before which Westerners should observe their own weaker, but still discernible, likeness. For Fromm, both East and West had succumbed to some degree to the threat of authoritarian dictatorship. He psychoanalysed the typical communist citizen who, through fear and submission, 'loses power to make use of all those capacities which make him truly human; his reason ceases to operate; he may be intelligent, he may be capable of manipulating things and himself, but he accepts as truth that which those who have power over him call the truth'. At the same time, however, the 'promise for development of man which is absent in any kind of dictatorship' is 'a promise only, not a fulfillment'.[94] Instead of a political dictator, Fromm argues, the West bows down to 'the anonymous power of the market, of success, of public opinion . . . and of [borrowing Mumford's metaphor] the machine whose servants we have become'.[95]

In terms such as these, Fromm outlined the crises of conscience – with respect to consumerism, capitalism, and conformity – that would preoccupy analysts of the United States's domestic scene for the next fifteen years. As the war ended, the United States – or the white middle-class United States at any rate – burgeoned into a nation of shoppers, spenders, and suburbanites whose men commuted to the city on a daily basis, maintaining, even as they transformed and diminished, the urban centre, and whose women quietly raised children in remote, interchangeable suburbs. Buttressed by a still-booming economy – some had feared that the end of war would reinstate the Depression – and by the GI Bill whose subsidised college study opened new professional worlds, middle-class men found new 'identity' in corporate and government bureaucracies, while women's record of accomplishment during the war years gained them little professional ground in the post-war period.

While thousands of American women – single, middle aged, even newly married or raising small children – 'riveted' their way through the war years with remarkably productive results to show for it,[96] returning veterans were quick to reach for the jobs women had held and lashed out intensely when women protested (see the following case study). Even before the war ended, FBI Director J. Edgar Hoover associated 'crime' and 'perversion' with a working mother's neglect of children; for Hoover, 'her patriotic duty is not on the factory front. It is on the home front!'[97] A commentator for the *San Francisco Chronicle* envisioned a post-conflict 'war on women' who attempted to maintain their current employment status. D'Ann Campbell observes that in the war years,

> [t]he labor unions, cresting in size and political power, yet fearful that postwar reaction would sweep away their astounding new gains, distrusted and even feared women. No one who switched into and out of the labor force, and who proclaimed primary loyalty to the family, could fit the intensely masculine image of the brotherhood banded together. The willingness of wives and single women to work for less pay than men demanded was even more disturbing.[98]

While the *Wall Street Journal* announced that three-quarters of working women planned to keep their jobs after the war, pressure was felt from every quarter – official, cultural, interpersonal – to return to domestic quarters.[99] Early in the war, the iconoclastic Philip Wylie published *A Generation of Vipers*, a massively influential polemic against mainstream American mores whose most famous argument, against 'momism', blamed women for the United States (that is, American men's) obsession to consume, succeed and conform. In fact, however, it is women who were manipulated by such obsessions – generated by men themselves – in an effort to return them acquiescently to housekeeping and child-raising. Gluck describes how advertisements in women's magazines prepared 'women for her [*sic*] postwar return to domesticity',[100] while May cites 'government propaganda during the war' as having 'laid the groundwork for the massive layoffs of female employees after the war'.[101]

Thus, the war was a national emergency that opened doors of employment and equality to large sectors of the nation's previously disenfranchised citizens, even as it was an exercise in ultra-patriotism that enabled intense commitment to capitalism, consumption, anti-communism, and the reassertion of old biases in the post-war era. Yet, despite the rightward shift that returned white women and Americans of colour to the ranks of the second class in the late 1940s and throughout the following decade, the roots of 1960s-era civil rights and feminist movements are directly traceable to the remarkable gains made during the war – and even more so to their frustrating loss in the late 1940s.

Modern Woman: The Lost Sex (1947)

In 1947, sociologist Ferdinand Lundberg and psychiatrist Marynia F. Farnham, published *Modern Woman: The Lost Sex*, a treatise on the 'crisis' in modern femininity as influential at that moment as it is notorious today. Responding to, and exacerbating, the backlash against women – especially the newly enlightened generation of war-era servicewomen and industrial workers – Lundberg and Farnham's 'historical' perspective roots the tragedy of liberated womanhood in the writings of the eighteenth-century feminist Mary Wollstonecraft, castigated by Lundberg and Farnham for supposedly originating the phenomenon of female discontent. Interestingly, these authors are as opposed to professional ('masculinised' or 'modern') women as they are to the hyper-feminised, overly made-up 'women of fashion' whose desperate attempts to 'trick themselves out'[102] for male approval indicate the depth of modern men's disinterest and distaste. Their woman of fashion is close to Philip Wylie's 'Mom', who stays at home developing her taste for material goods and mercilessly drives her husband and children to keep up pretentious, untenable appearances. Despite the threats posed, seemingly everywhere, by this new entity, Lundberg and Farnham indicate that feminists fool themselves when they tout a women's revolution: in fact, few women have worked or have wanted to work, even during the war;[103] few women control household finances as advertisers would have us believe;[104] and 'military women' constitute 'the utmost formal expression of free-flowing penis envy'.[105] In the authors' estimation,

> the WAC, WAVE, SPAR, WASP (air ferrying pilots), and women's Marine auxiliary were the masculinity complex institutionalised, pure and simple. All their work could have been done just as well without uniforms, military procedure, or barracks formation, which would, of course, have deprived the entire business of its chief attraction.[106]

Not surprisingly, Lundberg and Farnham cite the damage done to modern women's neglected, neurotic children and perhaps especially their beset fiancés and husbands. The authors are adamant – although amusingly elliptical – regarding the damage done by women's preference for the selfish, 'external' (clitoral), instead of natural, feminine (vaginal) organism. Limited in her enjoyment of the sex act by her 'unconscious wish herself to possess the organ upon which she must thus depend',[107] modern woman alienates herself from her husband, her own sexual enjoyment, and her procreative biological goals – without which sex cannot be fully experienced. Despite the trouble caused by women's 'infantile' pursuit of clitoral stimulation,[108] the authors are forced to admit that 'the percentage of women so oriented must be enormously high'.[109] In a complimentary moment, nevertheless fraught with racist implications, Lundberg and Farnham point approvingly to the 'uneducated Negro women' of Alfred Kinsey's first major study of sexuality, who report '100 per cent full orgastic reaction', as opposed to the neurotic, overeducated (that is, white, middle-class) women analysed elsewhere in Kinsey's data.[110]

Other egregious examples of these authors' patent ideological assumptions masquerading as unassailable science include their diagnoses of the 'celibate' woman as a 'homosexual',[111] the desire for contraception as a 'psychic disorder',[112] and the pregnant woman's bouts of nausea and vomiting as women's 'unconscious . . . attempt to rid themselves of the foetus'.[113] While this book was a bestseller in the late 1940s, Dorothy Parker critiqued its blatant double standard, Ethel Goldwater in a 1947 *Commentary* denounced it as a pseudo-scientific 'attack';[114] and Margaret Mead in her review for the *New York Times* found it 'disappointing'.[115] Writing for *International Socialist Review* in 1962, Hedda Grant called the work 'vicious', while a year later Betty Friedan regarded *Modern Woman* as seminal to the flood of anti-feminist writing found in women's magazines for the next fifteen years.[116] She dismissed its authors as two of many of 'Freud's popularisers', while letting the outrageousness of the material she quotes speak for itself.[117] *Modern Woman* codifies (and very likely was originally responsible for) much of the pathologising of normal female sexuality, as well as women's normal desire for freedom and equality, that occurred in the middle twentieth century. The damage it did to women as a class, and to a generation of individual women readers, is immeasurable.

Conclusion

As with the intellectual debates that characterised this decade, the cultural forms that flourished in this period, despite their status as escapism and mere entertainment, spoke with equal vitality on its major themes: isolationism, patriotism, equality for all Americans, the realities of war, and the sublimities and absurdities of the atomic age. In each of the chapters that follow, the role played by war's massive exigencies will feature prominently, as will the complex sensations of relief and continued (even worsened) fear that characterised the second half of the decade. Some of the decade's most popular genres (for instance, music and film) marked the split between war and post-war by undergoing striking transitions of their own, while others (for instance, fiction and radio) continued to develop (or, in the case of radio, give way to the inevitable takeover of television) with little sense of a clear break in 1945. Also, in contrast to the overall shift to the political right throughout the decade, modern jazz, post-war visual art forms, and even Hollywood's social problem films constituted progressive, if not radical, alternatives to the accessibility and patriotism of their war-era precursors. Thus, the politics of these forms are as dynamic and complex as are their artistic qualities; in this book, the major cultural modes of the decade – fiction and journalism (discussed in Chapter 1), radio and music (discussed in Chapter 2), theatre and film (discussed in Chapter 3), and serious and popular visual art (discussed in Chapter 4) – will be considered for their artistic and entertainment value, as well as for the role each played in responding to, challenging, and illuminating the major world events that defined their historical moment.

Chapter 5 explores the arts of sacrifice and consumption raised to new levels in the first and second halves of the 1940s, respectively. While I mean this term generally in both cases – in that, Americans rather excelled at both doing without during the war and revelling in material wealth immediately after – I also mean it specifically and literally: in the early 1940s, public displays of patriotism and sacrifice by the home-front population made a significant cultural statement, as did performance and installation art; in the late 1940s, the art of 'easier living' (design guru Russel Wright's coinage) was enabled by an array of technologies innovated during the war and by the offerings of that era's great designers, who beautified (or at least 'modernized') dishware, furniture, vehicles, public and private spaces, cityscapes, and lifestyle itself in momentous ways. While all of the cultural formats explored in *American Culture in the 1940s* respond directly or indirectly to the World War II and its aftermath, the artistic modes examined in Chapter 5 were inventions of the war itself. While their status as cultural 'by-product' compares poorly to the equality and freedom bloodily and finally secured in battle, they are 'the arts of war' that involved neither military strategising nor maximising enemy casualties, that helped win the war in the first place, and that continue in their diverse and dynamic ways to benefit and inspire.

Chapter 1

Fiction and Journalism

Novel-writing and news coverage during the 1940s had history in common, since novelists responded as intensely to the war and its aftermath – even if by shunning the topical in their work – as did the reporters who recounted the decade's major events day by day. The 'anti-war' sentiments of some major novelists, and especially of the professional critics who extolled their greatness, sprang much less from leftist, pacifist sentiments than from a conservative ahistoricist tendency towards 'universal' human themes that, it was felt, would ensure continuing relevance and significance for the work in question. This chapter will explore the trends in print culture that spanned the decade: novelists and critics eschewed 'politics' in literature (never mind that the war-themed novels they wrote and discussed overflowed with historical and cultural content and theme), while journalists revelled in the politics of the era. Publishers, editors, and columnists espoused strongly slanted views on the Roosevelt administration, World War II, the atom bomb, and the communist threat, while reporters risked their lives and performed invaluable national service by retrieving their stories from the theatres of war.

Two Critical Trends – Existentialism and New Criticism

Major American fiction of the 1940s flourished in two categories, the war being (not surprisingly) one of these, and the American South (perhaps quite surprisingly) being the other. I define the war novel as any canonical work from the decade focused on the war itself and/or on an alienated, seemingly shell-shocked, solitary male – often at war with (and often defeated by) an undifferentiated, uncaring mass society. These pushed-to-the-limit loners enlarge upon, or in certain cases anticipate, the specific intellectual phenomenon of existentialism that swept philosophical and literary circles in the United States (and especially France where it largely originated) throughout the decade. An important feature of existentialism is its emphasis on the individual's (in 1940s' parlance, 'man's') interminable, overwhelming solitude and the moral choices one is forced to make when one realises the pointless absurdity of lived existence. A figure whom Elisabeth A. Wheeler has described as 'the lone violent man' stalks ubiquitously through weathered urban environments and bloodied battlefields (in present experience or in traumatic, irrepressible memories), finding himself the only reliable resource in desperate circumstances yet often losing the pitched battle despite heroic attempts to survive.

Linked with cynicism, nihilism, and (in a specifically historical context), the traumas and tragedies of war, the existential gesture is observed in the hero's 'turning inward in an attempt at … self-discovery'.[1] This comment comes during Malcolm Bradbury's analysis of Saul Bellow's first novel, *The Dangling Man* (1944), in which Joseph, riddled with anxiety as he awaits the draft, 'looks to the army with relief, crying "Long live regimentation!"' when he is at last called to serve and perhaps sacrifice his life.[2] This puzzling sentiment is even more 'Existentialist' than is its speaker's inward turning, in that it enacts Sartre's description of 'bad faith', or the shrugging off of existential responsibility. Yet it is the protagonist's initial retreat into the self that defines the act of existential self-discovery during this period for Bradbury and for many of his fellow critics. From a sociological perspective, Frederick R. Karl (who also regards *Dangling Man* as a watershed novel) observed: 'That surface of life so beloved by the popular press and by *Time* and *Life* magazines drove an ever deeper wedge between the serious novelist (who appeared subversive, unpatriotic) and the more popular panderers of confectionary culture.'[3]

In literary criticism, this was the era of the New Criticism, an inward-turning interpretive method in its own right that, like the existentialist novelists it analysed, de-emphasised the historical and biographical aspects of a work's origins to focus exclusively (and some would say ultra-conservatively) on the work itself. While there is an important difference between turning one's back on a horrific war as a post-traumatic coping mechanism and turning one's back because of indifference or greed (the difference, in short, between shell shock and isolationism), in all cases, ahistoricism was read and celebrated as a prevailing trend in fiction of the 1940s. The body of literature that hailed from the seemingly insular, deeply conservative South only enlarged the trend: Lawrence H. Schwartz notes that critics shaped Faulkner, for instance, into 'an emblem of the freedom of the individual under capitalism, as a chronicler of the plight of man in the modern world. Faulkner was seen to exemplify the same values that Western intellectuals saw in capitalism that made it superior to communism.'[4] In his Nobel Prize acceptance speech, Faulkner, in fact, eschewed capitalist greed as heartily as he did communist repression, though he called upon fellow writers to ignore the distracting anxieties of the atomic age when embarking upon the artistic process (see the following case study).

For decades, Faulkner and fellow Southerners publishing in the 1940s – Carson McCullers, Katherine Anne Porter, Robert Penn Warren, and Eudora Welty – were read as fitting into this conservative tradition, bolstered no doubt by the conservative critical stance of the New Critics themselves, many of whom began their careers identified with the conservative Fugitive Poet and Southern Agrarian movements centred at Vanderbilt University in the 1920s and 1930s. Fugitive Agrarians who wrote in the New Critical tradition included Warren himself as well as John Crowe Ransom and Cleanth Brooks; Ransom published an inaugural volume of essays, *The New Criticism*, in 1941, and Brooks's major works from this decade include *Understanding Fiction* (1943) and *The Well-Wrought Urn* (1947). The New Critics' ensconcement in higher-learning institutions marked a shift of the task (and privilege) of literary taste-making to English departments from popular journals, especially those publishing H. L. Mencken who reigned as the nation's most noteworthy literary critic throughout the 1920s and 1930s. Their origins as poets themselves, as well as the reference in Brooks's 1948 title to Keats's canonical work, 'Ode on a Grecian Urn', indicate their interpretive focus on poetry; although they turned their methods upon drama and fiction as well, it may be argued that intensely concentrated, language-oriented poetry is the most 'inward turning' of all the genres and thus best suited to the New Critics' interpretive approach.

From the vantage point of the present day, it is difficult to ignore the vital historical contexts of the major novels of the 1940s. The war novels' depiction of the conflict is fundamental to our understanding of them, African American canonical works present an existential hero from a specifically black perspective, and white Southern novels focus on race, class, and sexual identity in essential ways. Regarding *Intruder in the Dust* (1948), Faulkner himself wrote that 'the premise [was] that white people in the south, before the North or the govt. or anybody else, owe and must pay a responsibility to the negro'.[5] His reference to humans' 'responsibility' to each other returns us to the radical aspect of Sartre's existentialism, regarding the burdens freedom placed upon each individual.

William Faulkner's Banquet Speech, 1949 Nobel Prize in Literature

William Faulkner's receipt of the 1949 Nobel Prize in Literature was a most auspicious ending to a decade that began with difficulty for an author now recognised as a master of the twentieth-century novel form. Mid-decade, in the midst of financial troubles, intensifying alcoholism and a stormy marriage, his flagging career was rejuvenated by the efforts of a devoted literary critic, Malcolm Cowley, who made an intimidating literary master more accessible to a wide readership with his aptly named *The Portable Faulkner* (1946). It is rumoured that Faulkner was drinking up until the day he delivered his acceptance speech in Stockholm; whether he was drunk (or hung over) as he spoke or not, the recording from that event captures his voice stumbling over and having to rephrase certain passages or rushing through others that might have been delivered with more resonance, irony or conviction.[6] In other words, the speech sounded somewhat *road*, and read rather carelessly, while the writing itself, minimally revised for publication in *Essays, Speeches, and Public Letters* (1966), is remarkable for its fine phrasing and the striking position it espoused. Although Faulkner's monotonous delivery disguised the fact in its original moment, the speech is a fist-shaking protest by an angry man, a passionate call – *not* to arms but to 'the young men and women already dedicated to the same anguish and travail [of writing], among whom is already the one who will some day stand here where I am standing'. Faulkner emphatically rejects what he perceives to be the preoccupying question of the moment – 'When will I be blown up?' – because writing focused on this matter, and all matters local, historical, and topical, result in literature 'ephemeral and doomed'.

In textbook New Critical fashion, Faulkner enjoins would-be laureates to turn their talents towards 'the old universal truths', which include honour, pity, compassion and sacrifice, in short, the only theme towards which all literature ought to tend: 'the problems of the human heart in conflict with itself'. William Moss notes that Faulkner's speech was the first of many he would make throughout the 1950s – as goodwill ambassador for the United States government as well as on his own behalf – regarding the need to protect individual freedom from government incursion of any kind. Moss notes that Faulkner 'came to see the great conflict not as one of competing ideologies but as a struggle for the integrity of the individual in conflict with any group or mass'.[7] While in the speech he regards as 'the basest thing' the 'physical fear' that distracts from a writer's higher calling, in fact Faulkner's turn from 'doomed' historical writing towards 'enduring' universal literature that will survive any catastrophe is itself a fear response, an answer to the bomb's imminent threat to annihilate humankind, leaving only its works behind.

Existentialism, Naturalism and the War

If in existentialist terms, the modern fiction hero is burdened by freedom and the responsibility to self and others this brings, in another sense he is simply constrained by forces beyond his control and shares some features of the naturalist protagonist of the 1920s and 1930s. For the leading men of Ernest Hemingway's *For Whom the Bell Tolls*, Norman Mailer's *The Naked and the Dead*, and Irwin Shaw's *The Young Lions*, the absurdities of war (and especially the military organisation) physically confine and mortally threaten; for the heroes of Richard Wright's *Native Son* (1940) and Chester Himes's *If He Hollers Let Him Go* (1945) it is race and a harsh oppressive city. Like Wright's Bigger Thomas, Algren's Frankie Machine (from *The Man with the Golden Arm*) is a doomed denizen of the underclass, addicted to heroin and chained by guilt – his drink driving resulting in his wife's paraplegia – in a loveless marriage. In their diverse ways, both Wright's and Himes's crime novels (especially Himes's) belong to the sensationalist detective genre of the era whose hard-boiled heroes included Raymond Chandler's Philip Marlowe in *Farewell, My Lovely* (1940) and Mickey Spillane's Mike Hammer in *I, the Jury* (1947).

In Hemingway's *For Whom the Bell Tolls*, his only novel of 1940s, traditional forms of combat are replaced by the manoeuvres of war machines (especially aeroplanes), making war-related wounds and death in the Spanish Civil War as dishonourable as they are inevitable. While Hemingway's hero, Robert Jordan, begins the story ready to sacrifice his life for the Republican cause, the meaning of this gesture is taken from him in the course of the story, and he is yet another disillusioned war hero in the existentialist pantheon of this decade. As Hemingway wound down a career that had flourished in the 1920s and 1930s and would end with the late, triumphant *Old Man and the Sea* (1952) and his suicide in 1961, Mailer and Shaw were two war-hardened young Turks whose combat experience served them well in the creation of first-time, best-selling literary works. Both *The Naked and the Dead* and *The Young Lions* present a diverse cast of soldiers who find themselves in conflict with each other and themselves as often as they are with the enemy. Mailer's hyper-masculine anti-heroes are Sergeant Croft and Major Cummings; their sadistic leadership creates an atmosphere of absurdity, cynicism, and doom that rings with existentialist overtones. *The Young Lions* features a young and honourable German soldier named Christian Diestl, along with two Americans – a sensitive Jewish youth named Noah Ackerman and a playboy playwright named

Michael Whiteacre. Despite the heroic qualities of Diestl, he kills
Ackerman at the end of the novel and is then done in by Whiteacre.
Both novels were made into successful films in 1958. Two exceptions to
the pessimistic bent of these forays into existential heroism are William
Saroyan's *The Human Comedy* (1943) and John Hersey's *A Bell for
Adano* (1944). Both are upbeat, despite their war themes: Saroyan tells
the story of a fourteen-year-old boy on the American home front who
delivers telegrams for the War Department, even one to his own mother
regarding the demise of his older brother, with indefatigable aplomb;
Hersey's focus is a war-torn village in Italy aided substantively by a
kindly Italian American soldier. Joyce Moss and George Wilson note
that 'critics wrote mixed reviews in response to the novel, a few of them
remonstrating that the characters were unrealistic . . . The works' characters are "good in a way that human nature is never good".'[8]

The crime-novel existentialist hero of the 1940s home front was a
war-worker (Himes's Bob Jones) or a veteran (Spillane's phenomenally
popular Mike Hammer); Wright's Bigger Thomas dreams of joining
the military early in *Native Son* but knows this opportunity is denied
to him (see the following case study). Still, Frederick Karl regards this
as Wright's ' "war novel", in which the consciousness of one man,
rather than a squad or platoon, becomes central'.[9] As Wheeler
observes, Bob Jones is also thwarted in his attempts not only to join
the war but even to get to his job at the plant: 'Bob Jones's leaderman
job is the pride and joy of his life, and yet his productive life is end-
lessly deferred. The novel becomes painful to read precisely because
Jones never gets to work.'[10] He is even hindered from the detective
work that is the novel's focus, prevented from the total freedom of
movement that is the noir hero's structural essence: 'The African
American hero cannot master the entire city. Although Jones swaggers
and tough-talks like a standard noir hero, his urban expertise becomes
racialised, limited to his knowledge of the colour line.'[11]

If Bigger's and Bob's existentialist isolation results from their exclu-
sion from mass (that is, white) society, Mike Hammer's is due ultimately to his superheroic superiority, his ability to outwit both
evildoers and well-meaning cops, and his singular willingness to use
unsanctioned violence to achieve justice. In *I, the Jury*, the first
Hammer novel (written solely for financial gain in the course of nine-
teen days), Mike involves himself as private detective and avenging vig-
ilante when a war buddy is sadistically gunned down. Jack Williams
had lost an arm to the 'Japs', saving Mike from a bayonet, and throughout the novel Mike labours to pay his debt, stripping and shooting the

seductive blonde (who had done in Jack) in the novel's final scene. In
almost anti-existentialist fashion, Mike revels in (instead of anguishing
over) his aloofness from ordinary men and even women, many of
whom he beds but all of whom he refuses to commit to. Yet Mike's
killing of Charlotte fails to even the score: he answers for Jack's murder
but Jack's disability (which left him vulnerable to attack in the first
place) is the persisting indicator of war's ability permanently to reduce
even superheroes like Mike to postures of eternal gratitude and indebt-
edness. Mike mentions the war at the outset of several early Hammer
novels, indicating that his entire career as a fighter of violence with violence is a post-traumatic response of some kind. In *One Lonely Night*
(1951), Mike narrates that 'it took the war to show me the owner of the
gun and the obscene pleasure that was brutality and force, the spicy
sweetness of murder sanctified by law'.[12]

Another hyper-individualist *Übermensch* of a very different sort is
Ayn Rand's rogue-architect Howard Roark from *The Fountainhead*
(1943), who triumphs over the pathetic attempts of plebian taste-
makers to destroy his career; his unpopular buildings, like his uncom-
promising self, enshrine the qualities of unapologetic individualism
Rand brought to a pinnacle in this work and in *Atlas Shrugged* (1957).
Spillane the brawler and Rand the philosopher thus provided something for right-wing readers across the intellectual spectrum; both
of Rand's novels were best-sellers, and today they rank number
two and number one respectively on the Reader's List of the twentieth
century's one hundred best novels, published by The Modern
Library.[13] In their heyday, the success of each of Spillane's Hammer
novels was phenomenal: his works have sold more than 225 million
copies worldwide, and seven of the fifteen all-time best-selling
American fiction titles are his.

Two leftist novels from the 1940s read often in naturalist terms are
John Steinbeck's *Cannery Row* (1945) and Ann Petry's *The Street*
(1946); they are thus often read as anomalous to this period though they
productively complement each other. Steinbeck's novel is sometimes
regarded as a late disappointment in a literary career that flourished in
the Depression-era 1930s; New Critic Chester E. Eisinger dismisses the
work as 'built on accepted propositions of the old liberalism . . . The
happy bums of Cannery Row . . . are superior to . . . the ulcer-ridden,
trussed-up, decent citizens of the community.'[14] Meanwhile, Hilfer
regards Petry's novel as 'one of the finest novels of the 1940s', forgotten by contemporary readers because of its seemingly outdated generic
qualities: 'Petry published a novel of naturalistic social protest just as

critics were busy declaring this form of fiction officially obsolete.'[15] The marked difference in tone and outcome between the utopian-comic *Cannery Row* and the dystopic-tragic *The Street* belongs in large part to the demographic particularities of each authorial vision. Despite the several suicides and acts of violence dotting the margins of Steinbeck's work, the story is primarily comic and optimistic, filled with rough-hewn roustabouts with hearts of gold who mean well and even eventually manage to do good. Petry's novel, the first by an African American woman author to sell more than a million copies, tells the story of race and sexual oppression; its heroine Lutie Johnson is exploited by white landlords and the black men in her life; trapped in her small, overpriced apartment and on Harlem's littered streets, Lutie's travails are many, and she is forced to lash out murderously against one black male adversary, simultaneously killing prospects for a better life for herself and for her son.[16]

Richard Wright's *Native Son* (1940)

Writing for *Dissent* in 1963, Irving Howe asserted that 'The day *Native Son* appeared, American culture was changed forever . . . [I]t made impossible a repetition of the old lies [and] brought out into the open, as no one ever had before, the hatred, fear, and violence that have crippled and may yet destroy our culture.'[17] Howe attributes to the novel 'crudeness, melodrama, and a claustrophobia of vision', all themes that have been retrieved by contemporary critics as they contemplate the philosophic influences and generic qualities of Wright's 1940 masterwork which, as Arnold Rampersad asserts, 'remain[s] the cornerstone of his success'.[18] Both Rampersad and Desmond Harding, exploring the novel's 'architectural determinism',[19] identify *Native Son* as a late entry in the canon of naturalism, especially 'urban naturalism'.[20] The naturalist reading follows the ways in which Bigger's environment – the cramped and decrepit black belt of Chicago's 1930s-era South Side – foreordains his eventual ignominy and demise. The famous opening scene, during which Bigger battles a rat that invades his family's cold one-room apartment, is noted for its naturalistic elements, especially the clear coding of the large black rat, its teeth bared and 'belly puls[ing] with fear', as an analogue for Bigger himself.[21]

Rampersad has also identified the pro-communist and proto-existentialist strains in Wright's novel, specifically, with respect to the former, its intense materialist critique of black exploitation, and, the latter, its 'gloomy sense of fundamental human relations' but also 'the power of the will in creating identity'.[22] Cornered (like the rat in the first scene) by the insensitive manoeuvring of his white employer's attractive daughter Mary and her well-meaning but naive communist boyfriend, Bigger is thrust into a compromising situation and takes matters into his own hands. To muffle her drunken cries, as he helps her to bed one fateful night, Bigger accidentally smothers Mary to death, then burns the body in the basement furnace to cover his crime. Trudier Harris refers to Bigger's crime as a 'creative act of violence [through which Bigger] achieves a higher level of consciousness, of self-reflection.'[23]

Rampersad observes that Native Son is much more, and much other, than an 'entertaining detective story',[24] but it indeed succeeds in this genre as well, while James Smethurst makes the convincing case for its Gothic qualities. Most provocative is Smethurst's connection of Native Son to James Whale's Frankenstein, enjoying a revival in 1938, as Wright was developing his novel: indeed, Bigger's being chased by a large contingent of Chicago police to the water tower where he is at last caught and for all intents and purposes condemned bears striking resemblance to the final scene of Whale's film, in which the townspeople bearing torches chase the monster to a windmill where he is trapped and perishes when the mill is set on fire. As Smethurst observes, 'Particularly significant for Wright's novel is the moment where the line between the monster and the man who created him is blurred. Bigger, then, is a monster created by a murderous society, initially marked not by an "unnatural" origin so much as by his physical appearance.'[25]

Rampersad notes the damage done to the Native Son's reputation by James Baldwin's dismissive critique, 'Everybody's Protest Novel' (1948), and when compared with the more sophisticated narrative technique demonstrated by Ralph Ellison in Invisible Man (1952). Despite these setbacks, Wright's novel is a canonical work that sold well immediately (more than 250,000 hardback copies) and remains a favourite with teachers, students, and general readers today. The publishing house Modern Library has placed it at number twenty on its list of '100 Best Novels of the Twentieth Century'.

Southern Literature

Among southern writers, Warren and Faulkner enjoyed 'major' status in their own era as Faulkner continues to do today; their regionalism complemented, but did not threaten, what were regarded as universal themes and narratives. State politics cause ideological conflict in *All the King's Men*, for which Warren won a Pulitzer Prize in 1947. Based on Louisiana's 1930s-era iconoclastic governor-then-senator Huey P. Long, Willy Stark runs for office and loses both his idealism and moral compass when he achieves great power. It is the transformation of the narrator, Jack Burden, that is the story's main focus, however; as Stark's aide, he not only sees the ways in which public good can come from political corruption but also adopts a philosophy of nihilism, famously disseminated through the novel as The Great Twitch, that

Figure 1.1 Richard Wright was an acclaimed novelist of the 1940s; his *Native Son* (1940) was adapted for the stage in 1941 with Canada Lee in the starring role. Library of Congress, Prints and Photographs Division, FSA/OWI Collection (LC-USZ62-121359).

allows him to perpetrate immoral acts himself: he digs up scandal against Stark's political foe, Judge Irwin, despite the fact that the judge is Jack's long-time friend and, it is finally revealed, his own father. Also, he tolerates the betrayal of his ex-lover Anne Stanton, who sleeps with Stark when she learns of corrupt acts by her own father (Stark's predecessor as governor). When Anne's brother Adam learns of Anne's sexual indiscretion, he guns down Stark in the state capitol, just as Long himself was gunned down on the steps of the Louisiana state house in 1935. The novel was adapted for Hollywood in 1949 and won three Oscars, including Best Picture. Eisinger regards it as 'one of the most distinguished novels of the period',[26] while Hilfer argues that it fails as a whole, with Jack's conversion from cynicism to decency ringing false.[27] These assessments reflect the general falling-off of Warren's reputation between the 1960s and the present day, although some have set about rejuvenating Warren's work in modern, new historicist terms.[28]

Faulkner's three major works of the decade were *The Hamlet* (1940), *Go Down, Moses and Other Stories* (1942), and *Intruder in the Dust* (1948); with other Hollywood screenwriters, he co-wrote two screenplays during this period, adapting Hemingway's *To Have and Have Not* in 1945 and Chandler's *The Big Sleep* in 1946. Hilfer posits that 'Faulkner's greatest writing years were behind him by 1943',[29] yet his career was revived mid-decade by Cowley, as noted above – a testament to the power of the critic to define greatness from one era to the next. *The Hamlet* is the first in Faulkner's 'Snopes Triology', also including *The Town* (1957) and *The Mansion* (1959), which narrates the conflict between Will Varner, a southern planter-aristocrat, and Flem Snopes, an unlikeable tenant farmer who cheats his way to land ownership and threatens the local sovereignty of Varner himself. Matthew Lessig argues that, despite his local origins, 'Flem combines the figure of the intrusive Northerner in the age of "abstract" sociological analysis and New Deal reform programs with the "industrialism" decried by the Agrarians as the antithesis of traditional Southern culture.'[30] According to Lessig, Varner's genial, paternalist approach to his own exploited tenants is just as bad.

Both *Go Down, Moses* and *Intruder in the Dust* narrate episodes from the saga of the Beauchamp–McCaslin clan, the Beauchamps being the black (originally slave) members of this complicated family tree, the McCaslins their insensitive owner–cousins. *Go Down* is a collection of closely related stories that take place in and near the McCaslin plantation: in 'The Fire and the Hearth', patriarch Lucas

Beauchamp plays a major role and will be falsely convicted of the murder of a white man in *Intruder*; in 'Go Down, Moses', Gavin Stevens is the semi-enlightened white lawyer who arranges to bring home the body of Samuel Beauchamp, the intelligent, well-spoken grandson of Lucas and Molly who is executed in an Illinois penitentiary. In *Intruder* Stevens rescues Lucas from the false murder charge. *Intruder in the Dust* was made into an MGM film in 1949 and has been singled out by contemporary critics as a rare of example from that era in which the black characters are allowed to perform roles with dignity and intelligence.

Eudora Welty is a southern writer whose essentially affirming vision excludes her from the war-related, grim naturalist, or existentialist contexts of her fellow writers of this decade, in addition to the Gothicism and sexual, racial, and class-based tragedies of her fellow southerners. It was a busy decade for Welty at the beginning of an exceedingly long career, during which she published two short fiction collections; two novels, *The Robber Bridegroom* (1942) and *Delta Wedding* (1946); and a short story-novel hybrid reminiscent of some of Faulkner's work, *The Golden Apples* (1949). The two traditionally styled novels tell stories of remarkable Mississippi families whose beautiful daughters find marital bliss, although *Delta Wedding* is complicated by issues of class disparity (Dabney is about to find her bliss with the overseer) and familial versus conjugal bonds. Faulknerian in style and theme, *The Golden Apples* is the darkest of these works, focused on social rebels and outcasts and the tight-knit communities that make differentness unbearable.

On the theme of the social outcast, two southern writers who are often paired in analyses of 1940s fiction are Carson McCullers and Truman Capote, sexual renegades whose frank address of sexual and racial issues makes their work especially relevant to contemporary readers. Both in their mid-twenties when their first novels appeared during this decade, McCullers and Capote told stories of rebellious rogues or lonely people who longed to connect; the stories are marked for various critics by their Gothicism, decadence, and psychosexual strangeness. In McCullers's *The Heart is a Lonely Hunter* (1940), a group of misfits pays visits to a charismatic deaf mute named Singer, each under the deluded impression that s/he connects with Singer in a special way. In truth, Singer loves another deaf-mute man who, being also insane, does not return his love. In *The Member of the Wedding* (1946), twelve-year-old Frankie Addams, like *Hunter*'s twelve-year-old Mick Kelly, is a tomboy on the threshold of sexual discovery.

Lonely and motherless, she determines to join her brother and his bride on their honeymoon and is enlightened as to the unlikelihood of her plan by the family's worldly black servant Berenice. In Capote's *Other Voices, Other Rooms* (1948), fourteen-year-old Joel Knox also loses his mother and journeys to a decayed southern plantation in search of the father he never knew. Instead he finds there his cousin Randolph, a transvestite, who initiates him into homosexual activity. *The Member of the Wedding* was made into a successful stage play in 1950 and film in 1952. In both, Frankie was played by a young Julie Harris, and Berenice by the versatile singer/actress/comedian Ethel Waters, who won a New York Drama Critics Award for her stage version in 1950.

Despite the good showing of canonical literary works in this decade, it is always partly the case that great books are determined by the narrow readership of critics and scholars who analyse and write about them. Many an average reader may have waited for the literary classic to come out in (shortened, often sweetened) cinematic format, and Richard R. Lingeman reports that, for much of the war, non-fiction outsold fiction. Memoirs, such as Kinnan Rawlings's *Cross Creek*, Ilka Chase's *Past Imperfect*, and Eliot Paul's *The Last Time I Saw Paris* (all 1942) sold well, as did comic takes on military life, including Marion Hargrove's *See Here, Private Hargrove* (1942) and Bill Mauldin's *Up Front* (1944) and *This Damn Tree Leaks* (1945). William L. White's *They Were Expendable* and Richard Tregaskis's *Guadalcanal Diary*, two hard-hitting battle memoirs from 1942, were widely read and later, along with Hargrove's, made into hit films. Wendell Willkie's *One World* (see the Introduction) 'became the fastest seller in publishing history, selling 1,000,000 copies . . . in a little more than two months and 2 million in two years'.[31] Two popular novels tinged with melodrama and sentiment were Betty Smith's *A Tree Grows in Brooklyn* and Jesse Stuart's *Taps for Private Tussie* (both 1942);[32] and overseas, Lingeman notes, publishers sponsored the Armed Service Edition programme, through which pocket-sized paperbacks were provided by the hundreds of thousands each month to the Army and Navy. Not surprisingly, it was not canonical literature but lightweight genre fiction (westerns, mysteries, racy humour) that soldiers and sailors wanted and what they were sent; like the comic books beloved by servicemen (see Chapter 4), 'the Army Service Editions . . . provid[ed] men with portable reading material – the ubiquitous books turned up everywhere, invasion barge, submarine, foxhole' and paved the way 'for the greater acceptance of [the paperback format] in the postwar years'.[33]

Twilight of an Empire: American Newspapers

The role of journalism during this decade may be better understood by considering less in-depth the output of America's major newspapers than the careers of its various weekly or monthly magazines – especially those that came to 'Life', burgeoned into national prominence, or waned into obscurity during this period. The major papers of the nation's largest cities, reading from left to right (geographically) were the *Los Angeles Times*, the *Chicago Tribune*, the *Washington Post*, and the *New York Times*; to consider the left-to-right political spectrum represented by these major organs, one might more or less simply reverse this list although, of the four, the *Tribune* has always been the most rightward leaning. Before the media consolidations that characterised the later decades of the twentieth century, the 1940s were times during which major cities supported many papers: in Chicago, the *Sun*, the *Times* (later merged by liberal Chicago magnate Marshall Field into the *Chicago Sun-Times*) and the *Daily News* competed with the *Tribune*; in New York, the *Times* competed with the equally distinguished *Herald Tribune*, the somewhat lower-brow *World Telegram*, the liberal *Post*, and the sensationalised Hearst paper, the *Daily Mirror*. In addition, hundreds of smaller cities in the United States published daily editions, and small towns had their weekly sheets of local doings. Historians view this period as an already rusting golden age, but one that still boasted enough independently owned journalistic enterprises to provide the general public with a true spectrum of news and opinion.

To read from a range of offerings – the liberal daily *PM*, the black news weekly the *Pittsburgh Courier*; the (white, middle-class) women's magazine *Ladies' Home Journal*; and 'mainstream' (once more, white middle-class) magazines as diverse as the *Saturday Evening Post*, *Reader's Digest*, *Time*, and especially *Life* – is to understand not only the public mood as this is reflected in these serials but also the ways in which the serials themselves shaped the habits of information gathering and leisure reading for the American public during this period.

Former *Time/Life* editor Ralph Ingersoll established *PM* in June 1940; journalism historian Paul Milkman observed that the thirty-two-page, tabloid-style daily strongly slanted to the left and was a thoroughgoing product of its times: avowedly pro-New Deal (and thus Roosevelt), pro-labour, and anti-fascist. As these were boom times for such opinions, the paper's tone was light and entertaining; on its second anniversary, 'the high point of its existence' according to Roger Starr, *PM* published voluminous congratulatory messages from politicians, Roosevelt most eminent among these. Milkman points out, however, that 'ironically, *PM* made entry into the world at precisely the moment when Roosevelt was abandoning New Deal politics to create an interventionist coalition'.[34] While the paper lasted until 1948, the seeds of its demise are discernible even in the president's subtle shift to the right in the early war years and by the even more drastic political shifts that occurred upon the occasion of his death: 'Though there are many reasons for the demise of *PM*, perhaps the most important was the cerebral hemorrhage suffered by Franklin Roosevelt in April 1945.'[35] The death knell was even louder in 1946, when the Republicans took over both houses of Congress and national interest became defined not only by impatience with labour demands but by vigorous anti-communism. Milkman observes that on election day 1946, the paper was forced to break with the innovation it had held to since its founding – publishing advertisement-free – and accept advertisements to boost revenues.[36] The paper changed ownership in its final years and, despite the gust of hope generated for the left by the surprise re-election of Truman in 1948, succumbed in June of that year.

Despite the relatively short life of this journal, Ingersoll's achievement continues to be reflected upon and appreciated. Its operation free from advertisers' influence is noteworthy in its own right; *PM* also housed an impressive collection of editorial-writers, including Max Lerner and I. F. Stone, and provided its readers with solid leftist journalism regarding the war (the most emphatically interventionist of all New York papers in 1940), integration and civil rights, labour, and the Soviet Union. In addition, it provided information on consumer prices and the best radio listings of any paper in the region. In fact, Ingersoll was instrumental in the invention of Luce's photo-magazine *Life*,[37] and Starr notes *PM*'s emphasis on pictorial coverage (theorising that 'PM' stands for 'photographic material',); Philip Nel (who suggests 'picture magazine' as the phrase behind the initials) credits the iconoclastic photojournalist Arthur Fellig (aka 'Weegee') with giving *PM* much of its distinctive photographic look. Ingersoll's first editorial stated the paper's mission: '*PM* is against people who push other people around'. Because of his outspoken views, Ingersoll, so he had always suspected, was drafted at the age of forty-one and served for three years (1942–45) in the war. When he returned, the paper was already in decline, and he became embroiled in staff in-fighting, which weakened the publication further. Still, Starr calls Ingersoll 'a magazine genius', and his smart little news daily vitally served its original readership as it continues to provide a portrait of this bygone decade to historians today.

African American and Women's Periodicals

The *Pittsburgh Courier* was founded in 1907 and shortly taken over by the gifted editor Robert L. Vann, who brought the paper to national prominence. Together with the *Chicago Defender* and *Baltimore Afro-American*, the *Courier* was a top-circulation and massively influential black paper throughout the first half of the twentieth century. The *Courier* (as well the *Defender*, *Afro-American*, *California Eagle*, and many other African American newspapers of the era) took an active role during the war, supporting Roosevelt's call to arms (even if not necessarily all of his presidential bids),[38] yet arguing against mistreatment of black soldiers in both official and unofficial forms: editors and reporters protested against black servicemen's limitation to support (instead of combat) roles in battle and objected strenuously to racist attacks while in training in the United States. They hailed Executive Order 8802, which forced war contract-holders to lift discriminatory hiring policies (see the Introduction) as well as Truman's desegregation of the troops in 1948.[39] Yet the *Courier* distinguished itself during this period for its inception of the wildly popular 'Double V' campaign, which promoted victory abroad and victory against fascist (that is, racist) elements at home. The logo developed by the *Courier*, one V nested inside another, was a design adopted in print, on clothing, even for hairstyles; photographs of prominent blacks and liberal whites making 'Vs' with the fingers of both hands accompanied a series of articles and updates about the campaign. The campaign was endorsed by politicians, Republican presidential contender Wendell Wilkie most prominent among these, and was yet another way – in addition to rationing, saving, and buying war bonds – that the *Courier*'s African American readership could show its support for the war.[40]

In the 1940s, *Ladies' Home Journal*, edited by the dynamic and forward-thinking Bruce and Beatrice Gould, had reached a pinnacle of artistic and journalistic excellence, not to mention reader and advertiser appreciation. In circulation, its numbers ranged only below those of *Reader's Digest* and *Life*, at the number one and two spots respectively;[41] while it would by 1960 be eclipsed by *McCall's* in a dramatic assault by editor Herbert Mayes,[42] the look and content of the *Journal* under the Goulds' leadership made the magazine 'an undisputed leader'[43] throughout the war and especially in the second half of the 1940s. Mary Ellen Zuckerman points to the ways in which the war, which affected all women's magazines, appeared in the *Journal*: a WINS (Women in National Service) campaign that encouraged women to keep up physical and mental health on the home front, then, later, support for women entering the war-industry workforce. The progressive, cosmopolitan Goulds were interventionists from the start, and employed prominent wartime women, including journalist Dorothy Thompson (see below) and Eleanor Roosevelt to write frankly about its meaning for American women. Zuckerman observes that the Office of War Information even began broadcasting vocal renditions of the *Journal*'s 'How America Lives' series as these featured more and more often families directly affected by war.[44] After the war, the Goulds hired presidential adviser Margaret Hickey to run the magazine's Public Affairs Department; both this and its 'Political Pilgrim's Progress' series encouraged women to become more involved civically.[45]

While the progressive, even feminist, stance of the Goulds marked the *Journal* as primarily leftist during this period, its sister publication under the Curtis media umbrella, the *Saturday Evening Post* spoke for and appealed to a traditional, middle-American conservative perspective. It spoke against the railroad union in 1939,[46] against entering the war in the 1940s,[47] and, together with its fellow conservative, the *Reader's Digest*, published red-baiting articles and editorials in the post-war period that sounded as paranoid as McCarthy himself.[48] It published an offensively racist cartoon, 'Ambitious Ambrose', about a dim-witted, incompetent African American grocery store clerk, during the early 1940s.[49] As David Reed notes, 'ironically, as the women's monthlies strove to generate understanding and compassion in the post-war years, the *Post*, *Digest*, and *Life* were all playing on ignorance and fear to whip up hatreds of such qualities when exercised in the political arena.'[50] Historically, the cultural and aesthetic heyday of both the *Post* and the *Digest* was behind them (in the 1920s and 1930s), yet both continued to enjoy top circulation during the 1940s (three million and a remarkable eight million respectively), so must have continued to respond to some national need. Despite its exaggerated anti-communism, the *Digest* may be credited for its emphasis on health issues, especially its early targeting of the carcinogenic properties of cigarettes;[51] the *Digest*'s focus on research and current events meant that it was well positioned to continue as a leader during this decade.

From Fiction to Non-fiction, from Words to Pictures

The war caused two tidal turns for popular magazines of all kinds – from fiction to non-fiction and from romanticised illustrations to realistic photography – that reflected the perspective of the battle-hardened 'veteran': even those who had never left the American shore had had a vigorous and revolutionary awakening during the first half of the 1940s to the goings-on of the wider world, answered with a deep desire to know, and especially to *see*, the unfolding international scene. The astounding success during this decade of *Look* magazine and two Henry R. Luce publications, *Time* and especially *Life*, all of which tapped into Americans' urge to ground themselves in the science, politics and history of the day, led almost all other popular serials to undergo (or maintain) a similar stance: the *Digest*, which had always focused on non-fiction coverage,[52] continued in this vein, while the *Post*, under the 1940s leadership of editor Ben Hibbs, threw over the revered stylistic traditions of George Lorimer, emphasising photography and scaling back what had been the *Post*'s mainstay for decades – a heavy commitment to fiction.[53] Reed observes that *Ladies' Home Journal* used colour photography to impart 'precise information' about 'fashion, food, and home decoration [which] are all visual topics'.[54] In this way the *Journal* used photography to turn housekeeping into a credible, productive science for its female readership.

While Luce's conservative stance meant that the editorial voice of both *Time* and *Life* could be as intently anti-communist as were those of the *Post* and *Digest*, his publications' forward-looking appeal to the latest in consumer tastes was anything but culturally or aesthetically conservative. Defining this new approach, historian James L. Baughman observes that 'Luce's formula involved little more than summarizing the week's news in print (*Time*) or pictures (*Life*) in ways that left readers with a concise, entertaining, and frequently inadequate version of an event or trend. Complex "running" stories were simplified. Normally, the *Time* entry emphasized "personality".'[55] Baughman observes that as the world became more complex in the post-war period, and as education and jobs became more specialised, leaving huge gaps in the average American's understanding of the big picture, 'readers, knowingly or not, surrendered to *Time* the right to sift through facts'.[56] Luce's publications succeeded astronomically throughout the 1940s by condensing complex information into a brief but seemingly complete report and, especially, by trading in the proverbial thousand words for the single striking picture (see the following case study). Ironically, print journalism's 1940s lunge towards the visual did little to stave off the rout it received in its own war with television at the dawn of the 1950s, after which advertising and subscription rates plummeted and never returned to their wartime highs.

Life Magazine and 'The American Century'

Henry Robinson Luce was a missionary's son, born in China in 1898, who had been proclaiming the inevitability of American world leadership since his graduation from Yale in 1920. With his fellow Bonesman, Brit Haddon, he founded *Time* magazine in 1923 and, at the behest of his wife, Clare Boothe Luce, and editor, Earl Ingersoll, *Life* in 1935; both publications enjoyed record popularity throughout the 1940s. 'The most read of any Luce publication in 1940 was his latest creation, *Life*. Published weekly, *Life* introduced its readers to photojournalism' and eventually reached a weekly readership of tens of millions.[57] Luce was a lifelong Republican and master capitalist; his *Time/Life* conglomerate also included *Fortune* magazine and 'The March of Time' newsreel series that opened for many a feature film throughout the 1940s.

As war approached, Luce's editorial position changed from objective neutrality – Hitler was *Time*'s Man of the Year in 1939 – to ardent interventionism. He saw the gains in business and politics to be made by decisive action in the world's latest armed conflict and promoted his thesis in an essay entitled 'The American Century' in *Life* in February 1941. Borrowing heavily from the writing of Walter Lippmann,[58] Luce called upon the United States 'to assume leadership of the world', drawing a sharp rejoinder from Vice-President Henry Wallace in 1942.[59] At the end of that year, two weeks after Pearl Harbor, Luce's 22 December editorial, 'The Day of Wrath', reiterated his world-leadership argument, calling for national unity and an end to isolationism. For Luce, the war was both the result of, and likely cure for, 'as pusillanimous an epoch as there ever was in the history of a great people: the twenty years between 1921 and 1941 . . . The epoch that is closing was much less tragic than it was shameful.'[60] Taking the opportunity to blast the liberal era of 1920s' feminism and sexual liberation, 1930s radicalism and labour organisation, and implicitly Roosevelt's several administrations, Luce may have been wrong to pin the war on the women's vote and the repeal of Prohibition, but he was correct in his prediction that it would swing the country sharply to the right for the next several decades. When he urged his readers to 'create the first American Century', he foresaw how the United States would climb to the pinnacle of world leadership during the war and the forty-year cold war that followed.

Unlike the daily publications, which brought immediate, frantic news of Pearl Harbor and all happenings related to war, *Life* both suffered from, and enjoyed, a lag in publication that gave it a different purpose. Its 8 December 1941 issue – having probably appeared on newsstands the evening before – had no coverage of Pearl Harbor but, even a week later, its treatment was meagre: 15 December's cover featured Patricia Peardon, sixteen-year-old star of Broadway's *Junior Miss*, with a story on 'Japan's reckless attack' saved for page twenty-seven. This article's enormous headline – 'WAR' – is oddly mitigated, surrounded by advertisements for hosiery and Christmas ham. It is only in the 22 December issue, touched off with a patriotic cover (a waving American flag) and the emphatic signed editorial referred to above, that war coverage went into high gear and, throughout the war, events (for instance, the Normandy invasion) were usually treated two weeks after the fact. Given these constraints, *Life*'s primary contribution to wartime journalism was much less often the breaking story than the elaborate text-photo overview. Both the temporal distance (the time lag between coverage and publication) and the long visual perspective provided by Luce's death-defying photographers and his reporter-researchers in the field and back at home situated and comforted readers with a sense of understanding and mastery. As bad as whatever the current crisis was, the reader got on top of it, literally, thanks to *Life*'s eagle-eye images and accompanying text.

Life covered the war both abroad and at home, praising towns and individuals whose sacrifices helped troops overseas and urging readers to conserve resources, seek work in war industries, and act with consideration: don't bother the doctor with minor ailments, he may need to treat a recovering soldier; don't ride the rails for frivolous reasons or cancel tickets at the last minute, as GIs may be trying to get home on leave. Advertising used the war to boost sales in every instance. An ad for Modess sanitary towels bragged that its improved design helped women workers stay at war plants longer.[61]

Not surprisingly, *Life* was there, if two weeks late, for the major events of the post-war 1940s: the revelation of concentration camp atrocities, the atom bombings of Japan, the return of refugees in Europe, American labour strikes in 1945 and 1946, the formation of the United Nations, the Nuremberg trials, the partitioning of India and Pakistan in 1947, and the Truman presidency. Despite its anti-Roosevelt stance, upon the president's death in 1945, *Life* wrote, 'Americans will not soon forget the jut of his chin, the angle of his cigarette holder, his smile. This gallant, fearless man, who could not stand on his own feet without help, bestrode his country like a giant through great and changeful years.'[62]

With its sprawling tabloid format and spectacular black-and-white photography, *Life* provided keen perspectives on the world's happenings throughout the decades of its publication, capturing images that endure today as iconic historical touchstones. Throughout the 1940s, *Life* advertised its enthralment to the visual with frequent write-ups of photography staff members; regular features including 'Picture of the Week', 'Speaking of Pictures' and 'Pictures to the Editor' (sent in by readers); and coverage of the human condition even in the extremity of death. Yet its disparate focus on life's tragedies and absurdities was lamented by cultural critic Dwight McDonald, who regarded *Life* as a primary example of homogenised mass culture: 'The same issue will contain a serious exposition of atomic theory alongside a disquisition on Rita Hayworth's love life; photos of starving Korean children picking garbage from the ruins of Pusan and of sleek models wearing adhesive brassieres.'[63] While historian George Roeder notes that 'race was the touchiest issue' in wartime imagery,[64] *Life*'s coverage of race issues seemed fairly progressive, with a glowing

feature on Joe Louis (by Earl Brown, 'one of America's foremost Negro journalists')[65] and the photo of an African American soldier dancing with a
white French girl in Paris's post-war Place Pigalle.[66] One Latina was illustrated in a story about California's female war workers,[67] yet the Asian
faces were much less often those of ordinary American citizens and more
often those of the smiling Chinese ally or the dying Japanese enemy.

Prominent Publishers and Editors

Like the publications they wrote for, the talented journalists of the
1940s defined themselves by their political slant (even as this shifted
radically from the beginning to the end of the decade) and distinguished themselves in their response to the war. They were publishers,
editors, columnists, and correspondents; the columnists were often
syndicated into hundreds of newspapers, enjoying readerships in the
millions and great national influence; the reporters delivered their
information to print and radio outlets; the editors worked for more
than one periodical (even simultaneously), or edited for one group
while reporting for another. The owner-publishers themselves made
headlines with their scandals and lawsuits and created media empires
out of what had once been a stirred-up sea of independent news enterprises. The two most powerful owner-editors were Luce and, establishing his empire a generation earlier, William Randolph Hearst.
Hearst was in the last decade of his life in 1941, having amassed by that
time more than thirty newspapers, a dozen magazines, two news services, a film company, and several timber holdings and mining interests. While his direct control of the news enterprises was mitigated by
court-ordered reorganisation the preceding decade, his radically conservative, sensation-laden media network continued as a force to be
reckoned with throughout the 1940s. In 1941, his rage over Orson
Welles's *Citizen Kane*, based on Hearst's life story, was national news;
Hearst used his papers as a platform from which to condemn Welles as
a communist and banned all RKO pictures (of which *Citizen Kane* was
one) from write-ups or advertising in the chain.[68] Baughman notes that
Citizen Kane 'showed Hearst's empire in decline and a new one emerging: Time, Inc.'.[69]

While not a media magnate like Hearst and Luce, Norman Cousins
was another editor renowned as much for his skills in publishing as his
role as public speaker and activist. Joining the *Saturday Review of
Literature* (later the *Saturday Review*) as executive editor in 1940,
Cousins, as editor two years later, transformed the journal from a

struggling literary magazine into a forum for public opinion with a circulation of over 600,000.[70] The *Review* appears to have been another major periodical of this decade that enjoyed increased circulation because of its shift in emphasis from fiction to non-fiction. While Hearst and Luce were staunch right-wingers, Cousins was a liberal and a humanitarian whose famous essay for the *Review*, 'Modern Man is Obsolete' (1945) – an impassioned plea for world government following the atom bombings of Japan – was later published in book form and sold widely (see the Introduction). Cousins is also famous for having co-sponsored, together with a large contingent of contributing *Review* readers, 'the Hiroshima maidens', twenty-four bomb-scarred Japanese young women who came to the United States for restorative plastic surgery, and for eventually legally adopting one of these young women.

Like Cousins, Charlotta Bass, owner-editor of the African American *California Eagle* was known for her left viewpoint and career of public activism; 'by the early 1940s [she] was an institution in black Los Angeles'.[71] Kathleen Cairns notes that Bass was active in city politics in the first half of the decade and ran the West Coast campaign for Wendell Willke when he ran for president in 1940. While she often supported Roosevelt as well, Bass's politics turned to the ultra-Left, specifically Henry Wallace's Progressive Party, after the war and especially after the death of her beloved nephew in battle against the Nazis.[72] She was later accused of being a communist by more moderate African American leaders. Throughout the 1940s, Bass spoke out emphatically against racial discrimination in Los Angeles and throughout the United States and was the first African American grand juror in a Los Angeles county courtroom in 1943. The *Eagle* was supported in this period during times of flagging advertising revenue by Bass's appreciative celebrity readers such as Dorothy Dandridge and Hattie McDaniel.[73]

John Sengstacke, nephew of the *Chicago Defender*'s founder-editor, Robert S. Abbott, ascended to his uncle's post in 1940 and held the position until his death in 1997. Throughout his long career, Sengstacke, like Hearst and Luce, acquired multiple newspapers, including the *Tri-State Defender* and the *Michigan Chronicle*; during the 1940s he raised the *Defender*'s circulation rate to record levels. He is remembered for an historic meeting in 1942 with Attorney General Francis Biddle, during which he brought to Biddle's attention black support for the war effort and staved off a sedition probe that the FBI may have been planning to mount against the black press.[74] Sengstacke also met Roosevelt to discuss the issues of black postal workers and White House press corps members; he was appointed by Truman to the committee that oversaw desegregation of America's armed forces. Also in 1940, another prominent African American newspaper, *The Pittsburgh Courier*, underwent an important change in leadership, as founder-editor Robert L. Vann passed away and was replaced by the *Courier*'s long-standing sports writer Ira Lewis. Under Lewis's leadership, the *Courier* enjoyed record circulation.

The Great Columnists and Editorialists

Hearst's staff of gossip columnists contributed greatly to his papers' popularity. Louella Parsons wrote for Hearst's *Chicago Record-Herald* and later for his *Morning Telegraph* where she kept up her column and took on the role of film critic, as she did for *Cosmopolitan* and *Photoplay*. Her arch-rival, Hedda Hopper, wrote for the *Chicago Tribune–New York Times* syndicate for thirty years and was famous for her outlandish hats and her running feud with Parsons. Hearst's most important writer in this vein, however, was Walter Winchell, who expanded his beat from Hollywood to true crime and crime fighters (especially his hero, J. Edgar Hoover) and became a powerful Washington player during the course of his career. As Winchell turned his nose for news against America's enemies abroad, Ted Gottfried observes that 'periodically, Winchell went to Washington and briefed the president on Nazi activities in the United States'.[75] Following the war, Winchell became a staunch anti-communist and McCarthy supporter, even after McCarthy's congressional censure in 1954; his influence with policymakers as well as readers (and listeners to his radio broadcasts), who once numbered in the millions, waned with the decade. Another columnist for Hearst's King Features Syndicate was Westbrook Pegler, an ultra-rightist with a razor tongue who hated the Roosevelts and lambasted the first couple as well as other political leaders and entertainers (and lost a libel suit to a fellow journalist in 1954). Perhaps not surprisingly, he advocated in 1942 interning Japanese Americans during the war, as became federal policy in April of 1943.[76] Pegler even attacked Hearst, a move that cost him his job in the early 1960s; despite the ignominious end to his career, Pegler began as a World War I correspondent, the youngest in American history, and actually supported Roosevelt in the late 1930s. Before World War II, he reported in a range of fields, winning a Pulitzer Prize for investigative reporting in 1941.[77] But, as Ted Gottfried observes, 'As Pegler drifted further and further to the right, his writing became harsher, less humorous, and more one-sided, and he began to lose readership.'[78]

Other columnists of a decidedly more substantive nature enjoyed national recognition as well. The dean of these learned policy analysts – the United States's first pundits – was Walter Lippmann whom many have considered the most influential journalist in American history. Lippmann's understanding of the big picture and his authorial skills drew intelligent readers and even lawmakers, who sought his advice throughout the middle decades of the twentieth century. In the mid-1940s, Lippmann coined the term 'the cold war' and incisively outlined its core dilemmas (see the Introduction). Inexplicably, his superior approach to the complexities of mid-century politics was marred by his vigorous support, along with the likes of Pegler, of Japanese American internment. In February 1942, Lippmann wrote three columns, syndicated to over four hundred papers, 'not only demanding internment, but offering a rationale for it that no one else appears to have thought of before. Lippmann travelled around the West Coast reporting back that it was a fact, not speculation, that the Japanese were about to attack the coastal states.'[79] Geoffrey Perrett assigns to Lippmann the 'open[ing of] the floodgates' that allowed countless other journalists to adopt the anti-Japanese American position. As otherwise distinguished as Lippmann was Max Lerner, an academic in the social sciences and a talented public intellectual; his career spanned many decades but, during the 1940s, he was a contributing editor to *The New Republic*, a columnist for the *New York Star* and *New York Post*, and little less than 'the voice of [*PM*]'[80] during most of that paper's career. James Reston was a consummate Washington insider and Pulitzer Prize-winning diplomatic correspondent for the *New York Times*, considered 'one of the most influential political columnists of the twentieth century'.[81]

The brilliant and iconoclastic I. F. Stone adopted the stance of a proud outsider to Washington power circles, challenging the administration gadfly-style with his marvellously researched exposés from the pages of *PM* and *The Nation*. During the war, Stone railed against American indifference to the plight of the Jews and travelled with displaced persons in their flight to the fledgling state of Israel in the months immediately following. His fascinating account of this journey, *Underground to Palestine* (1946), details multiple harrowing memories of the camp survivors who comprised the first waves of immigrants to Israel, as well as the drama that accompanied the illegal journey itself. Despite his intense sympathy for the Jewish plight,

Stone argued for fair treatment of the Palestinians and was accused of anti-Semitism by American Jewish groups. The *Pittsburgh Courier*'s renowned associate editor and widely respected columnist, George Schuyler, spoke out against discrimination against men of the armed services, Jim Crow laws, and a host of other race issues; in 1943 his article for the NAACP's (National Association for the Advancement of Colored People) *Crisis*, entitled 'A Long War Will Aid the Negro', argued that the war was draining white human resources in ways that would eventually require white Americans to rely upon the untapped energies of African Americans, opening opportunities in the process. Post-war, Schuyler moved sharply to the right, speaking out against communism and even writing occasionally for the John Birch Society. In 1947, he published *The Communist Conspiracy against the Negroes*. Regardless of political slant, Schuyler was a brilliant rhetorician with a sharp satirical wit; he was mentored by his stylistic forefather, H. L. Mencken, who regarded Schuyler as a master journalist.

For the African American news weekly the *Chicago Defender* and other publications such as *Negro Digest* and *The New Republic* Langston Hughes wrote incisive social commentary, providing the *Defender* with a regular column on a variety of subjects affecting the black community beginning in the early 1940s. Christopher C. De Santis observes the catalysing effect of the war: 'Eager to reach a wider audience and to comment on important events, Hughes on 21 November 1942 published his first column for the *Chicago Defender*, beginning a 20-year career with the black newspaper.'[82] In the *Defender* essay that led to him being offered the column, 'Negro Writers and the War', Hughes compares the war to 'a great big old juicy ham' that sails through the open window of an elderly, hungry slave woman. Hughes concludes the vignette with ' "Hallelujah!" she cried, shouting. "Thank God for this ham – even if the Devil did bring it!" '[83] and reads the war itself as a gift from the Devil that hungry African Americans must make the most of (through valour in battle, through defence industry jobs offered) if they are to advance in the post-war period. Hughes titled this column 'Here to Yonder' with the intent always to connect his community's local concerns to the larger picture: in this original instalment, Hughes warns aggrieved African Americans to consider the additional hardship to be faced under an Axis takeover, and therefore to give their utmost to the war effort.

About three months after his first column, Hughes gave birth to 'one of the best known literary creations in African American letters',[84] a fictionalised everyman named Jesse B. Semple (nicknamed 'Simple') who took frequent part in a dialogue-style column going over the day's pressing issues. In the original instalment, Hughes persuades Simple to not resist the draft, noting that even in the dreaded Jim Crow South, where he is likely to do his basic training, he is allowed to stay up late if he wishes – a habit Simple cherishes. If the Nazis come, Hughes warns, Simple would be curfewed into early bedtime: 'In fact, you would be hog-tied'. Hughes scholar, Blyden Jackson, celebrates the distinctly ordinary qualities of this American everyman: 'at the very heart of American racism there seems to be an assumption of the most dangerous import: to wit, that there are no Negroes who are average people'.[85] Donna Akiba Sullivan Harper notes the cathartic effect of the Simple columns' dialogue form: 'The Negro Press in general, and Hughes's column – especially the Simple stories – in particular, illustrate the value of such catharsis . . . By envisioning a just reality, and *by talking about it*, the speaker begins to really improve his situation.'[86]

Covering a wide range of subject matter, the celebrated editorial cartoonist Herblock won his first of three Pulitzer Prizes in 1942. Starting out with a Chicago paper just as the Depression struck, Herblock (the pen name of Herb Block) was politicised by this economic catastrophe (Katz) and maintained an adversarial stance (as did fellow political cartoonist, Theodor Geisel; see the Introduction) in response to Nazism and isolationism in the early days of the war. During the war, Herblock produced cartoons for the Army and moved to the *Washington Post*, where he enjoyed total freedom from editorial control, in 1946. In his work, Herblock targeted domestic and international examples of political corruption and the trampling of human liberties: in January 1947 he depicted the head of Senator Theodore Bilbo, a notorious southern racist, as a 'bad apple', dripping with pus, plucked from the barrel of 'American Representative Government'; a July 1949 cartoon showed Uncle Sam as a paranoid cave-dweller cradling his atom and refusing to sign the 'atom agreement' offered by a perplexed 'Britain'. The caption reads 'I'm not an isolationist anymore – It's just that I don't trust Anybody'.

Heroic Reporters and Photo-journalists

In the theatres of war themselves, columnists and reporters sent back regular word of an equally inspiring, instructive nature. In his seminal history of the genre, Benjamin Mott observes: 'Its reporting of the second world war to the American people was, all things considered, the greatest achievement of the American press in all its history, . . . outstanding in scope, quantity, variety, and reliability'.[87] In Europe, columnist Dorothy Thompson filed reports for *Ladies' Home Journal*, the *New York Herald Tribune*, and *New York Post* throughout the 1930s and 1940s; as with Stone, her pro-Palestinian sympathies after the war drew charges of anti-Semitism, and she was dropped from the roster at the *Saturday Evening Post*. Her position on this issue hampered the rest of her career, which ended in 1958.[88] Early in the European conflict Sigrid Schultz reported on Kristallnacht (9 November 1938) for the *Chicago Tribune*; and *Life* photographer Margaret Bourke-White filed written reports in addition to the photographs she captured.[89] She managed to remain in Russia after Hitler began his invasion, 'fill[ing] her hotel bathtub with developing trays and . . . smuggl[ing] to New York the first visual evidence of Russia at war'.[90] For *Collier's* the intrepid Martha Gelhorn covered the Battle of the Bulge, the Russians at the Elbe at the end of the European conflict, and the liberation of Dachau. Marguerite Higgins, who also witnessed the opening of Dachau (and Buchenwald), covered both Europe and Japan for the *New York Herald Tribune*. She would go on to cover the Korean War as well as the Vietnam War, win a Pulitzer Prize for war correspondence in 1951 and fatally succumb to a rare tropical fever while covering the Vietnam conflict in 1966.[91]

During the war, Ernie Pyle was very probably the most beloved reporter in America, embraced by ordinary readers for his faithful coverage of battles in European and Pacific theatres. Though he feared for his own life, Pyle resolutely accompanied the military into numerous battles and was killed in Japan shortly before war's end, only days after Roosevelt's death.[92] He especially praised 'the infantry because they are the underdogs. They are the mud-rain-frost-and-wind boys. They have no comforts and they even learn to live without the necessities. And in the end they are the guys that wars can't be won without.'[93] During the war his dispatches appeared in four hundred daily newspapers and three hundred weekly publications; following his death, Truman mourned his loss in a national broadcast.[94] General Omar Bradley once observed: 'My men always fought better when Ernie Pyle was around.'[95]

Another champion of the infantry underdog – he referred to them as 'dogfaces' – was Bill Mauldin, whose cartoons were featured in home-front newspapers and in *Stars and Stripes* where they were most appreciated by GIs themselves. Mauldin's Willy and Joe – hulking, stooped, bearded, and dishevelled – were infantrymen dealing with the

"Wisht I could stand up an' git some sleep."

Figure 1.2 'Willy and Joe'. Bill Mauldin was a cartoonist beloved by infantrymen for comically capturing the hardships of their service experience. Used with permission from *Stars and Stripes*. © 1944, 2007 *Stars and Stripes*.

frustrations and fears felt by all World War II servicemen. The cartoons poked resentful fun at naive civilians, overfed rear echelons, and inept commanders who made the front-line soldier's dangerous life that much more hazardous and aggravating. Mauldin's panels were filled with large figures draped in billowing uniforms that emphasised the weight of their excess fabric; heavily shaded backgrounds were criss-crossed with vertical and horizontal lines (representing drifting ciga-rette [or gun] smoke and whizzing bullets, respectively). Even the down times depicted in these drawings thus seemed noisy, dirty and chaotic.[96]

Alongside the record of service performed by the nations' commit-ted and often heroic wartime journalists must be recalled the counter-vailing force of censorship of overly disturbing wartime and post-war truths, applied as often by the government's Office of War Information as by newspaper publishers themselves. Historians of the era report the ways in which information was manipulated – held back or strate-gically released – to keep the public concerned and compliant (but not paralysed with fear) throughout the duration of the war.[97] There existed a military file of photographs too disturbing to disseminate to the press, known as the 'Chamber of Horrors', that nevertheless doc-umented the brutalities that would surely have vigorously swayed public sentiment – either in favour of escalating the war or abandon-ing the task immediately. Others have noted that, as the war wound on, toleration of graphic reports and images increased; what would have never been divulged in the earliest years was routine fare in late-war newspapers, as well as in newsreels, radio reporting, and even Hollywood films. Regarding coverage of the atomic bomb, Paul Boyer reports that journalists attempting to tell the truth about radiation poisoning saw their stories killed; in the immediate aftermath, despite medical evidence to the contrary, 'the *New York Times* categori-cally denied that radiation sickness was occurring as a result of the atomic-bomb attacks,' ascribing the story instead to 'Japanese propa-ganda'.[98]

Conclusion

Despite the hazards of both battle and bureaucracy, the war provided news reporters with a singular opportunity for adventure and heroism that would not present itself again until 1950, with the opening of the Korean War, and then more vividly with the covering of Vietnam in the 1960s and 1970s. The late 1940s, in their need for the analysis, stra-tegising, and sometimes fear-mongering invited by the Cold War, opened themselves to the talents of the news commentators, political scientists and Washington insiders who became the first full-time pundits. Also, the late 1940s witnessed the first wave of war-related memoirs and fiction, written by a new breed of scarred survivors, who combined love of language with first-hand knowledge of blood, violence and death for a curious and appreciative post-war readership. Across the decade, American novelists, correspondents, and photojournalists blended aesthetics and history to provide arresting, important narratives to readers of every intellectual level and political persuasion.

Chapter 2

Radio and Music

In the 1940s, Americans connected to the world through their radios, which offered on-the-spot information-gathering as had never been heard before (and had never been so important to hear), as well as a spectrum of news analysis, entertainment, and music so complete that one might never leave one's chair. As satisfying and sustaining as were the dramas (both real and fictional) played out each day, the involving serials, and thrilling live broadcasts from ballrooms around the country, 1940s radio inspired listeners to move – join the service, run for the fallout shelter, get up and dance – as often as it moved them to sit quietly, learn and enjoy. Meanwhile, the invisibility of radio, celebrated for the exercise it gave the imagination even while the listening body sat motionless, caused controversy when white actors were selected to play (or exaggerate) black roles; those few African American actors and musicians who were allowed to perform had to sound 'black enough' to reinforce the stereotyping assumptions of this aural medium. Finally the war necessitated advances in radio technology and in broadcast journalism that raised both to new levels of achievement, even as radio faced its last years of pervasive cultural influence, before television's advent at the end of the decade. The musical styles that cheered and distracted home-front and service-member Americans during the frightening, sorrowful days of the war would not even last the decade, seeing radical transformation, especially the waning of swing music and dancing, in the late 1940s.

Broadcasting the Blitz

While it had been a medium of entertainment and public service for two decades, radio as a source of international reporting and news analysis was in large part born in response to crises erupting in Europe in the late 1930s and early 1940s, especially Hitler's hostile takeover of Austria and the Sudetenland of Czechoslovakia and the German bombing of London.[1] Seminal incidents include H. V. Kaltenborn's live coverage of the Spanish Civil War in 1936 and Edward R. Murrow's historic broadcasts from London as the city took cover during the German Blitz of 1940–41. Kaltenborn, who had been analysing the news on radio since its inception in the 1920s, by the 1940s was hailed as the dean of radio commentators. He is famous for his twenty straight days of round-the-clock news analysis during the Munich Crisis of 1938. Though in his sixties by the time the war began for the United States, he broadcast from sites in the Pacific and visited soldiers on the Italian front.[2] Murrow is as remembered for the courage, style, and technical acumen involved in his production of the London broadcasts as he is for his televised attacks on Senator Joseph McCarthy in the 1950s. Kaltenborn, Murrow and many other first-generation radio journalists were fluent in French and German, using their language skills to interview leaders among the belligerent nations during America's neutral pre-war days and needing no interpreters to decipher Hitler's speeches.[3] As they sent home news in the months immediately preceding American abandonment of the isolationist position, the London correspondents helped forge a permanent and powerful alliance between American and British citizens and their governments, through their humanising, sympathising coverage of the British plight.

Many reported bravely during the war, from ships doing battle in the Pacific Ocean (for instance, Cecil Brown in 1941 and Leslie Nichols in 1945), from the beaches at Normandy and Iwo Jima, and form the liberated capitals of Europe in 1945. A military plane carrying Kaltenborn almost crashed in the Pacific, and a military plane carrying Eric Sevareid did crash in the Himalayas, while William Shirer was almost jailed by the Nazis for supposed espionage, and Richard C. Hottlet was for a brief time a Nazi prisoner. War historian Geoffrey Perrett calls the Normandy invasion radio's 'finest hour of the war. All commercials were cancelled. With the aid of short-wave, tape recordings and daring reporters, it brought into American homes the authentic sounds of battle and vivid descriptions of the desperate fighting on the Normandy beaches.'[4] Sevareid, Shirer, and Hottlet were part of an elite collective known (even in their own day) as the Murrow Boys, selected by Murrow for their records as scholars, daredevils or accomplished journalists to cover the war with him for CBS. The Boys also included two of the most fearless reporters of the war,

Bill Downs – 'Murrow's Ernie Pyle'[5] – and Larry LeSeuer, who sent back battle reports (not all of them received through radio's then faulty technology) and stayed close to advancing troops on Europe's front lines.

Dorothy Thompson, like Shirer, was forced to leave Germany because of her loudly spoken anti-Hitler sentiments. Upon her return to the United States, she continued her campaign of anti-Nazism, often in the midst of pro-Hitler and isolationist gatherings, drawing verbal and physical attack. In 1938 Thompson collected $40,000 for the ultimately unsuccessful defence of Herschel Grynszpan, a young Jewish Parisian whose assassination of a German diplomat triggered Krystallnacht. With her widely syndicated column, 'On the Record' and frequent broadcasts for NBC, she was regarded during the war as one of America's two most influential women – the other being Eleanor Roosevelt.

Upon her expulsion from Germany, she was offered newspaper as well as radio venues while Elmer Davis, another committed Hitler foe and later Roosevelt's appointee as director of the Office of War Information, moved from newspaper (where he wrote news, non-fiction, and even serialised fiction) to radio just as England declared war on Germany. While it is strange to credit the reign of Hitler with both the birth and the golden age of radio journalism, in fact, many risked their lives (as they inaugurated brilliant celebrity careers) in the 'air war' against him. Most striking is J. Fred MacDonald's assessment:

> Ironically, the end of World War II dealt a serious blow to the radio industry. Since 1939, and more dramatically after American entry into the struggle, commercial radio had been the most vital communications and entertainment medium in the nation . . . The cessation of the war left radio without purpose or direction, and in need of self-appraisal. Waging a crusade so intensely for so many years, by late 1945, radio personnel found it difficult to discover meaning in a new world.[6]

Note that McDonald refers not only to news programming but to radio in all genres, and indicates that the medium never recovered from the blow of war's end. After half a decade plagued by inertia and overused formulas, radio heard its death knell (sounded by television) in 1950. Many (for instance MacDonald) have noted,[7] in fact, that the first favour done for radio by the war was its disruption of development and distribution of television technology in the early 1940s, buying radio an extra decade of cultural significance.

Trusted Commentators

Between Kaltenborn, the radio pioneer, and Murrow who successfully made the transition from dying radio to newborn television in the early 1950s, were many men (and one or two women) who shaped the public experience of the war and early post-war period through their on-the-spot radio reporting and informed radio commentary. Some of these journalists began as newspaper correspondents and moved to radio; others flourished simultaneously in both mediums. Examples of the former include Kaltenborn, Raymond Gram Swing and Lowell Thomas, three of the most respected voices during the early 1940s; examples of the latter include Thompson, Drew Pearson and Walter Winchell, the most widely followed columnist/commentator in the nation in 1941. Like the columnists who filled the nation's op-ed pages during the 1940s, radio commentators occupied the political spectrum. The right was represented by Upton Close, Fulton Lewis Jr and, in its extreme form, the anti-Semite Father Coughlin. Moderates included Kaltenborn, Thomas, the eccentric and optimistic Gabriel Heatter, and the left-leaning Pearson who lashed out in his Washington-insider exposés at the Roosevelt and Truman administrations almost as often as at congressional conservatives. Walter Winchell shifted his political allegiances from far left to far right shortly after the war. Reliably on the left were Murrow, Thompson, Davis and Swing.

Kaltenborn and Davis were two commentators regarded as the most trusted authorities in news analysis, although their styles differed greatly. As Davis biographer, Roger Burlingame observed:

> . . . when Kaltenborn spoke one never felt his immediate presence. He was always talking from afar . . . Elmer Davis was right in your room . . . In that flat, even voice, the impact of the faintest up and down was stunning. And hearing it, you could almost see facial expressions: the slight raising of eyebrows, the slighter twist of the mouth toward the smile that never quite came.[8]

Davis's Midwestern tones, like those of Missouri-native Harry Truman's, reassured middle America, while Kaltenborn, whose patrician style probably reminded listeners of Roosevelt's own, is famous for being mocked by Truman at a dinner shortly after Truman's surprise presidential victory in 1948, and for being a thoroughgoing gentleman in his reaction to the barb.

Throughout his career, Raymond Gram Swing enjoyed access to a world stage: as New York and Washington correspondent for two

British periodicals, as radio commentator whose BBC and Mutual Network broadcasts were sent in multiple translations throughout Europe, and as the first political analyst for Voice of America near the end of his career, Swing was, as Fang argues, 'to foreigners . . . a radio Uncle Sam, communicating American policy and American moods'.[9] Fang observes that war's end brought declining ratings for Swing, whose 'solemn interpretations' of events were liked less than the lighter touch provided by Gabriel Heatter, Walter Winchell, and Lowell Thomas.[10] Thomas specialised in human-interest stories that made him popular for decades. He began broadcasting in 1930 and enjoyed successful radio and television careers until 1976, when he was eighty-four. While Heatter, imprisoned by anxieties and compulsions, was almost a recluse when not on air, Thomas travelled the world on a regular basis, having covered Lawrence of Arabia in the 1920s, the liberation of Buchenwald in 1945, and 'High Adventure' (the name of his mid-1950s television series) in New Guinea, the Arctic, and Tibet. Heatter did little in television, though he worked in radio and newspapers until the mid-1960s, and appeared rarely in films (most famously, as himself, in *The Day the Earth Stood Still*); when asked to take part in a film with Cary Grant, he declined. Both Thomas and Heatter did many of their broadcasts from fully mounted studios at home; Thomas's was part of his fifty-room mansion, Hammersley Hill, and was itself thirteen rooms, one of the many indicators of the luxury and largeness his life afforded him at the height of his career. Uncomfortable with the perquisites of wealth that his Lower East Side upbringing never prepared him for, Heatter's studio was a refuge from the outside world (and the attention it would bring) that he found so anxiety inducing.[11]

Heatter was known for his emotionalism on air and sentimental human-interest stories, his almost obsequious relationship with his sponsors and the products he sold, and his silver-lining approach to the worst developments during the war: his famous opening line, which brought comfort to millions, was 'Ah, there's good news tonight'. Easily moved, he cried during air time at the news of the fall of Paris and also in a cinema when touched by his portrayal in a Hollywood film (the one he declined to appear in himself) as well as on a train when he read a news report indicating that he was the favourite commentator of all nine justices of the Supreme Court. He insisted that a journalism award designated for him be granted to his sponsor instead, and an acerbic critic of his style once quipped: 'His equal anxiety over Dachau and dandruff, Japan and gingivitis made his commentaries ludicrous.'[12] Yet America adored his optimistic, heartfelt stories of personal courage and loyal dogs, the warmth and sympathy that bubbled into every personal interview and heart-rending update during the war. As Fang incisively notes: 'He was deeply impressed by the courage of others because he sensed so little courage in himself.' Throughout the war 'this fearful man continued to bring hope and optimism to his listeners'.[13]

Washington and Hollywood Insiders

Many have compared the careers of Drew Pearson, the consummate Washington insider, and Walter Winchell, in some ways the most influential personality of his era, with a listening/reading audience of fifty-five million at the height of his popularity. While Pearson is regarded by some as a top investigative journalist and Winchell as a trafficker in false innuendo that did little other than ruin people, in fact the term 'muckraker' may apply accurately to both. Robert Sherrill declared Pearson 'the greatest muckraker of all time',[14] and many regard Winchell as great in his own way, as one who rose from nothing to coin a lexicon and make kings and who has profoundly influenced our contemporary sense of celebrity and popular culture. Pearson and his co-columnist Robert S. Allen added radio as a venue for their already widely syndicated daily column, 'Washington Merry-Go-Round', just as the war opened for the United States; Winchell had done the same with his report in 1932. The ellipses that marked the rapid-fire breaks from one item to the next in both columns were replicated by Winchell in his radio broadcast by the sound of a rapidly (and randomly) struck telegraph key as he moved from one item to the next. Both shows were broadcast on Sunday evenings on NBC.

Pearson is famous for his involved (some would say scandalous) personal life among the wealthiest Washington elite and for his exposés of HUAC chairman John Parnell Thomas (for corrupt practices) in August 1948, of General George S. Patton (for slapping a shell-shocked soldier) in November 1943, and Harlem congressman Adam Clayton Powell (for various affairs and misappropriations) in the mid-1950s. He claimed he was proudest of having collected food for wartime European refugees on a cross-country rail campaign and for having helped rebuild a Tennessee high school that had been bombed after an order to desegregate.[15] He was considered by Arthur Cooper of *Newsweek* 'that rare combination of showman and newsman, and every day his pungent blend of punditry and titillating gossip would set off quaking shocks on the Washington seismograph'.[16]

Winchell is famous for his urgent delivery, accented as Gerald Nachman recalls as 'Good evening Mr. and Mrs. Nawth Americur and all the ships at sea. Let's go ta press!';[17] his invention of still-circulating slang ('making whoopie', 'scram', 'blessed event', 'belly laughs'); and his influence dealt through New York's Stork Club where he held court, with the most powerful politicians and celebrities of the 1930s and 1940s. Like Pearson, he married more than once and inflicted upon his children difficult childhoods. Pearson's daughter Eileen was kidnapped by his ex-wife before he finally won her custody; he and his second wife had to kidnap her son from the boy's estranged father; Winchell's daughter Walda went in and out of mental institutions, and his son Walter Jr, destitute and disaffected, committed suicide in 1968.

Another populariser (though some might say bastardiser) of the craft was Arthur Godfrey, a Washington-based announcer/entertainer in the early 1940s, assigned to cover Roosevelt's funeral for CBS in 1945. His emotional breakdown during the proceedings represented the nation's own grief; he was catapulted to stardom following the programme and given two daily programmes on CBS, during whose morning session he combined entertainment (ukulele playing, comedy); folksy delivery of news, human-interest stories, and sponsored advertisements; and news commentary, even editorialising. An influential supporter of military build-up, especially in the air force, during the early cold war, Godfrey personally lobbied Senator Lyndon Johnson for increased military spending and endorsed Eisenhower during the 1952 presidential election. *Time* magazine once noted that 'the thing that makes Arthur Godfrey remarkable as a hit entertainer is his remarkable lack of definable talent. He can neither sing, dance, act, nor perform with skill on a musical instrument. Yet today he is the top moneymaker and the outstanding personality of the air.'[18] Media historian Ted Gottfried observes that 'Godfrey was not a broadcast commentator analyzing the news. Rather he was an entertainer with opinions who became influential through the back door of high ratings. He remained an entertainer even as he manipulated his audience's politics.'[19]

The Example of Murrow

Just as influential as Winchell and Godfrey, though at the opposite end of the legitimacy scale, was the towering figure of Edward R. Murrow whose consummate class with respect to personal appearance and professional achievement has been admired by generations of broadcast journalists. While he was respected by his colleagues for his ability to gather, sift, and convey hard news, in the midst of his first and most famous assignment in London during the German Luftwaffe raids it was, as biographer A. M. Sperber notes, 'the reflective, impressionistic pieces that captured the public imagination and established his image as poet of the blitz'.[20] Like Thomas, Heatter, and even Winchell, Murrow divined that the human angle was what would capture his home audience's attention and their hearts. 'He spoke of individuals – an East End woman, her house gutted by incendiaries, clutching a dirty pillow . . .'[21] and sang the praises of ordinary British people, who heroically and stoically headed for the shelters each sleepless night and rose each smoke-filled morning to live another day. His placing of a microphone on the steps of St Martin-in-the-Fields to capture the very footsteps of these shelter-bound Londoners is remembered for its stylistic as well as its political importance: According to Murrow scholars Stanley Cloud and Lynne Olson, 'here was the Murrow method at its experimental best'.[22] He broadcast more than once from the rooftop of London's CBS headquarters and opened almost always with his trademark, tension-filled, 'This – is London'. In 1943, he flew on a bombing mission to Berlin and then told a vivid story of heroic pilots, missions accomplished, and near death in a lengthy and famous broadcast, known as 'Orchestrated Hell', the following day.

Murrow is credited with multiple innovations that enabled the medium to come of age. Dispatching to the capitals of Europe permanently placed, expert reporters in the late 1930s, he would call upon them in round-robin fashion to fill segments throughout the broadcasting day with developing news. Once the Blitz began, he did a similar thing, posting correspondents at key points around London and calling upon them in serial fashion to create a news roundup as the action unfolded. In the example provided by Sperber, Murrow began: ' "This – is Trafalgar Square." Positioned elsewhere around the city, awaiting their cues, Larry LeSueur at an air-raid precautions station, Eric Sevareid at a dance palace, Vincent Sheean in Piccadilly, and in Whitehall, author-broadcaster J. B. Priestly for wrap-up commentary.'[23] Despite Murrow's later lamenting 'the incompatible combination of show business, advertising, and news' that prevailed in the television age,[24] one cannot help but raise an eyebrow at the intensely orchestrated, even contrived, quality of this coverage. In Sperber's apt phrasing: 'The program was *London After Dark*, . . . starring the citizenry of London and the better part of 1000 uninvited guests [the nightly German invaders].'[25]

Despite the exhilaration of both the war and the birthing of radio broadcasting, Murrow, like all Londoners during this period, felt the strain. Sperber reports his inability to relax on rare weekends in the country, sulking alone, hearing crumbling bricks and mortar in the crunch of gravel, losing large amounts of weight, and surviving on 'adrenaline, black coffee, and cigarettes'.[26] Murrow smoked heavily, constantly, all of his adult life, yet Sperber notes that 'his smoking had intensified' during the Blitz, 'a chemical means of keeping down the pressure'.[27] His sleep was disturbed, during this period and for the rest of his life, and he died of lung cancer at fifty-seven in 1965. His super-human qualities failed him to the extent that he, like all those who shared this moment with him, succumbed to forms of post-traumatic stress that had lifelong (in Murrow's case, life-shortening) effects. After the war, Murrow continued to excel, developing shows for CBS, serving as one of its vice-presidents and its most respected vocal presence. Of the cold war scenario, Murrow offered this prescient metaphor: 'Both the East and the West are doing what they can to bunch themselves into one fist. Each side is labeling that fist as purely defensive . . . [But] it seems reasonable to expect that the forces contending in Europe will use their fists – economic, political, and propaganda-wise – to drive those areas [of Europe and the Middle East that had not yet chosen sides] into one camp or another.'[28]

A World of Entertainment

News programming was not all, or even primarily, what occupied radio airwaves during the 1940s. As in the preceding decade, radio in the 1940s provided a range of programmes in lengths of five and fifteen minutes (for news editorials and cliff-hanger soap operas), thirty and sixty minutes (for dramas, comedies, and game shows), and multi-hour formats (most often for music programmes). Like the television schedules of today, block programming, a concept developed by producer Frank Stanton, resulted in soap operas and other shows aimed at women being broadcast on weekdays, with children's and mixed adult fare in the evenings and at weekends. Most of these show genres (and many of the shows themselves) transferred directly to (or even enjoyed a simultaneous existence on) television in the 1950s: quiz shows, talk/news programmes, soaps, radio dramas, mystery/thrillers, crime stories, westerns, comic-book adventures, comedy/variety hours, and live and pre-recorded music in every form. Radio was such a relied-upon source of entertainment that there were even radio re-enactments

Figure 2.1 The well-respected radio journalist Edward R. Murrow is famous for his broadcasts from London during the Blitz. Digital Collections and Archives, Tufts University.

of actual news events (*The March of Time*, which began reporting actual news in 1942, *One Out of Seven*) and of recently released Hollywood films (*Lux Radio Theater*).

There is a quality of blatant commercialism associated with golden-age radio (and television) that takes much more subtle, discreet, some would say insidious forms today. The example of *Lux Radio Theater* is a prime example of sponsors' inclination to put their name first before the public – even though the word 'Lux' is the name of a soap that conveys nothing of the drama or interest that might actually invite listeners to tune in to the sponsored programme. For many years 'The Bob Hope Show' was officially designated *The Pepsodent Show*. Listeners did not tune in to 'Jack Benny' but instead to *The Lucky Strike Program*. This is despite the fact that Hope and Benny were two of radio's top comics, whose names attached to their shows might have done much more to sell the products in question than ever would the product name itself. There were even musical acts associated with these shows called the Champion Sparkers and the Vicks Vaporub Quartette. Yet the heavy-handed presence of sponsors throughout this era is explained by the way much early radio was programmed – through the production and supervision of sponsors themselves (or often their advertising agencies), who developed a programme's concept, wrote its scripts, cast and paid its performers, and owned all rights. When, for instance, Jack Benny's show was sponsored by Jell-O, Benny not only worked for Jell-O as a radio performer but as a familiar face on the company's magazine and grocery store advertising. In those same magazine pages, Bob Hope hawked Pepsodent, and on the programmes themselves, much of the faithful announcer's job involved pushing the sponsor's product at the beginning, end, and often mid-point of the show. The infamous 'middle commercial' was especially rankling to news commentators, many of whom despised having to interrupt serious news (especially war-related news) to sell cigarettes, tooth powder, or washing powder.

Radio Comedy

Groucho Marx's *You Bet Your Life*, a radio success from 1947 until 1956 and on television from 1950 to 1961 blended quiz-show formatting, cash prizes, and acerbic humour. Beneath Groucho's broad physical comedy and eccentric appearance (greasepaint eyebrows and moustache, rolling eyes, ever-twiddling cigar) was plainly discernible a sharp intelligence that relished wordplay, the outwitting of suckers, and biting insult. His sharp-edged comedy is a plain precursor to the rough sport that is stand-up and improvisational comedy today and may almost seem too smart (that is, to smart too much) for its wholesome, homespun original audience, who also laughed uproariously at styles of humour most modern listeners would find juvenile and inane. In fact, as with the political tendencies of the news commentators above, radio comedy was a full-spectrum phenomenon in the 1940s, one that included the sniping patter of Edgar Bergen and his wooden dummy Charlie McCarthy; the deprecation traded between Jack Benny and his radio rival Fred Allen; the wry jibing of Eve Arden as *Our Miss Brooks*, an under-appreciated

English teacher at a school full of philistines; and the warmer tones of family comedies such as *Fibber McGee and Molly*, *The Aldrich Family*, and *Life with Luigi*. The clownish vocal antics of Baby Snooks, the Great Gildersleeve, the Bickersons, Bob Hope, and Red Skelton and his alter egos 'Clem Kadiddlehopper', 'Willy Lump-Lump' and 'Junior, the Mean Widdle Kid', as well as scatterbrained-women routines perfected by George Burns and Gracie Allen, Goodman and Jane Ace, and the cast of *My Friend Irma* may seem dated now but made their original studio audiences roar.

And what the Radio Hall of Fame website refers to as the 'first and most successful morning program' was *The Breakfast Club* hosted by Don McNeill and enjoying the longest run in radio history, from 1933 to 1968. Its heydays (or hey-decades) were the 1940s and 1950s; listeners (the vast majority of them women) were drawn by McNeill's easy-going personality. Frequently McNeill made mention of, and occasionally visited on-air, his wife Kay and three sons; he figures as a forerunner to contemporary American daytime television stars such as Dr Phil and Regis Philbin, who attract women viewers in part through the development of their personas as loving family men. The show emphasised family, featuring not only a regular cast of performers but their spouses and children and referring to their vast listening audience as family members around a breakfast table. Broadcast before a live audience, the show 'was divided into four 15-minute segments for the "four calls to breakfast" and featured music, [skit] comedy, [and] inspirational verse.'[29] The second half hour typically began with a 'March around the Table', during which cast members literally got up and marched around to lively music. The show boosted its visibility by publishing annuals and family albums (containing photographs and reminiscences from the preceding year), issuing club membership cards, and undertaking regional tours, during which mobs packed major concert venues to see the show live.

While we may marvel that a show as old-fashioned-seeming as this was a cultural mainstay until the late 1960s, it is the case that enclaves of modern listeners continue to celebrate these and almost all programmes from 1930s and 1940s radio, as shown by an OTR (old-time radio) fan culture energised by its own publications, conventions, and most recently the Internet.[30] *Fibber McGee* and *Henry Aldrich* were the most popular comedies of the 1940s and have loyal fan bases today; comedy historians (for instance, Gerald Nachman) continue to marvel at Bob Hope's rapid-fire style of one-line (or even half-line) gags; and radio fan-site author Elisabeth B. Thomsen astutely observes that *Gildersleeve* (originating from a character on *Fibber McGee* – America's first media

Figure 2.2 Fred Allen was a popular but acerbic radio entertainer of the 1940s. Library of Congress, Prints and Photographs Division, NYWT&S Collection (LC- LC-USZ62-126226).

spin-off), 'was a true situation comedy, more sophisticated in style. There was a clear separation between the story and the advertising, with a true suspension of disbelief – no musical numbers, and no announcer dropping by the house to talk about the sponsor's product.'[31]

Fibber McGee is a frequently discussed example of a programme that, in its inception, repeated the vaudeville formulas the show's creators had put to good use in the 1920s. During a show from 1935, Fibber claims he can sell car polish better than can announcer Harlan Wilcox, and interrupts Wilcox's pitch to do so. By 1940 the show had stopped interrupting its sketches with musical numbers and joking

asides and developed the realistic format of sustained comic plot development, much to its audience's delight.[32] Variety programmes, like
those hosted by Hope, Benny and Fred Allen, and skit comedies, starring characters played by Burns and Allen and by Jim and Marion
Jordan (Fibber McGee and Molly), shared the stage with, and themselves solidified into, the single-plot situation comedy format that continues to define much televised comedy. Other popular shows of the
era included *Henry Aldrich* and *Beulah*, two shows about white suburban families although, in the former, it is the teenaged son and, in the
latter, the sharp-tongued maid who steal most of the attention from the
traditional leads (that is, the mother and father of the family).

Racial Controversy and Inequality

Equally dated (but also equally vigorously defended) is the phenomenally popular *Amos 'n' Andy*, a show about black migrants from the
rural south to industrial Chicago, their schemes, tribulations, and triumphs. What has been controversial about the programme since its
inception in the early 1930s was its creation by two white actors
Freeman Gosden, who played the upstanding but gullible Amos, and
Charles Correll, who played both the street-smart but shiftless Andy
and his scheming friend the Kingfish. Correll and Gosden played all the
male roles with various intensities of black dialect and with frequent
recourse to stereotypical characterisations and situations. Yet, as
Elisabeth McLeod, author of *The Original Amos 'n' Andy*, has noted,
the show, especially in its early years, featured black characters across
the class spectrum, many of them wealthy and/or solidly respectable
and/or lacking a discernible black accent.[33] McLeod notes that the show
was loved by working-class black audiences yet reviled by many in the
black middle class. It was hailed by *The Chicago Defender* (America's
top black newspaper) yet criticised constantly by Robert L. Vann, pub-
lisher of the *Pittsburgh Courier*. While the show peaked in popularity
in the 1930s, it remained a ratings-earner throughout the 1940s, hiring
black actors when it moved from Chicago to Hollywood yet also
switching in the late 1940s from (melo)dramatic serial format to situation comedy, which emphasised the laughable schemes of Andy and the
Kingfish and the exaggerated behaviour of its various 'coon' characters.

Perhaps not surprisingly, American radio in the 1940s was an overwhelmingly white environment. No persons of colour had roles to play
in the field of news reporting or analysis, despite the inroads being made
by black reporters for black-owned newspapers during the same period.

On the entertainment side, black talent was primarily 'coloured' musical acts such as a four-man group known as 'The Vagabonds', and referred to as 'the boys' in promotional literature advertising their appearance on *The Breakfast Club*. On *Fibber McGee*, the family's black maid Beulah was played for many years – to the shrieking surprise of its live audience – by a white man; other white male actors impersonated black male and female characters, and a white actress named Tess Gardella had two black maids on her resumé during this period. Only after *Beulah* became a show in itself in 1945 (*Fibber McGee*'s second spin-off) did a black actress, Hattie McDaniel, finally assume the role – but only after it had passed through its original and then a second white male impersonator. The rare black actor who had radio work in that era reports often having to strain to make his or her voice 'Negroid' enough to suit white producers' and listeners' expectations.[34] Jack Benny's indispensable valet, Rochester, played with broad humour by Eddie Anderson, represents a pinnacle in black achievement in radio in this era (see the following case study).

Two 'ethnic' comedies of the era, *The Life of Riley*, about a working-class man and his family, and *Life with Luigi*, about a hapless recently landed Italian immigrant, draw us back to the controversies surrounding dialect on radio at this time, and the prominence of accents used to create character and vocal range in this invisible medium. Finally, it mattered little whether the actor in question looked the part but meant a great deal if s/he could pull off the right vocal trick. William Bendix, who starred as the comically rough-spoken Riley in *The Life of Riley*, performed before his audience in a suit and tie; the heavily accented Luigi was played by an Irish American character actor, J. Carroll Naish. Only a few radio programmes of the decade were known to affect physical verisimilitude (that is, actors wearing costumes, using the props referred to in the script) that accompanied the vocal illusion created. The issue is indeed troubling in the genre of comedy: when an audience was encouraged to laugh throughout a programme, elements of caricature and mockery that demeaned vocal minorities were almost inevitable by-products (or main products) of the proceedings.

If we consider the dramatic genres, however, the issue becomes more complex: a German accent assigned to a villain (especially during the war) differed then (and differs today) from a black dialect exaggerated for laughs, and from a 'Jap' accent affected to suggest villainy during that same wartime era. In the remarkable but short-lived *One Out of Seven*, actor Jack Webb (later famed lead of the *Dragnet* series on radio and television) played all the roles in his fifteen-minute re-enactment of a

singular story from the past week's news. In one segment, Webb impersonates the racist southern drawl of the notorious segregationist from
Mississippi, Senator Theodore Bilbo, other southerners with more or
less offensive attitudes, *and* a gently accented, stoic black soldier writing
to his wife from the North African front. In another, commenting
ironically on the nation's failure to live up to the aims of 'National
Brotherhood Week', Webb impersonates a hypocritical minister, two
hostile anti-Semites, a softly spoken black witness to a race riot, and a
Jewish immigrant newspaper editor whose home is burned. In radio
throughout the decade, to save money, or perhaps simply to showcase
his talent, the radio actor was called upon to impersonate multiple voices
in the course of a single programme, and accents of various intensities
were often a means by which radio actors fooled (and dazzled) listeners.

Eddie 'Rochester' Anderson

The career of Eddie Anderson, the smart, comical valet Rochester on the
enormously popular Jack Benny show reflects interestingly on the role of
African Americans on radio in the 1940s. Anderson joined the show in
1937, in a walk-on role as a railway porter that earned him big laughs and
a permanent engagement. While actual black actors in black roles were
something of a rarity in the late 1930s, the character itself was less than
revolutionary, relying as it did on the traditional 'coon' comic situations
related to drinking, gambling, womanising, and razor-toting. Even in this
early guise, however, Rochester's cheeky dealings with his boss were readable as subversive of traditional power imbalances, as were the comic
turns provided by the African American actresses who came to inhabit the
Beulah role on radio (especially Hattie McDaniel, who also mastered the
technique with Oscar-winning success in the role of Mammy in *Gone with
the Wind*). In the late 1940s and into the 1950s, the early moments of the
civil rights era, the stereotyping gave way to a dimensionalising of
Rochester's character. His popularity grew so great that he achieved an
implicit second-billing or even shared-billing status with Benny; critics
have seen him as Benny's own Mammy (literally his mother) or wife, as his
actual wife and the show's sole female player, Mary Livingstone, played a
wisecracking secretary with Benny scripted as a perennial bachelor. Critics
such as Margaret T. McFadden have even read a homoerotic relationship
between Rochester and Benny's always effete character, especially in the
film versions of their coupledom, during which Rochester donned a flow-
ered apron and complained of all the cooking and cleaning he had to do.[35]

   At the height of his popularity, Anderson earned $400,000 a year and
was close to Benny throughout his life. Gerald Nachman tells the story of
an incident involving a racist hotel manager who asked Anderson to stay
at another hotel when a southern couple complained. The following

morning, the entire show, forty-four crew and cast members, decamped, taking their considerable business with them.[36] Benny's brother-in-law and manager, Hickey Marks, recalls another incident, in which a waiter refused to serve Rochester in a restaurant. When the waiter saw that it was Jack Benny's party, he was apologetic, but 'Jack just looked up at him in disgust and said quietly, "you had your chance" . . . And we all got up and walked out. Jack couldn't stand such insensitivity.'[37] In his own memoirs, Benny (who referred to Anderson as 'Rochester' even in off-stage moments) observed that 'Rochester became one of the greatest assets of the show. He was a master of the slow take. His timing became sharp as a razor.'[38] Benny was unapologetic about the show's heavy use of racial and ethnic humour, noting that that was simply the style of the era and averring that 'I didn't hire Rochester because I was fighting for equal rights. I hired him because he was good.'[39] He later admitted, however, that 'the black man's fight for equal rights and fair play' after the war raised the show's own consciousness: 'I would no longer allow Rochester to say or do anything that an audience would consider degrading to the dignity of a modern Afro-American . . . Rochester had to stop eating watermelon and drinking gin on radio and television after 1945.'[40]

Despite the gains enabled by Anderson's obvious talent and history-making run with the Jack Benny show, his role remains controversial, as do many of the roles played by black performers in 1940s radio. He was the only member of the cast required to adopt a stage name – everyone else played versions of themselves – and was introduced as 'Rochester' only at the start of each show. An infamous exchange between Rochester and Benny during which Benny searches for his pressed suit and is told by Rochester, 'Gee, I'm lazy. Don't I remind you of Stepin' Fetchit?' is read as subversively self-aware by Michele Hilms[41] but as a feature of the stereotyped character that 'came to embarrass Benny' by Nachman.[42] Anderson's success is thus controversial – not only because of its partial reliance on racial stereotypes but also because of its marked singularity in this era: in important ways, Anderson's career reflects not at all the reality of African Americans in radio in the 1940s, the vast majority of whom enjoyed nothing like Anderson's success, when they were allowed to perform at all.

Radio Drama and Other Genres

Family dramas included evening programmes such as *One Man's Family* and *The Goldbergs*, and occupied many daytime hours of 1940s' radio as well; primarily these were soap operas like *Ma Perkins*, about a noble widowed lumber yard owner and her troubling children, and *The Romance of Helen Trent*, about an ageing single woman who finds and loses marital prospects again and again. The melodrama exuding from these programmes was aided exponentially by the voice of a sympathetic male announcer, who served vitally in the show's opening moments to bring the listener up to date as to various recent exploits, and by the expressive chords of a Hammond organ, whose tones were by turns plaintive, scandalous, and pathetic and which underscored so effectively the plot's constant turning that it qualifies as a minor character in its own right. The organ was vital to a melodramatic sister genre, the horror/ suspense programme, whose outstanding examples include the Chicago-originated *Lights Out!*, *Inner Sanctum*, *The Shadow*, and *Suspense*. *Inner Sanctum* is famous for its gripping introduction – eerie organ strains and the creaking of a heavy door; *The Shadow* is warmly (or chillingly) remembered for its own haunting opener – the announcer creepily inquiring, 'Who knows what evil lurks in the hearts of man?' and answering with 'The Shadow knows' and a hollow laugh. *Suspense* was a thriller/mystery whose reputation was made early in its run by Agnes Moorehead's tour-de-force performance as Mrs Albert Stevenson in the original radio version of *Sorry, Wrong Number* (made into a successful film in 1948). Moorehead was asked to reprise her panicky shrew-turned-murder-victim several times throughout the *Suspense* series.[43] It is indeed a marvellous performance.[44]

It is impossible in the space provided to convey adequately the rich array that was radio programming during the 1940s. Dozens of shows in the genres already discussed (quiz shows, sketch/variety comedy, situation/family comedy, soap operas, thrillers) were broadcast in national and regional markets, as were children's programmes featuring The Lone Ranger, Red Ryder, Tom Mix, The Cisco Kid (all westerns), the Green Hornet, and Superman; crime stories and murder mysteries for youth and adults; patriotic and public-service programmes; and one-woman talk-show sensation Mary Margaret McBride.[45] Radio historian J. Fred MacDonald also reminds us that 'through its heavy diet of popular music . . . radio was playing an instrumental role in rejuvenat-ing national spirits following the Depression. As the austerity of the early 1930s gave way to a broader national confidence by the end of the decade, radio created for its audience . . . a "Make-Believe Ballroom".'[46]

The Rage for Swing

MacDonald observes further that 'the dance music called "swing" was largely popularised through radio. Network radio allowed a nation of jitterbugging "hep-cats" to hear remote broadcasts from the more important ballrooms and nightclubs in Los Angeles, Chicago, and New York City.'[47] In his indispensable guide to the genre George T. Simon notes that Camel cigarettes attempted even to blend the news and entertainment facets of radio, 'sponsor[ing] the Benny Goodman and Bob Crosby bands in series highlighted by weekly commentary on the news, called "Newsy Bluesies", composed and sung by Johnny Mercer . . ..'[48] Al Jarvis in Los Angeles and later Martin Block in New York (for whom Walter Winchell coined the term 'disc jockey') both hosted shows called *Make Believe Ballroom*, then-innovative all-record programmes that included pre-recorded applause and audience background, fully to replicate the live ballroom experience; *Lucky Strike's Hit Parade* (later known as *Your Hit Parade*) selected each week's most popular song. Swing was not the only musical format at the dawn of the 1940s, yet it was the overwhelming favourite with black and white Americans of all classes (especially the youth class). These jitterbuggers (named for the athletic dance style inspired by infectious swing rhythms) packed the clubs and ballrooms of major cities around the United States – the Hollywood Palladium, Palomar, and clubs on Central Avenue in Los Angeles; the Reno Club in Kansas City; the Hotel Sherman in Chicago; the Savoy and Apollo Theatre in Harlem; the Paramount Theatre, Strand, Astor Roof, and the clubs of 52nd Street in New York's midtown, and in Greenwich Village Barney Josephson's revolutionary Café Society, which opened its doors to black and white patrons and featured racially mixed acts from its inception.[49] Carnegie Hall also played a vital role, as the setting for Benny Goodman's groundbreaking concert in January 1938, jazz impresario John Hammond's 'From Spirituals to Swing' series of 1938 and 1939, and Duke Ellington's Russian War Relief concert in 1943, where he gave the premiere of the magnificent *Black, Brown, and Beige*, which lasted almost forty-five minutes and 'memorialised the military contributions of African Americans to the United States'.[50]

Swing got its start in the mid-1930s and remained a national mania through the war years. While music lovers of the early twenty-first century might wonder what there was to dance about during an era marked by economic depression and war, in fact, swing's elating rhythms were just the tonic sought after by the chronically underemployed and underfed of the later 1930s, as well as the about-to-be-inducted and the soldier on leave during the war years. As Kathleen Smith observes of this period: 'Preserving morale was as vital as manufacturing weapons, and the great booster of morale . . . was music.'[51] While Smith's focus is American songwriters' combination of stirring melodies with inspirational or even instructional lyrics that would 'mobilise and direct the public',[52] the point resonates with respect to instrumental genres such as swing as well. Each band's well-stocked instrumental sections – vibrant horns (trumpets and trombones), reeds (saxophones and clarinets) and rhythm sections (vibraphones, drums, string bases, and pianos) totalling seventeen, twenty or more pieces – created an exhilarating wave of ever-modulating sound, as various soloists imprinted the original score with their unique style, singers added aural and visual variety, and band leaders wowed the crowd with their own impressive instrument-playing, songwriting, and creation of a total, one-of-a-kind sensory experience.

In addition to radio – many of whose programmes still featured live performances in 1940 – the growing record, sheet-music, and juke-box industries in popular music production meant that opportunities for bands of local, regional and national renown abounded. Those who rose to nationwide (and even international) prominence in the 1940s are those best remembered today as having mastered the art form with respect to musicianship, stylistic innovation, and audience rapport. While it is impossible to single out specific band leaders, musicians and vocalists as 'the best' in a field crowded with excellence, jazz historians indicate that the bands of Count Basie, the Dorsey Brothers, Duke Ellington, Benny Goodman, Jimmie Lunceford, Glenn Miller, and Artie Shaw constitute a sort of upper echelon in the swing Olympiad, although close behind are the important cultural and artistic statements made by Les Brown, Cab Calloway, Lionel Hampton, Woody Herman, Earl Hines, Stan Kenton, Andy Kirk, Gene Krupa, Buddy Rich, Chick Webb, and even the International Sweethearts of Rhythm (see the following case study) – the band leaders themselves, as well as the musicians and singers who joined their organisations. As one can see from even this unfairly narrow selection, the swing era resounded with major talent whose contribution to popular culture continues to thrill an ever-renewing audience for swing dancing and the music that sets it in motion. When we consider that, in the 1940s, swing was a specifically pre-war and wartime phenomenon, experiencing a sharp decline in popularity as soon as the conflict ended, we may be even more amazed by the incredible range and significance of music enjoyed by grateful audiences in five short years.

The International Sweethearts of Rhythm

While jazz history (at least according to most jazz historians) is overwhelmingly male, feminist jazz historian Sherry Tucker reports that there were hundreds of all-women bands in the 1940s, and one of the most famous and mostly highly regarded of these was the International

Sweethearts of Rhythm. In fact, the band was much less international than multi-ethnic and, in later years of the 1940s, actually 'integrated' – meaning that white women were hired to play with a band that would have been otherwise designated as 'black' in the Jim Crow South and in the largely segregationist mindset prevailing throughout the country in that period. The band as it originated included African American, Asian American, Native American, and Mexican American female members; it began at the Piney Woods School in Mississippi, a boarding school for orphaned African Americans and other children of colour. While the school served both boys and girls, its principal (and the band's first director) Lawrence C. Jones, conceived of the all-girl roster in the late 1930s, as a novelty gimmick that would raise funds for the always financially ailing school.

Lawrence McClellan notes that the school provided the players with a tutor and a chaperone, the latter of whom 'saw to it that they were properly groomed and maintained good eating habits'.[53] While the band severed its ties with the school, once under professional management in 1940, Tucker observes that

> As with the Prairie View Co-Eds [another black school women's band of the period], the proud history of black education traveled with the Sweethearts, even after the band ended its relationship with Piney Woods. The Sweethearts reflected a history of African Americans providing basic education for poor black children . . . [and] served as reminders of the struggles of African Americans for education as a mode of resistance, freedom, and progress.[54]

According to McClellan, the original band members, all around the ages of fourteen or fifteen, began with little ability, improved rapidly in their early years and were well received by audiences from the start. 'When they performed at clubs such as the Rhumboogie in Chicago, there were three shows a night and seven shows a day. Crowds were turned away many times.'[55] They became known for their large horn section and hard-driving sound, inspired by Basie's jump blues style. In the early 1940s, Basie's arranger Eddie Durham joined the organisation, arranging music that suited the band's strengths and limitations, even writing solos that sounded like improvisations for soloists. The personnel – both management and talent – changed frequently during this period, and McClellan tells us that the Sweethearts were cheated out of much of their income by deceptive handlers. Nevertheless, they gained in ability and popularity throughout the decade, participating in 'Swing Battle of the Sexes' exhibitions with Jimmie Lunceford's and Fletcher Henderson's bands and changing sexist perceptions with each performance.[56] Like all African American performers of the era, touring in the South was fraught with hazards and humiliations; luckily the band gained enough financial security to own its own tour bus, where the young women did just about everything but perform, so limited were their options when travelling through the southern states. During the war, the Sweethearts were a popular favourite on Armed Forces Radio's *Jubilee*, a programme aimed at African American soldiers; they toured with the United Service Organizations (USO) in Europe in 1945.

Figure 2.3 Duke Ellington was a pioneer in swing whose innovations often went uncredited, because of racial prejudice. William P. Gottlieb/Ira and Lenore S. Gershwin Fund Collection, Music Division, Library of Congress.

Swing's Innovators

About the origins of the swing era, Simon observes:

> When the country started latching onto the big band sounds in the mid-thirties it was merely discovering the music that Duke Ellington and his band had already been playing for close to ten years – but to none of the rewarding hoopla or fanfare that greeted appearances by Benny Goodman, Artie Shaw, Tommy Dorsey and the rest of the white swing bands.

Such idolatry heaped upon those 'Benny- and Artie- and Tommy-Come-Latelys' must have been discouraging for Ellington, whose orchestra, even then was regarded by most musicians and jazz followers as the best of all the big bands.[57]

Simon describes here a scenario that characterised much of the swing era – if not much of American music at any time: namely, innovation and achievement by African Americans in a particular genre, later imitated by white counterparts, who then received the credit and fame. Simon notes that Ellington's lack of exposure was directly related to segregation: 'Duke's, like numerous other black bands of the thirties [and forties], was not accepted' in spots regarded as top venues for performance, listening, and dancing.[58] Nevertheless, Ellington is credited as a founding father of the swing style, and as a master composer, arranger, pianist, and leader of a band filled with talented sidemen (band members, especially those who emerged as star soloists in their respective instrumental sections). These include drummer Louie Bellson, bassist Jimmy Blanton, pianist-protégé Billy Strayhorn, and trumpeter Cootie Williams. Although Ellington is frequently described as ahead of his time, he wrote many popular tunes of the era, including 'Perdido', 'Don't Get Around Much Anymore', 'Black and Tan Fantasy', 'Mood Indigo', 'It Don't Mean a Thing if it Ain't Got that Swing', and 'Sophisticated Lady'. Strayhorn's 'Take the A Train' became Duke's crowd-pleasing theme.

Goodman, Shaw, and Jimmy and Tommy Dorsey are regarded as the white originators of, if not the sound, then the fad that swept the nation from the late Depression era into the war. The Dorseys shared a band in the late 1930s, but led separate groups in the 1940s, because of the brothers' different personality styles, especially Tommy's angry outbursts and demeaning way with his band members. While Tommy (on trombone) was regarded as the better musician (and was a shrewd businessman), Jimmy's band (led by his own saxophone- and clarinet-playing) was more popular in the early 1940s, selling more concert tickets and record albums during the period. Following the war and a general decline in audience interest and resources, the brothers reunited although the big band era, as it had been during the war, would never again be. Tommy died in his sleep in 1956, depressed over the declining state of his career and his marriage, following a (probably accidentally) large dose of sleeping pills, combined with a heavy meal that caused him to aspirate vomit.[59] His brother, dealing with widespread cancer and evidently heavy drinking,

followed six months later. While they were among the brilliant inno-
vators of the swing era twenty years earlier, their tragic deaths were
aided by, and sadly representative of, the striking decline of the genre
by the 1950s.

The Segregated Music Scene

Jazz historian Lewis A. Erenberg has singled out Goodman and Shaw
for their groundbreaking approach to integrated music-making in the
swing era. Goodman's four-man combo included himself, Gene Krupa
on drums (a white member of his big band), and African Americans
Lionel Hampton on vibraphone and Teddy Wilson on piano. Artie
Shaw hired Billie Holiday after she left the Count Basie Orchestra. On
his radio programme, Goodman featured Holiday, Basie, and the great
Ella Fitzgerald (Chick Webb's vocalist before moving on as a solo act),
as well as Hampton and Wilson; like the theatres and ballrooms of the
era, the doors of most radio studios were otherwise closed to black
musicians – largely because many show sponsors were tobacco and
beverage manufacturers based in the South.[60] Erenberg notes that,
despite his integrated combos in the late 1930s, Goodman's full band
'remained all-white. This compromise proved necessary to circumvent
the rules of segregated venues that might accept some black "guest"
players but were uncomfortable with a large integrated band that
symbolised permanent equality between the races.'[61] Significantly,
however, Goodman violated even this colour line by the end of the
decade, hiring pianist Fletcher Henderson and guitarist Charlie
Christian as big band members and Ellington's trumpeter Cootie
Williams and other African American players in 1941.

Yet, despite the inroads made by these white and black pioneers, the
segregationist mindset proved tenacious, especially in the South: the
touring experience for black and mixed bands in rural southern areas
was a nightmare that has been detailed by many who survived it,
including Billie Holiday in her autobiography, *Lady Sings the Blues*
(1956), where she indicates that she left Artie Shaw's band largely
because of the restrictions placed by Jim Crow on herself and her white
fellow members in the South and even in New York. The band had
trouble getting served in southern restaurants; as Holiday recalled, 'I
got so tired of scenes in crummy roadside restaurants over getting
served, I used to beg [one of Shaw's band members] to just let me sit in
the bus and rest – and let them bring out something in a sack . . .
Sometimes it was a choice between me eating and the whole band

starving.'[62] On one occasion Holiday was forced to wait in the women's lavatories between sets, so severe was the prohibition against black performers mingling with white audience members.

True to their creators' integrationist philosophies, Shaw's and especially Goodman's signature sounds were known for their black idiom intonations and harder-driving swing, which Erenberg and others have contrasted to Glenn Miller's softer, sweeter (whiter) sound, favoured by audiences during the rightward-shifting war years. By the same token, Ellington and Lunceford, two black band leaders, have been described as presenting a more sophisticated, urban (again, white) sound, and contrasted with Basie, who provided a rootsy, black-oriented 'regional and cultural authenticity'[63] characterised as 'swingin' the blues'. The great blues shouter and fellow Kansas City man Jimmy Rushing was Basie's vocalist starting in 1935 and for many years;[64] other famous Basie alumni include Clark Terry, Illinois Jacquet, and Lester Young, later 'one of the most important style setters of modern jazz'.[65] Basie reached a civil rights milestone when his orchestra played the Blue Room at New York's Hotel Lincoln – the first black band to perform there – in 1943.[66]

Miller's terrific success during the early 1940s – by which time, Erenberg argues, Miller's style had trumped Goodwin's as the trend-setter for commercial orchestras[67] – was owed not only to his smooth, controlled, even 'tame' sound and phenomenal hits such as 'In the Mood' and Miller's theme, 'Moonlight Serenade',[68] but also to the publicity generated when he joined the Air Force, then tragically disappeared over the English Channel in December 1944. Patriotic, conservative and musically non-threatening, Miller was the emblem of sentimentality and sacrifice, themes that pervaded the war years owing to generations of servicemen being separated from loved ones. Both Simon and Erenberg have used the term 'romantic' to describe Miller's well-orchestrated sound, a term fundamental to understanding the new direction big band was being asked to take during the war years – a direction that would spell its demise when the war ended. Erenberg considers the significance of a nation of single women, worried mothers and pining sweethearts influencing musical styles on the home front, seeking out what was patriotically or romantically stirring in modern instrumentals and especially in a burgeoning class of band-fronting vocalists, many of whom moved in the mid-1940s into successful solo careers. Surely, servicemen in the Pacific and European theatres, worried about their stateside sweethearts' fidelity and missing women in general, were also in the mood for love; Erenberg notes:

Harry James's Orchestra, for example, shot to the top in late 1942 with a syrupy trumpet, a string section, and beautiful ballads. Tommy Dorsey, Gene Krupa, and Artie Shaw followed suit, while Count Basie, noted *Variety*, 'discarded almost completely the typically-Negro rideout style' to become 'an outstanding example of the way swing bands are softening up more and more'.[69]

A musician's strike from 1942 to 1943 prevented musicians – but not vocalists – from making records, hastening the transition from big bands to the solo vocal performers who would dominate the late 1940s.[70]

Popular Vocalists

Band leader Harry James is famous not only for his great trumpet playing and band directing during the swing era but for his own romantic engagement with American GIs' favourite pin-up girl, Betty Grable, whom he married in 1943. He also gave a start to the most romantic and successful popular singer of the post-war period, Frank Sinatra. 'Old Blue Eyes' (though he was quite young, and extremely skinny, in this period) left James for Tommy Dorsey's band at the end of 1939, only six months after joining it, then left Dorsey for a solo career in 1942. During the war, Erenberg notes, GIs were resentful of Sinatra's 4-F status and jealous of his spellbinding appeal to female audiences, while the women themselves – primarily teenage bobby-soxers but women of all ages – swooned in the aisle at his concerts, creating the first heart-throb sensation in American music history. By contrast, the boys over-seas preferred the regular-guy persona and easy-going musical style of Bing Crosby, America's favourite vocal performer throughout the early 1940s and wildly popular after the war as well. Many have contrasted Sinatra's dramatic, even 'mooing' bel canto singing style with Bing's offhanded crooner sound; while Sinatra entertained at home, Crosby travelled to Europe in 1944 (as did Bob Hope; see the following case study), made inspiring films (in which he played the beloved Father O'Malley) throughout the war years, and sang Irving Berlin's 'White Christmas' in the 1942 *Holiday Inn*. It had sold thirty million copies by the time of Bing's death in 1977 and is estimated to be the biggest-selling record in American history.[71] Ironically, Sinatra struck many as a washed-up flash-in-the-pan by the end of the 1940s; it was not until the 1950s that he made his monumental mark with Capitol records, flour-ishing in partnership with composer-arranger-conductor Nelson Riddle.[72] At this time, as Henry Pleasants observes, 'The frail, pleading, moonstruck boyfriend was reborn as the confident, easy-riding, hard-driving irresistible and unchallenged Chairman of the Board, addressing himself to an audience of all ages and both sexes.'[73]

Other major vocal talents included the timeless Louis Armstrong, Rosemary Clooney, Perry Como, Sammy Davis, Doris Day, Ella Fitzgerald, Billie Holiday, Peggy Lee, Dinah Shore, and Sarah Vaughn. Blousy and maternal, even in her younger days, Kate Smith hosted a hugely popular *Kate Smith Hour* on radio, where she broke records for war bond sales and frequently belted out what came closest to being the United States's official 'war song' during the second world war, Irving Berlin's 'God Bless America' (1939).[74] Like Smith, the Andrews Sisters were also unaffiliated with big bands; their close vocal harmonies and airy bird-like voices charmed servicemen and their stateside sweethearts with hits like 'Boogie Woogie Bugle Boy' (1941) and 'Don't Sit under the Apple Tree' (1942) and numerous film appearances – often in uniform. Among the singers, Armstrong, Fitzgerald, Holiday, and Vaughn have been singled out by music historians for their mastery of the vocal arts in the jazz idiom: Armstrong (aka 'Satchmo') is known for his gravelly voice and tremendous innovations as a singer (and of course horn player) throughout the 1920s, 1930s, and 1940s; Fitzgerald (aka 'the First Lady of Song') for her brilliant vocal clarity and range as well as a remarkable ability to interact and improvise (especially in her patented scat style) with the instruments playing behind her; Holiday (aka 'Lady Day') for her soulful and unique spoken-sung musical style and heroin-plagued, tragically shortened life; and Vaughn (aka 'the Divine One') for her 'exceptional range spanning four octaves, from baritone to lyrical soprano'[75] and soulful, powerful overall style.

Bob Hope's USO Tours

Beginning with a performance at Riverside, California's March Field in May 1941, Bob Hope's popular *Pepsodent Show* functioned as a touring company sponsored by the United Service Organizations (USO) at army bases around the United States and overseas before, during, and after World War II. As television writer-producer Frank Buxton remembered, the company performed 'countless camp shows on makeshift stages, off the backs of Army trucks, on the decks of aircraft carriers – wherever there was a GI audience'.[76] For the shows, Hope and his writers developed a formula, similar to the one already filling his radio hours, to entertain military audiences throughout the remainder of his career – in Europe, Korea, Vietnam, and even in the Middle East during the Gulf War. His rapid-fire monologue began with, for instance, 'Hi, this is Bob "Mosquito Control" Hope', insert-ing each time a comic tag appropriate to the show's locale. The monologue itself was loaded with local, topical humour, specifically tailored to amuse beleaguered GIs. 'His monologues were . . . devoted to jokes about soldiers' gripes, crap games, officers, the food, and the location itself. . . . Wherever he was, he talked their language.'[77] The middle segments of the programme interspersed comedy, music, and attractive women: comic routines were performed by his regulars, Jerry Colonna, a bug-eyed, heavily moustached clown, and Vera Vague (played by Barbara Jo Allen), a plain Jane as man-crazy as Hope was girl-crazy. Hope often sang duets with the female singers in his crew, including long-time regulars Frances Langford, Dinah Shore and Doris Day. He famously trotted out the sex symbols of show business for appreciative GIs, including Rita Hayworth and Jane Russell, cracking jokes about 'what we're all fighting for' amid his audience's cat calls and applause.

Hope's first overseas performance was in Bristol, England (the city of this emigré's birth, as it turned out) in July 1943 for American and Allied soldiers. He later performed in North Africa, the South Pacific (covering more than 30,000 miles there, at some personal risk to himself and his crew), and in Berlin during the Berlin Airlift of 1948, when he presented the first of many Christmas shows. Peter W. Kaplan noted that 'as he traveled around the bases, and he saw the lonely and wounded soldiers, a deeper emotion entered his work. He allowed himself to do pictures that were slightly more serious,' and his lightning patter slowed and warmed.[78] In 1944, Hope wrote a best-selling book about his experiences, *I Never Left Home*, heavily pep-pering his recollections with jokes about military life lifted directly from his monologues

Hope died in 2003, at the age of one hundred, having received multiple honours and awards throughout his life: for the more than seventy USO tours he led from the 1940s to the 1990s, he was named an honorary veteran (the award that he said meant the most to him), honorary Knight Commander of the British Empire, and honorary Mayor of Palm Springs, California. Roads, hospitals, and military aircraft have been named for him, and he received a Congressional Gold Medal in 1962 and a Presidential Medal of Freedom in 1969. His papers, including numerous letters, photo-graph albums, radio and television scripts, and a compendious joke file are now at the Library of Congress, whose website, *Bob Hope and American Variety* (http://www.loc.gov/exhibits/bobhope/) provides a detailed overview of his life and work.

The Shift from Swing to Bop

In December 1946 alone eight bandleaders called it quits,[79] marking a significant transformation in jazz and the strengthening of the already-popular niche genres of blues, rhythm & blues, gospel, country and folk. Two splits are discernible in this period: the division of jazz

styles – which became evermore challenging and, some would say, eso-
teric – from the 'popular' modes and, unfortunately, something of a
resegregation of musical tastes (with white audiences choosing pop
vocalists, folk, and country styles, black audiences moving toward
gospel and R&B, with its own talented singers and instrumentalists)
that would not dissolve again until pioneer rock 'n' rollers (heavily
influenced by rhythm 'n' blues) brought black and white audiences
back together in the early 1950s. The only racially mixed fan base
remained jazz lovers, though again, this was more a left-oriented, highbrow minority willing to wrestle with the new form's complexities
than the national average by the late 1940s. Of all the cultural modes
examined in this study, it is music more than any other that so clearly
replicates the break in twentieth-century American history signified
by the end of the war and the beginning of the post-war, cold war, civil
rights, contemporary era.

Jazz in the late 1940s changed its name from 'swing' to 'bebop' (or
'bop') and was characterised by a marked shift in sound and even look.
Many of its chief practitioners were veterans of the big band era, prac-
tically all of them were African American, and all of them distinguished
their style by new forays into experimentation – in chord structure/
progression, rhythms, atonal melodies and harmonies, pacing, volume,
or whole-group dynamic. Not surprisingly, the groups themselves
became much smaller; the financial burdens of fifteen- to thirty-piece
orchestras, no longer supportable in the post-swing era, were blessings
in disguise for bop artists, who gained flexibility, intimacy and freedom
in smaller combos. Boppers – despite the frivolity of the designation –
regarded themselves as serious students of their craft, artists instead of
entertainers, who adopted a cool, even disaffected demeanour before
audiences, losing themselves in the depths of their music. Wary of the
long tradition of white exploitation of black musical styles, bop musicians determined to 'create something that they can't steal because they
can't play it'.[80] They eschewed, even disparaged, the clowning and
ingratiation effected by earlier jazz performers, especially African
American ones, reading an uncle-Tomism in such behaviour and even
distancing themselves from jazz greats like Armstrong, whose ready
smile they suspected.[81] The music was often too fast, and too difficult,
to dance to, but that was rather as it should be, as bop artists promoted
an environment in which patrons sat and attended quietly instead of
talking, drinking, and most especially dancing during performances. As
it turns out, unruly, tipsy, adulating jitter-buggers were something
of a thorn in the side of swing musicians throughout the preceding

period; bop was instrumental in turning jazz from a club into a concert experience.

Milestones of the bop era, which itself experienced a general collapse in 1950, include the performances of Dizzy Gillespie (on his famous bent trumpet) and Charlie 'Yardbird' Parker (on saxophone) – both together and as leaders of their own groups. Gillespie, in fact, worked several times with a large band but often in smaller groups as well; Parker led a combo featuring bop and modern jazz greats including Miles Davis and Max Roach in 1947. Diz and Bird teamed up in 1945, then split when, following a West Coast engagement, Gillespie returned to New York but Parker cashed in his air ticket to buy drugs. While out west, Parker generated interest in bop on that coast but was eventually hospitalised for his addiction. When released, he returned to New York where he paired again with Gillespie for a landmark Carnegie Hall concert in 1947. Other big-league boppers, including Dexter Gordon, Thelonius Monk, Chano Pozo (an innovator in Latin Jazz), and Bud Powell, played for or led groups in this era. The landmark numbers of the bop era belong primarily to Parker and include 'A Night in Tunisia' (1944), 'Salt Peanuts' (1945), 'Yardbird Suite' (1946), and 'Ornithology' (1946). Drafting his 1957 classic *On the Road* in 1948, novelist Jack Kerouac developed the idea of 'spontaneous bop prose' that would emulate the musical style in words. For Kerouac, bop prose 'describe[d] his efforts to reform fiction along the lines of avant garde jazz, where immediacy of expression and technical fluency combine to open new possibilities'.[82]

Other Music Genres

Rhythm 'n' blues, gospel, country, and folk appealed to the rural and middle-American masses during the 1940s – gospel and country being staples throughout the radio and recording era, and electric (or Chicago-style) blues and R&B developing out of the delta blues tradition with a strong following in the post-war period. Blues and R&B artists reached their audiences through 'race records', pitched specifically towards a black audience, juke box plays, and radio, particularly the show *King Biscuit Time*, a well-regarded forum for talented blues artists like Howlin' Wolf, Muddy Waters, Bo Diddley, and Sonny Boy Williamson during this period. Mahalia Jackson, mixing black church music and the blues, created a gospel sound distinct from the spirituals of earlier decades.[83] She toured the nation with gospel/blues pianist Reverend Thomas A. Dorsey and recorded hit records on the Apollo label. While the Clara Ward Singers, Roebuck 'Pops' Staples, and Roberta Martin (among others) were inspiring gospel acts of the 1940s as well, Pleasants notes that Jackson is regarded as the most famous gospel singer of her generation, 'the Gospel Queen',[84] not only because of her great talent but also because of her cross-over success; she moved from Apollo to Columbia Records in 1950 and played for more and more predominantly white audiences in the later decades of her career.

White gospel fans found church influence in the increasingly popular genre of country music (and the related 'cowboy', 'western', 'honky-tonk' and 'mountain' styles), as well as more secular themes such as romance, patriotism, folk heroism, and comedy. The *National Barn Dance* (broadcast from Chicago's WLS) and the *Grand Ol' Opry* were radio programmes beloved by country music lovers. Both had been hit shows from the 1920s; the *Barn Dance* ceased broadcasting in 1960s, and the *Opry* continues today as the longest-running radio programme in history. Nashville's large broadcasting area and especially WLS's 50,000-megawatt coverage of (on a clear day) great swaths of the entire mid-section of the United States meant that after the war (and especially following the wane of swing), the 1940s was an era during which 'country music first began reaching a truly national audience'.[85] Having formed the Blue Grass Boys in 1939, 'father of bluegrass' Bill Monroe was in the early years of his career in the 1940s. His hits from that decade include 'Kentucky Waltz' (1946) and 'Blue Moon of Kentucky' (1947); Blue Grass Boys alumni Lester Flatt and Earl Scruggs formed the Foggy Mountain Boys in 1948. While the Carter Family reigned as country music royalty in the 1940s (as they had since the late 1920s), the most influential country singer-songwriter of the decade was Hank Williams, whose honky-tonk, hard-luck, heartbreak musical themes have continued to define the genre. Williams is as legendary today for his 1940s-era charts, including 'Move it on Over' (1947), 'Honky Tonkin'' (1947) and his 1949 mega-hit 'Lovesick Blues', as he is for his tragically eventful life which included heavy drinking, notorious unreliability as a performer, two unsuccessful marriages and death from a substance overdose at the age of twenty-nine in 1953.

More than any other genre, country was known as well for its 'novelty' music – comic and incisively topical songs or performers whose lyrics function now as vital historical artefacts. Wayne W. Daniel has demonstrated how heavily themed were the wartime *Barn Dance* programmes themselves (salutes to American allies, to the red, white and blue), as well as many of the songs made popular through the programme. These songs encouraged petrol conservation, victory gardens and fidelity to faraway servicemen with catchy, comic, or romantic lyrics. The novelty act, known as the Hoosier Hotshots, was responsible for many comic routines and songs issued from the *Barn Dance* with lyrics enjoining Americans to drive less and 'park' (that is, make love in parked cars) more, 'save [their Victory Garden] scallions for Hitler's battalions' and laugh along to 'She's a Washout in a Blackout' (1942).[86] In the post-war period, the favourite novelty theme was the atom bomb, whose canon included, according to Charles K. Wolfe, a striking range of apocalypticism, pacifism and God-on-our-side jingoism. For Paul Boyer, the atomic theme in country music belonged to a long tradition that 'both celebrated and deplored the inroads of technology'.[87] Country star Fred Kirby, touring radio stations as the government's 'Victory Cowboy' during the war, wrote and performed both 'Atomic Power' in 1945 and 'When the Hell Bomb Falls' in 1950.[88] 'Atomic Power' was recorded by several groups in the late 1940s and spent several weeks as a chart-topping jukebox favourite.[89] Karl Davis and Harty Taylor recorded 'When the Atom Bomb Fell' in December 1945,[90] and the Sons of the Pioneers sang 'Old Man Atom' for audiences in 1947.[91] Comparing the popular tunes of Tin Pan Alley to 'hillbilly' music during the war, Ronald D. Cohen notes that, while the former favoured nostalgia over outright patriotism, the latter capitalised on both: 'country music could approach war topics in a more earthy manner while still dripping with nostalgia and romance'.[92]

Cowboy/western stars of the era included Patsy Montana, a singing cowgirl, whose 'I Want to Be a Cowboy's Sweetheart' (1935) was the first million-seller ever performed by a female country artist.[93] Don Cusic notes that by the 1940s ' "Western" music was alive and well . . . but increasingly the "western" came from the clothes [the performers] wore, not necessarily the songs they sang.'[94] The cowboy singer's look was on display in the 1940s most often when cowboy singers crossed over on to the screen, which happened frequently in the careers of Gene Autry and Roy Rogers, singing cowboys who were phenomenal Hollywood successes. Cusic relates the bitter irony involved in Gene Autry's entry into the military: 'Although Republic would . . . reissue some of Autry's . . . movies during the war, the studio reacted to Autry's departure by heavily promoting Roy Rogers as the "King of the Cowboys". The war would give Rogers, who stayed in Hollywood making movies, a big career boost.'[95] Red Foley, another cowboy singer of the period, was 'the most popular country singer of the late 1940s'[96] whose war-era, patriotically themed 'Smoke on the Water' was 'by far the most popular World War II song recorded by a "National Barn Dance" artist'.[97] Foley, like Eddie

Arnold, was regarded as a country crooner, whose sophisticated, almost urban style in part crossed over into the pop genre and may have appealed to a more middle-class, city-dwelling listener.[98]

Folk and Classical Styles

In folk music, the legendary Woody Guthrie was beginning his career in 1940, leaving a radio programme he had hosted in California to take part in performances, recordings and leftist protests in New York. His career intersected with all major players of the 1940s folk scene: he talked with, and sang for, the great folklorist and musicologist Alan Lomax who recorded these sessions for the Library of Congress; he recorded hundreds of records for Moses Asch (founder of Folkways Records in 1948) throughout the decade; and he performed with fellow folk artists Leadbelly, Cisco Huston, Burl Ives, Pete Seeger, Sonny Terry, and Sis Cunningham in New York. With several of these friends, Guthrie formed the Almanac Singers in 1940, a short-lived leftist folk group that re-formed as the Weavers in the early 1950s. Guthrie wrote the American anthem 'This Land is Your Land' in 1940, in part to counteract the jingoism he heard in Irving Berlin's 'God Bless America', an inescapable theme in the early 1940s. During the war, Guthrie shipped out as a merchant marine, performing mess duties but entertaining troops with his populist songs and even penning lyrics for a military pamphlet about the hazards of venereal disease.[99] Leadbelly, a blues-folk artist from the Mississippi Delta was miscast as a 'race' or blues artist early in his career, but did better in association with both Lomax and Asch in the New York 1940s folk scene. Burl Ives was a Broadway and film actor in addition to being a folk singer; his hits include 'The Wayfaring Stranger' (1944) 'Foggy, Foggy Dew' (1949) and 'Big Rock Candy Mountain' (1949). Sixties folk icon Pete Seeger began his career in 1940s New York, enjoying a hit version of Leadbelly's 'Good Night, Irene' in 1949. Because of their pronounced leftism, many folk performers came under Congressional fire during the red scare of the 1950s; Ives informed upon Seeger among others and continued his career unhindered, while Seeger refused to answer questions and was charged with contempt of Congress.

Classical yet popular, even populist, orchestral pieces composed by Aaron Copland in the 1940s enjoyed large audiences as well. These included 'Fanfare for the Common Man', *Lincoln Portrait*, and *Rodeo* (all in 1942), *Appalachian Spring* (1944) and *The Red Pony* (1948), a score for the film of the same name based on John Steinbeck's novel. Copland was a prolific scorer for Hollywood and widely influential among others in the trade, especially those writing for westerns. Borrowing jazz, folk and church melodies, he popularised and Americanised classical music in the 1940s, depicting the cultural and geographical landscape, especially rolling prairies and soaring peaks of America's rural territories. Also during the 1940s, the great conductor/composer/pianist Leonard Bernstein gained international fame. He held appointments with the New York Philharmonic and New York City Symphony Orchestra and composed his first large work, 'Symphony No. 1: Jeremiah' (1943). He collaborated with Jerome Robbins on two ballets, 'Fancy Free' (1944) and 'Facsimile' (1946), and with Betty Comden and Adolph Green on *On the Town* (1944; see Chapter 3).

Conclusion

Thus it was a great era for listening (and, whenever appropriate, dancing), thanks to the thinkers, talkers, singers, and musicians filling the airways and jukeboxes of the decade. While the news was not always good and the music sometimes challenging, radio and popular music brought Americans together over issues of national import and widely enjoyed entertainment styles. At the same time, each important event from the war received myriad critical interpretations, as journalists and commentators with a range of rhetorical emphases, stylistic innovations and political opinions presented their findings to early-1940s radio listeners. In entertainment, genres of radio programming and popular music proliferated to suit every taste and mood. If radio's dramatic stories, both real and fictionalised, exercised the imagination in ways that film and television never would, music broadcast over the radio and played live in hundreds of clubs and ballrooms around the country during the war exercised the body through the skilled and energetic dances it all but demanded of its eager listeners. Some of the real action described through radio news was too frightening to imagine, but its informed analysis by trusted commentators, as well as comforting radio entertainment and the mood-elevating jitterbugging, top-flight musicianship, patriotic anthems, and sentimental love songs of the era's popular music all helped Americans through the frightening dreams and tragic realities inflicted by war.

Chapter 3

Theatre and Film

The American theatre and film scenes changed dramatically in the 1940s; on Broadway, this change occurred on stage while, in Hollywood, changes made behind the scenes were as important, if not more so, than the thematic shift undergone on screen following war's end. In 1943, Richard Rodgers and Oscar Hammerstein II's *Oklahoma!* changed forever not only the look of the American musical but the tone and quality of stage entertainment as a whole. Thanks to Rodgers and Hammerstein, and many of their talented fellow composers and lyricists, the war era was as fine a time for song and dance on-stage as it was in the nation's ballrooms and radio stations. This trend continued after the war, although centre stage was claimed by major dramatists of the era, who dealt in remarkable ways with the disaffected Everyman and his tragic end. Film also got darker after the war – literally, as noir film styling led to a spate of classic films that, in fact, challenged both the guts-and-glory patriotism of the wartime Hollywood product and the mindless suburbanisation that then characterised the cultural landscape. Perhaps the trend towards dark filmmaking was primarily a reaction to the grim occurrences on the American political scene – Congressional hearings launched to persecute leftist Hollywood producers and screenwriters and new rules for redistributing the resources of Hollywood's industry monopoly. Despite the dark themes emanating from stage and screen throughout the decade, however, Broadway and Hollywood remained largely white environments, failing as badly as did radio to open their doors to producers, directors and performers of colour.

America's Theatre District

Historians regard the 1940s as the fullest flowering of a great era in American theatre, in large part because its greatest musical innovations occurred during this period. This is remarkable when we recall that Broadway is often less interested in innovation than the commercially successful sure bet. As the United States lacks a national theatre, and as most regional stages were not to raise curtains until the following decade or later, theatre in the 1940s originated almost entirely from a twelve-by-two-block strip surrounding Times Square on New York City's Upper West Side. There, some twenty-five playhouses, many built at the turn of the century, housed productions that, after brief out-of-town runs in New Haven, Boston or Philadelphia, made their debut on Broadway and succeeded or failed – almost always on the word of influential theatre critics. Many long-run shows were later packaged for a national tour with less elaborate settings and often casts of lesser fame. Many have been the show that was so poorly (or, conversely, so challengingly) conceived, performed or staged that it has closed out of town. Some did poorly as first runs but enjoyed successful restagings years or decades later (see discussion of Eugene O'Neill below). Some flopped horribly but live on through well-written scores, and others, even though closing shortly, are regarded by historians as historical – worth continued study and admiration – for myriad reasons. In 1946, the first off-Broadway theatres opened in the southern neighbourhoods of Manhattan; here much challenging, daring and innovative theatre has made its debut while, ironically, an off-Broadway show's move uptown is as often for the 'wrong' reason (its commercial viability) as for the right ones – its inherent quality and significance.

The War Off- and Onstage

Offstage, the theatre community of 1940s New York did its part to support the war effort. The famous Stage Door Canteen, housed in the 44th Street Theatre, was sponsored by an organisation begun by seven theatre women and known as the Stage Women's War Relief during World War I. At the start of World War II, the group renamed itself the American Theatre Wing and functioned for a while under the auspices of the Allied Relief Fund; shortly after US entry into the war it became an independent organisation. The Canteen (and seven others like it throughout America and in London and Paris) was open only to servicemen in uniform, who enjoyed food, entertainment and dances with pretty girls (all of which were served up by the leading lights of theatre and film) at a nightly rate of 3,000 troops:

> In an average night . . . the Canteen served 2000 sandwiches, 3000 slices
> of cake or doughnuts, 1000 half pints of milk, 80 gallons of fruit juice or
> cider, 25 lbs. of candy, six crates of fruit, and 5000 cigarettes. Theatrical
> luminaries gave of their time and talents in the Canteens. Katharine
> Cornell [a romantic tragidienne of the 1930s] gladly cleaned off tables,
> Marlene Dietrich frequently assisted at the milk bar . . .[1]

Theatre historian James V. Hatch observes that the Canteen was an
integrated club where Carl Van Vechten, who ran the operation two
nights a week, instructed the hostesses to 'dance with uniforms, not
with colours'.[2] Another popular Wing programme was the Lunchtime
Follies, a revue packaged for staging in the lunch halls of area war
industrial plants, by way of keeping up morale. In the plants, performers erected simple sets, performed topical skits and songs, and
often stayed around to entertain the 'lunch hours' of all three shifts.
The Wing also produced a hospital entertainment programme, entertained troops overseas, and raised money for the USO through its
popular radio programme 'Stage Door Canteen'.

   The Theatre Wing is best known today as the producer of the
annual Tony Awards. These were given for the first time in the Grand
Ballroom of the Waldorf-Astoria on 6 April 1947, with 1,000 people in
attendance. The award was named in honour of Antoinette Perry, a
Wing co-founder who served as its board chair and secretary during
the war years. The first Tony awards were not the medallions they
became in 1949 nor the medallions mounted on bases that we know
today but a scroll of recognition dandified with a cigarette lighter,
money clip or compact ('Tony History'). The original roll of award
winners included José Ferrer and Fredric March (both chosen in the
Best Actor Category), Ingrid Bergman and Helen Hayes (both
awarded as Best Actress), Arthur Miller (for his drama *All My Sons*),
Elia Kazan (for Best Director of that play), and Kurt Weill (Best
Composer for *Street Scene*). Special awards were given to Beck Theater
treasurer Dora Chamberlain 'for unfailing courtesy'; to Mr and Mrs
Ira Katzenberg for 'enthusiasm as inveterate first-nighters'; and to
Vincent Sardi, owner of a famous theatre hangout, for 'providing a
transient home and comfort station to theater folk at Sardi's for twenty
years'.[3]

   Perhaps not surprisingly by now, the war itself was a catalyst for
achievement, as musical theatre was a genre thoroughly appreciated by
soldiers on leave and by the sorrowing families of the home front;
almost any musical of the early 1940s is readable for its covert or overt

patriotic themes. Lightweight escapism was hailed by audiences, and even sometimes critics, desperate for the lift in spirits. *Follow the Girls* (1944), a military farce set at a servicemen's canteen, delighted reviewers who might have scoffed outside the war context; audiences loved the lowbrow revue *Star and Garter* (1942), starring vaudeville veteran Bobby Clark and famed stripper Gypsy Rose Lee, as well as Irving Berlin's higher-toned but purposely goofy *This is the Army* (1942). One top-quality military musical was Betty Comden and Adolph Green's *On the Town* (1944), about three sailors exuberantly on weekend leave. The show was loved especially for its lavish dance spectacle, choreographed by Jerome Robbins and set to Leonard Bernstein's marvellous score.

Non-military foolishness was also welcomed. Jule Style and Sammy Cahn's silly but nostalgic *High Button Shoes* (1947) starred the popular comic Phil Silvers and Broadway sweetheart Nanette Fabray, and featured a Keystone Kops ballet sequence also choreographed by Robbins.[4] At the end of the decade, Styne and Leo Robin scored (literally and figuratively) a zany hit with their adaptation of Anita Loos's novel *Gentleman Prefer Blondes* (1949), about Lorelei Lee, 1920s gold-digger. She herself scores big, in part because she was unforgettably portrayed by the one-of-a-kind Carol Channing, a leggy, dingy, comic genius in her first major role (played by Marilyn Monroe in the screen version of 1953). While wartime, war-themed dramas were also plentiful, they were less popular with audiences looking instead for military high jinks onstage and also compare unfavourably to the plays produced in the post-war period by the dramatic masters Eugene O'Neill, Tennessee Williams and Arthur Miller.

The Rodgers and Hammerstein Revolution

Entertainment-starved servicemen might have been happy with any excuse to watch pretty girls dancing and enjoy a comic's joke; many early shows were star vehicles, either designed especially with a star's talents in mind or designed with no special intent but relying upon the magnetism of the star personality to sell tickets anyway. When shows lacked their own spark and a top star, they folded quickly; weak shows rescued by a talented performer closed as soon as he or she left the cast. More than once, this was the beloved dancer-comic Ray Bolger who propped up Rodgers and Hart's *By Jupiter* in 1942 and Frank Loesser's early and not-so-impressive *Where's Charley?* (a musical remake of *Charley's Aunt* that required Bolger to spend much time in drag) in

1948. Similarly, Ethel Merman's departure from *Sadie Thompson* (1944) was its death knell.[5]

Musical theatre underwent a marvellous revolution on 31 March 1943. That night the curtain rose in the St. James Theatre, and Richard Rodgers and Oscar Hammerstein's *Oklahoma!*, a deceptively simple story of love, jealousy and reunion with two romantic leads, an engaging supporting couple and a host of feuding farmers and cowmen, commenced. *Oklahoma!*'s book (the dialogue script), score and choreography came together in ways that had never been dreamt of, let alone attempted, before. As Ethan Mordden notes, 'the songs pop out of the script so naturally that the singing is like dialogue, only more so'. Prior to *Oklahoma!*, 'songs tended to block the action, stop it dead. *Oklahoma!*'s songs convey it.'[6] The same went for Agnes DeMille's balletic choreography which, instead of being mere visual diversion, 'heightened the drama by revealing the subconscious fears and desires of the leading characters'.[7] This innovation began a raging trend – many musicals in the succeeding decade (especially Rodgers and Hammerstein's) would not have been complete without their ballet sequences. Finally, 'everything in *Oklahoma!* kept faith with everything else. "The orchestrations sounded the way the costumes look" is how Richard Rodgers explained it: integrity';[8] 'what was unique about *Oklahoma!* was the synthesis of its component parts into a complete theatrical entity of great beauty and imagination'.[9]

Based on Lynn Riggs's stage comedy *Green Grow the Lilacs*, purchased for production by the financially ailing Theatre Guild, the show seemed jinxed from the start, with trouble finding backers and an untested song-writing team. Out-of-town reviews were mixed, but the producers and performers moved quickly from relief to elation on opening night; in Hammerstein's own recollection, the audience fairly glowed in delight,[10] and critics could not stop raving the next morning. Not surprisingly, the show exploded previous records for the number of performances for a musical, quadrupling what previously had been considered an astounding success with 2,248 consecutive performances, or five years and nine weeks beyond its premiere. It toured nationally for a decade and has been revived frequently on Broadway – and performed almost constantly by regional and local theatres nationwide – ever since.

Perhaps the last measure of this show's superlative place in American theatre history is the shadow it immediately cast upon everything that had been written before it and everything that was to come. During a decade plagued by missed hits, Cole Porter gamely admitted that, in the late 1940s, 'the librettos are much better . . . and the scores are much closer to the librettos than they used to be. Those two [Rodgers and Hammerstein] made it much harder for everybody else.'[11] And imagine the sorry lot of the first show to debut in *Oklahoma!*'s wake. Abe Laufe reports that 'a musical farce, *Hairpin Harmony*, opened, received brutal reviews, and closed after three performances. One reviewer said that any show that followed would, by comparison, make a better impression.'[12] That show, Kurt Weill's *One Touch of Venus*, opened six months after *Oklahoma!* and starred Mary Martin as a beautiful statue brought to life by the man who falls in love with her. Indeed it had merit but ultimately 'the production disappointed critics who compared it with *Oklahoma!* . . .'[13] The next actual hit was the completely different – and in long retrospect, vastly inferior – *Follow the Girls*, the military farce referred to above, probably helped to its 882-performance run by striking such a resonant political chord and opening an entire year and a month after *Oklahoma!*. By then, audiences were ready for another smash, and perhaps the best way to achieve such success was to abandon altogether the high-prestige neighbourhood now ruled by Rodgers and Hammerstein. Even, or perhaps especially, the golden duo themselves would suffer the trial of measuring against, when their next joint venture, the also fine but not-quite-so-stellar *Carousel* opened in 1945.

Great Musicals of the 1940s

Despite the tendency to regard pre-*Oklahoma!* productions as somehow lacking, many fine shows appeared in the early 1940s. These include two by Rodgers and Hart, *Pal Joey* (1940) and *By Jupiter* (1942), Vernon Duke and John Latouche's black folk musical *Cabin in the Sky* (1940), and Kurt Weill and Irving Berlin's psychoanalytic, expressionistic *Lady in the Dark* (1941). King of 1920s operetta, Sigmund Romberg, had a last hit in 1945 (*Up in Central Park*, about the Boss Tweed scandals of the 1870s that plagued the park's construction). Following his best decade (the 1930s), Porter's early 1940s showings – *Panama Hattie* (1940), *Let's Face It!* (1941), *Something for the Boys* (1943) and *Mexican Hayride* (1944) – were solid hits, secured in large part by star turns by Ethel Merman (Porter's favourite leading lady, for her ability to articulate his complex lyrics), Danny Kaye (another silver-tongued, comically gifted enunciator) and comedian Bobby Clark. Still, they appeared thin; '*Oklahoma!* happened and suddenly Porter's *Mexican Hayride* looked tacky, though it, too, was a smash';[14] Porter contributed to a disastrous revue (*The Seven Lively Arts*, also in 1944), and his collaboration with Orson Welles in a musical adaptation of Jules Verne called *Around the World* closed after seventy-five performances. Happily, Porter completed the decade with a strong comeback in 1949: the sophisticated and comical *Kiss Me, Kate*, about a feuding theatre couple's reunion during their performance of Shakespeare's *Taming of the Shrew*.

Irving Berlin was another 1930s-era stalwart made nervous by the new standard set by Rodgers and Hammerstein. Following his successful *This is the Army* (1942), during which Berlin, dressed in his World War I uniform, reprised his 1917 soldier's anthem, 'Oh, How I Hate to Get Up in the Morning', he did no composing until he was asked – by none other than producers Rodgers and Hammerstein themselves, to write the score for *Annie Get Your Gun*. Despite misgivings, Berlin accepted the job and created a smash in 1946, which ran for more than 1,100 performances. He is known in this show for having 'made a lady' of Ethel Merman,[15] who had been cast in the past as the tough-talking dame but got to display tenderness and vulnerability as the sharp-shooting heroine Annie Oakley. Berlin's late-1940s *Miss Liberty*, about a search for the model who posed for the Statue of Liberty, was less meritorious, regarded by historian Ethan Mordden as a 'total disaster'[16] especially for its plodding book by playwright and FDR speechwriter Robert E. Sherwood, but is appreciated by Stanley Green for Berlin's stirring music.

Cabin in the Sky is regarded as an important 1940s musical (and an important forerunner to *Oklahoma!*) for its complex characterisation and its dramatisation of serious subject matter that was nevertheless well complemented by its musical numbers. It is significant for being an all-black (though white-authored) production that featured radio and stage-comedy star Ethel Waters, in her only dramatic-musical role, as the devout, long-suffering wife of a well-meaning but weak-willed husband (Dooley Wilson) tempted by the siren Georgia Brown (dancer-choreographer Katherine Dunham, played by Lena Horne in the 1943 film). In 1944 Yip Harburg and Harold Arlen (who also co-wrote the score for *The Wizard of Oz* [1939]) produced the charming but challenging *Bloomer Girl*, about the nineteenth-century feminist effort to achieve equality through the wearing of pants (or in this case, pantalets). The show's political themes – not only the feminist angle but an abolition subplot that involved two African American actors as slaves – came couched in the inviting music of Harburg and Arlen and the inviting performances of first Celeste Holm and then Nanette

Fabray in the title role. Harburg explicitly linked the black rights theme to the wartime context: 'he felt [that] audiences of 1944 could accept the theme as pertaining to the struggle for freedom everywhere'.[17] Arlen's next project, co-written with Johnny Mercer, was *St. Louis Woman* (1946), an all-black musical that, while unsuccessful, featured the popular comedy duo the Fayard Brothers and gave Pearl Bailey her star debut, during which she wowed audiences with the comic songs 'Legalise my Name' and 'A Woman's Prerogative'.[18]

Harburg teamed with Burton Lane for *Finnian's Rainbow* (1947), yet another racially themed story of a leprechaun who comes to 'Missitucky' (combining the southern states' names of Mississippi and Kentucky) to search for gold, evidently buried under Fort Knox. In one sub-plot, a racist southern senator mistakenly makes a wish that is granted by his turning into a black person; ultimately this sub-plot resolves but not before demonstrating 'the inanity of racial intolerance'.[19] At the end of the decade, Kurt Weill teamed with playwright Maxwell Anderson for *Lost in the Stars* (1949), an adaptation of Alan Paton's novel of South African apartheid, *Cry, the Beloved Country*. Theatre historian Allen Woll notes that the foreign context of *Lost in the Stars*, similar to the vogue for black-themed stories set in the Caribbean during this period, is significant: 'the critique of race relations in South Africa rarely caused reviewers to muse about race relations at home'.[20] Examining both segregation and integration on twentieth-century Broadway, Woll concludes that mid-century all-black musicals exemplify segregation but so also did the appearance of stars such as Ethel Waters in otherwise white revues, 'whose routines were clearly separate from those of the [white] stars'.[21] More promising were the post-war gestures towards integrated casting, as occurred in Harold Rome's *Call Me Mister* (1946), a revue about returning GIs; Duke Ellington's *Beggar's Holiday* (also 1946);[22] *Bloomer Girl* and *Finnian's Rainbow*, as indicated above; and even *Kiss Me, Kate*, which featured African American supporting actors in several roles.[23]

Even Rodgers and Hammerstein got on to this bandwagon, first when Hammerstein staged his modernisation of Bizet's *Carmen* (as *Carmen Jones* with an all-black cast in 1945), then when both adapted James Michener's short stories as *South Pacific* (1949). Its heroine is a bigoted US Army nurse who learns better in the course of the show; one sub-plot involves an inter-racial romance between an Ivy League soldier and his island love interest, and the island girl's mother, Bloody Mary, sings some of the show's most memorable songs (including 'Bali

H'ai') and was portrayed originally by the African American classically trained singer and character actress Juanita Hall. (Hall won the Best Supporting Actress Tony for this role in 1950.) For theatre historians, *South Pacific* contends with *Oklahoma!* as Rodgers and Hammerstein's masterpiece. Most lean slightly towards the former in their assessments, turning to its outstanding theatrical run (three hundred fewer performances than *Oklahoma!* but the highest gross receipts of any Broadway musical) and its Pulitzer Prize for evidence. Significantly, this award was for Best Drama, as *South Pacific* is primarily a dramatic tale that includes (though includes perfectly) music. The drama (even tragedy) set to music was part of the Rodgers and Hammerstein revolution from the outset; in *Oklahoma!* the story's villain is killed on stage, in *Carousel* it is the conflicted hero Billy Bigelow who succumbs at mid point while, in *South Pacific*, the secondary but heroic Lieutenant Cable dies in the course of anti-Japanese strategic manoeuvres. The background theme of war and the always-weighty topic of racism made *South Pacific* dramatic fare. Certainly there were comedic numbers, but even with these, 'there was no choreography for the production'.[24] As Mordden notes, *South Pacific*

> embodies the forties style in musicals. It may be a summit, perhaps an index, full of the decade's entries: the war theme, of course, so of the time . . . that no major fifties musical dealt even with the peacetime military; the mixed-race casts of *Beggar's Holiday* and *Finnian's Rainbow*; the mixing of legit and musical-comedy voices . . . that leads to a sound comprising the vernacular and the exalted.[25]

Indeed, the 1940s encapsulates the learning curve that transformed the musical into a truly excellent American art form: Rodgers and Hammerstein broke all rules in 1943, by the end of the decade many others (Porter, Berlin, Bernstein) were on board, and *South Pacific*, which raised the standard higher yet, promised only good things for the next decade. While less well-structured escapist fare would always have a chance at popular success, a tradition in musical theatre was established that Americans could point to with pride in a period during which its self-image and international reputation were vital. Its record of racial integration onstage, equally important to the American international profile during this era, improved during the 1940s. Yet this was something of a golden, fading moment in American theatre history, as integrated casting shamefully 'dwindle[d] in both the drama and the musical on Broadway during the 1950s'.[26]

Popular Dramas

The non-musical plays of the 1940s also traversed the spectrum from the dramatic (even tragic) to the comically farcical. Once more, war was a perennial theme, although one that tended to indicate a play of lesser quality; Lillian Hellman's drama *Watch on the Rhine* (1941) and Thomas Heggen and Joshua Logan's serio-comedy *Mister Roberts* (1948) are among those few that stand out. *Watch* focuses on the American in-laws of an anti-Nazi German emigré who must come to terms with their indifferent response to the war in the days before Pearl Harbor. *Mister Roberts* was beloved by audiences; it starred Henry Fonda in both the stage and 1955 film versions and ran for 1,157 performances. The story satirises the inept, authoritarian leadership on board a Navy cargo ship. It ends with Roberts's heroic death when he is at last released from his backwater military post to serve on a destroyer and is killed in action. One grim drama unrelated to war was the stage adaptation of Richard Wright's *Native Son* (1941) with the charismatic Canada Lee in the title role; despite its bleak violence, which distressed even African American playgoers, 'it was inevitable that history be made with such a play, or the white man's style in the "black folk play" would remain the only black style anyone knew of'.[27] Mid-decade *Deep are the Roots* (1945) described inter-racial romance; *Strange Fruit* (1945) told the story of a young black woman who has a white man's child, and was praised by Eleanor Roosevelt in her syndicated column for women's magazines.[28] That same year *Anna Lucasta*, about an African American waterfront prostitute, was a milestone of its own kind (see the following case study). Maxine Wood's *On Whitman Avenue* (1946), also starring Lee, focused on the problems a black veteran's family has in finding housing in a white neighbourhood. *Our Lan'* opened in 1947 and was the second 1940s' drama by an African American (the first being *Native Son*); it narrates the crises of land ownership endured by newly freed blacks during the US Reconstruction period.

Anna Lucasta and the American Negro Theatre

In August 1944, *Anna Lucasta*, the story of a waterfront prostitute first rejected then sold out by her pious but opportunistic father, opened on Broadway and ran for more than two years. Noted as 'the first all-black production with a non-racial theme',[29] the production moved downtown five weeks after it had opened in Harlem under the auspices of the American Negro Theater (ANT). Anna was portrayed by the beautiful actress and civil rights activist Hilda Simms and, in the supporting role of Anna's tough-talking co-worker, was novelist-playwright Alice Childress, who joined the company in part because her 'complexion was too fair for commercial black roles'.[30] The film version (1959) starred Eartha Kitt and Sammy Davis Jr.[31] Wolcott Gibbs of *The New Yorker* called the production 'dignified and exciting',[32] while Lewis Nichols of the *New York Times* liked everything but the 'occasional jarring costume' and praised the acting of Simms and Childress, as well as ANT founder Frederick O'Neal and Broadway leading man Canada Lee, who also had parts.[33]

In 1940 O'Neal and his co-founder, playwright Abram Hill, established the uptown theatre collective in the basement of the Schomburg Library at 135th Street and Lennox Avenue. Its mission was to enable black play-wrights, actors, and stageworkers to ply their trades without having to compete for the rare spot offered by the 'integrated' production on Broadway. The co-founders selected the group's name as much for its acronym as its spelled-out significance: while tiny and powerless as indi-viduals, the 'ants' were a hard-working and mighty aggregate who paid dues and pooled financial resources to produce locally written plays for dramatic talent.[34] Over the next nine years, 50,000 playgoers attended ANT productions; it expanded to include a theatre school (whose graduates included Harry Belafonte, Ossie Davis, Ruby Dee, and Sidney Poitier) in 1942.[35]

Originally a novel about a Polish American family by the white author Philip Yordan, *Anna Lucasta* was briefly a white-cast Broadway drama *and* a now-obscure white-cast film starring Paulette Goddard, John Ireland and Broderick Crawford in 1949. After leaving the stage for the first time, however, it was optioned by ANT producers whose adaptation was an immediate success. While the play's move to the Mansfield Theatre on Broadway was one of many marks of distinction for ANT, it regrettably caused more trouble than benefit and signalled the demise of the company: ANT actors who were not cast for the Broadway production were resentful, and most damaging of all, 'ANT received royalties of less than two-percent . . . and none at all for the tour or the film'.[36] While the original contract was fairer to the Harlem producers, this disappeared mysteriously after the show caught on downtown.[37] In addition, this initial contact with the Broadway environs encouraged ANT's directors to pursue other white-authored plays, in the hope of similar success, losing its vital connection to the Harlem community as it did.[38] Co-founder Hill recalls, 'I couldn't stand all the acrimony. They didn't want any show that did not have a Broadway potential. We had nearly three hundred members. Women came in looking for Hilda Simms roles; guys looking for Poitier roles.'[39] Despite the downturn of the company itself, the American Negro Theatre launched many important careers and is part of an illustrious Harlem tradition whose twentieth-century milestones included the Harlem Renaissance of the 1920s and the Black Arts Movement of the 1960s.

Comedies unrelated to war succeeded better than dramas did, especially Joseph Kesselring's *Arsenic and Old Lace* (1941), about two
sweet old ladies who poison unhappy widowers and allow their unbal-
anced nephew, convinced he is Teddy Roosevelt, to bury them in the
basement; Mary Chase's *Harvey* (1944), about the friendship between
an eccentric tippler and a six-foot rabbit; and Garson Kanin's *Born
Yesterday* (1946), about a dizzy blonde – the marvellous Judy Holiday
in a breakthrough role – who comes out on top. More substantial was
Thornton Wilder's *The Skin of our Teeth* (1942), the second of his two
great plays, the first being *Our Town* (1938). The play's title indicates
its thesis, 'that humanity can and will survive anything, if only barely',
a position that 'must have been particularly welcome to its wartime
audiences'.[40] Postmodern in its self-consciousness, actors get 'out of
character' at certain points – to criticise their performance from the
night before or complain to the audience about the story's obscurity
and irrelevance. Pieces of the set collapse, and the characters shift
abruptly from ordinary American family members to cave-dwelling
types, ark-building types and warriors locked in inter-generational
conflict. Gerald M. Berkowitz points to a certain dead-end quality to
the experiment – after Wilder tried it, there were no imitators – yet
regards the play's anti-realist qualities as key anticipators of 'the movement from political to psychological and spiritual subjects' that prevailed in the 1940s and 1950s.[41]

Leading Dramatists: O'Neill, Williams and Miller

Eugene O'Neill travelled a similar path, from his experimental dramas
of the 1920s and 1930s to his more realistic (and less political, more personal and psychological) later plays. Interestingly, he had no theatrical
success in the 1940s, yet all of his major late works were written during
this decade, then performed successfully later. In 1941, O'Neill completed his bravely autobiographical *Long Day's Journey into Night*,
which did not open until 1956, three years after his death. *A Moon for
the Misbegotten*, a sequel to *Long Day's Journey*, closed out of town
in 1947, but was revived successfully in the 1970s. O'Neill's first production of the 1940s, *The Iceman Cometh* (1946), lasted less than six
months but was revived in 1957 to critical acclaim with America's
quintessential interpreter of O'Neill, Jason Robards Jr, in the lead. In
the story, a collection of regulars at a 1912 saloon drink themselves into
daily oblivion, cushioning the ride with comforting 'pipe dreams' of
success they will achieve one day – if they can ever get off their bar

stools. They are first cheered and then dismayed by the arrival of Hickey, who usually buys everyone a round but on this day challenges his compatriots to set down their drinks and delusions and begin living life. When it is learned that Hickey's liberation has come at the expense of his wife – whom he has murdered out of shame and rage for forever disappointing her – he is led away by the police while the barflies return to their happy, hopeless habits. Challenging and revolutionary, the play solidified O'Neill's most important themes: tragic enslavement to circumstance, humans' obsessive tendencies, the inevitability of wounding loved ones and the need to forgive (both self and others) because sins against others, damaging as they are, cannot be avoided.

Long Day's Journey and *Moon for the Misbegotten* is a two-part saga whose Tyrone family closely resembles O'Neill's own. *Long Day's Journey*, 'the single greatest American play',[42] features O'Neill's alter-ego, the sensitive, consumptive poet, Edmund, bullied and buffeted by his charming-skinflint father, morphine-addled mother, and loving but resentful older brother Jamie, each turning traumatically from the tragedies of their past, yet in failing fully to leave these pasts behind, continuing to threaten each other emotionally and physically. In *Moon for the Misbegotten*, the now independent Jamie mourns not only the passing of his mother but his raffish behaviour while she lived her last moments. When the earnest young woman he encounters convinces him that his mother loved and forgave him as she herself will be able to, Jamie is not reformed but at least momentarily at peace. O'Neill wanted *Long Day's Journey* kept under wraps for twenty-five years after his death; his widow, to whom the play had been dedicated as an anniversary gift in 1941, overrode that wish three years following his passing, with a staging first in Stockholm – in thanks for O'Neill's Nobel Prize in 1936 – and then in New York.

Drama historians regard Tennessee Williams and Arthur Miller as worthy successors to O'Neill; they borrowed his experimental and realist modes for their tragically visionary plays in the post-war period. Like O'Neill, both presented realism (or, as often, the death of illusion) but with experimental touches designed to push at the boundaries of conventional theatre: legends and scrims, half-walls and mood music, heavily laden symbols. Williams's *The Glass Menagerie* (1945) was the first production from either dramatist to indicate the calibre of things to come. The story is autobiographical to the extent that it outlines a cultural phenomenon formative of Williams's own outlook: personal and national memories of a genteel but decadent southern past overcome by the heedless aggression of the industrial North. There are

elements of the alter ego in intellectually, sexually frustrated Tom
Wingfield and his shrinking-violet sister Laura who, by turns, embody
Williams's outsider status as sensitive, talented and gay in a society that
regarded those as eccentric, even aberrant, traits. Laura's mark of out-
siderism is her mild limp, magnified into a pathologic shyness and
accompanying tendency to get childishly lost in her collection of glass
figurines; her overbearing mother, the pretentious former belle,
Amanda, keeps up appearances in the family's shabby St Louis apartment and coerces Tom to bring around romantic prospects for Laura.
When Tom's charming co-worker, who went to school with Laura,
takes the bait but reveals his already spoken-for status by the drama's
end, Laura's dreams are crushed, Amanda faces reality, and Tom breaks
free physically while remaining haunted by his betrayal of his tragically innocent sister.

A *Streetcar Named Desire* (1947), which won a Pulitzer Prize and
Drama Critics Award, was regarded by Williams – and many who follow
him – as his best play.[43] Its riveting heroine, Blanche Dubois, combines
Amanda's pretension with Laura's shrinking-violetism (Blanche's main
pretence) and conflicts verbally and physically with her brutish brother-
in-law, Stanley Kowalski (played definitively by Marlon Brando in both
stage and screen versions). Here, epic struggle occurs between illusion
and reality, refinement and vulgarity, the broken dreams of a beautiful
but decadent Anglo-Southern past and the inexorable realism of the
ethnic-immigrant future. Like Laura, Blanche, by play's end, has lost her
chance at romantic fulfilment yet tragically has no sense of this loss, as
the rape by Stanley that followed her desertion by Mitch (the gentleman
caller from Stanley's poker circle) has driven her insane. Williams's last
play of the decade, *Summer and Smoke* (1948), was more effectively
staged, as was O'Neill's *Iceman*, at Circle in the Square in the mid-1950s,
when Geraldine Page assumed the lead role of Alma in 1953. In yet
another variation of the southern heroine, Alma is sexually repressed but
led, through association with the town's earthy physician, to a healthy
acceptance of her sexual self. Williams followed up in the 1950s with
many more such striking southern heroines and a host of famous productions including *Cat on a Hot Tin Roof* (1955) and *Suddenly, Last
Summer* (1958). Many were adapted for film in the 1950s, and many were
directed on both stage and screen by the prolific director, Elia Kazan,
who also founded the left-oriented Actor's Studio in the Old Labor Stage
in 1947. The Studio established a school for actors and was famous for
propounding the Method Acting techniques developed by the Russian
dramaturge Konstantin Stanislavsky.[44]

Figure 3.1 Marlon Brando, Kim Hunter and Jessica Tandy in *A Streetcar Named Desire* at the Barrymore Theatre, New York City, 1947. Tennessee Williams's *A Streetcar Named Desire* did much to modernise American drama. From the collections of the Wisconsin Center for Film and Theater Research.

Miller's two major plays of the 1940s – also both directed by Kazan – were *All My Sons* (1947) and his masterwork *Death of a Salesman* (1949); while we may equivocate on the decision, the former was selected over O'Neill's *Iceman* for the Drama Critics Award, and we may recall, the original Tony Award for Drama, in that year, while the latter is regarded by many as the best-written American tragedy ever staged. Both deal with the crisis of misguided fathers making tragic sacrifices for lost sons; *All My Sons*'s Joe Keller sells defective parts to the military to support his family during the war, then must reconcile this noble motivation with the many airmen's lives taken by his swindle. Ironically, Keller's own son Larry kills himself out of shame when the crime is exposed. In *Death of a Salesman* (starring Lee J. Cobb in the role he was born to play), Willie Loman is an American Everyman, doing his part to keep the machine of capitalism humming but in middle age is chewed up by its grinding gears and discarded. His sons Biff and Happy, fed on Willy's grandiose philosophies of achievement through sheer personality, are ungrateful ne'er-do-wells; even his wife, Linda, drained by a life of self-sacrifice in the service of three self-absorbed men, 'can't cry' at Willy's burial, until she confronts the irony and shame of his having killed himself to collect insurance money, enabling her to live debt-free but alone from now on. Like Rodgers and Hammerstein, Williams and Miller presided over what many see as a golden era of dramatic theatre that would last until the early 1960s.

Hollywood in Transition

On the other coast the American film capital in 1940s Hollywood bore witness to momentous change; the war catalysed production – of films that 'brought the war home' and those that provided a few hours' escape – and, after the war, two government interventions, the 1947 House Un-American Activities Committee (HUAC) inquiry into communist influence in Hollywood and the 1948 Paramount Consent Decrees, upset the industry in irrevocable ways. The Decrees were a series of Supreme Court decisions that found the major film studios in violation of anti-trust laws. They were forced to divest themselves of some of their holdings and became much less powerful in the process. The Decrees heralded the end of Hollywood's studio system, whereby production houses of various size, wealth and levels of prestige had, for decades, owned exclusive contracts with leading and featured actors, directors and technicians; assembled production units that turned out pictures with the regularity of an assembly line; and owned the nationwide theatre chains that served as outlets for their products.[45] The 1948 ruling required the studios to sell the theatre chains; this loss, coupled with the advent of television, reduced big studios' profitability and led to what some regard as a decline in film quality in the decades following. The 1940s are thus readable as the swan song of classic Hollywood; in 1946, cinema attendance reached record proportions and, until the last months of the decade, film-going was a vital, enthraling pastime for the vast majority of Americans.

At the very beginning of the decade, John Ford's adaptation of John Steinbeck's great 1939 novel, *The Grapes of Wrath* (1940), reflected grimly on a decade of oppression and radicalism, standing as 'perhaps Hollywood's finest contribution to the cult of social consciousness and represent[ing] the culmination of the decade's social problem cinema'.[46] That same year Hattie McDaniel won a Best Supporting Actress Oscar for what some have deplored and others have celebrated as her iconographic portrayal of Mammy in *Gone With the Wind* (1939), and Charlie Chaplin's *The Great Dictator* (1940), about a humble Jewish barber who uncannily resembles the Führer (both roles played by Chaplin), satirised Hitler in the last months before it was impossible to find anything funny about Nazism and ended with an impassioned plea for intervention.[47] One way, thus, to examine the films of the 1940s is to consider the ways in which they perpetuated the stylistic traditions and/or progressive politics of the 1930s, and the ways in which the war itself, and the nascent cold war that followed, moved the Amercian cinematic product to the right, anticipating the cultural and political conservatism of the next decade.

As indicated elsewhere in this study, the war signalled much less a curtailing of democratic gains than a honeymoon period between the radicalism of the 1930s and the paralysing hysterias of the post-war period. During this period, the United States took the world stage in opposition to fascism and was forced to examine its own claims to freedom and equality. Because film was America's most influential medium for representation to its own and world audiences, implicit in Hollywood's mission during this era was the reflection (and prescription) of best behaviours: international intervention for moral instead of financial reasons, self-interest subordinated to collective action, sacrifice as a personal responsibility, racial tolerance, recognition of women's contribution and all-round good neighbouring. While there remained throughout the war a moratorium on film exports to enemy and occupied nations, many around the world (including legions of American troops overseas) continued to receive the cinematic message and form clear impressions of the United States from it. Ironically, the war films so warmly welcomed by stateside audiences were often met with derision by American soldiers and sailors, who laughed at the unrealistic renderings of combat and pleaded instead for more escapist fare.[48] The year the United States entered the war, one of its all-time greatest films, Orson Welles's *Citizen Kane* (1941), could not have chosen a worse moment to open: hailed by film-lovers today for its stylistic innovation, complex structure and artistic integrity, its dark expressionism offered neither the heroism of war nor the escape of comic relief sought after by its original constituency. At the 1942 Oscars it was nominated for nine awards but received only an Oscar for Best Screenplay and, 'when Welles's name and his film were mentioned [during the ceremony], they were booed'.[49] It lost the Best Picture contest (as did another innovative but dark classic, *The Maltese Falcon*) to the wholesome, affirming – or as the original film noir critic put it, 'admirable but profoundly boring' – *How Green Was My Valley* (see the following case study).[50]

Orson Welles and *Citizen Kane*

One could argue that Orson Welles was simply too clever for the formulaic tendencies of Hollywood filmmaking, not to mention the low-brow entertainment seekers perceived as Hollywood's most loyal audience. Yet, looking back on a film career fitfully executed and studded with box-office failures, one might also claim that Welles simply never worked out how to make sophisticated films that also appealed to the general public, as others of his generation, and more recently, have managed to do. The example of *Citizen Kane* (1941) is paradigmatic: hailed today for its intellectual content and complex style, regarded by *Sight and Sound* reader polls, the American Film Institute, and influential critics like Roger Ebert as the greatest film ever made, it was markedly under-appreciated in its original moment, failing to meet any of the needs the public turned to films to fill in that period. Also, its intrusive, critical depiction of newspaper magnate William Randolph Hearst (and other mogul-capitalists Welles was interested in as an American type) caused Hearst to lever his powerful press against cinemas daring to show the film and against the RKO studio itself, which consigned the film to an extremely limited first run. Similarly, Welles's second project, *The Magnificent Ambersons* (1942), did poorly with preview audiences at the same time that his South American documentary, *It's All True* (1942), filmed in support of FDR's Good Neighbor Policy, hit its own snags and was never completed. By then, Welles had not only lost the right to his films' final cuts but had trouble convincing RKO that he was any sort of a bankable director. For the remainder of the war, he paid his bills mainly through radio appearances and expressed his staunch leftist opinions (for very little pay) in the pages of sympathetic newspapers. Even in these venues, 'creative differences' between the iconoclastic Welles and his always-more-conservative employers often resulted in release from contract.

After the war, Welles's long-held propensity for chiaroscuro lighting and dark themes dovetailed perfectly with the noir stylings of the late 1940s.[51] His *The Stranger* (1946), *The Lady from Shanghai* (1947), and *Touch of Evil* (1958) are critically esteemed and did well with mainstream filmgoers when they originally appeared. In 1949 Welles starred in Carol Reed's noir classic *The Third Man*, based on the novel by Graham Greene; his nefarious sociopath Harry Lime impressed filmgoers indelibly. *The Stranger* is read by R. Barton Palmer as 'testimony [that Welles] could work ably and profitably within the constraints of the studio system'.[52] In the film, Welles plays a post-war Nazi biding his time in a quiet Connecticut town, whose attempt to hatch a neo-fascist plot on American soil is his undoing. In classic noir fashion, this action leads not to a happy ending but to the emotional devastation of his duped wife, played by Loretta Young. *The Lady from Shanghai*'s femme fatale was Welles's then wife Rita Hayworth, her signature red tresses bleached and bobbed, her career dimensionalised by the dramatic (distinctly unsympathetic) role and by her first and only chance to die on screen.

Despite *Citizen Kane*'s initial commercial failure, it is from its first frames a masterwork of stylistic innovation, as well as an engrossing detective story that unfolds in complex fashion. In the opening scene, a wealthy recluse dies in his eerie mansion, uttering the enigmatic expression 'Rosebud' as he does. Learning of the story from a newsreel screened in his office, an editor sends a reporter to unravel the mystery of the life and death of media impresario Charles Foster Kane (played by Welles). The reporter interviews persons important to Kane – a supervisor from his youth (whose memoirs he reads), a sympathetic business associate, a protégé turned adversary (played by Welles's Mercury Radio Theatre colleague Joseph Cotten), and his embittered second wife (read by viewers in the know as Hearst's young mistress, film actress Marion Davies). Each reveals a different facet of the charismatic but ultimately vanquished man who attempted to win the hearts of the masses but had failed even to win the affection of a wife. The reporter gives up his search for the meaning of Rosebud but, in the final frames, workmen clearing Kane's now worthless possessions toss a sledge named Rosebud into the fire – the very sledge he was riding the day his mother (played by Mercury Theatre alumna Agness Moorehead) announced she was abandoning young Kane to the care of the uncaring supervisor.

The film is hailed for both its visual and sound innovations, such as its low-angled shots that required set designers actually to build ceilings (stretched muslin mimicking plaster) and its deep-focus filming technique, which allowed action and characterisation to develop simultaneously in the foreground, middle range, and deep background of any one scene. Gerald Mast notes the marked stylistic shift in each of the first three scenes: 'Welles shatters the dark mood of death [in the opening scene] with the blaring music, and glaring, overexposed images of the newsreel documentary.

[This is followed by] a scene played entirely in shadow, drenched in smoke, backlit by shafts of light from the projection booth . . . Three sequences, three completely different film styles.'[53] Mast and others remark upon Welles's use of montage to indicate rapidly the passage of time (for example, the years of Kane's first marriage that begins well but ends in animosity) and sound (laughter in the background of a scene during which Kane and his second wife argue). Mast notes, 'Welles's . . . years in radio made him aware of sound's dramatic power, an advantage he enjoyed over those directors who graduated to sound from the silents'.[54] As Sklar aptly observes, 'By the sensationalism of its style and the controversy over its content, *Citizen Kane* made obvious to everyone what intellectuals and critics had begun to speculate about more and more, Hollywood's role in forging the nation's cultural myths.'[55] Emphasising the striking biographical similarities between Welles and Hearst and the enigmatic Kane, Sarah Kozloff emphasises the film's politics, its suggestion that 'people become isolationists or fascists when they lose their mothers, or – more generally – suffer from an inability to love.[56]

The War on Screen

While each boasted its headlining star, war films emphasised the ensemble supporting cast, often well mixed with respect to ethnicity and even race, and emphasised said star's ascent to heroic status only through suppression of his rogue tendencies. James Cagney and John Garfield played outsiders who learn just this lesson in various films – *The Fighting 69th* (1940) for Cagney, *Air Force* (1943) and *The Pride of the Marines* (1946) among others for Garfield.[57] A war sub-genre, which crossed the spectrum from melodrama to farce, involved the reluctant soldier who learns to reconcile his pacifist (or cowardly) ways with the need to serve a higher cause. In 1941, Gary Cooper's Sergeant York overcame religious proscription in a film of the same name; in the home-front melodrama *Since You Went Away* (1944), the sensitive character played by Robert Walker is mocked by his ex-military father until he bravely joins up and is killed in action.

In several war comedies, shirking clowns such as Bob Hope and Eddie Bracken in *Caught in the Draft* (1942) and Preston Sturges's *Hail the Conquering Hero* (1944), as well as the comedy duo Abbott and Costello (who found themselves running from Frankenstein and Dracula even more often then from the prospect of induction) deploy tactics to keep themselves in civilian garb, comedy ensuing. Even Fred Astaire in *You'll Never Get Rich* (1941), Gene Kelly in *For Me and My Gal* (1942), Cary Grant in *Mr. Lucky* (1943), Alan Ladd in *Lucky*

Figure 3.2 Though it was booed on Oscar Night, *Citizen Kane* (1941, starring Orson Welles) is regarded by many as the best American film ever made. RKO/ The Kobal Collection.

Jordan (1942) and *China* (1943), and Daffy Duck in *Draftee Daffy* (1945) dodged the draft for comic and dramatic purposes, but all (except Daffy) saw the light and behaved heroically by the film's end.[58] Bernard F. Dick observes that in both of his films, 'Ladd is radicalized by a woman. Women, as Hollywood had discovered, could bring out the avenging knight in the least chivalric of men.'[59] Probably 'the most famous reconstructed neutral and the coolest patriot in movie history was Rick Blaine',[60] the world-weary club owner of *Casablanca* (1943), portrayed by 1940s film icon Humphrey Bogart. Rick honourably returns the love of his life (Ilsa Lund/Ingrid Bergman) to her devoted husband, an agent in the French Resistance, then decides to join the Resistance as well, with his Algerian compatriot (Captain Renault/ Claude Rains) in the film's last scene. While the Office of War Information (OWI) fretted that Rick remained neutral for too long, that 'neutrality had no place in the war against fascism',[61] the film was an immediate popular and critical success and claimed Best Picture, Best Director and Best Screenplay Oscars in 1944.

Primarily, however, great war films of the decade depicted bravery and camaraderie, even if not always victory. The classics of the genre include *Guadalcanal Diary* (1943), based on war correspondent Richard Tregaskis's best-selling non-fiction account of the same name; *Bataan* (1943), about an ethnically integrated but doomed patrol of American soldiers who die one by one at the hands of massively outnumbering Japanese adversaries; *Thirty Seconds Over Tokyo* (1944), the story of the first Japanese bombing raid; *Objective Burma!* (1945), in which Errol Flynn leads a group of intrepid (again ethnically integrated) fighters to destroy a Japanese radar station behind enemy lines; *Command Decision* (1948), notable as US Air Force Major Clark Gable's first post-service film; and *The Sands of Iwo Jima* (1949), an 'extremely popular [and] stirring tribute to the marine heroes of World War II' starring John Wayne.[62] Despite the 'realism' these films were known for, they were rife with historical inaccuracy. British audiences objected to the Americanisation of the personnel in *Objective Burma!*, and the idea that US platoons harmonised despite ethnic difference is highly questionable. As military units were not integrated until 1948, the idea that wartime combat formations included black soldiers is both poignant wish fulfilment and misleading fable.

Race Issues in War Films

One creative solution to the racial dilemma occurred in the film *Sahara* (1943) in which the African American actor Rex Ingram plays a Sudanese Allied soldier guarding an 'Italian' prisoner of war (the Irish American character actor J. Carrol Naish of *Life with Luigi* fame – see Chapter 2), who himself comes to support the nobility of the Allied cause. In the post-war era, a film version of Arthur Laurents's stage play *The Home of the Brave* (1949) featured a character named Moss (Jewish in the play, portrayed by the black actor James Edwards in the film) who grapples with survivor guilt when a war pal (Lloyd Bridges) hurls a racist epithet just before dying in Moss's arms. While the subject of white racism is lauded by Bernard F. Dick in his valuable study of war films,[63] film historians Harry Benshoff and Sean Griffin argue that this and other social problem films dealing with racial trauma almost always presented the white point of view: 'Hollywood obviously felt that this formula – dealing with racism from a white perspective – was necessary to draw white audiences'.[64] A refreshing departure was a documentary produced by the War Department under the direction of Frank Capra, *The Negro Soldier* (1944). A 'ground-breaking recognition not only of black contributions to US history but of the urgent problem of inter-racial friction within the supposedly united services',[65] the film was so popular among the troops that it crossed successfully into the main-stream,[66] and was hailed in the black press.[67]

Asian characters and actors suffered different, though equally regrettable, forms of misrepresentation in Hollywood war films. Because most Japanese Americans (especially on the West Coast) had been relocated to inland settlement camps for the duration of the war (see the Introduction), Asian Americans of other extractions were often called upon to play the 'inscrutable' enemy in films such as *Gung Ho!* (1943), *Behind the Rising Sun* (1943), *The Purple Heart* (1944), and *Blood on the Sun* (1945), in addition to *Objective Burma*, *Bataan*, and *Thirty Seconds over Tokyo*, mentioned above. Chinese American actors Richard Loo and Keye Luke, and Korean American actor Philip Ahn 'sacrificed ethnic pride to contribute to the war effort as morale-enhancing villains'.[68] Loo, featured prominently in many war films based in Japan, is especially remembered as having given 'a face to the enemy that wartime audiences . . . loved to hate'.[69] Thomas Doherty, in his marvellous history of narrative and documentary World War II films, notes that newsreel filmmakers were required by the OWI and the Production Code administration to minimise graphic combat depictions. And yet as the war dragged on,

> . . . the newsreels extended coverage and picked up speed [and] also became more explicit and cold-blooded . . . Though the full horror of combat and its grisly impact on the human frame never reached the homefront screen, the depiction of death and destruction was hardly sani-tised or 'Disneyfied'. Naturally enemy dead . . . were more emotionally

acceptable and widely showcased than American dead. Naturally, too, given the peculiar ferocity and racist cast of the war in the Pacific, Japanese dead were a special occasion for unblinking satisfaction.[70]

Clayton Koppes and Gregory Black note that Edward Dmytryk's *Behind the Rising Sun* is a singular example in this period, containing Japanese characters who emerge as individuals; otherwise, racist stereotypes prevailed in Japan-themed war films.[71]

War Films for Women

Not surprisingly, most of the women's pictures relating to war dealt with home-front issues and, as with the male-oriented pictures, dilemmas of sacrifice confronted the characters, who wrestled with the inconvenience of rationing and the tragedies of losing husbands or sons to war. Although soldiers smirked at this production as well,[72] *Mrs. Miniver* (1941) was an early example of the genre that set the bar high, dominating the Academy Awards of 1942 and returning American viewers to their original impulse for entry into the war – strong regard for their noble British allies. Two years later, *Since You Went Away* (1944) was embraced by its original audience and remains a valuable artefact for its broad exposition of the wartime context: stoic Mrs Hilton (Claudette Colbert) and her two daughters (Jennifer Jones and Shirley Temple, by now a teenager) undergo home-front hardships in paradigmatic fashion: preserving foodstuffs, selling war stamps, collecting scrap metal, tending victory gardens, rolling bandages, welding in a munitions plant and peaceably enduring a railway journey plagued with delays, even though it means missing a meeting with their beloved husband/father during a brief stateside visit. Selfish characters, including a society matron played by the great supporting actress Agnes Moorehead, are mocked by the film's perspective and rebuked by the major players. The film's bright conclusion, news received on Christmas Eve that Captain Hilton is alive and on his way home – was criticised by at least one critic, Philip Hartung of *Commonweal*, on behalf of those families who would never receive such miraculous reprieves.[73] Heavier burdens were borne by the women of *Tender Comrade* (1943), especially by the lead character Jo, played by Ginger Rogers, whose husband is killed in battle. The film caused controversy later in the decade, when the mother of star Ginger Rogers was, for some reason, sought out by HUAC to condemn the film's communist themes (see the following case study).

Sacrifice was also a theme in women's military pictures, especially the major releases *So Proudly We Hail* (1943), *Cry Havoc* (1943), and *They Were Expendable* (1945), a traditional (men's) war film with Donna Reed in a major role. Significantly, all of these women's war films take place in the doomed Pacific theatre of Bataan, where soldiers abandoned by General Douglas McArthur when he was ordered by Roosevelt from Asia to Australia were sacrificed in a catastrophic rout. *So Proudly We Hail* was based on the story of American nurses rescued from Bataan–Corregidor to Australia while escape was still possible. This plot enabled the film to intermix hospital scenes with romantic and comic high jinks and was criticised by one reviewer for 'the studiously disheveled glamour of the Misses [Claudette] Colbert, [Paulette] Goddard, and [Veronica] Lake'.[74] Meanwhile, the film ends with the Veronica Lake character's self-sacrifice by grenade, taking several Japanese attackers with her. MGM's *Cry Havoc* is regarded as the more serious film, because of its more down-to-earth leading lady (Margaret Sullavan), more dramatic tone, and a plot that forces its lead characters to come to terms with their fates – 'sweating, starving, and dying' by the end of the story.[75]

HUAC in Hollywood

By 1947 the cold war had begun, bringing with it intense fears of the Soviet threat and hysterical intimations, known as the Red Scare, that legions of home-grown subversives were undermining American schools, government and entertainment sectors. Founded in 1938 to prosecute Nazi propagandists and Ku Klux Klansmen, the House Un-American Activities Committee (HUAC) quickly turned its attention to supposed communists instead. In 1947 it raised the alarm in Hollywood, according to Ring Lardner Jr, one of its Hollywood targets, for the sake of increasing its audience and influence. According to Larry Ceplair and Steven Englund, 'in truth, their main target was the populist and liberal themes which, in HUAC's eyes, appeared all too frequently in the films made by the artists, intellectuals, and Jewish businessmen who dominated an industry which in turn dominated the public imagination.'[76] HUAC's friendly witness list during its Hollywood hearings would eventually include right-wing studio heads Jack Warner, Louis B. Mayer and Walt Disney; Russian-born screenwriter and conservative novelist Ayn Rand; actors Robert Taylor, Gary Cooper and Ronald Reagan; and, for reasons indiscernible in the archival material, Ginger Rogers's mother Leila, an aggressive side figure in Hollywood with strong opinions of her daughter's films. In the early 1950s, several film and theatre workers with long resumés in Left politics, including Elia Kazan, Robert

Rossen and Budd Schulberg, would testify to HUAC against fellow leftists, so as to settle old scores and protect their own careers. To defend what many regarded as acts of cowardice and betrayal, Kazan directed and Schulberg wrote the Oscar-winning *On the Waterfront* (1954), in which a heroic longshoreman (played by Marlon Brando) informs on mobsters attempting to take over the docks.

In October 1947, HUAC hearings took place in Washington where Warner, Mayer and Disney testified in part so as to hit back at unions whose strikes and internecine conflicts had caused violence (and reams of bad press) during the war and immediately after. These and other moguls deter- mined that labelling unions as being communist influenced disabled them. Rand lambasted the inaccuracies of MGM's *Song of Russia* (1944), saying that the opening scene, during which a US flag fades into a hammer and sickle, made her 'sick'.[77] Robert Taylor complained about having had to star in the film, produced under Mayer's own supervision, though, through- out the hearings, Committee Chair J. Parnell Thomas (a Republican from New Jersey) attempted to place blame for all wartime pro-Russia films on the Roosevelt administration;[78] Warner testified that his *Mission to Moscow* (1943) was basically an FDR production.[79] Reagan was there mainly on principle, later informing to the FBI, as president of the Screen Actors' Guild, on communist activities within the Guild. In her testimony, Ginger Rogers's mother castigated Ginger's war-era *Tender Comrade* (1943), indicating that her daughter, under contract with RKO, had been basically forced to mouth the script's propaganda – especially the line 'Share and share alike – that's democracy'. Leila wanted the committee to know that actually 'that's socialism', yet shared responsibility and self- sacrifice were little less than national values, universally endorsed by the American home-front constituency, a few brief years earlier.

Tender Comrade was directed by Edward Dmytryk and written by Dalton Trumbo, two of the ill-fated Hollywood Ten, an aggregation of writers, directors and producers with leftist sympathies called upon to testify, cited for contempt of Congress – for refusing on First Amendment grounds to answer whether they 'were or ever had been members of the Communist Party' – and sentenced to prison. (Sentences for the Ten ranged from six months to a year; Dmytryk was sentenced to twelve months but served fewer than that, Trumbo served eleven months.) The other members of the Ten were screenwriters Alvah Bessie, Lester Cole, Ring Lardner Jr, John Howard Lawson, Albert Maltz, and Samuel Ornitz; director Herbert Biberman; and producer Adrian Scott. Several of the Ten, and many others who were blacklisted in the next half-decade, never worked in Hollywood again, although some of the writers – using pseudonyms or fronts (col- leagues willing to pose as the writers of scripts in fact generated by the blacklisted themselves) and earning much lower salaries – somewhat maintained their careers.

During the first week of the 1947 hearings, friendly witnesses levelled their accusations; during the second week, one unfriendly witness after another found himself in the congressional hotseat. Robert Sklar argues that the belligerent attitudes of the unfriendly witnesses, especially of the deliberately abrasive, arrogant and unruly John Howard Lawson, who testified first, 'cost the Ten critical support within the industry'.[80] At the hearings' conclusion, the Ten were indicted and, that November, sentenced by Congress. Days later the industry itself capitulated to Congressional and public hysteria; studio financial officers based in New York convened at the Waldorf Hotel to issue their 'Waldorf Statement', which declared that the Ten would be dismissed or suspended without pay and that the film industry would undertake its own crusade to eliminate subversives within its ranks.

In June 1950, the right-wing journal *Counterattack* published a pamphlet called *Red Channels* in which 151 additional writers, journalists, poets, singers, dancers, choreographers, and composers were named as communist subversives or supportive 'fellow-travelers'. The more famous among these included composer/conductor Leonard Bernstein, actor John Garfield, novelist Dashiell Hammett, playwright Lillian Hellman, actress/singer Lena Horne, poet Langston Hughes, actor Edward G. Robinson, and wunderkind Orson Welles. Both Welles and Charlie Chaplin (another blacklisted filmmaker) embarked on self-imposed exile in Europe, Garfield died of a heart attack in 1952, and others on the list died early, drank themselves into oblivion or at the very least saw their careers destroyed. Historians Paul Buhle and David Wagner observe that 'premature strokes and heart attacks were fairly common [for blacklisted film workers], along with heavy drinking as a form of suicide on the installment plan'.[81] Also those who had turned informant or otherwise aligned themselves with conservative forces suffered early death or psychological torment, including Rossen, actors Sterling Hayden and Burt Lancaster, and even director Kazan, who admitted to wrongdoing before receiving a highly controversial Lifetime Achievement Oscar in 1999.[82] HUAC was discredited during its hearings in the late 1960s, when unfriendly witnesses Jerry Rubin and Abby Hoffman mocked the proceedings by wearing outlandish costumes and blowing bubble-gum bubbles during their testimony, and attacking HUAC's scare tactics in the media. The Committee disbanded in 1975.

A Break from the War for Servicemen and Home-front Audiences

Not to be outdone by its patriotic brethren back east, Hollywood's pantheon, led by iconic co-founders Bette Davis and John Garfield, opened the Hollywood Canteen to entertain uniformed servicemen six months after the opening of Broadway's Stage Door Canteen, on 3 October 1942. Located in what had been an old barn at 1451 Cahuenga Boulevard in Hollywood, the interior was styled as a rustic lodge with service area, a few tables and a stage. Photos from that era indicate that the operation was a stunning success – servicemen on leave packed the room, crowding stars with their autograph books in hand, and lined up by the hundreds outside, awaiting their turn to enter. As in New York, all Hollywood's luminaries worked the room as entertainers (singers and comics especially), servers, dancers, and mere presences among the star-struck men, whose encounters with their screen idols would have cheered them through many difficult months of service to come. Davis had her last best decade in the 1940s, starring in twenty films in ten years, including *Now Voyager* (1942) and *Deception* (1946) and enjoying renown as a leading lady unafraid to adopt the mortifying disguises of the character actress. Garfield, regarded as 'the quintessential Hollywood social victim',[83] as well as 'Red Hollywood's leading personality'[84] and 'the great proletarian actor',[85] played a variety of loner/outsider characters in the 1930s and 1940s and often starred in films with a notably leftist slant.

Occasionally, service and home-front audiences sought a break from the war, and Hollywood responded with escapist fare. Several have observed that even non-war films of the early 1940s – in their heart-warming, uplifting, nostalgic, or otherwise patriotic guises – commented upon the war nevertheless. Probably the war was finally all-but-impossible to escape, in cultural representation as in lived experience, no matter how hard America's dream factory attempted to oblige. Yet many directors tried, including that accomplished purveyor of universal human sentiment, Frank Capra, whose 1940s features included *Meet John Doe* (1941) and the Christmas classic *It's a Wonderful Life* (1946) and starred respectively his two most popular leading men, Gary Cooper and James Stewart. These films, like several he had made during the 1930s, affirm the integrity and significance of the common man, who stands up to corrupt social forces and wins. During the war, Capra enlisted and made documentaries for the Army. *The Negro Soldier* is discussed above, and *Prelude to War*, first in his six-part government-sponsored 'Why We Fight' series, won an Oscar for Best Documentary in 1942.[86] Stewart also volunteered and achieved the rank of colonel in the US Air Force, flying twenty combat missions in Europe and receiving the Croix de Guerre for his role in the liberation of France. Ironically, in *It's a Wonderful Life*, Stewart plays George Bailey, a man frustrated by life's limitations, including being designated 4-F (physically unfit to serve) by the local induction board. Bing Crosby was another star of the era, whose sentimental films, including *Holiday Inn* (1942), *Going My Way* (1944), and *The Bells of St. Mary's* (1945) touched hearts and inspired cathartic tears.

Not surprisingly, music and comedy were effective means by which to lighten a wartime film experience, and Hollywood mined Broadway deeply for its hit shows, casting them most often with Hollywood figures in the major roles although some stars, like Gene Kelly and Ethel Waters, were renowned on both coasts and reprised their roles. Meanwhile, as on Broadway, Hollywood perpetuated the segregation of black and white musical elements, with – thanks to the editing techniques enabled by film – even greater sleight of hand. As Allen L. Woll observes, the all-black musicals, once again *Cabin in the Sky* (1943) and the Hollywood-scripted *Stormy Weather* (1944), were seen by some as sops thrown to black audiences. In the words of the prolific and influential film critic Manny Farber, they depicted 'niggertown[s] . . . exist[ing] in a vacuum' that reinforced social segregation.[87] As on stage, black dancers and singers often entered the scene of a show-within-a-show apropos of nothing preceding or following, performed their routines, and were shown off stage by a swinging curtain. Such scene arrangements enabled editors to cut black performances from versions of the film sent to the American South without disrupting narrative continuity. Also, reports Woll, 'in *Holiday Inn*, when Bing Crosby sings his praise of the Great Emancipator in "Abraham", Louise Beavers joins him in song but remains in the distant kitchen as the camera cuts from room to room. Bing is even unaware that his maid is singing, even though the melody is ostensibly a duet.'[88] Woll notes as well that publicity stills for *You'll Never Get Rich* show Fred Astaire joining a group of black GIs for a song and dance when they find themselves in the brig together. Yet there is no correlative scene in the film itself: instead, 'Fred dances throughout the cell, while the camera cuts to the corner of the cells where the blacks are playing their instruments'.[89]

As the war and the changing American context made Hollywood newly aware of its tendency to stereotype black characters, ironically, 'the easiest way for Hollywood and OWI to deal with racial problems was "writing out" – simply eliminating the troublesome [black] character'.[90] The most successful non-Broadway musical of the era was probably Vincente Minnelli's *Meet Me in St. Louis* (1944), the endearing story of an early twentieth-century family facing a life transition – from St Louis to New York – starring Judy Garland. Yet the most memorable inter-racial musical moment of the decade probably belonged not to any classic vocalists but to Humphrey Bogart and Dooley Wilson (lead actor of Broadway's *Cabin in the Sky*) who, as club piano player Sam in *Casablanca*, shared key scenes with Bogart and a relationship of mutual respect.

For very different reasons, the 'Good Neighbor Policy' films of the period – daffy musicals set in Central and South America and almost always featuring the Brazilian Bombshell Carmen Miranda – succeeded as well. Miranda was a Portuguese-born Brazilian nightclub singer, known in the United States for her offbeat appearance (high heels, heavy make-up and jewellery, and turbans topped by towers of fruit) and off-colour comedy. Like her Cuban counterpart, percussionist/band leader/later television producer Desi Arnaz, part of her comedy derived from her heavy accent and misuse of English. Unlike Arnaz, however, she was never cast as the romantic lead but rather as the over-the-top man-crazy comic relief. Miranda's films of the decade include *Down Argentine Way* (1940) and *The Gang's All Here* (1943). These films, in keeping with official policy, stretched a friendly hand across southern borders by way of solidifying hemispheric unity in a time of world conflict. In addition, they cultivated a South American film market as restrictions across war-torn Europe limited distribution in that region. Each film took care to distinguish various Latin cultures, especially Cuban, Argentine, and Brazilian, and featured the Latin rhythms – including the samba, conga and rumba – sweeping American dance floors at the time as well.[91]

In one respect, the magnificent career of Alfred Hitchcock escaped the war by being so much more than a product of that period or even of that decade. A British auteur at work in his homeland since the early 1920s, before making a seemingly effortless transition to Hollywood in 1940, Hitchcock would go on for several decades past the war, thrilling viewers with tales of the intriguing and the bizarre – one suspects with similar effectiveness had the war ever happened or not. Roughly half of his wartime output, including *Rebecca* (1940), *Suspicion* (1941), *Shadow of a Doubt* (1943) and *Spellbound* (1945), have little if anything to do with the war and, often when the war is enlisted as a theme, as in *Foreign Correspondent* (1940) and *Saboteur* (1942), the deployment seems more opportunistic than specifically political: the war was at hand, as a theatre of provocation and betrayal among desperate adversaries, as would be on other occasions sexual jealousy, psychological aberration and later the cold war and its hidden universe of intelligence-gatherers. In Gerald Mast's assessment, Hitchcock 'deliberately refuses to cloud a good story with ideology'.[92]

Yet other film historians have discerned political intent within Hitchcock's wartime films, not only his marked stance in support of the Allied cause but in the example set in his inter-racial casting of

Lifeboat (1944), featuring Broadway leading man Canada Lee. Hitchcock allowed Lee to rewrite the offensive, stereotyped dialogue of his character, a steward on board a torpedoed passenger ship that is abandoned by an irregular cast of personalities and political persuasions for the wooden dinghy of the film's title. Lee received praise for both the revised script and his acting in the film; among black GIs, Lee's role 'was the symbol of changing times'.[93] *Lifeboat* features a Nazi character that drew criticism for being stronger, smarter and more capable than the Allied nationals all in the same boat, yet Sam P. Simone argues that Hitchcock 'neither underestimated the military strength of Nazi Germany nor closed his eyes to the political weakness of the Allied Powers'.[94] Simone also argues that *Foreign Correspondent* and *Saboteur* explicitly target the Nazi threat, abroad and at home, respectively.[95] Hitchcock's late-1940s films include the classics *Notorious* (1946) and *Rope* (1948); as with his early-1940s pattern, the former is specifically political (ex-Nazis intrigue with atomic secrets) while the latter is less political than philosophical, questioning human culpability in Nietzschean terms.

Post-war Readjustment: The New Social Problem

After the war, there flourished two genres whose roots were locatable in the 1930s and early 1940s and whose popularity boomed in the post-war context: the social problem film, a perennial species whose post-war emphasis was the trauma induced by both war and homecoming, and film noir, whose dark and brooding atmosphere, doomed men and wicked women tapped the anxiety of a shell-shocked post-war society threatened by new arrangements between the sexes, new enemies overseas and new fears for long-term survival. Benshoff and Griffin observe that, like the social-problem film, film noir, with its greedy, weak-willed, desperate villains *and* protagonists, 'questioned the ideals of American capitalism that citizens had just been fighting to preserve'.[96] Both film genres suffered in popularity in the more conservative 1950s.[97]

One might regard every picture made about the war, its dilemmas and its tragedies, as a social problem film but the term more ordinarily refers to a range of films produced from the 1930s onwards that examine domestic troubles which plague the American family (and the American city). Immediately after the war, the trials of readjustment became a prime focus, exemplified by William Wyler's Oscar-winning story of three soldiers returning to beloved but alienating home contexts, *The Best Years of Our Lives* (1946). Each veteran carries his own scars and faces different readjustment problems: the well-heeled banker played by Fredric March has difficulty returning to his settled, bourgeois existence and is disoriented by his children's growth during his absence. The working-class Fred Derry, played by Dana Andrews, faces limited professional opportunities despite his intelligence and distinguished war record. He comes home to an unfaithful wife and winds up attached to the banker's daughter (played by Theresa Wright). Lower middle-class Homer Parrish, played by Harold Russell, a real-life double amputee veteran, fears rejection by his family who, in fact, react with shock and sadness at the sight of his hooks for arms. The film won seven Oscars, including Best Picture and Best Supporting Actor for Russell. Other returning-soldier films include *Till the End of Time* (1946), in which the main character overcomes depression following the loss of his legs in battle; *From this Day Forward* (1946), in which the protagonist deals with feelings of social isolation and professional irrelevance; and *Home of the Brave* (discussed above), in which the black veteran Moss must face post-traumatic stress, racism and survivor's guilt.

Racism was a theme of other returning-soldier films; during the conflict, Hollywood prided itself on its ethnically mixed platoons yet afterwards interrogated the racism that reinstates itself in 'peacetime' and acknowledged that the battlefield might not have been such an egalitarian paradise after all. *Crossfire* (1947) tells the story of violent anti-Semitism among soldiers and veterans; a few years later, *Bright Victory* (1951) involved a blinded veteran's overcoming of both self-doubt and the racist attitudes instilled in him by his southern culture. With the love of the right woman, a recurring trope in this sub-genre, Larry looks forward to a professional career and re-establishes his friendship with Joe, a black fellow veteran whom he offended when they went through rehabilitation together at a hospital for the blind. The major statement on anti-Semitism in this era was made by Elia Kazan's *Gentleman's Agreement* (1947), in which Gregory Peck plays Phil Green, a magazine reporter who poses as a Jew, for first-hand experience for his story on anti-Semitism. The film stands out as a treatment of subtle ('normal') anti-Jewish sentiment, as opposed to the virulence on display by the anti-Semites in *Crossfire*. Even Phil's love interest is exposed as a bigot, though she redeems herself with the help of Phil's actual Jewish friend, Dave, played once again by John Garfield.

No fewer than four 'Negro problem' films appeared in 1949: *Home of the Brave*, *Lost Boundaries*, *Pinky* (also directed by Kazan), and

Intruder in the Dust, based on William Faulkner's 1948 novel (see Chapter 1). Film historians Peter Roffman and Jim Purdy observe that the first three of these films disappoint with respect to their continued insistence on the white perspective: the main black characters are acceptable on white terms – as ' "white" black characters';[98] Moss, for instance, 'is [almost] always in the company of whites' and proves himself worthy of white audience sympathy by being successful in his modest profession and of reserved demeanour. The protagonists of *Lost Boundaries* (a mulatto physician seeking work in Atlanta) and *Pinky* (a mulatto nurse with a white fiancé) are literally white, with white actors (Mel Ferrer and Jeanne Crain, respectively) cast as passing, light-skinned blacks whose main trouble is their tragic mixed-racedness, not the prejudice that limits their lives. *Intruder in the Dust*, considered 'by far the best of the 1949 cycle',[99] treats Lucas Beauchamp as a multi-dimensional character and describes the problem as racism instead of blackness. The film may have failed commercially because of this pointed critique.[100]

In contrast, the critical and popular success of *The Lost Weekend* (1945), starring Ray Milland and winning several Oscars, indicates that, in fact, 'social problem' films of the 1940s may have fared better when they shifted the problem in question from the sphere of social responsibility into the realm of the personal, individual psyche. In the story, Don Birnam's alcoholism is less associated with any social limitation (for instance, poverty or lack of education) than with the quirks attending his talents as a writer and status as tortured artist. He lies pathologically to his loving fiancée – increasing our sense that he is psychologically deranged by alcohol instead of traumatised by social factors, such as the war. Indeed, Don's evident lack of military service – suggested through his self-hating confession that 'I've never done any-thing'[101] – positions him opposite the shell-shocked veteran, to whom society owed an obvious debt, but at no less a disadvantage. Overall, *The Lost Weekend* fits well 'with the general trend toward problems as individual neurosis and held out a logical solution – going on the wagon – which could provide the necessary optimistic ending'.[102] Roffman and Purdy observe that even America's mentally and physically disabled veterans were often enjoined in returning-soldier films to solve their troubles through personal reconversion to a peace-time mentality instead of placing blame on government or public neglect: 'in *Pride of the Marines* [the story of real-life World War II veteran, Al Schmid, who was blinded during combat] John Garfield's failure to fit into society lay in his own psychological trauma'.[103] Similarly, the

Figure 3.3 Ray Milland in *The Lost Weekend* (Paramount 1945). Billy Wilder's *The Lost Weekend* was a post-war social problem film for disaffected veterans. It won the 1945 Academy Award for Best Picture. From the collections of the Wisconsin Center for Film and Theater Research.

focus in *The Best Years of Our Lives* is on the personal journey undertaken by the three veterans to acclimatise psychologically to an environment utterly divorced from wartime experience.

The Challenge of Film Noir

Yet, if diagnosing mental instability, self-destructive behaviour, and both racial victimisation *and* race hatred as personal, psychological problems instead of crises of the social sphere suited the conservative mood of the era, such reassuring attitudes were effectively undermined by noir's own bold politics. A body of cinematic work and a style pervasive to late-1940s filmmaking as a whole, film noir, despite its focus on criminal minds and distorted mental outlooks, questioned the post-war value system that was settling rapidly into place. While critics argue about which is the first noir film (with Hitchcock's *The 39 Steps* [1935] and John Huston's *The Maltese Falcon* [1941] often cited) and even about a consistent definition of the term, noir films in general reverse the traditional moral perspective. One finds oneself in sympathy with desperate men and dangerous women, hoping for their success as murderers and thieves, pulling for their eventual getaway and the consternation of authority figures attempting to track them down and root out the truth. In noir, the motives of adulterers and killers are made plain, even understandable; one is distanced from the ivy-covered wives and upstanding employers – the cornerstones of bourgeois respectability – manoeuvring obtusely in the background. Sometimes it is shell-shock that accounts for the sociopathic protagonist's heinous crimes, though more often it is a generalised boredom with workaday, middle-class, married life. Film noir's mood of cynicism and disillusionment is displayed in its marked visual style: low-key lighting creates dramatic shadows that shroud the bodies and faces on screen, draping them in menace and mystery or trapping them within webs or prison bars of light and darkness. The camera positions figures at disorienting angles or in tight close-up, intensifying the atmosphere of entrapment and desperation; night scenes predominate as do seedy urban locales.

In noir, characters – even lovers – use each other as means to an end, effecting devotion and passion as it suits their plots, turning on each other (sometimes with guns drawn) in the final frames. Seen as one more source of menace in a maze of danger and intrigue, the noir hero/ine realises that appearance is utterly deceptive, that whom to trust is impossible to determine. Women as well as men are subject to such treachery, and critics debate whether the femme fatale – and all she has coming to her – gained ground in the struggle for women's equality or intensified the backlash that occurred during this period. While some critics admire the active (however negative) roles undertaken by women actors in films noir, many regard these seductive but deadly women to reflect (and confirm) men's anxieties in the post-war period. Noir commented on these anxieties not only through its femmes fatales but also through, as Leighton Grist observes, the recurring use of homoeroticism as a sub-theme: 'It is a feature which can once more be related, historically, to the threat posed by female sexuality and the concomitant breakdown of stable patriarchal organization.'[104] Paradigmatic for Grist is the relationship between the lead and supporting male characters of Billy Wilder's *Double Indemnity* (1944), who end the film in a bloody embrace, declaring their love for each other.[105]

In R. Barton Palmer's assessment, '*Double Indemnity* is a masterpiece of dark filmmaking because of the fruitful collaboration by a number of talented people,'[106] many of them European émigrés who

Figure 3.4 Fred MacMurray and Barbara Stanwyck in *Double Indemnity* (Paramount 1944). The scheming lovers of Billy Wilder's noir classic called into question middle-class propriety and pretension in the post-war period. From the collections of the Wisconsin Center for Film and Theater Research.

brought a cynical, war-hardened sensibility to 'the Horatio Algerism of Hollywood as a whole'.[107] In the story, a seemingly respectable insurance salesman (played by Fred McMurray, an actor with an unassuming, even bumbling and comic film persona) is convinced by a sexy housewife (Barbara Stanwyck) to murder her husband. The husband is depicted as boorish and abusive, slanting viewer sympathy in favour of the plotting lovers. Yet, while passion is part of their motive, money is the main attraction for both: Phyllis Dietrichson (Stanwyck) is mercenary and two-timing; even mild-mannered Walter Neff (McMurray) acknowledges that he had been planning to cheat his company for some time and had been merely waiting for the opportunity to do so. In a complicated plot involving body doubles, the ensnarement of Dietrichson's daughter and her boyfriend, and the detective work of Edward G. Robinson's character (an insurance investigator), the couple commit the crime but then turn upon each other. Each fatally shoots the other, Neff surviving only long enough to narrate his lurid tale in tortured flashback. The Production Code's persistent influence – specifically its mandate that crime does not pay – is on view in this tragic ending;[108] yet also as Palmer observes in his reading of its familiar settings (living rooms, supermarkets), 'the film . . . domesticates crime, makes it an element of family life and its discontents . . . [Finally] the illicit couple cannot escape a world defined by family responsibilities and ties, the rhythms of stifling everyday life.'[109]

Conclusion

Theatre and film production of 1940s thus reflects the complex and shifting nature of the nation's political climate, even as one may chart a steady ascent in the artistic quality of the theatrical product and numerous cinematic high points throughout the decade. The war brought out both the ridiculous and the sublime in 1940s dramatists and filmmakers and set the scene for progressive (both interventionist and pacifist) and rightist–jingoist viewpoints. Patriotism, which had no (or perhaps encompassed all) politics in this era, was a ubiquitous theme that played out in overtly themed war dramas, military comedies, and nostalgic retreats into a celebrated American past. Strikingly, the issue of African American racial equality was that which most inspired leftists playwrights and screenwriters, even in otherwise conservative contexts such as gung-ho (and anti-Japanese) war films and the HUAC-hysterical late 1940s. One might also observe that in theatre the subject of war was more often tangential, and sometimes downright threatening, to the achievement of greatness in musicals and plays, which succeeded more often with nostalgic returns to the past or with the exploration of 'universal' human themes related to family, betrayal and death. Conversely, war seems much more integral to the great films of the 1940s (with some work by Welles and Hitchcock as exceptions); during the war, the inherent drama and significance of the conflict were zealously and stirringly transferred to the silver screen, and post-war the phenomenon of nationwide shell-shock flourished in the challenge to middle-class values and self-sacrificing patriotism in the social-problem and noir genres of the period.

Chapter 4

Visual Art, Serious and Popular

This chapter follows a culturally constructed scale from the 'highest' art of the 1940s to the 'lowest'. The terms implicitly divide the 'best' from the 'worst' in visual arts, with even such contrasts as 'serious' versus 'popular' and 'easel' versus 'commercial' hinting to the viewer to appreciate the former and dismiss the latter. Yet the 'popular' brings great non-intellectualised pleasure to its viewer, listener or reader, and also fundamentally defines – and in this case illustrates – a particular historical period. The most serious artists of the 1940s, abstract expressionists, can indeed thrill the viewer with their enigmatic, dynamic and contemplative works, yet they achieved a sort of ahistoricity that many novelists of the 1940s, who sought such a status, could not. Most of the artists of this school, whether they had fled Europe before the war, emigrated many decades earlier or had always been an American citizen, did no military service during the war and avoided depicting this subject – or indeed any subject – in their work. Of all the genres of culture discussed in this volume, theirs belongs least to its own war era. Only when one descends the first step in the visual arts hierarchy, to visit the great representational painters of the 1940s, does one feel the significance of the war and world events in general. The visual arts of the decade fairly well showcased African American practitioners, who mastered the representation of war and other major events from United States history. Self-taught artists of the period also allowed the war and aspects of history to come through in their work, and often brought their 'simple' rural visions to the 'complicated' New York arts scene. Commercial illustrators and comic book artists, consigned to the lowest rungs on the aesthetic ladder, did even more to define and interpret current events for their vast American audiences; Norman Rockwell's *Four Freedoms* series from 1943 is emblematic in this case, but so is the image of Captain America beating Hitler in a fist fight.

The Influence of the 1930s

In the early days of the 1940s, the world of art began to relocate its capital city from Paris to New York. The move speaks as much to an Americanisation of the art aesthetic – specifically the revolution issuing from the New York School that came to be known as abstract expressionism – as to an internationalising of the New York scene, as émigrés from the occupied nations of Europe joined European brethren (such as Arshile Gorky, Mark Rothko and Willem de Kooning) who had been in the country for many years. If the war was a key factor in consolidating the United States, especially New York, as the new heart of technical and philosophical artistic innovation, an earlier influence was the Depression-era support provided by the Federal Arts Project, a division of Roosevelt's Works Progress Administration, through which artists were paid (however minimally) to maintain their creative output, often through mural-making in railway stations, airports, and post offices. While the term abstract expressionism was not coined by art critic Robert Coates until 1946, the movement got under way in the early 1940s and has shaped our opinion about visual arts ever since – perhaps most notably in the continuing contest between abstraction and representation.

Abstract expressionism both reacted against certain American traditions and followed upon various European precursors. Styles in vogue in the United States in the 1930s – an 'American scene' style infused with affection, humour, even occasionally satire, known as regionalism; a more urban-based protest style referred to as social realism; and a draftsman-like celebration of modern architecture and industry called precisionism – struck painters of the 1940s as artistically and politically passé: regionalism's 'cultural isolationism ran counter to the growing internationalism, and its artistic conservatism to the increasing tendency toward abstraction'.[1] Social realism, exemplified in Ben Shahn's acerbic attack, *The Passion of Sacco and Vanzetti* (1931–32), and Alice Neel's affecting *T.B. Harlem* (1940) carried a message, an implicit call for change, that the artists of the 1940s rejected with cynicism and despair. Discredited as well were the 'hopeful rationalism' and 'technological advances' celebrated by the precisionists: 'the generation which began to paint in the 1930s and early 1940s was in a desperate frame of mind. A new approach was urgently needed to resolve what was seen as a crisis of subject matter.'[2]

Yet forerunners to the movement abounded, including 1920s surrealism (specifically, its reliance on a subconscious-guided automatism to achieve artistic breakthrough), Jungian myths and archetypes, European expressionism (its attempt to represent the mental state), eastern arts (especially calligraphy), existentialism (its emphasis on the responsibility of the individual) and even 'the art of children and psychotics'.[3] While the abstract expressionists distinguished their methods from modernist cubism, the influence of Picasso and Miró (especially his biomorphisms) is obvious. The 'white writing' of north-western artist Mark Tobey as well as the avant-gardism of the Russian Wassily Kandinsky and German Paul Klee pointed the abstract expressionists away from the artwork's 'centre': both its rules of composition with respect to centre and margin and its pointed messages, associations and meanings. As Anthony Everitt observes, 'many painters began to concentrate on the act of painting itself, unimpeded by anything save the decision to paint'.[4] There was a general abandonment of representational technique, even so much as that signified in a suggestive title, and new emphases on gesture, action and process.

As art critic Harold Rosenberg defined the movement in 1959, abstract expressionists 'started to consider the canvas an arena to act in instead of a space in which to reproduce, redraw, analyse, or "express" a real or imagined subject. The canvas was therefore no longer the support of the painting but, on the contrary, an event.'[5] The sense that the artist had literally entered his work during its composition was aided by the new scale adopted by this school. Large surfaces enabled Jackson Pollock – who often laid his canvases on the floor to work – to move all around (and sometimes across) a broad space in a frenetic dance; the largest work by Barnett Newman, a staunch adherent of the gestural approach, was *Anna's Light* (1968), twenty-eight feet (8.6 m) wide and nine feet (2.7 m) tall. Once on display, 'very large canvases altered the relation of the spectator to the work: he was no longer able to "take it in" or frame it with a single glance. In fact, he was often overtaken by an expanse of colour which stretched beyond his range of vision.'[6]

Masters of Abstraction

Art historians point to Arshile Gorky as a bridge figure both between European and American contexts and between abstract expressionism and its many precursors, almost all of which Gorky experimented with in pre-1940 phases of his career. Born Vosdanig Manoog Adoian in Turkish Armenia in 1904, Gorky's family was abandoned early in life by its draft-dodging father. Following the Armenian genocide of 1915, they fled to Russian-controlled territory where Gorky's mother died of starvation – a trauma said to have affected Gorky deeply throughout the remainder of his short life. Following his arrival in the United States in 1920, he studied in Boston and New York and went through 'Cezanne' and 'Picasso' periods before moving into his mature phase in the late 1930s and early 1940s. His important *Garden in Sochi* series of the early 1940s, 'marks [his] transition from the biomorphic version of Surrealism to Abstract Expressionism'.[7] In addition to the scene suggested by the title, 'its swelling forms are also breasts and buttocks, metaphors for the female body'.[8] Similarly, *The Betrothal II* employs biomorphic forms to represent 'a sexual cycle'.[9] Following a series of mid-life tragedies – a fire in his studio that destroyed everything, cancer surgery, a paralysis-inducing car accident and the break-up of his marriage – Gorky hanged himself in 1948.

Willem de Kooning is regarded, along with Pollock, as a leading abstract expressionist, yet approached and departed from pure abstraction throughout his career; his most famous works were the controversial *Woman* series that he developed over several decades, portraying recognisable – and some say savagely rendered – female figures, whose large breasts and bared teeth predominate. In the 1940s, de Kooning married Elaine Fried, who took her husband's last name and became a major artist in her own right. They experienced a period of extreme poverty, during which de Kooning's lack of access to artist's pigments required him to paint a series of black-on-white and white-on-black abstractions (using household enamel) that is well regarded today. Following his first one-man show in New York in 1948, his fortunes improved, and his work was in demand until, and beyond, his death in 1997.

Like de Kooning in certain phases, Jackson Pollock is regarded as a principal practitioner of 'action painting', yet another famous concept from critic Harold Rosenberg, coined in 1952. Pollock's intense engagement with the gestures of painting shows forth in canvases that burgeon with complex movement and feeling. He experimented with paint-pouring in the early 1940s and employed his famous 'drip method' in the late 1940s when he and his wife, artist Lee Krasner, acquired a home on Long Island with a studio in the grounds, a converted barn on whose floor Pollock spread his canvases and developed his technique.[10] In his action paintings, Pollock 'turned [his] canvases into allover-fields by means of a lattice of brushmarks or drips';[11] his was 'a kind of "landscape" in which everything depended on the physical gesture and the pictorial material'. While doubtful to the casual viewer, some critics have claimed that 'nothing was accidental in his work'.[12] Pollock's renowned drip paintings include *Cathedral* (1947) and *Blue Poles* (1953); in 1949 *Life* magazine suggested he was 'the greatest living painter in the United States', though he abandoned his signature method by 1953, returning to forms of representation, and was dead three years later in a car accident at the age of forty-four; inebriated and at the wheel, he was killed together with one of his passengers. Pressure to keep up with demand for his work had caused Pollock in his final years to retreat more deeply into the alcoholism that had plagued him for much of his adult life.

The exuberant styles of de Kooning and Pollock are distinguished from the placid monochromatism of colour-field painters such as Adolph Gottlieb, Robert Motherwell, Barnett Newman, Ad Reinhardt, Clyfford Still and perhaps, most famously, Mark Rothko. Throughout the 1940s, Gottlieb created his 'Pictograph' series in each of which a grid design displays 'diverse [images] into a nonhierarchical, decentralised array'; these works are appreciated as 'a cultural leveling device, a destroyer of distinctions'.[13] In the late 1940s and early 1950s, Gottlieb turned his interest towards the figurations of earth and sky of *Frozen Sounds No.1* (1951) or sun-like discs hovering over 'exploding patches' as in *Burst* (1957) and *Brink* (1959). Everitt observes that in these 1950s works 'Gottlieb has nearly arrived at a colour field position', yet consistently 'refused to banish [the pictographical sign] altogether'.[14] Both Motherwell and Newman were noted art critics, in addition to being painters, who explained and defended their artistic movement with eloquence and force. Newman's figurative tendencies of the early 1940s gave way in 1948 to a general 'abandon[ing] of subject matter' with his noted *Onement* series, in which thin vertical stripes, which he called 'zips', cross otherwise vacant colour fields. In paintings of the 1950s, he returned to subject matter to explore his Jewish roots but did not achieve fame until near the end of his life in 1970.

Motherwell, Still and Reinhardt were all drawn to the expressive powers of the darker palette, even black, in their work: Motherwell's famous *Elegies to the Spanish Republic* (a series of over two hundred beginning in 1949) repeats the pattern of 'bulbous [black] shapes compressed between [black] columnar forms' that seem to obscure, even extinguish, some image in the white background.[15] This contrast 'may be read as an indirect, open-ended reference to the experience of loss and the heroics of stoic [republican, anti-fascist] resistance'.[16] Both Reinhardt and Still moved from rich colour into experiments in black;

Reinhardt's geometrical patterns in warm pinks and blues gave way to monochromatic colour paintings in the early 1950s, then finally to his all-black *Ultimate Paintings* which he painted exclusively from 1953 until his death in 1967. Curator Nancy Spector notes that 'These canvases – muted black squares containing barely discernable [*sic*] cruciform shapes – challenge the limits of visibility.'[17] They represent Reinhardt's 'final minimal style, which, with their close values and barely discernible rectilinear divisions, are deliberately made almost impossible to reproduce'.[18] Some of Still's early colour experiments, such as *Painting 1948-D* (1948), disrupt a warmly hued canvas with a gash of black pigment; Still's jagged marks, which became more and more prominent, have been compared to tongues of flame, or to the effect of the colour being torn off to reveal other layers of colour (or blackness) beneath. Mark Rothko's colour-field paintings stand apart from these, as they are noted for their warm, calming, contemplative palette and composition. Even his late *Black on Grey* (1970), painted the year he committed suicide, suggests the silence and serenity of the lunar surface, although Everitt biographically reads the darkening colours – again, black is prominent – and senses a mood 'bleakly pessimistic'.[19]

In architecture Frank Lloyd Wright and Bauhaus originals Walter Gropius and Mies van der Rohe continued through the 1940s in long and illustrious careers. Wright was seventy-three in 1940 and began work on the Solomon R. Guggenheim Museum, regarded as his most well-known large-scale work. In keeping with Wright's love of natural settings, the Guggenheim's distinctive shell shape is a bold stroke of nature in the midst of the crowding high rises of Manhattan's Fifth Avenue; inside, visitors drift up a spiralling ramp, admiring the well-spaced works exhibited on the walls. Both Gropius and van de Rohe took American citizenship in 1944, having both fled to the United States from Nazi persecution in 1937. Gropius founded and directed the German Bauhaus school of design from 1919 to 1933, promoting clean lines, industrial materials, and the all-round embrace of mechanised, forward-moving modernism. As an émigré he settled in Massachusetts and directed the Harvard Graduate School of Design. Van de Rohe is regarded by Edward Lucie-Smith as 'the émigré architect who established himself most successfully in the US, and who in turn exercised the greatest influence on architecture there'.[20] He headed the architecture school of the Illinois Institute of Technology and designed skyscrapers and private homes in the Chicago area (and around the world) from the 1940s to the 1960s. His masterpiece, the

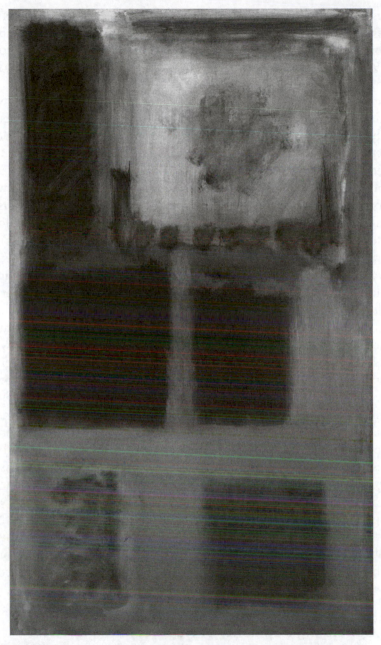

Figure 4.1 *Untitled No. 10* (1949). Mark Rothko's calming colour-washes epitomise the contemplative style in abstract expressionism. Gift of the Mark Rothko Foundation, Inc. Image courtesy of the Board of Trustees, National Gallery of Art, Washington DC.

Farnsworth House (1946–51), featured exposed industrial steel and glass walls and is today an area landmark and public museum. Inspired by this design, Harvard architect Philip Johnson created 'Glass House' (1949) on his estate in New Canaan, Connecticut. Today it, too, is an historic landmark.

Sculpture explored the realms of abstract expressionism as well, moving away from representation to free-form and formal abstraction. Easily the most famous American sculptor of the post-war era – a constructivist who built his work from pieces (mostly of metal) and not a traditional carver of solid objects – was Alexander Calder. At a French exhibition in 1931, Marcel Duchamp christened Calder's work 'mobiles', a term invented specifically for what Calder did: working mainly with wire and flat, biomorphic metal pieces in bold colours, Calder drew upon his love of nature (especially the astral bodies) and his training as a draughtsman and engineer to work these materials into delicately balanced sculptures that danced around an axis by means of cranks and motors or, later, of just air current. By the 1940s, Calder was world renowned and in his artistic prime: he enjoyed exhibitions in the United States and abroad, including a mid-career retrospective at the Museum of Modern Art (MoMA) in New York in 1943 and showings at Gallery Louis Carré in Paris in 1946 and the Buchholz Gallery in New York in 1947. For the Buchholz show, Jean Paul Sartre wrote an essay for the exhibition catalogue in which he said: 'A "mobile", one might say, is a little private celebration, an object defined by its movement and having no other existence . . . A general destiny of movement is sketched for [mobiles], and then they are left to work it out for themselves.'[21] During the war, Calder switched from metal – because of scrap shortages – to wood but resumed his metalwork following the war; in 1945–6 he made *Silver Bedhead* for the great art patron Peggy Guggenheim, whose Art of This Century gallery operated in New York from 1942 to 1947 and whose works by Calder – including the headboard and a set of mini-mobile earrings among other jewellery – belong now to the Guggenheim collection (see the following case study).

The Continuing Popularity of Representational Art

Despite abstract expressionism's domination of the art scene in the 1940s United States, representational painters continued to create great work – and continued to draw large, appreciative crowds – throughout the decade. In 1948, *Life* conducted a round-table discussion of

Peggy Guggenheim and Art of This Century

Peggy Guggenheim experienced the dysfunctional childhood, whirlwind social scene, world travel, and failed marriages of many an American heiress but managed to make a fundamental impact on the world of twentieth-century art as she did so. As at home in Europe as she was in the United States (indeed more so), Guggenheim spent most of her life in Paris and Venice and was a New Yorker most prominently only during the 1940s. As the war was an unlooked-for boon to the American art scene in many ways, so it instigated the Guggenheim art collection that eventually became world renowned. Guggenheim's granddaughter, Karol Vail observed, 'the uncertainty of war meant that although artists were more anxious to sell, there were fewer buyers; artworks were more readily available and the prices were quite cheap'.[22] Guggenheim learned business acumen as she learned the importance of modern art, and was able to amass a larger and larger private collection, even as she was financing the flight of various French refugees from Europe to the United States. Working from a list compiled by her friend and mentor, Herbert Read, Guggenheim attempted to purchase 'a picture a day' and secured works by Brancusi, Dali, Giacometti, and Héllon (her future son-in-law).[23] 'However, she had no luck with Pablo Picasso, who mistook her for a bourgeois housewife with her shopping list and dismissed her abruptly from his studio.'[24] During the war, Guggenheim hid her collection at Musée de Grenoble in the Swiss Alps.

Following her return to the States, Guggenheim opened Art of This Century, a museum gallery that drew appreciative art lovers and many of that decade's principal artists. It was located on the top floor of 30 West 57th Street and featured four spaces, most painted in blue and turquoise (Guggenheim's favourite colour), though the surrealist gallery had a black ceiling and floor and, at first, lights going on and off in random order over various works . The gallery often suspended its showings from cat's cradle-like rope contraptions that caused them to sway gently at eye level; it featured interactive displays such as a mechanised belt upon which works by Klee were visible and a peep-hole through which viewers observed works by Duchamp.[25] As Jacqueline Bograd Weld observes, 'it was a carnival of the *outré*, a theatre for painting . . . '[26]

Many of Guggenheim's biographers have noted Art of This Century's opening night on 20 October 1942. Says Weld, 'Her hair dyed a shoe-polish black, her startled cerulean eyes staring relentlessly above a large and bulbous nose, her lipstick running and always out of place, Peggy, said a friend, looked more like one of de Kooning's women than a doyenne of modern art.'[27] All recount that she wore that night 'a different earring in each ear: one, by Alexander Calder, represented abstract art, while the other, by Yves Tanguy, designated surrealism. She was trying to say she embraced them both.'[28] Guggenheim presented an important all-woman show in 1943 and was an early champion of Jackson Pollock, whom she supported financially throughout the mid- and late-1940s and provided with his first solo exhibition in 1943.

The end of the war brought an end to Art of This Century, as Guggenheim determined to return to Europe and closed the space in 1947. Laurence Tacou-Rumney (a granddaughter-in-law) notes that 'Before leaving, she had Art of This Century completely destroyed. This was the end of the magical gallery that had given birth to a whole generation of artists that Peggy called her "war babies," where pictures floated in space, in tune with the spirit of the times.'[29] Critic Clement Greenberg declared Guggenheim's departure 'a serious loss to living American art'.[30] In 1946, Guggenheim published *Out of this Century: The Informal Memoirs of Peggy Guggenheim* and settled in Venice by 1948, at the Palazzo Venier dei Leoni, which housed her private collection and provided adequate garden space for her beloved dogs. In May 1949, Guggenheim began the tradition of asking the many luminaries who visited her Venetian estate to sign a guestbook, many of whom 'signed' with humorous or beautiful sketches. In so doing, Guggenheim 'amassed a startling collection of [her guests'] signatures, drawings, sketches, comments, reminiscences, poems, and musical bars'.[31] In the late 1940s Guggenheim continued to collect art – though often pre-Columbian and African, as she could no longer afford and, in fact, disdained the later offerings of the New York art scene.[32] She died at the age of eighty in a hospital in Camposanpiero, near Padua, in 1979, while her surviving child, Sindbad, rescued her collection from rising canal waters that threatened the palazzo during a season of heavy flooding.

modern art, during which 'Fifteen Critics and Connoisseurs' levelled their opinions. Partially in response to this discussion, Russell Lynes wrote the influential essay 'Highbrow, Lowbrow, and Middlebrow' for *Harper's* the following year, in which he entertainingly outlined three stations on the cultural hierarchy that continue to be of great use to cultural critics today.[33] Thus highbrow practitioners of abstract expressionism would consign painters such as Edward Hopper, Jacob Lawrence, Georgia O'Keeffe and Andrew Wyeth to the category of the middlebrow or, worse, the 'popular' – a loaded expression that connotes broad public acclaim but also a sort of pedestrian or even philistine accessibility that producers and consumers of the avant-garde dismiss. And if artists of the calibre of these belong to the popular, then surely magical realists such as Paul Cadmus (whose gay themes stirred controversy during his career) and George Tooker; local-scene painters such as Archibald Motley; 'primitives' like Grandma Moses, Bill Traylor, and William Edmondson; and perhaps most especially a ubiquitous cultural presence like Norman Rockwell all rest even lower on the scale of artistic merit. What is evident in such

attempts to distinguish serious from popular is the futility of erecting
a stable barrier between the two. Much depends upon one's definition
of artistic merit; of the group discussed here, only Rockwell might be
universally consigned to the popular, yet general cultural (not art) historians of the era would do well to consider Rockwell the most influential American visual artist of the first half of the twentieth century.

Thus it may be simpler to distinguish between 'easel painters' and
commercial artists (also known as illustrators) who packaged their
work specifically for mass consumption but who, in fact, did much to
bring art to the masses. As Steven Heller and Louise Fili observe, 'The
American magazine cover was a museum of the street, a highly visible
outlet for painters, illustrators, cartoonists, and graphic designers to
exhibit their diverse talents.'[34] Also many in this group contributed to
the war effort in ways that far outdid the generalised cries of displea-
sure and protest voiced by their abstract expressionist brethren. It
seems that, for the abstract expressionists, the Spanish Civil War was a
much more inspiring crisis than World War II – when they bothered
to address in their work any social issue at all; as Baur notes, 'World
War II [is] not as prevalent a theme as its cataclysmic nature would
seem to warrant . . . [George] Grosz and [Philip] Evergood . . .
adopt[ed] a symbolic treatment. [Jacob] Lawrence alone of this group
attempted to convey the many-faceted impact of war on the common
soldier.'[35]

In fact, the animosity between abstraction and representation was
very much a two-way street. O'Keeffe and Wyeth physically removed
themselves from New York; Wyeth, like Hopper, adopted the stance
of the resolute outsider. The sculptor Elizabeth Catlett observed that
'non-objective art, for me, has many valuable aesthetic qualities but has
been used to create a snob group in the arts, both of creators and
observers';[36] while North Carolina artist Ed Wilson was 'appalled by
"the decline in communicable content"' in modern art.[37] Art historian
Cedric Dover noted in 1960 that within the African American artistic
idiom, represented here by Catlett and Wilson, the general rejection
of abstract expressionism related to a counter-trend: the 'refining of
forms and pigments to the pressing claims and complications of
modern life'.[38] Meanwhile, it is the case that many within the social-
critical, American-scene and other representational schools of the
decade combined abstract, expressionist, impressionist and figurative
styles in their work. This is certainly true for O'Keeffe, regarded
as semi-abstractionist by many; for Romare Bearden who went
through abstract and abstract expressionist phases before settling into

his well-known collage work of the 1960s; for the 'dean of African American painting' Aaron Douglas; for the noted muralist and art educator Hale Woodruff; and for Lawrence himself, despite his commitment to chronicling the black serviceman's experience and other subjects of historical significance. Thus, the line between abstract and figurative is as difficult to draw as that between the serious and popular, although it is interesting to note the tensions and divergent perspectives elicited by both cultural divides.

Masters of Representation

It is inaccurate to regard prolific artistic masters such as Bearden, Lawrence, O'Keeffe, Hopper or Wyeth as painters of the 1940s, as their careers spanned many decades. Yet, in the early 1940s, Bearden's work was taking a turn similar to that of many visual artists of the decade – away from the social realism of Ben Shahn and the influential Mexican muralist Diego Rivera towards the abstractions of the New York School. He had his first one-man show in 1940, in which he exhibited his realistic gouaches and watercolours, the most famous of these being *Interior* (1939). Following the war (he served between 1942 and 1945 in a segregated Army unit), Bearden moved into a Picasso-style abstractionism, followed in the 1950s by a decidedly abstract expressionist phase. His noted works from the 1940s belong to series, *The Passion of Christ* (1945) and the Lorca-inspired *Death of the Bullfighter* (1945), but also include single works such as *Sharecroppers* (1940), *The Visitation* (1941), and the patriotic *Factory Workers* (1942). In 1945 he became represented by the prestigious Kootz Gallery, where he took part in several group and solo shows and met on a monthly basis the Kootz collective (including Gottlieb, Motherwell and William Baziotes) to discuss art and aesthetics.[39] During the 1940s, Bearden was also part of the important 306 studio, named for its location at 306 125th Street in Harlem. Many artists and writers lived and worked there, challenging and inspiring each other. Like Motherwell and Newman, Bearden was a noted art critic; late in life he completed with Harry Henderson the monumental *History of African American Artists* but, in 1946, he controversially criticised the Harmon Foundation, a philanthropic centre for African American artists since the 1920s, for sponsoring 'mediocre' art. Dover rejoindered that 'it would be unwise for [such] an encouraging organisation to pontificate on what is good and bad', that in fact, 'most of the artists for whom the Foundation opened doors were doing just what Mr. Bearden required'.[40]

The Harmon Foundation, the Julius Rosenwald Fellowships, the Public Library at Harlem's 135th Street and Cleveland's Karamu House were a few of several philanthropic institutions that encouraged study and achievement in black arts during (and before and beyond) the 1940s. In 1940 the WPA (Works Progress Administration) and City of Chicago sponsored the Diamond Jubilee Exposition (also known as the American Negro Exposition) celebrating seventy-five years of achievement for African Americans since emancipation in 1865. While artistic production was not the only focus, the Exposition's art exhibit was widely influential, bringing dozens of established and emerging artists to national attention.[41] Months following the Exposition, Alain Locke published *The Negro in Art* (1940), followed later that decade by James Porter's important history *Modern Negro Art* (1943). The late 1930s and early 1940s witnessed the establishment and growth of art departments in historically black colleges and universities through the United States, headed by noted artists of the era. These included Aaron Douglas at Fisk University, Hale Woodruff at Atlanta University, the muralist John Biggers at Texas Southern University and (among others) James Porter and Loïs Mailou Jones, the marvellous interpreter of French street life, at Howard University.[42] In 1940 the legendary Augusta Savage also began teaching, her moving and monumental *Lift Every Voice and Sing* sculpted for the 1939 New York World's Fair being her last major work. At Atlanta University, Woodruff instituted an annual exhibition of black artists that occurred from 1942 until 1970.

For Jacob Lawrence, another member of the 306 group, the 1940s were years of accomplishment and recognition, shaped in part by the war – beginning with Pearl Harbor which occurred the day before he and several other black artists were to be featured in a multi-gallery exhibition. His sponsor then was the famed Edith Halpert, whose Downtown Gallery proceeded to present the work of Lawrence and others, despite the new national crisis. Prominent at this showing was Lawrence's *Migration* series (1940–41), a sequence of sixty panels depicting the move from the rural South to the industrial North undertaken by thousands of African Americans in the early decades of the twentieth century. Working in gouache and later egg tempera, Lawrence innovated and perfected the multi-panel format (often accompanied by verbal descriptions gleaned from his study of history), which Dover describes as 'amazing . . . historical novels in tempera or gouache'.[43] Gates and West observe, 'often accompanied by text, his paintings are epic, sweeping narratives of the everyday experiences of forgotten and ordinary folk'.[44] Lawrence was influenced by the great muralists of the era, including José Clemente Orozco, who was working in New York when Lawrence met him in 1940; his multi-panel series are equally historically instructive and emotionally moving, but simply more movable, than the murals produced during this era. Lawrence preceded *Migration* with series depicting the lives of Haitian liberator Toussaint L'Ouerture (1937–8), Frederick Douglass (1938–9) and Harriet Tubman (1939–40), and followed with series on the life of abolitionist John Brown (1941), on Harlem (1942–3) and on World War II (1946–7).

War interrupted Lawrence's career once more when he was assigned to a segregated Coast Guard ship in 1943. Yet his commander was a progressive thinker who unilaterally desegregated his crew, proving to the Navy that they could function well in battle as an integrated troop. Lawrence was assigned to produce patriotic, morale-boosting artwork in addition to his other duties and painted as well a laudatory portrait of Commander. Skinner; he later remembered the ship as 'the best democracy I've ever known'.[45] In the late 1940s, Lawrence taught at Josef Albers's prestigious Black Mountain College; however, racial tensions (in part experienced while at the North Carolina school) and mounting success overwhelmed Lawrence; he checked into a psychiatric hospital in Queens to recuperate in 1949. From this experience Lawrence not only regained sound mental health but also created a moving series, *Hospital* (1950), depicting the despair and confusion of the setting. Important single works from the 1940s include *Tombstones* (1942), *Pool Parlor* (1942) and *Seamstress* (1946). In this last work, among many others, the seated, sewing figure has 'oversized hands . . . symbolic of labor, tenacity, and strength in Lawrence's designs'.[46]

In 1940, Georgia O'Keeffe purchased Ghost Ranch, 120 miles north of Albuquerque, New Mexico, her frequent and then permanent home for the remainder of her long life. Having visited New Mexico since 1929, O'Keeffe became fascinated with the sublime grandeur of the landscape and is associated with this region most often, despite her dual role as a New York artist with a clear interest in the abstractionist style. In 1946, her husband, the photographer Alfred Stieglitz, whom O'Keeffe loved very deeply, died suddenly, initiating her permanent move to New Mexico by the end of the decade. In the 1940s, O'Keeffe continued to paint the large, luxurious, even erotic flowers she had painted for many years, as well as surrealistic works featuring the sun-bleached animal bones she had collected from the desert around her home. Her *Pelvis* series – close-ups of animal hip sockets through which the vivid blues and yellows of skies or sunsets were visible – was executed in the mid-1940s. Also in the mid-1940s, she enjoyed two one-woman retrospectives, at Chicago's Art Institute in 1943 and New York's Museum of Modern Art, the first woman artist ever to be honoured in this way by this institution, in 1946.

By 1940, Nyack, New York-native Edward Hopper was well known as a painter of desolated American rural and urban landscapes, peopled by individuals physically distanced from each other or emotionally isolated even when in close proximity. Like Rockwell, he focused frequently on the American heartland, though the grim moods created in his works form the perfect counterpoint to Rockwell's affectionate, affirmative representations. Though he lived and worked for much of his life in New York City, he opposed himself to the artistic insiders of 1940s and 1950s; 'in particular, the rise of Abstract Expressionism left [Hopper] marooned artistically, for he disapproved of many aspects of the new art', and he painted less and less in the later decades of his life, dying in 1967 'isolated if not forgotten'.[47] His most remarkable works from the 1940s include *Gas* (1940), in which a station attendant on a deserted country road symbolises human (or American) isolation, and *Nighthawks* (1942), in which late-hour denizens sit dejectedly around the service counter of a diner, its bright lights less a comforting beacon than the glare that exposes inner pain. Hopper's influence seems strikingly on display in the works of African American artist Hughie Lee-Smith, among these *Boy with Tire* (1955) and *Impedimenta* (1958).

During this decade, Andrew Wyeth created *Christina's World* (1948), one of his two most famous paintings; the other is *Braids* (1977), the cover of the exhibition catalogue for the famed 'Helga Paintings', made during the 1970s and early 1980s but not revealed to the viewing public nor, evidently, to Wyeth's wife until 1985. Wyeth also distanced himself physically and philosophically from the New York School, having always 'present[ed] himself as a reclusive outsider',[48] instead seeking inspiration in the farmlands of Chadds Ford, Pennsylvania (his birthplace) and Cushing, Maine.[49] Still living and working in these regions at the age of ninety, Wyeth is drawn not only to the landscapes themselves but also to their inhabitants, using his friends and neighbours (of whom Helga was one) as models and muses. Christina Olson was a neighbour of his wife's in Cushing, affected by a debilitating disease (perhaps polio) in response to which she preferred dragging herself around her farm to using a wheelchair. In fact, Wyeth's wife Betsy posed as the model for the picture; 'only the arms and hands were modeled by Christina herself',[50] and much of the setting has been recomposed or entirely fabricated. Yet 'Wyeth perceived the Olson house, which had never been modernised, as a time capsule from another era' and in Christina's loneliness and isolation recognised a kindred soul. As Anne Classen Knutson observes, 'the powerful sense of loss in *Christina's World* suggests the artist's nostalgia for old New England but also resonates with his incessant longing for his father',[51] the artist-illustrator N. C. Wyeth who was killed in a car crash three years earlier. John Wilmerding regards Hopper and Wyeth as the two greatest realists of the twentieth century, noting that the two met in 1942.

> In Hopper's [and Wyeth's] art, there is a similar consciousness of the psychological and sexual beneath the surface of things; a concentration on architectural fragments and an association of structures with personalities; a brooding emptiness in the landscape and strong abstract design underlying the realist view; and a vision attuned to modern loneliness and alienation.[52]

Knutson credits Hopper's influence in Wyeth's rendering of 'lone figures lost in thought and seen through or beside windows', noting that 'Hopper is one of the few artists whose influence Wyeth acknowledges'.[53]

A great representational sculptor of the era is Richmond Barthé whose career reached a peak in the 1930s and 1940s. Denied admission to art schools in the South because of his African American heritage, Barthé distinguished himself at Chicago's Art Institute although, interestingly, he studied there as a painter and began sculpting only to improve his three-dimensional technique on canvas. Yet he excelled in this field, working effectively in brass, marble, terracotta, wood, stone, and clay cast into bronze. His first solo shows were in New York in the early 1930s but a large 1939 exhibition, consisting of eighteen bronzes, won him Guggenheim fellowships in 1940 and 1941. During the war, Barthé sculpted as an 'artist for victory',[54] sensing that his race was as useful to the Office of War Information, which made a film about him, as were his moving works.[55] In 1943, *The Boxer* was purchased by the Metropolitan Museum of Art. During the decade Barthé specialised in busts and full-figure sculptures of unknown and well-known African Americans, including Booker T. Washington and Paul Robeson in his role as Othello. He sculpted other Broadway celebrities of the era, including Katharine Cornell and John Gielgud.

Yet, as happened to Wyeth and Hopper after the war, Barthé fell from favour because of the rage for abstract expressionism, a mode Barthé also rejected. He removed himself to the Caribbean where he felt better accepted and continued to work on commissioned busts as well as on official projects for the island of Haiti (including several coins that are still in currency). When he returned to the United States in the late 1970s, his work found appreciation again but he grew too old and infirm to continue working and had no savings with which to live out his later years. Lacking a work history, he disqualified for Social Security (a situation made bitterly ironic by the fact that one of Barthé's most famous sculptures is a large eagle outside the Social Security Building in Washington DC). Now a resident of Pasadena, he met and became friends with the actor, James Garner, who saw to his financial needs later in life but his end in obscurity, occasioned by his literal ousting from the New York (and American) art scene because of changing trends, was tragic. Of Barthé's monumental *The Negro Looks Ahead* (1940), Cedric Dover opined, 'all Negro history, potentiality and hope broods in [this work]'.[56] The piece was procured in 2007 by the Amon Carter Museum (Fort Worth, Texas), whose curators observed:

> It seems to capture a fleeting moment – a young man in mid-thought – that expresses the aspirations of an entire community rather than a particular individual. In a 1979 letter to the New York Public Library, Barthé recalled that his inspiration for the work was President Franklin D. Roosevelt. 'I believed that the Negro advanced more under him than any other President since Lincoln', he wrote in the letter, 'so I did this piece of the Negro emerging out of his rough background with hope in the future.'[57]

Self-taught Artists

A third provisional division is that between the formally schooled and the self-taught artists of this period. It may seem simple to divide those who trained at the major centres of Chicago, New York, and Europe and went on to distinguished, well-patronised careers from those largely rural, often impoverished practitioners who plied their craft in rare leisure moments or only after retirement, in the last years of life, and whose materials and technique convey a crudeness or flatness that does not diminish but instead enhances the thematic richness and emotional honesty of their work. Yet this distinction is complicated in the context of African American art, where many traditionally schooled painters, among them sculptor Sargent Johnson and painters Irene Clark, Aaron Douglas, William H. Johnson and Jacob Lawrence, 'turned primitive' after total immersion in the classical tradition, in a gesture of solidarity with their cultural heritage.[58] And what to say about the thoroughly schooled Richmond Barthé whose course work was almost *all* in painting except that, as a sculptor, he was largely 'self-taught'? Similarly, so-called primitive artists were hardly strangers to the New York art scene simply because they had not come up through the ranks as students of old masters. Pennsylvania native Horace Pippin, who was a favourite self-taught artist of New York art critics, is a case in point (see the following case study). James Porter, in his chapter on 'Naïve and Popular Painting and Sculpture' in *Modern Negro Art* (1943), stirred controversy when he 'promoted the work of Horace Pippin . . . for its presumed "authenticity" in comparison to what one called the "sophisticated primitivism seen so often among school-trained pretenders".'[59]

Nevertheless, four African American folk artists at work in the 1940s were wood-carver Ulysses Davis of Savannah, Georgia; stone-cutter William Edmondson of Nashville, Tennessee; wood-carver Elijah Pierce of Columbus, Ohio; and draughtsman Bill Traylor who died in Montgomery, Alabama in 1947. Both Davis and Pierce so happened to have been barbers as well as artists and so happened to have produced works quite similar in style – specifically rectangular wooden plaques with carved and painted relief. Like Lawrence and Pippin, Davis rendered World War II in his work; in the relief work *Farmhouse with Airplanes* (1943) an ominous tone is set by three aircraft dividing among themselves a midnight-blue sky that seems to drip (or bleed) into the orange-toned scene of rural serenity below. Other notable works from the 1940s include the wood figure *Abe Lincoln* (1944) and *Jesus on the Cross* (1946) whose crown of thorns was completed with toothpicks.[60] Pierce's plaque works are full of activity, reminiscent of Lawrence's many panels conveying a single narrative. The densely populated *Crucifixion* (1940) is not relief but wood figures – Christ and the two thieves, half-a-dozen Apostles, and several demons dressed in dark business suits – attached to a wood panel. *Pearl Harbor and the African Queen* (carved and painted wood, 1941) divides into rough quarters, one depicting Uncle Sam at Pearl Harbor, one of a man apparently at his induction ceremony, and then, below, a dog with a bone beneath the caption 'Duty' and two enigmatic African Queens.

Both Edmondson and Traylor have achieved top notoriety among critics and collectors in recent years; they were featured in *Black Folk Art in America, 1930–1980* at the Corcoran Gallery in 1982 and more recently in *Bill Traylor, William Edmondson, and the Modernist Impulse* at the University of Illinois in 2004–5. Traylor, the older of the two by twenty years, was born into slavery in 1854 and spent his life as a labourer in Alabama. In 1939 at the age of eighty-five, following the death of his wife and the scattering of his twenty-five children, he moved to Montgomery where he found basic shelter in the back room of a funeral parlour and spent his days on the sidewalks of his neighbourhood, developing his art form – pencil and crayon drawings on scraps of cardboard he had found – for the first time. Because of the war, in 1942 he moved north to be with some of his children but returned to Montgomery in 1946 where he worked simply and doggedly until his death in 1949 at the age of ninety-five. In his trickster animal figures and revelling stick-men, art critic Phil Patton sees visual analogies to African folk tales and to African American blues. Like Traylor, Edmondson began as a manual labourer, doing hospital janitorial work in the early decades of the twentieth century, then taking up stonecutting – as an apprentice to a gravestone-maker – when the hospital closed in 1931. Nearing sixty at the time, Edmonson progressed quickly from trade to craft; like his trained brethren in the urban North, Edmondson developed his technique as a WPA-employed artist in the late 1930s and early 1940s. His output, by his own account divinely inspired, consisted of preachers, angels, brides and animals in simple rounded forms. Sims points out, 'Traylor's [gyrating, imbibing] subjects tended to be profane and worldly. Edmondson focused on religions figures . . . and more genteel citizens of our society.'[61]

Charles Shannon was a young Montgomery artist and gallery owner who saw Traylor at work and featured him at his New South art centre in 1940. This led to a showing at the Fieldston School in New York in 1941, and a rather condescending piece in *Collier's* in 1946;[62] yet it was not until the late 1970s, when his next New York showing took place, that his significance in American art was firmly established. Edmondson was the first African American to enjoy a one-man show at MoMA, drawing national attention; unlike Traylor, his work stayed in vogue, taking part in a Paris exhibition after his MoMA debut and enjoying attention from Fisk University and the Cheekwood Center (both in Nashville) during the 1960s and 1970s. For the *Collier's* feature, Allen Rankin likened Traylor's work to 10,000-year-old cave paintings, yet more recent commentators indicate that both Traylor's and Edmondson's permanence comes more from the ever-renewing modernism pervading their art.[63]

Of course, not all self-taught artists are African American, and the most famous white artist of the era was Anna Mary Robertson Moses whose name was changed by her agents to Grandma Moses, as it was easier to remember. It is the case that Grandma Moses was, in the last two decades of her century-long life, both a big celebrity and big business. While she lived simply and rarely left her home in Eagle Bridge, New York, she was covered constantly in the media. As Jane Kallir reports: 'Moses became the subject of numerous "firsts". . . . Edward R. Murrow's 1955 interview with Moses was one of the few television programs at the time to make use of colour, and one of only two episodes of CBS's legendary series, *See It Now*, to receive commercial sponsorship that year.'[64] Her sweet-old-lady persona was as attractive as her remarkable art, and she won over her first New York audience by chatting about home-made preserves.[65] Her work was discovered in 1939 by an art collector travelling through Moses's upstate environs, and who saw her work on display in a drugstore. In October 1940, at eighty, she was given an exhibit at Galerie St. Etienne and signed to an exclusive contract shortly thereafter. Kallir notes of her style, 'the hallmark . . . is the integration of flat, almost abstract vignettes in a remarkably naturalistic landscape setting'.[66] She drew two-dimensional buildings and figures with childishly drawn faces, then gathered these into well-composed groupings arranged around her landscape and separated by roads and rivers; thus, many of her works have the pieced-together look of a quilt. In counterpoint, her landscapes display a perspectival sophistication. As Kallir notes, they 'were meticulously detailed and carefully observed from nature'.[67] While she began her career copying images from calendars and greeting cards, her own work was featured on greeting cards from 1946, and she received an award from President Truman in 1949. She was photographed for the cover of *Life* on her hundredth birthday in 1960, and she died a year later on 13 December. Her works from the 1940s include *Hoosick Valley* (1942), *Catching the Thanksgiving Turkey* (1943), and *The Thunderstorm* (1948).

Norman Rockwell, 'American's Greatest Illustrator'

Despite the idea that the illustrator serves merely the writers, editors and advertisers employing him or her, many regarded themselves, and

Horace Pippin, Self-taught Master of the 1940s

Horace Pippin was born in West Chester, Pennsylvania and returned there as a young married man in 1920, after an impoverished childhood spent in Goshen, New York; a stint as a working man in Patterson, New Jersey; and a World War I tour of duty serving alongside French troops, during which he sustained an injury to his right shoulder. At Armistice, Pippin was awarded the French Croix de Guerre but did not receive a Purple Heart until 1945 (a year before his fatal stroke at fifty-eight), 'after another world war needing black support made the omission too conspicuous'.[68] While fighting in France, Pippin kept an illustrated journal of what he saw and experienced, noting on one occasion that the war 'brought out all the art in me'.[69] Returning home, Pippin lived on disability benefits and his wife's income and, in the early 1920s, began making art – first by wood-burning then painting with oils – as physical therapy for his impaired right arm. Photographs of Pippin at work show his remarkable two-handed technique: 'he used his "good" left hand to guide his crippled right hand, which held the paintbrush, across the canvas. It took him three years to finish his first painting.'[70] While slow to produce his earliest works, Pippin gained speed and produced a hundred and fifty paintings during his brief career, half of these in the 1940s.

He is known for both his warm, convivial renderings of folk life (many of these staged in simple interiors), and his grimmer responses to historical events, including war and American race relations. Like Lawrence, whose work he knew, Pippin interpreted the life of abolitionist John Brown, as well as Abraham Lincoln and scenes of lynching. More than once he depicted the soldier's life in the trench-violated fields of France in moods both quotidian and tense. Many of his works of the 1940s are widely known and highly regarded, including *Domino Players* (1943) and *Interior* (1944), both set in stove-warmed interiors, depicting respectively the enjoyable interactions and solitary pursuits of thoughtful women and contented children. *Harmonizing* (1944) is an outdoor scene, set on a street corner in Pippin's West Chester neighbourhood, where a male quartet stand together in perfectly composed harmony before a church steeple and worn wooden fence, alongside the accenting vertical of a street light. His famous depictions of World War I include *The End of the War: Starting Home* (1930–33), *Dogfight Over the Trenches* (1935) and *The Barracks* (1945); it is interesting that several of Pippin's earliest works relive his experiences of war, indicating that painting for him was as psychologically therapeutic as it was physically. At the start of World War II, Pippin was disturbed by the conflict occurring overseas as well as by an elevated racial crisis at home. His three-part *Holy Mountain* series is dated 6 June (D-Day, 1944), 7 December (Pearl Harbor's third anniversary, 1944), and 9 August (the atom bombing of Nagasaki, 1945). Each replies to Edward Hicks's nineteenth-century *Peaceable Kingdom* paintings, depicting lions and lambs at ease with each other, tended by little children, as originally envisioned in the Book of Isaiah. *Holy Mountain III* (commemorating Nagasaki) is regarded as the most complex, and includes pastoral elements but also cockatrices (bird-serpent death harbingers also described in Isaiah) in the foreground and images of lynching and trench warfare in a darkly wooded background. It is easy to read the soldiers as ready to advance upon the peaceful scene in the foreground, ominously poised to destroy it. Judith Zilczer observes that 'letters published . . . about the *Holy Mountain* paintings reveal that [Pippin] was deeply troubled by human evil' but looked forward in his work to days of everlasting peace.[71]

Success came rapidly to Pippin in the late 1930s, as he moved from a local showing in 1937 to inclusion of four pieces in MoMA's 'Masters of Popular Painting' exhibition in 1938. Aided by his unflagging supporter, gallery owner Robert Carlen, Pippin gained critical recognition and an avid customer base, including stage and screen celebrities John Garfield, Charles Laughton and Clifford Odets. His work was featured in *Newsweek*, *Time* and *Life* and his still life *Victory Vase* (1942) appeared on a nationally distributed greeting card.[72] He had ambivalent contact with the realms of commercial art, including *Vogue* magazine and Hollywood, as the pressure to fulfil such commissions left him in 'physical and intellectual discomfort'.[73] Fellow artist Claude Clark felt that he had been 'exploited to the hilt'.[74] At the height of his career both creatively and financially, his marriage began to deteriorate, and he once told an admirer that he painted out of loneliness, to ease his moods of sadness. The personal and professional setbacks were troubling only as they impeded his marvellous work, which remained significant and well in demand throughout his regrettably short life and well beyond. Selden Rodman considered that 'among American popular masters he is without rival';[75] Bearden and Henderson celebrate Pippin's 'extraordinary quality of aesthetic consciousness' and observe that 'in contrast to other important self-taught US painters, who tended to repeat themselves, Pippin explored many different facets of black life and expressed humanity's yearning for universal peace'.[76]

were regarded by millions of admirers, as America's most important creators of visual art. Within the pages and on the covers of the immensely popular periodicals of the 1940s, especially *Collier's*, *Ladies' Home Journal* and *The Saturday Evening Post*, the artist illustrated little less than the zeitgeist, the national mood. Norman Rockwell's career as 'America's greatest illustrator' does not belong to a single decade,[77] although magazine historians point out that the 1940s were for illustrators in general and Rockwell in particular the last great decade of artistic and commercial success: beginning at the turn of the twentieth century, when printing methods had advanced enough to make colour reproductions of oil and watercolour works affordable to mass produce, picture magazines enjoyed a half-century heyday that ended only when the onslaught of television caused magazine editors

Figure 4.2 *Interior* (1944). The artist of this work, Horace Pippin, was the best-regarded self-taught artist of the 1940s. Gift of Mr and Mrs Meyer P. Potamkin, in honour of the fiftieth anniversary of the National Gallery of Art. Image courtesy of the Board of Trustees, National Gallery of Art, Washington DC.

to turn more and more frequently to photography, both to simulate the television-viewing experience and simply to say 'modern' to their young and forward-moving post-war readership. Beginning in 1916 Rockwell's work was featured on the cover of the *Saturday Evening Post* 322 times, more than any other artist.[78]

His works are known, ironically, for their photographic quality, their extraordinarily realistic detail in the rendering of both human figures and the evermore detailed settings he produced in later years. He loved to paint children and old people,[79] although he was interested in the human condition, and often the human foible, across the age spectrum. Almost always his context was small town and/or nostalgic; he was dismissed, since his earliest days, by critics who scoffed at the shaved necks and apple cheeks of his sentimentalised characters, and even those who recognise the value such sentiments had for Americans

struggling through the Depression and World War II question whether
his attitude was less affectionate than sardonic. The latter idea is supported by the artist's tendency to exaggerate facial expression and to
contort bodies to emphasise the rump, although Rockwell often stated
that this manner of over-drawing was necessary to convey to his
viewer quickly, within a matter of seconds, the story contained in the
illustration.

Rockwell was a progressive interventionist who felt deeply com-
pelled to contribute something to the war effort. His recurring character was a GI named Willie Gillis, who 'took shape as an unimposing,
slightly goofy young man with a shock of reddish hair, a somewhat
bewildered smile, and a still developing, gangly body ... Readers
loved the reassuring image of their everyman son, brother, lover,
neighbor, or friend.'[80] Inspired by the 'four freedoms' outlined by
Roosevelt in his speech to Congress in January 1941, Rockwell determined in early 1942 to produce his most famous contribution to the
cause – a poster campaign that would embody each of Roosevelt's four
somewhat abstract freedoms – of speech, of religious expression, from
want and from fear. He agonised, as he always did,[81] over just the image
for each instalment, and delivered the series to his clamouring editors
(and public) at the end of that year.

Freedom of Speech depicts the sort of town meeting Rockwell and
his wife regularly attended as residents of Arlington, Vermont where
they had moved from the artsy New York suburb of New Rochelle in
the summer of 1940. Centred is a rugged but thoughtful-looking man
in a plaid jacket, standing among his neighbours evidently in the coura-
geous act of voicing a contrary opinion. The range of facial reactions
from his fellow townsmen, from supportive to adversarial, but all suffused with respect for the dissenter's right to speak, tells the story even
more pointedly than does the drama of the lone protester. *Freedom to
Worship* is a collage of prayerful profiles, hands folded or clasping
articles of devotion, bowed heads covered respectfully according to
the dictates of various faiths. The painting features notably African
Americans in the upper left and lower right corners. *Freedom from
Want* depicts a Thanksgiving dinner presided over by an elderly couple
who administer a turkey to their happily gathered relatives, and
Freedom from Fear is a sentimentalised bedtime scene, parents lov-
ingly tucking in two sleeping boys, the hush of the nursery contrasted
with the chaos in the newspaper held in the father's hand.

Despite Rockwell's regrets – only the first in the series truly pleased
him – the four paintings were a phenomenal success; 'harnessing the

original oils to a tour, cosponsored with *The Saturday Evening Post*, of sixteen cities, seen by 1,222,000 people, [the US Treasury raised] $133 million in war bonds . . . The *Freedom of Speech* painting illustrated the commemorative covers for war bonds and stamps sold during the show.'[82] All four works were combined into a single poster which also sold many millions. Rockwell was presented with a Distinguished Service Award from the Treasury in 1943. Even when he was not painting specifically in support of the war, Rockwell can be credited with producing work that reminded Americans again and again of 'what they were fighting for'. His cheering depictions, which had warmed hearts throughout the despairing 1930s, now inspired his fellow citizens to think (however inaccurately) of American culture as a golden ideal worth the ultimate sacrifice to preserve and promulgate. His emphasis on children, in particular – in their combined vulnerability and resilience – drew out his viewer's protective instincts but also instilled the empowering sense that the United States, like these youthful figures, constituted the irrepressible, inevitable future. As Rockwell biographer Laura Claridge writes, Rockwell 'felt his talent lay in convincing the Americans at home that they were investing in their vision of what the country stood for in its very Yankee entrails: freedom'.[83] Towards the end of the war, Rockwell's remarkable *Homecoming* (*Post*, 26 May 1945), was *Post* editor 'Ben Hibbs's favourite Rockwell cover'.[84] It featured a young man in uniform returning home to his urban tenement, welcomed with open arms by his family and by joyful waves from his racially diverse neighbours.

Despite their incredible success, the *Four Freedoms* posters index helpfully Rockwell's controversial position within the world of art. His works were selected by the Office of War Information (OWI) for its 1943 War Loan campaign instead of those submitted by the social realist painter Ben Shahn, whose graphic themes of Nazi atrocities were deemed too disturbing for government-sponsored distribution. Shahn shot back with a satirical poster of the Statue of Liberty raising not her torch but a bottle of Coke, under the caption *The War that Refreshes: The Four Delicious Freedoms*. Following the rejection of Shahn's work, as well as what were deemed acts of artistic cowardice by the OWI's board of administrators, many leftists within the agency resigned.[85] Rockwell was mocked on artistic as well as on political grounds, epitomising kitsch for Clement Greenberg (though even *The New Yorker* was 'high-class kitsch'),[86] who popularised the term in an essay for *The Partisan Reader* in 1946. Modern assessments are more philosophical and favourable overall; Ned Rifkin compares him to his fellow sentimentalist Frank Capra,[87] and illustrator Brad Holland called him 'the American Dickens'.[88] Laurie Norton Moffatt writes, 'he was an anachronism for most of his career, and he knew it',[89] though Steven Heller contends that 'Rockwell ran one step ahead of cliché, while his acolytes lagged a mile behind'.[90] Holland notes that, unfortunately, Rockwell is 'more highly regarded for his sentimentality than for his genius with faces' and that 'one has to overlook much of what made him popular to realise just how good he was'.[91] Defending his rich realism, journalist Paul Johnson observed, 'critics dismiss Rockwell for the usual trade union reasons. They have nothing to say about pictures which explain themselves. Rockwell gave them no intermediary function.'[92]

Rockwell himself weighed in on the controversy with his usual wit and narrative complexity. *The Connoisseur* (1962) poses a well-dressed middle-aged man before a Pollockesque work of multi-coloured splashes. While the art patron's back is to the viewer, his stiffened, slightly arched pose conveys the consternation and indignation – or is it the elation and enlightenment? – we are to assume registers even more clearly on his unseen face. Wanda M. Corn reports that letters to *Post* editors the week following this picture's appearance on the cover ran the gamut. Some thought Rockwell was wasting paint rendering abstract expressionism, even in satire, others thought it not a bad emulation of Pollock's style: 'In [*The Connoisseur*] Rockwell makes clear that he knows something about abstract art, and he details for his audience the difference between his very literal style and the abstract one of the modern artist. He found a way to illustrate for a popular audience the different demands that Abstract Expressionist canvases and the covers of *The Saturday Evening Post* made on their viewers.'[93]

Despite the personal tragedies of the 1940s – a fire in his barn studio in 1943 that, as with Gorky above, destroyed every career-related item in his possession up to that point, and his wife's descent into mental illness and alcoholism – throughout the 1940s, and into the early 1950s, Rockwell was at the height of his professional and artistic success. His most famous non-war-themed works of the 1940s include the *Tom Sawyer* series (for Heritage Press, 1940), the prize-fight scenario on a unique horizontal canvas, *Strictly a Sharpshooter* (for *American Magazine*, 1941), *The Meeting* (for *Good Housekeeping*, 1942), and *Charwomen in the Theater* (for the *Post*, 1946). In 1949, collaborating with fellow illustrator Albert Dorne, he began the Famous Artists correspondence school, which was a marked success throughout the next decade.

Illustrating the War and the Home Front

Other illustrators of the era did their part to support the war, or simply left their marvellous stylistic mark, offering viewers (and shoppers) a means of visual escape as effective and appreciated as that provided at the local cinema. The War Department's Art Advisory Committee conducted a short-lived campaign to send soldier-artists into the theatres of battle, to sketch and paint historical action by way of developing a national archive on the war.[94] McClelland Barclay painted beautiful women for General Motors in the 1920s and 1930s but was stationed in the Pacific as a Naval Reserve Lieutenant Commander during the war. In the service, he painted posters, illustrations and officer portraits before being listed as missing in action when his ship was torpedoed in 1943. Another casualty was Gilbert Bundy, whose risqué illustrations for *Esquire* were set aside when he went to cover the war in the Pacific for King Features. Traumatised by the harrowing scenes he had witnessed there, Bundy took his own life in 1955.[95]

On the home front, Ernest Hamlin Baker was a great self-taught painter of world leaders, whose portrait of George C. Marshall among some four hundred others decked the cover of *Time* magazine throughout the 1940s. Rockwell's neighbour and close friend Mead Schaeffer painted battle scenes for the cover of the *Post*; when another Rockwell friend and colleague, Jack Atherton, was not painting homely covers for the *Post* he was winning 'Artist for Victory' competitions – specifically for his strikingly surrealist *The Black Horse* (1943) – as a respected 'serious' artist. Howard Scott portrayed the war-worker for the *Post* in 1941, and the fantastic visions of Boris Artzybasheff, his humanoid war machines often in the act of vanquishing Axis powers, promoted steel for the Wickwire Spencer Company and generally provoked reader interest for *Life* magazine in 1941. In a slightly more realistic mode Artzybasheff, like Baker, provided portraits for the cover of *Time*, including a famous one, after Hitler's suicide in 1945, of the Führer's face with an off-centred red X scratched across. Almost all of the painters in this group – including Rockwell – turned their talents to the selling of specific products: for instance, Parker Pens (Artzybasheff), Sanka Coffee (Dorne) and Kellogg's Cornflakes (Rockwell).

Howard Scott was well known for creating twenty-four-sheet posters (aka billboards) for Esso Gasoline and the Ford Motor Company; *American Artist* reported in the early 1940s that 'Scott calls his ideas for posters "scenarios" and refers to the posters as "one-act plays". The scenario must be direct as an arrow, aimed at a single idea; and it must reach its mark as unfailingly as a good cartoon gag.'[96] Similarly, Catherine Gudis describes the aesthetic of poster art that all in the industry agreed was never to be achieved simply by transferring a magazine layout to the twenty-four-sheet poster: 'most of all, designers were encouraged to capture a sense of motion in their work, to lure viewers into the scene and quickly back out of it again'.[97] Elsewhere in the genre of roadside visual art, the Burma-Shave campaign which, in 1925 began treating motorists to five- and six-panel series, each sporting one line of a folksy rhyme that always ended in 'Burma-Shave', was in its second decade of immense popularity in the 1940s. Wartime supply shortages – not only in sign materials but in rubber and gas, which reduced the number of cars – caused a hiatus in new signage in the early 1940s; instead, there was an increase in streetcar signage, with the entire jingle printed on one poster.[98] As a whole, the 1940s was a topical decade for the company, inspiring jingles against Hitler, 'Japs', and failing to buy enough war bonds. In 1948, they penned for a roadside series: 'We don't / know how / to split an atom / But as to whiskers / Let us at 'em. / Burma-Shave'.[99] While driving conditions, road beautification groups and public satiation led to a downturn in the signs' popularity during the 1950s, in 1947 there were six million users of the 'brushless shaving cream', and in 1949 more than 52,000 entries in the annual jingle contest, sent in hope of a $100 grand prize and roadside stardom.[100]

The Decade of the Comic Book

The popular art belonging so specifically to the 1940s that the decade is now regarded as this form's Golden Age is the comic book, a distant cousin to the comics panel or strip found in erudite magazines like *The New Yorker* and newspapers nationwide. Even within this family of illustrated or graphic narrative, there emerged a hierarchy, well delineated by Kirk Varnedoe and Adam Gopnik. Strip artists such as

> Fisher and Tad and Herriman and Goldberg were gents, popular figures, men about town who had a lot of money and a surprising social cachet. But Siegel and Shuster [who invented *Superman* specifically for the comic book trade], even after their success, remained Depression-era drudges, working for ten dollars a strip, their copyright long since sold away. The comic strips had been court jesters in the empires of Hearst and Pulitzer; the comic book was the pornography of the prepubescent.[101]

The comic strip, like all the art discussed in this chapter so far, was signed by its creator, who became well regarded accordingly as not only an artist but often as a philosopher and 'novelist'. The first art exhibition to honour the 'The Comic Strip, its History and Significance', was sponsored by the American Institute of Graphic Arts in 1942.[102] Despite the low status accorded the comic-book form, it is readable as the ultimate visual arts rage of the decade: comics historian Bradford W. Wright reports that in 1943, comic book sales were at twenty-five million copies a month, generating $30 million in sales that year.[103] In 1945, Market Research Company of America determined that '70 million Americans – roughly half of the US population – read comic books';[104] even by the end of the decade 90 per cent of young children remained avid readers.[105]

The comic book genre began inauspiciously by compiling and reissuing newspaper comic strips in tabloid form, sold by news companies at newsstands or offered by manufacturers as give-aways to lure buyers. Its full flowering occurred almost literally overnight when two aspiring strip artists from Cleveland, Jerry Siegel and Joe Shuster, approached a fledgling comics concern known as DC (for *Detective Comics*, their first serial) with a red-caped hero in 1938. *Superman* was an instant and total success, for its publishers if not for its creators, who regrettably sold their rights in the character for a miniscule sum when they were first hired at DC. As Wright notes,

> Siegel and Shuster, however unconsciously, had created a brilliant twentieth-century variation on a classic American hero type . . . Whereas heroes of previous centuries, like Daniel Boone, Natty Bumpo, and Wyatt Earp, could conquer and tame the savage American frontier, twentieth-century America demanded a superhero who could resolve the tensions of individuals in an increasingly urban, consumer-driven, and anonymous mass society.[106]

Almost immediately *Superman* sold nearly a million copies a month and was adapted as a syndicated newspaper strip. It was a radio show and film cartoon series in the 1940s, a television programme in the 1950s, and a film hero many times over in the decades that followed. Within months of the series' debut, a like-suited pantheon of copycat superheroes hit the stands, inaugurating new series, shops (aggregates of comics writers), and publishing concerns in the process. As historian Robert C. Harvey notes, 'superheroes and comics were made for each other . . . Comic books were the ideal medium for portraying the exploits of super beings,' since novels and film technologies of the era both failed in this regard.[107] Yet all of DC's titles – in crime, detective, jungle, action and animal genres – sold well, as did those of competing comic book houses. Finally, *Superman* seemed little more than the excuse young America was looking for to plunge itself into the comic-book craze that abated only when, once again, television radically reorganised the cultural spectrum.

Superman was followed quickly in timing and in popularity by two other DC superheroes, the noirish *Batman*, created by Bob Kane in 1939, and the so-called girls' series *Wonder Woman*, designed by William Moulton Marston (a Harvard PhD with credentials in psychology and ties to the advertising industry) in 1941.[108] Batman's partner in crime-fighting, Robin, spawned the fad in youthful side-kicks, who gave young readers a direct point of identification in narratives built around adult-sized prowess, speed and danger. Wonder Woman used a magic lasso to snare her adversaries, but she was also the first in a long line of scantily clad, voluptuously drawn queens and goddesses who wound up masochistically enthralled to male and female dominators at least once every episode. These cheesecake hero-ines proliferated during the war when comic books were popular, not only with juvenile readers, but also with servicemen hungering for cheap, lightweight entertainment at military bases overseas.[109] In fact, soldiers loved comics of all kinds and greatly expanded the genre's adult readership during the war; various comics' series were even used as instruction handbooks for the Army.[110] As Harvey notes, 'soldiers could read a comic book quickly without concentrating much, and that was just the sort of mildly engaging diversion young men needed to survive military routine'.[111] DC's rival, Marvel Comics, entered the fray with the Human Torch and the Sub-Mariner, and Fawcett Publications with Captain Marvel (whose youthful sidekick Billy Batson was actually himself before utterance of the transformative magic word, 'Shazam!').

Most successful of all, however, even outselling *Superman* during the war, was Marvel Comics's *Captain America*, created by Joe Simon and Jack Kirby, who took the concept of a caped crusader in a new direction: instead of fighting crime and defending the downtrodden in generalised terms, *Captain America*'s first issue featured on its cover the masked superhero delivering a knockout punch to Hitler himself. Significantly, this series was launched in March 1941, nine months before the United States would declare war on Japan and Germany. In addition to emphasising the evil of Hitler and, to a lesser degree,

Japanese adversaries, Captain America and his fellow superheroes 'betrayed [their] interventionist leanings' by attacking isolationists as pacifists and spies;[112] their creators, many of them Jewish and all of them decidedly left wing, created American avatar-ideals already, explicitly at war with fascist adversaries months before the war began for the United States. Following Pearl Harbor, these superheroes' avid patriotism was well in step and escalated only during the conflict. 'In that time of national crisis and overheated passions, the super-patriot captured an audience immediately.'[113] After the war, comics' creators sensed the need for a new tack by which to keep readers interested and shortly were forced to de-emphasise both the crusading content and the leftward political slant of their wartime series: 'In a vague sense, the [post-war] decline of the superheroes reflected a postwar public mood that had grown conservative and weary of reform';[114] DC's ultra-progressive Green Lantern bowed out in 1949.

In late-1940s series such as *Radar*, *International Policeman*, *Atoman*, *Johnny Everyman*, and various numbers of *Captain Marvel*, post-war realities and responsibilities continued to trickle through to young readers, couched in a liberal perspective (see the following case study). Yet more and more, politically neutral content filled the pages – of resurgent western series starring real-life cowboy heroes (even those no longer alive), of 'teen comics' dominated by the Archie series; and of underworld/crime series whose graphic depictions of sexual subjugation, torture and violence reached new lows. As comics' historians Reinhold Reitberger and Wolfgang Fuchs observe, 'the Second World War had a brutalising effect on the output of all the mass media, including comics. Things that would have been judged sadistic in 1940 were deemed accurate reporting in 1945.'[115] Even the bomb was de-politicised, as 'the comic-book contribution to folklore centered on advancing the idea of a benign Bomb, a friendly Bomb, a Bomb that would never hurt anybody unless we willed it – and certainly it would never hurt us.'[116]

The western series were adaptations of radio and film series starring Gene Autry, Roy Rogers, Hopalong Cassidy, Red Ryder, and the late Tom Mix – even John Wayne, whose *John Wayne Adventure Series* took him from his ranch to Korea and around the world.[117] As William Savage notes, the comic-book cowboy 'stood for law and order, peace and quiet, God and country, Mom and apple pie, just as he always had . . . Unlike the [comic-book] soldiers of Korea, the comic-book cowboy rode herd on no neuroses.'[118] Archie and his pals (half-asleep Jughead, vixen Veronica, sweetheart-next-door Betty, and ne'er-do-well-nemesis

Reggie) came to life in the house of MLJ Publications in 1941, but boomed in 1946 when MLJ changed its name to Archie Comics in response to Archie's huge post-war popularity. The Archie gang lived an idyllic life in Riverdale, suffering the minor humiliations of adolescence but keeping well clear of the temptations and hazards of inner-city delinquency. As Wright notes, Archie 'offered an idealised, tranquil, and nostalgic vision of high-school life primarily for boys and girls who had not yet experienced it . . . [He] offered young readers a safe glimpse into teen life, while carefully observing the rules of adult society.'[119]

The hyper-realised violence of the underworld series, most prominently *Crime Does Not Pay* – unfortunately, it paid bountifully until the very last bullet- and blood-filled frames – drew criticism from parents, schools and social reformers that became so vociferous that it finally had a terminal effect on comics' publishing in this era. Fredric Wertham, a child psychologist who would make headlines with his anti-comics polemic *Seduction of the Innocent* in the mid-1950s, began speaking out against comics' negative influence in the late 1940s. As founder and head of the first mental health clinic in Harlem, Wertham studied delinquent populations of all races and found a high correlation between early violent crime and comic-book use. That 90 per cent of children of all classes and moral tendencies were in thrall to the medium did not cause Wertham (or the millions of worried parents who looked to him for guidance) to question the parameters of his study. Following Congressional hearings and half-hearted attempts at self-policing on the part of comics' publishers, there set in a downturn in comics' sales from which the industry never recovered.

The 'Critical Internationalism' of *Johnny Everyman*

While certain series (especially the Green Lantern) occasionally promoted total democracy through racial equality, many others depicted evil Asian (specifically Japanese) adversaries during the war and child-like Latins and Africans, in constant need of rescue by white jungle heroes and heroines, throughout the decade. Beginning in 1944, the progressive hero Johnny Everyman presided over one-page public service comics that appeared in DC's World's Finest Comics and Comics Cavalcade series. Designed to fend off criticism of comic books' negative influence on impressionable young readers, educational pages like these served the additional purpose of promoting leftist values like racial toleration at home and international governance abroad in the politically and culturally conservative climate that had set in as the war ended. Johnny's adventures took him around the globe and back home again: 'Abroad, [he] combated the idea that Chinese could not be good airline pilots and highlighted the efforts by Belgians in Ohain to save Jews, while in the United States he both debunked prejudice faced by African Americans and gave hope to a returned black soldier who feared that racial discrimination was too persistent to overcome.'[120] In 'Meet Henry Wing' (1945), some white American boys disregard their Chinese American counterpart, until Johnny brings them together in an encounter of mutual recognition and respect.[121] In 'Room for Improvement' (1946), a dark-complexioned Russian boy comes to the United States and sees its racial prejudice is as bad as Soviet repression. Johnny's own perspective is even more slanted: 'After having extolled the virtues of Russia's cooperative society, Johnny turns a critical eye toward American society.'[122]

The series was developed by DC in partnership with the East and West Association, a humanitarian organisation founded by the novelist Pearl S. Buck to promote 'critical internationalism'.[123] Buck's sympathetic portrait of Chinese peasants in *The Good Earth* (1931) encouraged the pro-China sentiments that flourished in America during the war. Buck's name inside the cover of comics featuring *Johnny Everyman* episodes is a singular example not only of East meeting West but high meeting low culture in this era. As Wright notes, 'for preaching messages of tolerance and cooperation, the series won some rare praise from the *New Republic* and *Wilson Library Bulletin*, publications not noted for their endorsement of comic books'.[124]

In addition to the appearance of the series in DC Comics, historian Robert Shaffer notes that 'the association also printed hundreds of thousands of copies . . . on its own for use by school districts; the Seattle Public Schools distributed 45,000 copies of one series, and junior high schools in New York City circulated 80,000 copies'.[125] Buck was delighted to have reached this far into the ordinary alleys of cultural exchange. As she had written to an official at the more academically oriented Institute of Pacific Relations: 'I want to get down into the level of people who don't and won't listen to your programs and read your books . . . I want to get down to the level of the comic strip if I can, and I cannot imagine the Institute there!'[126] A columnist for an African American newspaper in Norfolk, Virginia, praised the series for 'touching the kids in their pliable years and instilling in them a sense of racial understanding that will do more good, I am sure, than a hundred inter-racial meetings'.[127] Before the anti-comics backlash generated by psychologist Frederick Wertham and his followers (see above), *Johnny Everyman*, and several others were singled out in an article in *Time* for their edifying properties: *Johnny* 'explore[d] and deplore[d] racial sources of racial prejudices' and comics of all kinds increased reading comprehension.[128] Despite the gains the series may have made, it was too educational for long-term success and folded in 1948.

Conclusion

For a variety of reasons, World War II is more tangential to the field of 1940s visual art than to any other cultural mode examined in this study.

Perhaps not surprisingly, the elevated preoccupations of the abstract expressionists – their purposeful turn from subject matter in general – created a silence in their work on the subject of world conflict. In addition, most of the major artists of the era seemed to have avoided service in the armed forces, even in the various stateside artists corps assigned the task of building military and civilian morale with inspiring, instructive art. Even Superman had to be rated 4-F by his induction board: so eager was he to pass the exam that he mistakenly used his X-ray vision to read the eye chart in the *next* room: his creators feared that, were the Man of Steel ever to enter the conflict, he would rout the Nazis in days if not hours, a scenario hardly squaring with the grave challenge the Axis enemy actually presented. Interestingly, many of the veterans among the 'serious' visual artists – Bearden, Lawrence and Pippin – were African American; they reflected in their work their experience of war, as did many among the commercial illustrators, who served both as soldiers and artists and turned their talents towards celebrating American heroism, as well as condemning the loss war inflicted. Yet to say that much art of the era was unrelated to war is not to say that it should be dismissed or forgotten, therefore. It is likely that the visual artists of this period who eschewed the topical did so for the express purpose of creating works that would excite and challenge viewers throughout the decades, regardless of the context in which they were encountered, and they have surely succeeded in this.

Chapter 5

The Arts of Sacrifice and Consumption

This chapter continues the discussion of popular art begun in the Chapter 4, but recasts the popular, that is, the populace itself, from observer/consumer to performer/participant in the home-front enterprises of playing a role to win the war, then embracing its opulent aftermath. The sacrificial and consumer art forms inspired by the war, like the visual arts discussed in the preceding chapter, ranged from the profound to the absurd; during the war, home-front artists made public displays of everything from their rusted scrap metal to their Victory turnips to their deepest grief. Post-war, a vast spectrum of new consumer goods included groundbreaking furniture and office design, drip-dry synthetic fibres, and TV dinners. While certainly Americans' finest moment, as artists themselves, belongs to the war era, the suburbanisation of the US landscape provided many of them – at least if they were white – a brand new canvas on which to display their material acquisitions, their modern lifestyle and their proud arrival in the burgeoning middle class.

Performing the Arts of Sacrifice

While one might argue rhetorically that Americans – like many nations engaged in the conflict – raised the gesture of sacrifice to an art form, I mean literally to consider the popular, collective works – the installations and performance pieces of immense communal effort – that emerged in response to the call to war. These works were created not only in the amassing of salvaged materials that marked the local landscape with temporary, yet memorable, even record-setting displays, but also in the intricate orchestrations of bodies in motions never executed before – in long, patient lines to donate blood or buy war bonds, in choreographies of simulated disaster that luckily never materialised, and perhaps most strikingly in countless, minute acts of consideration for fellow citizens who were utter strangers but whose fates were now tied inextricably with one's own. Thus, even a new mindset was created through both public, and perhaps especially private, unremarked acts of sacrifice and consideration – a new ethic of courtesy, foresight and honour that warms the American memory as a peak historical experience even sixty years after the fact. Commentators on this phenomenon have used film and stage analogies,[1] seeing those millions making their home-front contribution as bit players in an enormous theatrical production, directed by the federal government and starring their fighting loved ones on location in remote lands. Perry R. Duis compares this massive effort with 'a form of team sport, with neighborhoods and assorted organisations vying to [do] the most'.[2] My related analogy of performance art is meant to call attention not only to the individual actors or players in this drama but also the ways in which the town, the neighbourhood and the home were transformed into works of collaborative art whose function was to encourage (even insist), reward, cheer and inspire.

These publicly mounted, aesthetically significant communal works were often made in response to a closely related art project of the era, government-issued propaganda, which created a total media environment of instruction, information and inspiration. In town, posters covered lamp posts, buses, undergrounds and streetcars; corporations and commercial establishments sponsored drives and awareness campaigns; the local theatres were veritable hot beds of patriotism (about which more below); and at home one was touched by news of war – and what *you* can do – with every turn of the radio dial or newspaper page. The letter V (for Victory) and V-shaped objects (it was even stitched into women's clothing and worked into their hairdos) became a ubiquitous cultural icon, and historian George Roeder describes a 'Back the Attack' campaign that accompanied the Fourth War Loan drive. The Office of War Information (OWI), the major organ of war-related propaganda, directed local officials to plaster the slogan everywhere – 'by stenciling it on sidewalks and the sides of buses, painting it in red, white, and blue on fire hydrants, having businesses print it on their stationery, and placing posters on factory walls, delivery trucks, telephone poles, and lampposts'.[3] One wonders now whether Americans were driven to distraction by this barrage or came to see it as key to their wartime identity formation and maintenance. As Allan M. Winkler observes, 'as Americans became increasingly aware of propaganda, many began to feel uneasy about its implications . . . Propaganda to some seemed to have an unlimited force – the power to capture men's hearts and to bypass their rational processes'.[4] Winkler notes that Americans looked with scepticism at the rise of propaganda within Hitler's regime, as well as the rise of coercive American advertising in the years since the Great War, and had even more reason to be 'morbidly fascinated' by its potential.[5]

The Power of Propaganda

The OWI was formed in 1942 at the dissolution of several related federal agencies, such as the early-1940s Office of Facts and Figures headed by poet Archibald MacLeish, and came under the direction of the respected news commentator Elmer Davis during the war. Yet no sooner had the OWI consolidated than it began to subdivide; it was an enormous operation with separate bureaux for radio, print material and awareness campaigns; the OWI, along with other agencies, such as the Army Signal Corps, made films for civilian and military consumption, as well as monitoring and influencing, through their Bureau of Motion Pictures, the output of Hollywood. Also, there was burdensome infighting between the leftist intellectuals, who staffed the writers' division and favoured straight talk and plain style, and the businessmen and advertisers who ran the various drives and campaigns and preferred the manipulative, emotional appeal. In the last chapter, we learned that the writers' division resigned en masse over the adoption of Norman Rockwell's *Four Freedoms* posters in 1943. In fact, as Winkler reports, the conflict was more complex: 'The crisis peaked over a pamphlet dealing with the food question . . . [specifically] a grim assessment of the food supply.'[6] When some within OWI complained that the publication would give farmers unfair leverage in the commodities market, the writers refused to soften the bad news and the pamphlet was cut from the publication schedule. Their walkout indicated the general shift in the OWI's personnel and ideology as the war progressed; citing the need to 'conserve paper,'[7] the OWI relied less and less on writing's black and white and more and more on electrical media such as film and radio, on large-scale publicity events and on the more entertaining, emotional tones appropriate to such productions.

Americans' fears of the coercive subtlety of the propagandist arts was not unfounded in this era. As Roeder observes, the OWI and War Department carefully 'rationed' disturbing images of war, hiding them in classified files (known as 'the Chamber of Horrors') in the early days of the war but releasing them in manageable quantities whenever public sentiment grew sceptical (about sugar-coated reporting) or complacent (with the sense that the Germans were easy foes, that the war would soon be over). At one point, newspaper editors accused the OWI of attempting to 'alternately dose the public with stimulants and depressants in accordance with the mood they desire to create',[8] and, in fact, this is exactly what they did. Reading not only the powerful transformation in the look of the fighting soldier but of war weaponry itself, Paul Fussell notes that: 'One poster of 1942 depicts [African American heavyweight champion] Joe Louis charging with a slim, long bayonet . . . attached to a long, slender Springfield rifle. He wears a clean field jacket, properly buttoned. We half expect a necktie.' An illustrated poster from 1944, however, is much 'more shocking . . . a dead paratrooper's body just settling to earth, his head hanging with closed eyes, his toes just beginning to drag across the dirt. Blood is conspicious on his jacket and his hand.'[9] Fussell observes yet another notable shift in 1945, at which time graphic photographs came to replace the moving illustrations of imperilled soldiers of earlier years.[10]

Most powerful, because most unfamiliar in an American context except during times of war, was indeed the poster art whose style was as slanted and whose effect was as mesmerising, and even accusatory, as any produced by the regimes of Hitler or Stalin. Often the posters effected upon their viewer a humiliating harangue, a Big Brotherian, guilt-tripping chewing-out that invoked such discomfort in the viewer that 'better behavior' immediately and thenceforward was almost certainly the outcome. Like the dead-paratrooper example described by Fussell above, many in this genre explicitly linked a soldier's death, graphically portrayed, to the damning verdict that 'Someone Talked!' (spilled military or industrial secrets to infiltrating spies). One poster issued by the Government Printing Office in 1942 (artist Frederick Siebel) features a soldier floundering in dark waters, reaching out in desperation, but also in a defiant attempt to pull into the water with him the suspect viewer, the war-industry blabbermouth whose death is on his head.[11] In a 1944 Printing Office issue (artist identified as Yegley), embarrassment occurs in the moment required to recognise what the sentimental picture – a saddened dog and empty uniform draped over a living-room chair – is meant to connote. The picture's caption, 'Because somebody talked!', is printed in lacy, feminine script, as if they are the words of an aggrieved mother or sweetheart, initially disguising the tragic, accusatory message couched therein.[12] Biting irony is on display in another *trompe l'œil* poster from the Printing Office in 1944 (artist Steven Dahanos). A foreshortened fist and forearm (in Nazi uniform) extends toward the viewer, a swastika medal dangling between the fingers. This accolade from the enemy has been issued 'For Careless Talk' and has a surreal aspect – the hand has distinct claw-like features – that requires a moment's contemplation and startled, embarrassed implication.[13]

Despite propaganda's manipulative, authoritarian and hence distinctly un-American qualities, it is the case that such images – coupled with many Americans' self-generated desire to do something, anything, to help win the war – performed a remarkable task. Propaganda organised and directed the energy, anxiety and even guilt and animosity felt by those on the home front; while many of these efforts were largely wasted,[14] and contributed directly to the material and moral support of the war in no way whatsoever, public performances of sacrifice and consideration achieved the vital end of occupying, distracting and orienting this home population – even its youngest, oldest and most disenfranchised members – whose acceptance of the war was vital to its continuation. Some of the salvaging and sacrificing did result in recycled or re-allocated resources, and continued financial sustenance – the purchase of bonds eventually totalling $185 billion – kept the war machine vitally supplied with cash.

Self-fashioning for Victory

The lives of Americans on the war-era home front were refashioned in every way. Starting with fashion itself, the 'victory' look extended beyond an occasional hairstyle or embroidered detail. Fabric shortages meant that men's suits lost their pleats and women's hemlines rose, from mid-calf to just below the knee. For women, the silk and nylon shortages meant that their more exposed legs would simply go bare, protected only by a 'seam' up the back, sketched expertly with eyeliner, to mimic stocking construction. At the same time, women's jackets adopted a broad-shouldered look that not only mimicked the uniforms of their fighting loved ones but indicated women's own new muscularity, as competent, dedicated Rosie the Riveters in the wartime workplace. As Roeder reports, the uniform look came into style for non-serving men as well: 'Employees of war plants proudly wore their identification badges around town and many workers of all sorts requested adoption of uniforms at their workplaces. The socially and politically prominent, some of whom held military rank although their duties were in the civilian sector, also took pride in being seen in uniform.'[15] Air raid wardens were assigned tin helmets and other paramilitary insignia; as we recall from Chapter 1, some even attributed the boom in women's auxiliary organisations like the WAACs (Women's Army Auxiliary Corps) and WAVES (Women Accepted for Voluntary Emergency Service) to this uniform mania.[16]

National adoption of military clothing enabled home-front Americans to share the experience, and the responsibility, of their enlisted loved ones to whatever extent they could. In the corporate sector, Campbell's Soup, Coca-Cola and Lucky Strike cigarettes changed their packaging to appear more patriotic and even in-uniform,[17] and an advertisement for Kimberly Clark depicts a soldier throwing a grenade and a boy throwing a newspaper in identical poses.[18] Similarly, an advertisement in *Life* for Greyhound Bus juxtaposes the image of a pilot, having completed a mission, walking happily from his plane with the image of that same pilot just returned home, alighting from a Greyhound bus.[19] While the latter image suggests a 'now-and-later' sequence, the former may suggest a time lapse (the boy grown into the fighting man) or may suggest the boy as the home-front counterpart for whom the soldier fights. This is also the case in a poster encouraging civilians to walk instead of drive, to save both petrol and rubber. There a woman burdened with several packages cheerfully insists, 'I'll carry mine'. Silhouetted in the background, a soldier bearing his weapons and gear walks alongside, so to speak, his march alleviated to some degree by the woman's thoughtful, identical actions at home.

Donation and Deprivation

Civilians were called upon to give of their material surplus and even to do without that which they needed; they scoured their attics and garages, and children artfully canvassed the alleys and wasteland of their neighbourhoods for rubber, scrap metal, and paper;[20] during the shellac shortage, records were donated, and to hurt Japan before the war, silk and nylon were boycotted then done without once war began. Often entertainment outlets encouraged donation by trading one admission for so many pounds of salvage; thus one popular cultural form (for instance a film screening) encouraged and enabled another (the found-object/scrap installation piece). Country music historian Wayne W. Daniel recalls that 'the price of admittance to a *Barn Dance* show in the summer of 1944 in Normal, Illinois . . . was 100 pounds of scrap metal or 50 pounds or more of scrap rubber. The 7500 fans who attended donated 600,000 pounds of scrap metal and nearly 60,000 pounds of scrap rubber'.[21] Also, 'as early as 1942, *Barn*

Dance artists were diligently participating in the Victory Garden program [instituted to alleviate fresh food shortages] . . . Since most of the *Barn Dance* performers had grown up on farms, tending a Victory Garden was an activity at which they could excel. And they did.'[22] Not only did cinemas offer free admission with the purchase of a war bond, but the cinemas themselves were the sites of scrap collection and communal support. As Thomas Doherty notes, 'in many American towns the local Bijou was more of a locus for community than the church or city hall. As such, theaters were natural places to disseminate information, sell war bonds, hold rallies, solicit money for charities, and collect scarce goods for the war effort.'[23] In New York 'the 1943 Harvest show [where Victory Gardeners exhibited the fruits of their labours] was held in the lobbies of RKO theatres in all five boroughs'.[24] The pictorial record of the salvage drives features child participants with striking regularity; junk collectors by nature, at home in their roles as delivery boys among bundled newspaper, children were ideally suited in both strength and size to the scavenging and hauling of light articles such as bicycle tyres, smaller metal scraps, and stacks of old books.[25] Women were enjoined to save kitchen fat (for the making of nitroglycerine), dig the family's Victory Garden and volunteer with the Red Cross. For men who served through industry instead of fighting, the 'Beat your Promise' campaign encouraged war workers through poster art to exceed production goals on a regular basis. Home-front historian Richard R. Lingeman regards the Victory Garden programme as 'the most popular of all the civilian war effort tasks. At its peak, there were nearly 20,000,000 Victor gardens in the United States, producing 40 percent of all the vegetables grown in the country.'[26] The annals of this period abound with examples of collection goals readily met and exceeded,[27] indicating not only a nation of junk hoarders more than willing to clean the house while supporting the war but also, once more, the exuberance with which the home-bound populace sought to do its meagre share.

While such stockpiling occasioned communal gatherings, enjoyable bragging rights, free admissions and sources of local pride, the government-imposed deprivations – with respect to rationing of food, petrol, rail travel and housing – were the harder burden to bear. Subject to a complex system of ration books, coupons and blackout dates, consumers often went without coffee, sugar, butter and meat (though supplied expensively and unpatriotically by a thriving black market). As Donald I. Rogers observes, 'Americans had meatless Tuesdays and

Figure 5.1 Salvage in Yard. Scrap piles testifying to Americans' willingness to help took on the form of public monuments, even installation art. Library of Congress, Prints and Photographs Division, FSA/OWI Collection (LC-USF34-083761-C).

meatless Fridays and learned to make substitutions. Eggs were plentiful. So was fish. Young wives of the mid-forties learned to stretch their meat dishes just as their mothers had done during the Depression years.'[28] One more manifestation of the Victory campaign was its deployment as a term for a rationed, substituted or absent commodity. Victory Casserole might feature a bit of Spam and large helpings of tinned vegetables; to conserve fuel the official Victory Speed on American highways during the war was 35 miles per hour.[29] Adhesive tape, especially 3M's Scotch brand, may have been missed by women almost as much as were nylons. In the decades before the throw-away-and-replace postwar era, tape was essential to the home-repair work women regularly engaged in, and the Editors of *Consumer Reports* point out that 'before the age of Tupperware and plastic wrap [see discussion below], transparent tape could help with many food storage problems'.[30] Yet from keeping medical supplies fresh to repairing aircraft, the Allies veritably

Figure 5.2 Salvage Worker. A citizen-artist at work. Library of Congress, Prints and Photographs Division, FSA/OWI Collection (LC-USF34- 100061-E).

taped the war together and needed every available inch of commercially supplied adhesives to do so. The Editors quote a 1942 article in *Business Week* that criticises unpatriotic customers of the black market as 'Ladies who utilise sleep time to smooth out wrinkles and restore sagging facial contours' by taping their faces with the adhesives needed by the military.[31] Thus adhesive tape had many more roles (no pun intended) around the home in the war era than it may have today, indicating the nature of the inconvenience, and often the loss, incurred by its war-era absence.

Also, once petrol became too difficult to find, it was easier to donate the family car's four tyres to the next rubber drive. When old cars wore

out, there were no new ones to be had, as car-makers switched entirely
to tank and plane production during the war, and the only car produced was the jeep.[32] Posters exhorted travellers simply to stay home –
not to take unnecessary rides on trains, or cancel tickets at the last
minute, as such acts hindered soldiers' ability to report for duty or
enjoy a few precious days' leave. Women were exhorted to monitor
their kitchens and dining rooms to avoid wasting food; while such
waste would lead more directly to hungry, disaffected family members
than to the depriving of GIs, one poster announced, 'Food is a
Weapon! Don't Waste it! Buy Wisely – Cook Carefully – Eat it All'.
People ate last week's vegetables and unidentifiable meat or sacrificed
coffee or the Sunday drive, in the hope that, across the country or on
the other side of the world, a GI would benefit; they became acutely
aware of the subtle interconnectedness of humanity in this era – that
each loose-tongued whisper, monopolised official or hoarded lump of
coal aided an enemy and jeopardised an ally halfway around the world.
In this remarkable environment of all-out thrift, responsibility and
selflessness, people realised that their every action had a potentially
fateful reaction yet, oddly, this was an insight that did not paralyse
Americans with the fear of making wrong moves but mobilised them
more effectively than ever. Spurred not only by the vital role they felt
they played but also by a mood-enhancing prosperity gained through
lucrative war-industry jobs, Americans found time to plant and tend
Victory Gardens, serve as air raid wardens and Red Cross volunteers,
and maintain family and professional obligations.[33]

Duis observes that privacy was the scarcest commodity of all during
the war. Newly married women or young wives with babies returned
to the homes of parents or in-laws for financial and moral support;
families of servicemen were encouraged to communicate via V-mail,
which was microformed and printed out by third parties overseas; and
housing shortages in urban centres led to close confinement with total
strangers. But even those communal gestures of service and sacrifice
that I have been reading as collaborative art had their intrusive qualities; civil defence programmes often fingerprinted and background-
checked volunteers,[34] and 'one of the duties of the civil defense block
captain was to gather information about everyone in the jurisdiction'.[35]
To avoid suspicion as a draft-dodger, enemy agent or unpatriotic
shirker, 'compliance with the ideals of home front unity sometimes
required public forms of patriotic behavior to demonstrate one's
private loyalty'.[36] As correct as Duis's assessment surely is, it remains
helpful to consider the occasions of pride and self-affirmation created

in these public displays of individual and familial honour. Homes themselves were decked with such promotional signs, as 'colourful window stickers and posters told neighbors that a family bought bonds, contributed to scrap drives, planted Victory Gardens, and had someone serving in the armed forces'.[37] One flag-motif sign read 'Quiet Please – War Worker Resting'.[38]

The most meaningful window treatment of the era involved the service flags issued to families (although visual and verbal rhetoric often associated these with women, especially mothers) whose children served in the military. The flag displayed one star for each service member; flags with blue stars were displayed for those on active duty, and gold stars displayed when a son or daughter had died in the service. Many flags contained multiple blue (or, tragically, gold) stars, and government codes regulated the placement of gold and blue on the family's flag. There were rules, too, regarding the Service and Gold Star Lapel Pins worn by proud, worried or grieving family members; because multiple stars in this overtly decorative medium would seem frivolous, only one blue star (and/or one gold star) was worn, regardless of the number of offspring serving or lost. Considering the terms proposed by Duis above, the enjoinment to use one's window or overcoat as the canvas on which to display not only one's significant sacrifice (in the case of family proudly serving) but one's unbearable grief (in the case of offspring killed in action) seems indeed to have constituted an inextricable mix of violated privacy and therapeutic burden sharing; enshrining a dead son or daughter in this manner attached his or her potentially senseless, outrageous death to a public, national and thus necessary cause. In the neighbourhood at large, honour rolls of local servicemen and women were prominently displayed; in Chicago, 'by November 1943, . . . hundreds of dedication ceremonies . . . designat[ed] intersections nearest the homes of those killed in action as "memorial squares" '.[39] On a lighter note, patriotic occasions, from the Fourth of July to scouting, were, not surprisingly, vigorously celebrated in the war years; the annual I Am an American Day, recognised often with a rally or parade, was the occasion of both local (that is, ethnic) and national pride (see the following case study).

Shameful Displays

This was a vital context for both the advancement of democracy, even within the socially and racially divided United States, and the hysterical

I Am an American Day, 1940–52

In 1940 Congress declared a new national occasion, I Am an American Day, to take place on the third Sunday in May and to recognise newly naturalised citizens and native-born Americans who had recently achieved voting age. It was also intended as an observation of all Americans' rights and responsibilities as citizens of a democracy and a general celebration of things American; on the threshold of war, it was added enthusiastically to the patriotic calendar. In 1941 crowds in their millions turned out in major cities and small towns across the country, and attendance was high throughout the war. Parades, rallies, speeches and entertainments marked the day each year.

New York was a focal point of celebration. In 1941 hundreds of thousands jammed Central Park for the event, culminating in a mass recitation of the Pledge of Allegiance. At Yankee Stadium, an American Day baseball game was preceded by patriotic music, a speech by the Bronx Borough President, and the singing of 'The Star Spangled Banner' by opera diva Lucy Monroe.[40] In Atlantic City, the Variety Club presented George Washington Carver, famed Tuskegee University agronomist and educator, and in his eightieth year, with an award for achievement. A year later, Irving Berlin sang 'God Bless America' and Joe Louis addressed a racially mixed Central Park crowd, numbering more than a million.[41] In 1944, the well-regarded federal judge Learned Hand presided over the Central Park festivities. Before he led the group Pledge, he delivered a speech on the nature of liberty whose line – 'The spirit of liberty is the spirit which is not too sure that it is right' – has inspired moderates and anti-jingoists ever since. As Jeffrey F. Liss reports, 'Hand's [speech] was later printed in the New York Times, The New Yorker, and Reader's Digest. The Hand Papers at Harvard Law School contain hundreds of letters praising [it], asking for reprints.'[42] Historian Elisabeth Blackmar observes that for Central Park, which has been a key site for large-scale political protest for decades, these annual events represent 'the first direct politicisation of Central Park's use as a place for a mass audience'.[43] In San Francisco Walt Roesner's orchestra entertained crowds at the Civic Auditorium in 1945. That celebration was marked, too, by an address from Governor Warren and an appearance by Jack Benny and harmonica-player Larry Adler. Richard M. Fried's comments about the New York celebration of 1941 seem well suited to these nationwide events throughout the war: 'The message was double-edged – plenty of star-studded clowning, but admonitions too that "we live in dangerous times".'[44]

The message of I Am an American Day was not only about civic participation but also a general celebration of American unity through ethnic diversity. In Baltimore which, according to the available historical record, made an especially big deal out of the occasion each year, the congregation of the Greek Orthodox Church of the Annunciation gained greater recognition through its participation in I Am an American Day parades, as well as 'recognition of Greek Independence Day by city and state officials'.[45] In his history of Baltimore, Michael Olesker recalls that the day, complete with parades and pageantry, was 'a standard civic feel good exercise, a chance to include one's own group in a few hours of mainstream America'.[46] He recalls the Sons of Italy, the Polish Women's Alliance, and the Marching Hibernians demonstrating pride in their heritage but also willingness to subsume their respective European backgrounds into proud, forward-moving Americanism. In San Francisco, Chinese Americans were prominent players in the I Am an American Day pageant of 1943; as historian Scott Wong notes, Chinese Americans – intent upon distinguishing themselves from the Japanese (American) 'enemy' – made numerous such gestures 'to demonstrate their loyalty to the United States and raise funds for the war effort'.[47] Italian and German Americans were equally keen to prove their loyalty and also used these annual occasions to acknowledge their ethnicity but assert their superseding American identity.

As Fried helpfully observes, 'Conceived on the cusp between the demise of the New Deal and America's entry into World War II, I Am an American Day accommodated both conservative and liberal persuasions.'[48] Indeed, it was a sort of large-scale 'America-First' party whose main message was the inevitability of war. Its nationalist underpinnings were proud, even arrogant, while it took pains to spotlight each immigrant and racial group in American history, even Native Americans. It was the marginalised American's moment simultaneously to adapt to the new, and celebrate old-world, custom and, though such occasions are the traditional province of flag-waving conservatives, the event was vigorously promoted by Roosevelt himself, and presided over by leading leftists and moderates of the day. The holiday was thus one of several occasions during the war through which Americans submerged their internal disagreements and forced themselves to acknowledge that the same activity provided fun and self-affirmation for many across the political spectrum.

Not surprisingly, recognition of I Am an American Day reached its peak through the war years but trailed off in the late 1940s. After crowds numbered a million or more during much of the war, New York City's attendance records for 1946, 1947 and 1948 were 300,000, 150,000 and 15,000 (partly due to rain) respectively.[49] In 1952, President Truman renamed the event Citizenship Day and moved the observance to 17 September, the date of the signing of the Constitution in 1787. It was redesignated by Congress in 2004 as Constitution Day and Citizenship Day; despite its once-enormous significance, the event is almost entirely unrecognised by Americans today.

intensification of interracial suspicion and animosity fomented by world conflict. The forced removal of Japanese Americans from the West Coast to the desert West was one such outcropping of hysterical misaction; in an attempt to secure the coast from Japanese attack, Californians took complex (though again, ultimately unnecessary) steps to perfect the art of the air raid drill and the total urban blackout. More misguided was the gesture to remove their Japanese fellow citizens because, not only was the Japanese enemy never a presence on Californian shores, but Japanese Americans were never in the least proven to be the fifth column they were feared to be. Ironically, and despite the success of the Victory Garden programme, fresh vegetable shortages occurred throughout the war because many of California's farm-labourers were deported in this relocation programme.[50] While there is no way to read Japanese Americans' mass expulsion and relocation as anything resembling a work of art, the American citizens subjected to this injustice performed their roles heroically, with dignity and acceptance, and thus made to the fullest the only contribution they were allowed to make. Chinese Americans did demonstrate more political and cultural ties to their native land but it was fitting for them to do so because, during this period, China was under Japanese attack, and it was thus possible as a Chinese American to strike back at Japan in a gesture that supported both the old country and the new. The trick, alas, was distinguishing oneself, as a Chinese American, from the mistrusted and abused Japanese American counterpart. Non-Asian Americans, largely ignorant of the cultural and physical differences among Asian ethnicities, and, in fact, ignorant of foreign cultures in general, were provided with poster campaigns that enabled them to identify 'your friends' by both facial feature and uniform. African Americans and Mexican Americans attempted to do their part, as did many in this era, by working and living in racially mixed environments created by the war industry, as well as in many other acts of volunteer work and service. Where peace at the workplace and in the neighbourhood prevailed, we might locate the greatest performance art works in the home-front context; once more, propaganda materials attempted to demonstrate racial harmony but were criticised by southern officials for – the irony seemingly lost on them – promoting 'disunity'. Also, these communal performances were marred by frequent riots over housing and general animosity in American cities throughout the war years.[51]

Despite the racial unity between black and white workers promoted in several federal poster campaigns, it remained the case throughout the war that posters, closely resembling their cousin genre, the political cartoon, used a stylistic shorthand, to gain the attention of and to frighten the viewer, that depended often on racist caricature. While Hitler's distinguishing features were sometimes exaggerated for dark humour, more often the German threat was depicted in a much more menacing (and thus less satirical, more abstract) mood; the image of the swastika – sometimes in shadow looming over the American landscape – was a ubiquitous element in poster propaganda. Japan's distinctive flag, with its red-orange, well-centred rising sun, served a similar purpose; yet, seemingly indispensable to almost all anti-Japanese propaganda was the comic-yet-frightening monkey-like Japanese figure, with his prominent teeth, squinting, bespectacled eyes and contorted poses of surreptitiousness and surveillance. The 'sneaky Jap' stereotype was the thematic counterpart of many don't-talk campaigns. One poster, captioned 'All the Earmarks of a Sneaky Jap' depicts the sun icon at the centre of the Japanese flag as the hole through which a Japanese adversary secretly listens while careless workers divulge industry secrets in the foreground. In these posters, the Japanese caricature is the universal bogeyman whom all Americans might more or less believe was actually hiding under the bed, so alien and ineffable had this figure always appeared to the racist national imagination. Thus, despite the comic aspects of the exaggerated renderings, they retain their ability to frighten and motivate; the race-based animosity encouraged by these images exemplifies the varieties of hysterical mass action constituting a shameful obverse to the organised, meaningful and, finally, artful communal gestures of sacrifice and fellow-feeling that otherwise characterised America's collective response to war.

A New World of Material Goods

World War II historian Perry R. Duis observes that 'the war had made Chicagoans – and Americans in general – willing to accept what might be called a "substitute culture" of temporary replacements for artifacts, institutions, and social relationships. In the consumer goods that were still available, plastic and wood often replaced the iron, steel, brass, and aluminum needed to make the weapons of war.'[52] Yet it is the case that wartime plastic and plywood 'substitutes' became the new 'modern' standard following the war and were eventually embraced by many – among consumer and producer classes – as beautiful and worthy in their own, lighter-weight, lower-maintenance less expensive way. As Jeffrey Meikle observes, plastic 'was free of traditional preconceptions regarding its use and could be molded into any shape a restless drive for novelty might conceive . . . Plastic not only offered a perfect medium for this material proliferation. It

conceptually embodied and stimulated it.'[53] Thus, as with the 'arts' of
sacrifice and deprivation discussed above, we may speak here of the
post-war situation rhetorically – as soon as the war ended, Americans
made consumption into a veritable art form – but also literally: the
boom in materials acquired through war's necessities, as well as the
radical transformation to 'easier living' sought after by vast numbers
in the burgeoning suburban middle class, enabled their own art
forms: industrial design as a discipline unto itself (established more
or less *ex nihilo* in 1945)[54] and artful new ways to organise life, speed
up production, and make over the self and home. Some never found
any loveliness in the way post-war Americans laid out their environment, built homes, designed clothes or set the table; they were totally
disturbed by the mind-numbing suburbanisation of contemporary
life in ways that resembled not at all the provocative, stimulating disturbance that occurs when viewing, for instance, a challenging work
of abstract art. But many others saw the artistic significance of materials and designs that had been in the works since the late 1930s and
came to represent little less than the irresistible future of the post-war
generation.

One cannot underestimate the importance of the 1939–40 New
York World's Fair in the process of turning Americans towards this
inevitable, intensely attractive tomorrow. While the great majority of
the Fair's 'educational' exhibits were barely disguised advertising
campaigns for the product or technology sold by the sponsoring corporation, what these producers offered must have seemed attractive
enough for American consumers to wait for throughout the war
and then accept, even clamour for, as soon as American industry
switched back from swords to ploughshares (see the following case
study). In addition the third item in the Serviceman's Readjustment
Act (aka the GI Bill of Rights), signed into law by President
Roosevelt in June1944, did much to transform the post-war look of
American life. Veterans' guarantee of low-interest home loans signalled a revolution in living patterns that had kept families of multiple generations living nearby (even under the same roof) in urban
centres for decades. With these low-cost home loans, young families
felt free (felt the need) to flee the urban 'old country' for suburban
terra incognita, initiating the United States's endless 'love affair with
the automobile' and presenting to newly-weds a world of choices in
everything from landscaping to child-rearing that was completely
unrelated to the way in which their parents and grandparents had
done things.[55]

The 1939–40 New York World's Fair

At the height of the Depression in 1935, a group of New York businessmen came together to plan an exposition, an internationally sponsored and attended event that would boost the local economy and, through detailed displays of the future defined by modern science and business, point the way out of the nation's economic crisis. The Fair was designed to entertain, educate and inspire, to nudge the nation towards a more economically viable future by whetting its appetite for the products and services of Tomorrow. In the years leading up to the opening, the Fair's Board of Directors tirelessly promoted the event: abroad, they enlisted sixty western nations to host pavilions and borrowed five hundred paintings and sculptures, valued at more than $30 million, for the 'Masterpieces of Modern Art' exhibit; at home, they stitched the Fair's iconic Trylon (a 610-foot [186 m] spire) and Perisphere (a 185-foot-diameter [56 m] globe) on to Yankee, Dodger and Giant uniforms, and Howard Hughes promoted the Fair during his attention-getting national and international flights. The world's leading architects transformed a former rubbish dump outside Flushing Meadows, Queens, into a colour-coded wonderland of novelty structures, flag-lined avenues and bridges, sculpture gardens and fountains.

Opening day was a very hot Sunday in April 1939, commemorating the 150th anniversary of George Washington's presidential inauguration, which occurred in New York. FDR gave a welcoming speech, and attendance was 198,791 people. Through its two years, the Fair was open daily from 9 a.m. until 10 p.m., with the popular amusement park area open until 2 a.m. After dark, light and fireworks displays enchanted visitors and clearly anticipated the wonderland feel recreated each night by Walt Disney at his Disneyland theme park, opened in Anaheim, California, in 1955. In addition to FDR, specially recognised dignitaries on various days included the British Queen and Albert Einstein; theme days promoting each of the sixty sponsoring nations as well as Ford Day, Superman Day and others encouraged tourists to return for special celebrations.

The Fair ran for two seasons, from April to October of 1939 and 1940, and each season had its own personality. One difference was the change in leadership from the more education-oriented Grover Whalen, first chairman of the Board, to the more entertainment-oriented Harvey Dow Gibson, who played up the Fair's tawdry Amusement Area and sensationalised the language of the official guidebook. 'In its second season, the fair strove for folksiness. It was just one "super country fair", Gibson explained. A few weeks before the 1940 opening, a character named Elmer was introduced as the star of a nationwide advertising campaign . . . Elmer was a "beaming, portly, average American", about fifty years old. A New York actor who had previously posed as Stalin played the part.'[56] The other was the entrenching conflict in Europe which, by 1940, had caused two now-Nazi-occupied nations, Norway and Denmark, almost completely to withdraw from participation and several others, including Poland, Finland,

Czechoslovakia and Britain, to politicise their pavilions with pointed inclusions of national and ethnic cultural artefacts. As a University of Virginia website devoted to the Fair observes, 'the majority of the national buildings were dedicated less to the promotion of the future [than] to the best of that nation's particular cultural traditions, including food, dance, and art . . . [I]n a very real way the pavilions of Czechoslovakia and Poland became the only remaining icons of independent ethnic identity in the world.'[57] Elsewhere, the Virginia historians note that by the time of the Fair's second season, 'the mind of the nation was no longer on the future of 1960s but on the possibility of war. The momentum of 1939 and the allure of the new had subsided, and in the words of historian John Crowley, "It was the same fair, only the heart seemed to have left it".'[58]

Despite the gathering clouds over the Atlantic, the Fair drew massive crowds throughout its two-year run, they flocked not only to the mindless amusements but also to the intensive lessons in social planning and technological advance offered to them in the various corporate-sponsored exhibits. Its massive 3½-mile layout included the centrepiece Theme Center where the Trylon and Perisphere were located, six official zones (Communications and Business Systems, Community Interests, Food, Production and Distribution, Transportation, and Government) and the Amusement Area, all connected by various themed avenues and dotted with restaurants and watering holes. The Government Zone (where the international pavilions were), Communication and Business Zone (highlighting the earliest televisions and computers and IBM's own impressive collection of art) and Transportation Zone have received the most attention from Fair historians. In the Transportation Zone, the Railroads Building was the largest at the fair and included a 160- by 40-foot (49×12 m) diorama demonstrating a functioning railway. Actual locomotives were parked outside in the exhibit's multi-acre 'Trains of the Day' display. The General Motors pavilion highlighted designer Norman Bel Geddes's revolutionary 'Futurama', a 15,000-foot (4,572 m) display of a miniaturised city of the future, *circa.* 1960. In it, fifty thousand scale-model cars (one-fifth of which actually worked) dotted and cruised a landscape of interstates, on and off ramps, and urban–suburban metroplexes. Completing the picture were 500,000 miniature houses, more than a million trees of eighteen different species, and various bridges, farms, rivers and snow-capped mountains. Visitors to the exhibit, 322 at a time, sat in a long row of moving chairs, which carried them past the vignettes of the scene as they listened to a deep and god-like voice intoning the car-driven future. In minute increments, the exhibit increased in scale until full-scale GM cars functioned as the grand finale; each leaving participant was given a badge that read, 'I Have Seen the Future'.

As noted above, it is difficult to extricate the science from the sales pitch contained in each of these corporate displays; blending them thrillingly were the artistic talents of many of the day's leading industrial designers, including Bel Geddes, Raymond Loewy, Henry Dreyfuss and Walter Teague, all of whom staffed the Fair Corporation's Board of Design and created the Fair's streamlined, futuristic look. As the Virginia historians describe it, the Fair was 'part ideological construct, part trade show, part League of Nations, part amusement park, part Utopian community, . . . a literal laboratory for a group of industrial designers who considered themselves both artists and social theorists . . .'[59] Bel Geddes's 'Futurama', Dreyfuss's 'Democracity' (another scale-model cityscape housed in the Perisphere, which visitors walked around instead of being carried through), Loewy's locomotives and Russel Wright's food exhibits were of a piece with the better-living manifestos many of them had published at other times in their careers; 'it was Teague, in fact, who wrote that "Industrial design offers the only hope that this mechanised world will be a fit place to live in".'[60]

In contrast to the philosophising undertaken elsewhere at the Fair, the Amusement Area contained a plethora of cheap thrills, including an all-midget townscape and multiple girlie shows featuring, seemingly without controversy, plenty of public toplessness. A Ferris wheel provided a grand view of the Fair's environs, and the Lifesaver Parachute Drop was later transferred to Coney Island. Despite the popularity of this and many of the Fair's remarkable, history-making exhibits, its two-season run garnered only $48 million in ticket sales, a paltry sum when put against the original $160 million investment. The Fair Corporation declared bankruptcy shortly thereafter but this sorry financial outcome does not reduce the sheer momentousness of the Fair's historical importance. As the Virginia historians aptly observe,

> its cultural legacy has lasted well into the late twentieth century and has helped shape and define the commercial, cultural, and political climate of post-World War II America and the world. In a sense, we have lived through The World of Tomorrow, and the Fair has kept many of its promises, for better or worse.[61]

What also came into vogue in this era was 'streamform' – the sweeping, aerodynamic lines that made cars and trains go faster on less fuel but also made refrigerators and sugar bowls look more sleek and up to date: transport engineers thought about the way air slipped around vehicles in motion, and kitchen designers offered easy-to-clean, hygienic surfaces that were smooth, biomorphically rounded at the corners, and all of one piece. Finally, a host of technological advances (some briefly interrupted by the war, some entirely invented by it) transformed Mother's kitchen, as well as Father's garden, the children's school clothes, and the family holiday. The great chemists and industrial designers of the era – especially Wallace Carothers (who invented nylon), Norman Bel Geddes (whose World's Fair 'Futurama' exhibit for GM literally mapped out American, car-driven modernity), Walter Dorwin Teague and Henry Dreyfuss (who designed the interiors of many modern airliners), Charles and Ray

Eames (whose distinctive furniture for home and office, often co-
designed with Eero Saarinen, are iconic emblems of the 1940s and 1950s),
Raymond Loewy (who masterfully streamlined transport, kitchen technology and cigarette packaging) and Russel Wright (see the following
case study) – all created enduring designs for industrialists and ordinary
consumers; even pieces from Earl Tupper's line of marvellous, burping
'wonder bowls' belong today to the Museum of Modern Art.[62]

John Morton Blume points out that, in fact, the entire decade of the
1940s was a period of increased personal wealth and avid consumer spending, that war-industry jobs made home-front Americans wealthy and
acquisitive, resulting in a shift from saving (or Depression-era deprivation)
to instant gratification that has characterised the average American's personal economy ever since. As true as this is, post-war spending increased
even more: returning GIs found good jobs (thanks to their GI Bill-sub-
sidised college educations) in the generally booming economy, and a
plethora of goods that had not been available during the war, or never available before, poured on to the market. Historians of this era speak often in
terms of a 'pent up' impulse to spend and enjoy that Americans expressed
with abandon in the late 1940s and through the next decade. A Public
Broadcasting Service (PBS) website related to the *American Experience*
instalment on 'Tupperware!' observes that post-war Americans wanted
'machines that would help them *modernise* their lives. Between 1945 and
1949, Americans purchased 20 million refrigerators, 21.4 million cars, and
5.5 million stoves, a trend that continued well into the 1950s'.[63] Elsewhere,
'in the first five years after World War II, the amount of money spent on
household furnishings and appliances rose by an incredible 240 percent'.[64]

Another founding father of the era was William Levitt, an ex-Navy
Seabee (CB – Construction Battalion) who learned during the war how
to put up large amounts of service quarters very quickly. Developing an
assembly-line technique in an abandoned potato field on Long Island in
1947, Levitt's crew put up a thousand structures at a rate of thirty-five a
day, establishing the first 'pre-fab' suburb – known for better or worse
as Levittown – in American history: 'In line with Levitt's twenty-six-
step master plan, a thousand concrete slabs were laid down; a thousand
'plumbing trees' were planted; wires were connected by a team of elec-
tricians; and so on.'[65] Reviewing important inventions and transforma-
tions of the last half of the twentieth century, the editors of *Consumer
Reports* sum up the crisis in art and culture caused by this phenomenon:

In their ticky-tacky hutches, their boxes blazing in the sun, as Frank
Lloyd Wright described the architectural genre, Levittowners were

ridiculed for their homogeneity, conformity, dullness, dependence on the auto, and plastic flamingos in the front yard. But Levittowners bred and flourished. Due largely to them and their kind, ownership in single-family homes in the United States grew more in the decade following World War II than it had in the last 150 years.[66]

If pressed to explain themselves, the original suburbanites might have admitted that seeking refuge in treeless, unpaved uniform suburbs was less about aesthetic fulfilment than about ugly politics – specifically, their understandable fear of atomic attack on concentrated urban centres at the start of the cold war and their irrational fear of non-white urban neighbours. They might acknowledge that the car itself was very much the cowardly, conservative alternative to newly desegregated buses and commuter trains, and we must observe that none of these ugly politics is argued away by describing the artistic achievement sought after and sometimes realised by this new white suburban class. To the degree that one appreciates at all the look, feel and significance of the post-war suburban lifestyle, one only regrets that large sectors of American urban classes, especially African Americans, Hispanic Americans and Asian Americans, were denied access to the 'American Modern' until they were allowed to undertake their own suburbanising in the years following the struggle for civil rights, at which point, of course, the arts of the 1940s had faded into the past.

Russel Wright's *American Modern*

In 1939, the thirty-five-year-old industrial designer Russel Wright, whose beautiful spun-aluminum bar- and tableware sold well among the upper middle classes of the Depression era, launched a line of casually styled, open-stock ceramic dinnerware in warm, convivial colours such as 'bean brown', 'cantaloupe', and 'sea foam' which he named *American Modern*. Produced by Steubenville Pottery of East Liverpool, Ohio, from 1939 to 1959, it sold over eighty million pieces and is 'one of the most popular tableware sets ever designed'.[67] The affordably priced line featured rounded forms and lush curves, biomorphic indentations, streamlined simplicity and a signature water-jug strongly resembling a colonial-era coal-scuttle. As *American Modern*'s palette was full of complimentary colours, the line invited mix-and-match creativity and a daring departure from traditions dictating sixteen (or twenty-four or thirty-two) pieces marching in identically patterned step. Wright's *American Modern* furniture in maple, designed in 1935 in shades of honey and 'blonde' (a term coined by

Wright's astute wife Mary), offered buyers the same challenging choices: 'His furniture designs liberated middle-class consumers for the first time from the convention of pre-chosen "suits" of furniture, and encouraged them to assemble rooms that were at once expressive of their tastes and adaptable to their own particular needs.'[68]

Wright scholar William J. Hennessey observes that the sheer quality of Wright's work 'raised the public status of the industrial design profession to a level approaching that enjoyed by such "fine arts" as painting and sculpture'.[69] In addition, both Wright and his wife perfected the art of public relations in ways that established and enlarged Wright's personal status as a known celebrity and that attached value to his signature upon his work. Both Wrights made regular public appearances in department stores introducing Wright's products, and were interviewed by the periodical press and answered questions over the radio. Wright insisted that his name be attached not only to the products themselves but, significantly, to their advertising campaigns. Where the product itself had always been an advertisement's focal point, highlighting the creator in this fashion transformed him from humble, anonymous manufacturer into artist, the item itself into work of art, and the purchaser into sophisticated connoisseur. Wright's designs were beloved by brides and housewives nationwide: 'Within two years [of launching the *American Modern* ceramic line] the factory was unable to keep up with the demand . . . At one point during 1940, demand for it was so great that a two-by-four inch [5×10cm] newspaper advertisement announcing the arrival of a shipment at Gimbel's New York store produced block-long lines and a near-riot.'[70]

In 1939 Wright's design of the New York World's Fair Food exhibit was yet another example of his signature style. In a darkened hall, fairgoers moved from one display to the next, each of which contained a diorama of food production viewed through a biomorphically shaped window. Though it failed within two years, owing to logistical complications and the onset of war, Wright established in 1940 the 'American Way' line of household goods, including the work of sixty-five American craftsmen and styled as a patriotic celebration of the native heartland. The line began auspiciously at Macy's, where Eleanor Roosevelt presided, yet created demand that could not be met and thus died away. Wright saw the loss as a demoralising setback in his vital mission to lead Americans away from stuffy, outmoded European styles and towards acceptance of what the contemporary American context had to offer.

Despite this failure, *American Modern* dinnerware continued to sell strongly throughout the 1940s. Wright introduced the Iroquois Casual line in 1946 and the Residential (plasticware) line in the early 1950s. So successful were these wares throughout the decade that Russel and Mary published their *Guide to Easier Living* in 1950, a handbook not only to the placing and use of various *American Modern* pieces but also to the Wrights' own Asian-inflected philosophy, feminist-inspired politics and mid-century-modern art of contemporary living. The *Guide* not only offered advice on housework and on throwing a party that was so detailed as to seem intrusive in the end, even burdensome but – much more valuably – a sort of manifesto of simplified living that encouraged men to share women's chores, women to forego much traditional housekeeping and families to build and furnish houses with simple objects that encouraged focused thinking and peace of mind.

The *Guide* criticised outmoded European traditions and decor, as well as promulgators of outdated etiquette rules, such as Emily Post.[71] In a representative section titled 'What, no Victorian?' the Wrights lament that

> for many generations the bedroom has been considered the sentimental core of the home, and, through the dictates of fashion and etiquette, has become a veritable Valentine chock-full of all the feminine goodies, the classic models being the Victorian, Colonial, and French bedrooms so popular today . . .
>
> If you are so enamored of the charm of other centuries that you can stand the gruesome, tawdry look of such rooms each morning and then do the work of other centuries to restore order – then have such a room. But if you really want to save work, and to have a room that properly fulfills its intended functions, you'll have to give up your dreams of living in another age and enjoy your own twentieth century.[72]

'Paving the way for such lifestyle interpreters as Martha Stewart and Ralph Lauren',[73] the Wrights suggested to readers of their work and buyers of their wares a mental outlook and a physical environment which were as profound as they were stylish, casual and fun. As design historian Catherine McDermott observes, 'more than any other American designer, the work of Russel Wright has come to represent an image of informal living in the 1940s'.[74] Wright 'design[ed] in layers from the very core of home life – the table – outward toward furnishings, interiors, architecture, and landscape. From his earliest line, . . . his work sought to improve people's everyday lives.'[75]

War's Innovations

As noted above, war halted the development and dissemination of certain technological advances yet initiated many others. If television, refrigerated transport, transistor, and waste-disposal technologies were all somewhat interrupted by the war, they appeared in hearty profusion immediately thereafter; antibiotics, 'super' glues, duct tape, Saran Wrap, nylon, and polystyrene (branded Styrofoam by Dow Chemical in 1954) all owe their discovery and/or refinement to the war itself – as do two great mid-century children's toys, Silly Putty and the Slinky.[76] Expensive, complicated but rudimentary prototypes of television appeared throughout the 1930s; at the 1939–40 World's Fair the Radio Corporation of America (RCA) provided an exhibit of its own version, which the public largely ignored. The year after the war, televisions found their way into eight thousand homes; by 1949, this

Figure 5.3 American Modern pottery. Russel Wright's *American Modern* line was well loved by housewives and brides-to-be of the 1940s. Manitoga / Russel Wright Design Center.

number was an astonishing one million, which looked quite puny next to the 160 million figure that described television ownership by the end of the next decade.[77] Surely supporting America's television addiction was the advent of TV dinners – pre-made entrées, side dishes and desserts that just required oven heating in their own partitioned trays – and a variety of other frozen foods that allowed cooking mothers (and thus dining families) to get out of the kitchen and back in front of the television that much more quickly, or sanctioned families' forgoing of the round-the-table eating experience altogether.

Earlier in the decade, because of the rationing of fresh, and even canned, foods, as well as women's need to spend more time in the war plant and less time preparing food, 'the war . . . made frozen food acceptable, even patriotic'.[78] Thus, late-1940s' improvements in freezer technology – transporting frozen foods to the grocery shop, maintaining them there, and keeping them ice cold in enormous deep freezes and in the freezer compartments of modern refrigerators in women's kitchens – 'improved' Americans' bond with television as well. Many seemingly minor technical advancements had such broader impacts; transistors, for instance, marketed in portable radios in 1948, encouraged garden, beach, holiday and other leisure activities; canned fizzy drinks (starting with Pepsi, also in 1948) did the same. Hand-held drills, power lawn mowers and latex paint, all introduced (especially to male consumers) in the late 1940s, fuelled a trend in do-it-yourself, a trend, in fact, largely initiated in women's magazines. Preaching a gospel of 'togetherness' that encouraged husbands and wives to take on projects such as gardening, repairs and even home expansion in partnership with each other, the suburban household arts of this decade played with the layouts of men's and women's traditional spaces, as well as with their spheres of activity.

We might say that TV dinners and power drills encouraged modern families to break old rules about home permanence and room function in post-war suburban America; as gardens resembled the kitchen (especially a kitchen Dad could manoeuvre through without threatening his masculine role) more and more each year, interior designers encouraged women (and their husbands) to renovate living spaces to break down physical (and ideological) barriers between kitchen and living room. While this ethic of togetherness had its latent feminist aspect, there are many ways to read the boom in consumer goods of this era as simply reinforcing traditional gender roles: men had their manly new toys to play with, and women were deluged with foodstuffs and gadgets (such as deep-fat fryers, rotisseries, electric roasters and frying pans, mixers, blenders, and coffee makers) designed to distract them from their new reality: after the war, they were no longer needed, and no longer welcome, in wartime jobs they may have found mentally and physically, as well as financially, rewarding. Also, these innovations allowed the entire family to cut corners (in terms, for instance, of both food preparation and face-to-face communication) and still feel, perhaps undeservedly so, like an American ideal.

Waste disposals, as well as penicillin, which 'saved its first life' in 1942;[79] fluoridated water, which successfully reduced dental decay in Newburgh, New York, and Grand Rapids, Michigan, in 1945;[80] and a range of new cleaning products and appliances were part of a subclass of consumer goods fuelling this period's obsession with personal health and hygienic housekeeping. Such products often caused controversy, however; fluoridation's (in fact, minimal) health risk inspired picketing at reservoirs, and many town-wide referendums opposed fluoridating water throughout the 1950s and 1960s.[81] Regarding waste-disposal units, 'sanitation engineers and public works officials [wondered] about whether mixing garbage and sewage was a good idea'.[82] Still, 'the real test came in 1950, when the town of Jasper, Indiana, voted to require the installation of garbage disposers in all homes. They were motivated by health issues, as there had been an outbreak of cholera from garbage-fed hogs, and a polio epidemic was thought to have been fostered by the municipal garbage dump.'[83] Less controversial were improved laundry technologies; the detergent known as Tide was an immediately best-selling 'washing miracle',[84] and fully automatic washing machines sold like hotcakes throughout the late 1940s.[85]

The Synthetic Revolution

Tide was not the first synthetic washing powder, but it was the first to perform well in hard water. Proctor & Gamble developed an effective combination of surfactant (a soap-like molecule that emulsifies oil and grease) and water softener (an alkaline chemical) during the war and released Tide in 1947. 'By 1949 [it] was a fixture in one-fourth of America's laundry rooms.'[86] Such success was replicated on many occasions when the shortages of war taught industrialists that the wholly synthetic product was not only more reliably supplied but may also perform better. This latter claim is somewhat debatable in the field of synthetic fibres. As rayon and acetate, in use throughout the 1920s and 1930s, were both derived from cellulose (plant fibre), DuPont's nylon was the first entirely chemically constituted fibre which, throughout the 1940s, was embraced as a fitting substitute for silk. In 1940, 'the demand for nylon stockings caused 64 million pairs to be sold',[87] though during the war, nylon was commandeered for the ropes, tents and parachutes of battle, and women's bare-leggedness – see discussion above – was one more example of their patriotic willingness to do without. Black market stockings sold for $10 a pair, and 'movie stars, like Betty Grable, auctioned nylon hose for as much as $40,000 a pair in war-effort drives'.[88] One fashion historian of postwar America credits women's war-industry coveralls with paving the way for trousers in women's fashion,[89] yet this shift was gradual, and in the immediate post-war years there was evidently a rush to return to conventional dress and stockinged legs to accessorise this look. The archive includes pictures of post-war women storming the barricades of shops with nylons for sale and sitting on curbs outside the stores, donning their purchases before they get home.[90]

Rayon also remained a huge seller in the 1940s, outpacing wool and silk fibre consumption at that time, and showing up in 'ties, evening dresses, gloves, raincoats, draperies, ribbons, and exquisite upholstery fabrics'.[91] Seemingly less affected than nylon by war's exigencies, rayon boomed throughout the decade, with a peak production of fifty-two million pounds (23,600,000 kg) from DuPont's Old Hickory plant in 1951.[92] Dacron was discovered by two British chemists in 1941 and developed by DuPont for commercial use in the early 1950s. As opposed to the slinkier fabrics made with rayon and nylon fibres, Dacron lent itself to tailored items such as women's and men's suits and men's dress shirts. It blended well with wools and cottons, wore better through many washes and reduced wrinkling, which tumble driers (introduced into American homes in the early 1950s) tended to produce. While preferences in recent decades have shifted away from the plasticky feel of synthetic fibres (which, in fact, belong to the petroleum-based, plastics family) back towards the basics of cotton, silk and wool, the synthetic fibres introduced in the late 1940s and early 1950s had their fleeting aesthetic caché, as well as their own latent feminist aspect: 'Acrylic, polyester, and others . . . suited homemakers who spent up to twenty hours a week ironing clothes, tablecloths, draperies, and bed linens of "natural" fabrics. No surprise that by 1952, "wash and wear" was becoming a household term.'[93]

Like the petrochemical fibres that revolutionised clothing construction in the post-war period, plastics developed as petroleum by-products were less revolutionary materials than they were important improvements of old traditions. There had been plastics developed previously, courtesy primarily of the Belgian (but New York-based) chemist Leo Baekeland, who invented both Bakelite and Formica in the early twentieth century. Both were hard-surfaced, plastic-like materials that eventually served as brightly coloured kitchenware; Bakelite made utensil handles (as well as jewellery and the housings of radios and telephones), and Formica was a popular bar and countertop surface that resisted cigarette burns and food stains with equal ease.[94] Tupper named his resealable food storage bowl the 'wonder bowl' as he peddled it unsuccessfully in Macy's department store. It was transformed into Tupperware as it found its faddish niche in the 1950s home-demonstration party industry and improved upon the plastic homeware tradition in several ways: the plastic itself, a refined derivative of polyethylene slag, was nearly transparent and more pliable than older plastics, thus resisting breakage and cracking yet receptive to Tupper's marvellous 'burp' technology. Tupper patented the Tupperware seal in 1949, which allows the user, by stretching a lid over a container, forcing out additional air, and applying pressure to achieve the final seal, to keep food spill proof and fresh much longer than glass or ceramics could.[95] As with frozen foods, housewives at first resisted this seeming degradation of their kitchen craft, rejecting the earliest Tupperware marketing campaigns on aesthetic grounds, even though the science behind the bowl and seal construction offered improved food quality. Soon, however, they were persuaded as much by incontrovertible evidence as by the glamorous and vivacious Brownie Wise, who gave the first Tupperware party in 1949 and headed Tupper's home-party organisation throughout much of the next decade.[96]

Modern Home and Office Design

Wise's high-gloss approach to the kitchen revolution was of a piece with that taken by numerous industrial designers of the era. Her role as the 'business end' of a technological enterprise, whereby the male partner stayed home, so to speak, and developed the product, and the female partner brought it to the world, is replicated in the instance of numerous male–female design teams of this era. In fact, Tupper turned out to be quite a disgraceful partner in the late 1950s, unceremoniously dumping both Wise and his wife of twenty-seven years when he sold Tupperware to Rexall Drug and absconded to an island in Central America with his large income, renouncing American citizenship so as to avoid paying taxes on his wealth.[97] Almost all of the other design relations of the era were more harmonious; Henry Dreyfuss was so devoted to his wife, Doris Marks, that the two committed suicide by carbon monoxide poisoning in 1972, after Marks was diagnosed as having liver cancer. Russel Wright's wife Mary is widely credited with the business acumen that provided her husband's designs with national recognition, similar to the Tupper–Wise 'marriage' outlined above. In the case of Florence and Hans Knoll, Hans masterminded Knoll International, a furniture company established in 1938, while Florence was as active in promoting the business (especially after her husband's death in 1955) as she was in designing corporate America's modern look: in Florence Knoll's interior designs 'the plain geometry of cupboards, sideboards, and storage cabinets co-exists with the more vessel-like forms for chairs and rounded planes for tables'.[98] A student of van der Rohe, whose *Barcelona Chair* (1929) she mass-produced for public consumption after the war, Knoll was instrumental 'in selling modern European furniture design to postwar corporate America'.[99] In addition, Knoll International sold the work of important fellow designers such as Eero Saarinen and Harry Bertoia; Saarinen is known for his Womb Chair, with tubular steel legs and wool upholstery (1946) and Tulip Chairs and Tables of the early 1950s. Bertoia's steel-mesh Diamond Chair (1952) also sold in huge numbers.

Saarinen partnered Ray and Charles Eames to develop moulded plywood home and office seating, a genre they largely invented in the

early 1940s. The Eameses married in 1941, when they were both
students at the Cranbrook Academy of Art, a prestigious design/
architecture school founded by George and Ellen Booth in the plush
Detroit suburb of Bloomfield Hills in 1932. Other Cranbrook faculty
alumni include Saarinen, Bertoia, and Florence Knoll. In 1941 the
Eameses moved to Los Angeles where they built their famous Eames
House (1949), a Bauhaus/Mondrian-inspired, two-part structure fabricated from large industrial steel components. While architectural
projects were Charles Eames's focus in the 1930s, in the 1940s he
joined forces with his wife and with Saarinen to develop comfortable
furniture of resolutely modern design. Charles and Saarinen developed
a single-piece, moulded plywood chair for a competition held at the
Museum of Modern art in 1940, winning prizes that resulted in their
museum-piece prototype entering into mass production. During the
war, the Eameses manufactured splints for the US Navy, having access
to high-tech glues and moulding equipment, which taught them much
about crafting and mass-producing moulded plywood that they put to
use after the war.[100] While the Eames Storage Unit 421-C (1949–50)
failed commercially, it is recognised as hugely inspirational to many
better-selling 'copycat versions'.[101]

Much more successful were the Eameses' Dining Chair Metal
(DCM) and Dining Chair Wood (DCW), made of two pieces of
moulded plywood for seat and backrest and aluminum-tube or
plywood legwork and sold through the Herman Miller Furniture
Company showrooms and catalogue, beginning in 1946. These chairs
were hailed as 'the most advanced furniture being produced in the
world'.[102] Eames scholar Pat Kirkham observes that their design 'was
an attempt to make a chair's seat appear to float in the air . . . The float-
ing rhomboidal elements attached to one another by thin metal strips
referred . . . to the mobiles and paintings of Joan Miró, Alexander
Calder, and Hans Hoffmann'.[103] As the Knolls promoted the careers
of their stable of talent, in the manner of any devoted gallery owner or
arts patron, so the Herman Miller Company may be credited for its
productive partnership with the Eameses as well as with Saarinen,
Isamu Noguchi (designer of the bracingly minimalist Coffee Table IN-
50) and George Nelson who served as Herman Miller's design director from 1946 to 1966, creating a modular office system known as
Action Office during that time. Throughout her valuable biography of
the Eameses' lives, Kirkham takes pains to stress the active role played
by Ray in almost all of the couple's creative enterprises, as many
wound up attributed primarily or solely to Charles. Regarding, for

instance, the 1946 MoMA 'one-man' furniture exhibit celebrating the Eameses' work, Kirkham notes that 'this particular exhibition was the first of many that would focus attention on Charles at the expense of Ray and the staff'.[104] Many of these staff members resigned as a result, although Ray 'accommodated' and found 'reassurance in Charles's public statements about her contributions'.[105]

Jean Bienfait, the wife of Raymond Loewy, who emigrated from France to the United States in 1929, remained a partner in Loewy's design firm and maintained a cordial and productive relationship even after their war-era divorce and her return to France.[106] It seemed that Jean, however, like the other partners in the firm, managed accounts of her own within Loewy's organisation, as all of the designs associated with his name belong fairly clearly to him alone. Alternating with the Eameses, Loewy is regarded as the most important designer of the middle (or even entire) twentieth century; where the Eameses worked out one chair at a time, Loewy's distinctive designs for transport (specifically Pennsylvania Railroad trains, Greyhound buses, and Studebaker cars, although his style influenced a generation of American car-makers) sat all Americans within revolutionary vehicular environments whose every line suggested speed and forward motion – in short, mid-century modernity. Loewy decried squared corners, visible rivets and seamed-together components; his large-vehicle housings suggested (and mostly were) solid pieces of moulded or welded steel dropped over the mechanical works as were chassis on car assembly lines.[107]

His locomotive designs came mainly before the 1940s, as did his gorgeous remodelling of Sears Roebuck's Coldspot Refrigerator in 1934 which design historian Catherine McDermott notes 'was no longer just a machine, but a thing of beauty, a piece of modern design'.[108] Loewy's major projects of the 1940s include his redesign of the Greyhound bus (in 1940) and the Lucky Strike cigarette pack (in 1942) whose background he changed from green to off-white. He redesigned the interiors of locomotives, grocery shops and other retail establishments, and he modernised tractors, large and small appliances, soda-fountain dispensers and even car batteries. Like the cultural critics of the avant-garde and the kitsch, cited in Chapter 4, Loewy comically laments the persistence of 'Borax' design in his entertaining autobiography of 1951:

Usually upholstered with loud, sleazy fabrics, [Borax] is loaded with golden curlicues and polychromatic reliefs and sold to the lowest income group in staggering amounts. To the recently arrived Polish miner or the Croat foundry worker still obsessed by the misery of his Balkan background it represents materialistic splendor. They buy the stuff ravenously, take snapshots of the family sunken in upholstered American luxury, and mail them to Gdynia.[109]

The elitism in such opinions is plain but it is also the case that Loewy, like many of his fellow designers and even the high-brow artists and critics of the abstract expressionist scene, hoped to benefit the American Everyperson by bringing beauty and simplicity into the average home. The phenomenon of popular and 'affordable' art has its laudable ends, even as it is something of a contradiction in terms, even as it fills the bank accounts of its artist–manufacturers and creates a uniform look within a demographic context already fighting (or all-too-readily accepting) mind-numbing conformity. Design historian Penny Sparke observes a continuing conflict between the 'democratiz[ing of] consumption'[110] and 'aesthetic degradation'[111] enabled by the post-war market-flooding of cheaply made goods; the hardships of the Depression meant that 'the enthusiasm and optimism associated with the advent of new materials in the USA was unequalled elsewhere'.[112]

Conclusion

Finally, there is no denying that the great product designers and lifestyle philosophers of the period did marvellous work. That their wonderful product lines, whose extant pieces are now rare, revered and highly valued, were once readily available and modestly priced for all Americans seem fitting reward for the half decade of conservation and sacrifice undertaken by them. Yet the early 1940s are only partially readable as a period of missed material comforts, as Americans took significant comfort in the rearrangement and reapportionment of their material goods and habits of living so as to support the war. They could point with pride to the heaps of salvage massed at the centres of their towns, with pride in the level of collective wealth that (even through economic depression) left on hand such large mounts of scrap, and with pride in their willingness to part with even much-needed, well-loved salvageable items to bring home loved ones safe and soon. How many of these donated items ever directly translated into bullets and lifeboats is difficult to determine and perhaps beside the point, as the gesture of sacrifice was its own fulfilling sustenance, that which

Americans took nourishment and energy from when meat, coffee and car tyres were not to be had. If through this diet of sacrifice and consideration, Americans were in peak fighting form in the first half of the decade, their embrace of the easier, flabbier post-war lifestyle, their shift from the role of producer to consumer of popular industrial art, is understandable given the gorgeous array of new materials, technologies and commodities waiting at war's end to carry them from the traumas and sorrows of the past into the hopeful future.

The 1940s in the Contemporary American Imagination

Interestingly, the first half of the 1940s is as deeply enshrined in the contemporary American imagination as the second half is entirely forgotten. From the late 1940s, there remain some hazy memories of Dewey defeating Truman (or was it the other way around?) and Jackie Robinson obliterating baseball's colour line, but the period of 1946 to 1949 is otherwise a black hole of significance for twenty-first-century Americans. With remarkable regularity, histories of 'the postwar era' begin their analyses 'in 1950' or with 'the early fifties'; one comes to sense that everything happening on American soil in the late 1940s (for example, suburbanisation, communist hysteria, atomic fear) occurred with more significance and a better soundtrack in 'the fifties' – the next culturally resonant historical moment for which contemporary Americans have a ready repository of terminology, iconography and understanding.[1] Indeed, many of the momentous happenings of the late 1940s occurred outside United States borders; they involved the complex reconstruction of Europe, the dividing of world spoils between Western and Soviet blocs and the formation of the present-day crisis in the Middle East – foreign policy manoeuvrings that, despite their historical significance, lack the popular narrative (we might even say the Hollywood treatment) that would have established them in American memory. One might also explain this amnesia through the speculation that late-1940s Americans themselves were in great need of a sleep and a forgetting of the traumatising immediate past. The late 1940s are readable as years of rest, recuperation and a catching of breath whose biggest fads, fears and defining moments simply cannot compare with the massive work of war that had just been completed. Or more accurately these years are readable as a time of holding breath, as a hiatus of historical and cultural innovation that ended – if one believes 1970s' representations, such as the television show *Happy Days* (1974–84)and the film *Grease* (1978) – only at the dawn of the next decade.

Positive and Negative Reassessments

Thus, this final discussion, of 'the forties' as the decade is remembered and represented today, will be unavoidably, lopsidedly focused on the first half. Our interest will turn instead to diverse ways the war has been represented in print, film and public monument in the decades since its conclusion; the obscuring of World War II's afterglow by the humiliations of Vietnam is also included. Indeed, in the course of the Vietnam era itself, the 1960s and 1970s, there emerged a genre of World War II rehashing that resembles very little the ponderous valorisation almost universally accorded the subject today. What Philip D. Beidler has characterised as two categories of war writing – 'The Good War' and 'The Great SNAFU' – divide the field of textual response primarily in terms of thesis and tone. Good War stories start from the premise that World War II was for the Allies a necessary and honourable enterprise whose participants acted bravely even when unsuccessfully and whose stories deserve preservation (often in their own words) with the utmost care and seriousness. SNAFU stories, derived from a light-hearted or even cynical point of view, focus on the hopeless efforts and even criminal misdeeds of officers, enlisted men and civilians during the war and stress war's aspects of futility, absurdity and (often) overwhelming violence. In the former sub-genre war is seen to bring out the best in humankind; in the latter, the worst. In the former the actors are heroes while in the latter they are fools. As the years have rolled on, both types of text have tended to become more candid and graphic regarding war's carnage. Thus, a cynical, damning assessment such as Paul Fussell's *Wartime* (1989) and 'pro-war' films such as Steven Spielberg's *Schindler's List* (1993) and *Saving Private Ryan* (1998) and Clint Eastwood's *Flags of Our Fathers* (2006) and *Letters from Iwo Jima* (2006) spare no horrendous detail. And to say that these films are 'pro-war' is not at all to indicate (at least at this point) that any one of them speaks in jingoistic favour of the war having taken place. This many decades after the fact, and again, thanks to the sobering lessons of Vietnam, war of any era is rarely portrayed by serious film-makers as a guts-and-glory, all-American rite of passage. Eastwood's and especially Spielberg's visions are exceedingly grim, yet their films are 'pro-war' to the extent that they convey towards their subject matter the utmost respect and use their cinematic texts to honour the memory of those who fought and fell.

Figure C.1 United States Marines of the 28th Regiment, 5th Division, raise the American flag atop Mount Suribachi, Iwo Jima, on Friday, 23 February 1945. This 1945 photograph from the Battle of Iwo Jima was hailed by wartime viewers and remains profoundly significant for many twenty-first-century Americans. Associated Press/ Wide World Photos.

By contrast, Beidler identifies the mocking and challenging tone of what he terms the SNAFU stories. His examples are novels – Joseph Heller's *Catch 22* (1961), Richard Hooker's *M*A*S*H* (1969), and Kurt Vonnegut's *Slaughterhouse Five* (1970) – all of which became hit films in the late 1960s and early 1970s and for all of which, despite their World War II plot-lines, 'the real catch was now Vietnam'.[2] Beidler notes that Heller's novel languished somewhat in the early part of the 1960s; it was an era during which the reading public did not know what do with a cynical recollection of a major American victory. Yet the irreverent, rebellious mood of the late 1960s, fuelled not only by intense anti-war sentiment but also by civil rights movements for African Americans, women, homosexuals, and other American minorities; drug and hippie cultures; and rock and roll provided the perfect context for the embrace of Heller's work. 'As Heller himself suggested, his political text had finally found its political context and vice versa.'[3]

While the point is debatable, Paul Fussell contends that 'the real war is unlikely to be found in novels', even hard-hitting narratives like Mailer's *The Naked and the Dead* and James Jones's *The Thin Red Line* (1962), 'for they must exhibit, if not plot, at least pace, and their characters tend to assume the cliché forms demanded by Hollywood . . .'[4] For that reason Fussell's interest, as mine will be, is on non-fiction accounts; his own anti-war treatise, *Wartime*, will be discussed below. Two non-fiction texts from the 1970s that, in very different ways, focus on the mis-steps of war-era civilians and soldiers are Richard R. Lingeman's oft-cited history of the American home front, *Don't You Know there's a War On?* (1970), and John Ospital's less well-known collection of anecdotes from his own service experience, *We Wore Jump Boots and Baggy Pants* (1977). Both Lingeman and Ospital look upon the actors in their narratives more fondly than critically, yet each is free to accentuate the negative (Lingeman) or the ridiculous (Ospital) in ways that many more recent authors would regard as tasteless and disrespectful.

Irreverent Recollections

Lingeman, for instance, provides a valuable account of the Detroit race riot of 1943, in the course of which black and white participants are seen to give in to the mob mentality and initiate violence. He similarly surveys Irish Catholic anti-Semitism in Boston and anti-Mexican and anti-Japanese sentiment in California; while academics are at home with the issue of racism at all points in American history, mass reader-ships, at whom this book was originally aimed, are less comfortable with the subject of white guilt, especially when the ostensible subject is the heroic home front of World War II.[5] More striking is Lingeman's chapter on wartime scarcities, which he tellingly titles 'Shortages and Mr. Black'. Remember that the emphasis in Chapter 5, supported by the preponderance of writings on home-front culture written in recent years, was on the zealous willingness of Americans to pitch in, go without and compete with one another to contribute, collect and sacrifice the most. By contrast, Lingeman's focus is on the widespread resistance to the rationing and impositions necessitated by war, manifested in acts of panic buying (complete with 'punching [and] shoving'),[6] hoarding, stealing, lying and patronising the black market. Lingeman collects news items and single-panel cartoons, both of which feature thieves breaking into homes in search of sugar and butter instead of money; he reports that 750 of a thousand sugar wholesalers were found in violation of standard practices regarding pricing guidelines and inflation control.[7]

Lingeman points out that 'the black market was not a clandestine place like a speakeasy or a brothel, through whose doors slunk furtive citizens. Nor was it a little man saying "Pssst" from a doorway and opening his shabby coats to reveal pendant steaks, butter, canned pineapple, and other precious items.'[8] Rather, the black market occurred whenever a customer – often of long-standing – sought out goods beyond the allowable ration through the payment of higher prices and any time a purveyor accepted the arrangement. Based as it so often was on what during peacetime were cherished American business practices – free-market pricing and relationships of trust and consideration between sellers and their best customers – the black market appears in Lingeman's assessment as little more and little less than 'business as usual'. Perhaps most dispiriting of all, even when Lingeman's Americans manage to comply with wartime commodity restrictions, they do so begrudgingly, as they are frequently heard griping, complaining, harassing merchants or, like the women who didn't want to slice their own bread, 'send[ing] up a wail of protest'.[9] Despite Lingeman's admissions that Americans 'for the most part compl[ied]' with rationing[10] and that 75 per cent of Americans refused to patronise the black market,[11] his striking selection of facts provides the opposite impression, creating a record of dishonourable if not criminal behaviour on the wartime home front.

In the tradition of *Catch-22* and *M*A*S*H*, John Ospital promises 'zany antics' from the military annals in the Author's Note,[12] and is strictly focused on the comic side of European conflict throughout his work. Such a curious emphasis seems partly derived from the fact that Ospital (or his alter-ego paratrooper Jean La Coste) wound up cooking his way through much of his service term, but also partly derived from Ospital's patent disinterest in writing a depressing memoir of the war.

Ospital–La Coste trains as a paratrooper in the opening passages but is
frequently lifted out of battle by supervising officers who learn of his
skills with a frying pan. Much of the narrative involves his setting up
kitchens in various European villages and securing posts therein for
buddies. The reader always feels a touch of envy for the complete tour
of charming locales La Coste and his compatriots undertake; the battle
scenes are always skipped over, clearing the way for the zany antics of
chasing signorinas, pig-roasting without leave and befriending hungry,
cute Italian children. A typical (though somewhat rare) reference to
actual combat transpires thus: 'A behind our own lines jump to bolster
the sagging beachhead at Salerno was the order of the day. After it was
secured we took a little boat ride along the scenic coast line of the
boot.'[13] Later, 'we are in a city in Holland named Nijmegen, and the
objective of the division in this campaign was to secure the bridge in
the town that spanned the Waal river. This was successfully accomplished and then we became part of this city for some days.'[14] The politics of such writing are ambivalent and complex: La Coste's flouting of
military authority and Ospital's rejection of the hushed tones and
sacred themes of war memorialising constitute a radical approach to the
subject, in keeping with the text's original left-oriented times. Yet
the insistent passing over of war's horrors minimises and romanticises
the combat experience in ways that would only ratify and encourage
hawkish solutions to international problems.

Paul Fussell is a prolific author who has by now cornered the
market on the irreverent response to World War II. His vision is darkly
comic only when it is not bitterly demoralised; if Lingeman amasses
the data of civilian foibles in amounts that are finally embarrassing,
Fussell reconstructs an oral and written record of criminally sadistic,
tragically inept and pathetically misguided actions on the part of military commanders, officers and enlisted men that make the war – even,
or especially, Allied participation therein – into a botched and pointless travesty. In *Wartime* Fussell details the disasters of so-called pre-
cision bombing, the intricacies of military 'chickenshit' (enforcing
protocol for the express purpose of harassing and humiliating enlisted
men), the disfiguring injuries and violent deaths of soldiers in combat
and the horrifying realisation that, for virtually all those inducted too
close to the beginning of the conflict and not close enough to the end,
the three routes of discharge, honourable or otherwise, were disabling
injury, mental breakdown or death. In Fussell's estimation, no one
who joined the battle in the early years survived physically and mentally intact; Fussell points repeatedly to combat units 'replaced' at rates

of 100 and 150 per cent. Yet again, home-front constituencies are criticised; the fellow feeling and generosity described (and applauded) in Chapter 5 are read as false and 'high-minded' by Fussell, who rails especially against the waning of the sharp tongue in war-era American letters.[15] His contempt for the insanities and inanities of the military mindset; for 'sanitised and Norman Rockwellised, not to mention Disneyfied' mass media;[16] and the 'pap-fed mass public [unable] to face unpleasant facts'[17] fuels his polemic. Finally, it is not Fussell's relentlessly grim assessment that distinguishes his war writing from the traditional account, but his refusal to underwrite his exposure of the atrocious with any reference to an honourable and necessary cause or a meaningful and glorious end.

Fussell (dis)credits a popular text that appeared the same year as Ospital's memoir with defining the over-enthused, blatantly sanitised genre of war memorabilia for contemporary readers: 'The peruser – *reader* would be the wrong word – of the picture collection *Life Goes to War* (1977), a volume so popular and widely distributed as to constitute virtually a definite and official anthology of World War II photographs, will find even in its starkest images no depiction of bodies dismembered.'[18] Where earlier (see Chapter 1) *Life* magazine was read both in terms of its enormous public influence and its willingness to capture in pictures the human condition even in the death throes, Fussell's observation, that *Life* still withholds images of American dead and graphic depictions of dismemberment and disembowelment cannot be denied. Significantly, the late 1970s in the United States constituted a transitional period between the rebellious preceding decade and the intensely conservative 1980s and only slightly less conservative 1990s; while one locates valorising, glorifying memoirs of World War II at all points between 1945 and the present day, the genre that so vigorously called into question war's aims and meaning had its vogue in the 1960s and 1970s and has for the most part (again, Fussell being one persistent exception) died out.

Respectful Recreations

One major early-1980s text that helped solidify the genre of 'pro-war' writing was Studs Terkel's '*The Good War*' (1984). It is difficult to miss the oxymoron of the title (complete with its own scare quotes) and the irony inherent in any reference to war's goodness. A comment from the Introduction conveys the same ambivalence: 'They all came back home. All but 400,000.'[19] If Terkel begins where Fussell leaves off, countering the assertion that all but the luckiest last-called-up were killed, yet again the irony rings in his mention, seemingly as an after-thought, of the high death count. Thus Terkel hesitates to make explicit his support of World War II but, apart from this hesitation, the 580-page work is an otherwise attentive and respectful visit to this impor-tant moment from the American past. Through the testimonies of dozens of ex-servicemen, home-front families and war-workers, Terkel sets out to correct a grievous contemporary cultural lapse: 'the disremembrance of World War II [which] is as disturbingly profound as the forgettery of the Great Depression'.[20] While, in his interviewees' recollections, the war appears to have been constituted of equal parts anguish and glory, yet remembrances such as Terkel's – sprawling, democratic and filled with the voices of no one but heroes – are their own glorification. Easily achieving best-seller status, Terkel's book – both its title and content – reminded the American public that, despite the defeat of Vietnam (the 'bad war' the title implicitly refers to), World War II could be reached back for and brought into the con-temporary imaginary as an enduring source of comfort and pride. Embracing Terkel's book and many others, American readers have done so ever since although the sting of Vietnam is dull enough by now that many may not even recall its vital role in inaugurating the genre.

Thus has proliferated throughout the succeeding decades a boom in World War II personal and collective histories numbering into the hundreds, written by servicemen, nurses, home-front wives and sweethearts, historians, journalists of the war years and journalists of today with yet more to say about the event. In addition to Terkel, celebrity authors on the subject include CBS's commentator-curmudgeon Andy Rooney, who published *My War* in 1995 and reis-sued it in 2000 (see the following case study) and NBC news anchor Tom Brokaw, who has been to this thematic trough on three occasions with the popular *Greatest Generation* (1998), *The Greatest Generation Speaks: Letters and Reflections* (1999) and *An Album of Memories: Personal Histories from The Greatest Generation* (2002).

Andy Rooney's *My War* (1995)

Promotional copy for Andy Rooney's bestselling *My War*, recounting his wartime role as a soldier-reporter covering the European conflict for the United States Armed Services newspaper *Stars and Stripes*, notes that 'Rooney's unmistakable voice shines through on every page'.[21] Indeed, anyone familiar with Rooney's weekly commentary on the long-running CBS television series *60 Minutes* may have trouble silencing the wry, often snide, tone of voice indelibly associated with Rooney's persona as s/he reads. While Rooney often addresses serious subject matter on *60 Minutes*, it is almost always through the smirk of cynical humour, felt most sharply in his signature parting shot. Many of the anecdotes in *My War* are structured in a similar manner but, even when the content of the 'zinger' is no laughing matter (segregated buses in the American South, liberated Jews at Buchenwald) the reader (or listener) half expects a punchline.

The issue of necessary seriousness pervades a reading of this work, starting with the cover photograph – Rooney propped casually against some stockpiled bombs, smelling a bouquet – that 'must have seemed like an amusing picture to send home when [he] posed for this'[22] and must have struck the author sixty years later as a worthy cover image. In fact, it tellingly depicts Rooney's somewhat dilettante connection to the combat in his vicinity from 1942 to 1945. From early in the narrative, when he caves in to segregation policy in St Augustine, Florida, because he does not want it discovered that he has been AWOL (absent without leave) from his base for much of the past several weeks,[23] to his reluctance to accompany the Eighth Air Force on a raid over Germany,[24] to his several references to staying behind the lines, one is not surprised by his description of war as 'glorious',[25] nor by his announcement at the outset that 'I've gone for months without thinking about the war' and 'I'm not haunted by the horrors of war of which I saw so many'.[26] While surely Rooney bore witness to much carnage and atrocity, there is an after-the-fact quality to almost all of his arrivals on the scene that surely protected him from the trauma that characterised the war for combat-service members. Emblematically, he is on leave in New York during the winter of 1944, when a last-ditch German counter-attack stranded the 101st Airborne Division with disastrous consequences in the woods of Bastogne. When he returns to Paris, 'it was as if the Bulge [the Battle of Bastogne] had never happened'.[27] While several of his fellow correspondents were killed in action, Rooney was luckier and seems to have taken fewer risks; in *My War* he often uses his sneering throwaway lines to defend such a position, or at least to indicate his thoroughgoing unwillingness to apologise for it. There is a sort of combative, territorial quality even to the title of his book – suggesting both that his war will look rather different from the average soldier-memoirist's and that the reader can like it or leave it.

The narrative offers an entertaining rendition of events – Rooney is as clever in print as he is before the camera – and a worthwhile history of *Stars and Stripes*, its original staff of reporters and editors and its 'decline' near war's end, because of a takeover by features-oriented military types.[28] Through much of the war, he found himself well placed for viewing the action and filed hundreds of stories for the newspaper that were surely appreciated by their original readership and comprise a valuable archive today. And certainly no one can blame Rooney for the skin-saving impulse that would be almost anyone's under such circumstances; it is laudable

that he survived each day to tell the tale, as well as the tale he tells in his
late-published memoir. What rankles is his willingness to criticise the likes
of Ernest Hemingway, active with the French Resistance, whom he reads
as blustery, pretentious and 'having the time of his life playing war'.[29] In an
Afterword added to the 2000 edition (the text was originally published in
1995), Rooney is glad about the boom in World War II recollection perpetuated among the younger generation by media-makers such as Tom
Brokaw and Steven Spielberg. Yet his critique of those writers seeking to
'cash in' on the memoir craze rings hollow when we wonder how his purposeful reissue of *My War* is readable any differently;[30] despite his balking
at Brokaw naming the World War II generation as 'the greatest,'[31] his last
'zinger' is a somewhat shameless plug, letting the reader know that higher-
tech wars of the future 'won't make for good reading'.[32]

The celebrated (and, at the end of his life, regrettably discredited) historian Stephen E. Ambrose is responsible for more than a dozen
single- and co-authored works dealing in part or whole with World
War II, including *D-Day: June 6, 1944* (1994), *Citizen Soldiers* (1997)
and *The Good Fight: How World War II Was Won* (2001). His *Band of
Brothers* (1992, reissued 2001), about a company of paratroopers who
landed at Normandy but were required to function as hard-slogging
infantry fighters during the war's last desperate months, was later made
into an acclaimed HBO (Home Box Office) cable television series produced by director Steven Spielberg and actor Tom Hanks (see the case
study below). It was praised by, of all people, Paul Fussell, who
admired both the series' and the book's emphasis on the absurdities of
war. For Fussell, Ambrose is America's pre-eminent war historian,
despite 'a tendency to romanticising and sentimentality'.[33] From
Fussell this may seem like charitable praise indeed, especially when
others have criticised Ambrose for just the sort of disneyfication of
history that Fussell has decried on other occasions. Online journalist
David Plotz called him a 'cheerleader for America'[34] and, more damn-
ingly, a 'history factory',[35] because of the rapidity of his publication
schedule (towards the end, a major work each year, despite a calendar
filled with speeches and television appearances). In early 2002 it was
revealed that, among several other titles, both *Citizen Soldier* and
The Wild Blue (2001, about former presidential candidate George
McGovern's wartime career as a B-24 bomber pilot) contained numerous passages lifted directly, without quotation marks, from the works
of others.[36] The scandal outlines not only the hubris of one famed historian, appreciated by many as the chief populariser of World War II
for contemporary readers, but the rush to cash in on the 'history

factory' that public interest in World War II commemoration has continued to encourage.

While commercial interest might be said to cheapen any history-writing exercise, in fact each commemoration text published since the war offers its reader a worthwhile perspective, focused frequently on major (often ill-fated) battles, branches of the military (especially the Marines), war technology (for example, fighter planes), commanders beloved and notorious (especially Roosevelt and Churchill, Patton, Eisenhower and MacArthur), and the prisoner-of-war experience (often originating from the still-traumatising Bataán Death March, which occurred from 9 April to 18 April 1942). Material ranges from the archival (for example, unedited interviews with ordinary veterans recounting their specific experiences) to the broadly orchestrated (for example, by non-veterans such as Ambrose and Brokaw working heavily with secondary sources and research teams to bring to readers the epic sweep of war). One combat veteran whose writing talents have been praised is E. B. Sledge, author of the early *With the Old Breed at Peleliu and Okinawa* (1981) and the more recent *China Marine* (2001), about Sledge's experience in the reconstruction of the Chinese mainland after Japan's rout, with a forward by Stephen Ambrose. Sledge has been singled out by both Fussell and Fussell's protégé, Clint Willis, who included a long excerpt from *With the Old Breed* in his war anthology *The War* (1999).[37] What Willis and especially Fussell admire about Sledge is his willingness to narrate incidents in which the Marines behave deplorably – scavenging the Japanese enemy's body for military insignia and gold teeth, even before the enemy has actually died.[38] Among contemporary historians, wartime journalist Ernie Pyle is a hero and originator of the genre (see Chapter 1); his famous 'Captain Waskow' column from January 1944, in which men mourn the loss of a beloved leader in their various ways, is especially recalled and appreciated.[39] While almost all of these works search diligently for (and usually bring to light) what is most frightening, violent, gory or demoralising about the narrative subject matter, all work from, and return unerringly to, the 'good war' premise that motivates their very existence.[40]

HBO's *Band of Brothers* (2001)

HBO's ten-part miniseries played to great critical acclaim, winning six Emmy Awards in 2001, including those for Outstanding Miniseries, Outstanding Casting and Outstanding Direction. For *Slate* magazine, Paul

Fussell applauded the programme's exposure of war's indecencies, even when perpetrated by the Allies: 'a clinically sadistic commander, people who can't say anything without the assistance of the f-word, officers who kill prisoners for the fun of it and also run away in battle, and looters (virtually everybody), together with cowards, anti-Semites, and drunks'.[41] While some of Fussell's assessment is correct, in many ways, the series goes the usual distance to blunt the evils of both military hierarchy and combat violence; never is the audience challenged to disengage with a major sympathetic character (either through him becoming villainous or dying) and always is the audience reassured as to the prevalence of honourable behaviour, sound military strategising and moments of glory relative to those of despair.

The series follows the dashing and colourful men of 'E' (Easy) Company, 2nd battalion of the 506th Parachute Infantry Regiment, who landed behind enemy lines on D-Day, routed Nazis firing on Utah Beach at Brecourt Manor, assisted with the ultimately failed drive through Holland known as Operation Market-Garden, held the line at Bastogne (the Battle of the Bulge) until Patton's Third Army arrived, and were somehow – the issue remains in dispute – instrumental in the taking over of Hitler's Eagle's Nest in Berchtesgaden following his suicide in the spring of 1945. In each episode a different character or characters come to the dramatic fore; several are wounded, then heroically rejoin their units after recovery, and many are promoted throughout the course of the story, distinguishing themselves as brave soldiers and exceptional leaders. An early episode, the rout at Brecourt Manor, sets the tone for much of what is to come: outnumbered almost five to one, Easy Company plays a pivotal role in the Normandy invasion and is decorated auspiciously for its actions: eight Bronze Stars, three Silver Stars and the Distinguished Service Cross for Lt Dick Winters who rises through the ranks throughout the series to become a wise and well-loved, though still youthful, major by the last episode. While I wish in no way to minimise the historical Easy Company's heroism and success, the issue regards the decisions made by the text-maker in the first place – when he sets out to narrate for contemporary audiences the actualities of war, then sifts the historical archive for originating subject matter – in this case, why 'E' (Easy) Company instead of 'D' (Dog) Company? Why the 506th Parachute Infantry Regiment and not the 411th Infantry Regiment?[42] – and selects on purpose stories of mostly lovable, heroic figures destined for both survival and triumph.

Band of Brothers is a striking example of modern-day war commemoration because it is made of many intertexts and may be evaluated on scales of political efficacy (whether it makes a persuasive, inspiring or even entertaining anti- or pro-war statement) and historical accuracy. The complex cultural status of Stephen E. Ambrose was considered above; while the charge at that time was plagiarism, not fabrication, all would acknowledge that his books sell well because they tell good stories. For each, facts were selected, arranged, emphasised or left out to keep the reader well positioned and the story driving forward. When *Band of*

Brothers was transformed from 'history' to 'mini-series', the filmmakers heard from veterans whose lives were portrayed in Ambrose's story and who added details not provided in Ambrose's book. At the end of each episode the following disclaimer was printed, its paradox left for the reader to unravel: 'This film is a true story. Certain characters and events have been altered for dramatic purposes.' Even the series' own documentary elements call attention to its various untruths. Late in the dramatised series, Major Winters is offered but refuses the personal side arm of a surrendering Nazi officer. Yet in the series' final instalment, a sequence of interviews with surviving members of the historical Easy Company, the real Major Winters displays the recovered sidearm, which he did, indeed, accept from his Nazi counterpart. Another documentary moment – a title card following the third episode stating that the frightened soldier depicted in the story died of his neck wounds in 1948 – is utterly false. The soldier in question served bravely in Korea and died of a perforated ulcer in the late 1960s.[43]

Fussell is correct that the issue of looting is frankly dealt with throughout the story. Even the sterling Major Winters is seen raiding a posh Nazi hotel in Berchtesgaden, and he is not even caught in the act of filching meaningful memorabilia (such as a weapon, flag or historical document) but pieces of silverware, like a housewife at a department store fire sale, to which a fellow officer also helps himself so that he can treat his girlfriend to a special gift. The biggest kleptomaniac in the group is the steely but valorous Lt Speirs, who sends home pounds of absconded sterling from Austrian mansions without batting an eyelash. Yet interestingly, his thievery is set in the context of 'rumors' that circulate throughout the later episodes regarding the lieutenant's history of offering prisoners of war cigarettes then shooting them in cold blood. In fact, we even 'see' this incident in the second episode, when an Easy Company member befriends an American-born Nazi soldier then watches in horror from down the road as the prisoners are cruelly dispatched. It is something of a feint for the viewers to be screened from this heinous event in the first place, then doubly duplicitous of the film-makers to show a character witnessing the crime whose actuality is later entirely undermined. The rumours are demonstrated to be baseless; Lt Speirs is a thief but no murderer, and an excellent fighter in any event. Later, an on-screen shooting of prisoners is pointedly perpetrated by foreign-speaking Allied soldiers.

Pacing controls viewer access to the other horrors that Fussell congratulates the programme for exposing: while the men sustain horrific injuries, their bloody stumps and gushing arteries have their moment then leave the scene; the story never follows any of these wounded men for more than a couple of moments (and often only for a second); the biggest losses occur over Normandy, as the troops' transport aircraft come under attack, but these deaths occur quickly and in total darkness – and to a collection of characters we hardly know and do not miss. The terrifying randomness of sniper fire and mortar attack is well represented but always against the bodies of total strangers; again, the viewer neither knows nor cares about these dead, all of the major sympathetic characters survive, and even the sadistic battalion leader is left behind after the first instalment. Stylistically, each episode is suffused with Michael Kamen's stirring music and a palette of muted browns and greens, suggesting both the revered military uniform and the sepia-toned past.

Remembering World War II through Film

In his reading of *Life Goes to War*, Fussell incisively observes the potential of images to bring home even more graphically than can words the shocking, eviscerating damage war does to the human mind and body. Yet

[i]n the popular and genteel iconography of the war during the bourgeois age, . . . the bodies of the dead, if inert are intact. Bloody, sometimes, and sprawled in awkward positions, but except for the absence of life, plausible and acceptable simulacra of the people they once were.[44]

Fussell's reference here is to the reserved tone of wartime photojournalism, yet it holds just as well, if not more so, for the even more influential and thus possibly even more heavily censored genre of Hollywood film. While certainly 1940s-era films never got close to the realities of war injury and death, even in the current context of acclimatisation to, if not outright demand for, graphic displays of violence, filmmakers face the prospect of a profits-jeopardising 'NC-17' rating, not if the violence is excessive and stylised but if it is, as Fussell calls for here, realistic and emotionally disturbing. Thus, while modern filmmakers may feel free to include graphic violence for viewers evermore desensitised to such displays, still the mainstream war-themed spectacle (Jerry Bruckheimer's and Michael Bay's *Pearl Harbor* [2001] emblematic in this case) adheres to traditional codes – inflicting stylised harm on the barely glimpsed enemy and playing up the 'romance' aspect of men in uniform and the women who love them.

Ironically, America's 'bad war' (in Vietnam) has inspired many great films; its more or less disastrous outcome was instrumental not only in the nation's but also Hollywood's coming of age. Following this conflict and the many revolutions of the late 1960s, a sanitised approach to cultural representation was no longer possible, and a string of critically acclaimed, darkly realised films made in the fifteen years following – Hal Ashby's *Coming Home* (1978), Michael Cimino's *The Deer Hunter* (1978), Francis Ford Coppola's *Apocalypse, Now* (1979), Roland Joffé's *The Killing Fields* (1984),

Oliver Stone's *Platoon* (1986), Stanley Kubrick's *Full Metal Jacket* (1987), and again Stone's *Born on the Fourth of July* (1989) – set a new standard for war cinema. If World War II was the 'good war' in political and moral terms, it suffered aesthetically from a legacy of melodramatic 1940s- and 1950s-era mistreatments. Worse, a 'World War II picture' meant to some the wholesome, feel-good song-and-dance extravaganzas starring Judy Garland and Fred Astaire that belong to the war era, were fine films in their own right, but compare not at all with the grimly realistic, artistically superlative film texts presented by great directors of the modern era. Thus, the influence of Stone on Spielberg, for instance, is strong; as Terkel, Brokaw, and the other war commemorators urged their readers to reclaim World War II as a locus of proud Americanism, so Spielberg and others have sought to rescue the topic from the cloying sentiments and false action of the studio era to reconstruct it for contemporary viewers in its original horror and significance.

Fussell favourably compares Spielberg/Hanks's authentic and hard-hitting *Band of Brothers* to their work together in *Saving Private Ryan*, which 'after an honest, harrowing, 15-minute opening visualising details of the unbearable bloody mess at Omaha Beach, degenerated into a harmless, uncritical patriotic performance apparently designed to thrill 12-year-old boys'.[45] Fussell seems focused here on what several critics also read as a clichéd and sentimental script, complete with protagonist John Miller (played by Tom Hanks) exhorting Private Ryan (played by Matt Damon) to 'earn this . . . earn it' as Miller succumbs to battle wounds in the final frames. Equally negative was *The Chicago Reader*'s Jonathan Rosenbaum who called the film 'Spielberg's 1998 exercise in Oscar-mongering' and found most of it 'phony and hollow'. Both *The Los Angeles Times*'s Kenneth Turan and the *Chicago Sun-Times*'s Roger Ebert acknowledged the false-sounding dialogue but praised the film's strong acting and unprecedented renditions of battle; the basic plot, in which a group led by Captain Miller must retrieve the well-ensconced Ryan for return to the States as a publicity stunt, following the killing in action of Ryan's three brothers, also calls into question the military's priorities during the war. Turan called attention to precisely the kinds of inter-battle action, executed by inept US officers and cruel or cowardly US enlisted men, that Fussell seeks out in war representation.[46]

Most other critics did not even mention the weak script but focused solely on the film's gruelling battle scenes, especially the tour de force opening sequence recreating the D-Day landing, which the *New York*

Post's Rod Dreher called an 'excruciating masterpiece'.[47] In the opening twenty minutes, the first echelon of forces lands at Omaha Beach, vomiting in fear as they do, assaulted by chaotic noise and movement throughout, and experiencing visually if not viscerally the agonies of war-induced death throes of every sort: drowning, once wounded, under the enormous loads of waterlogged gear; losing limbs, heads and innards; falling – most humiliating of all – within seconds of embarkation. David Edelstein's observation, that the film has managed 'to make violence terrible again'[48] hits upon what may be read as this film's main contribution to the contemporary dialogue: perhaps expecting the typical Hollywood approach most often (though not always) associated with Spielberg, Hanks and Damon films, the millions of American viewers who attended this film's theatrical run (where the big-screen viewing experience had that much more impact) were assaulted by war's atrocity intensely, immediately and unforgettably. Despite the disturbing effect of the sneak attack, *Saving Private Ryan* was the top-grossing film (at $216 million) of 1998, though both it and the well-regarded adaptation of James Jones's 1962 novel *The Thin Red Line* lost the Oscar for Best Picture to the artsy but romantic *Shakespeare in Love*. Conversely, Spielberg's even more disturbing *Schindler's List* fared less well at the box office (ninth top-grossing film of 1993 with only $96 million) but won the Academy Award for Best Picture.

Spielberg was not the director but the producer of two companion pieces, *Flags of Our Fathers* and *Letters from Iwo Jima*, directed by Clint Eastwood and released within two months of each other in late 2006. Both centre around the bloody and decisive thirty-six-day battle for Iwo Jima, fought between US Marines and Japanese soldiers who defended their tiny but strategically important stronghold from within 18 miles of tunnels and underground bunkers in February and March 1945. While World War II is clearly of interest to both filmmakers, Spielberg's war epics belong both temporally and temperamentally to the left-leaning Clinton era while the more politically and artistically conservative Eastwood presented in the same year – a year embedded, as were the preceding three, in its own disastrous war enterprise – two war films that resonate with the more conservative political and cultural environment administered by George W. Bush.

Certainly Eastwood is at pains on both occasions to highlight in graphic detail the horrors of war and the psychological damage inflicted even upon physically intact survivors. Yet both films are pro-war and attenuated artistic endeavours in their failure adequately to challenge

Figure C.2 Steven Spielberg's *Saving Private Ryan* (1998) renewed interest in World War II for modern filmgoers. Dreamworks LLC/ The Kobal Collection/David James.

and instruct their viewers. While critic David Edelstein reads this as an accomplishment, his comparison of *Flags of Our Fathers* with Spielberg's *Saving Private Ryan* aptly describes the problem: as opposed to the battle scene that opened the earlier film, 'the way Eastwood backs off from splattery spectacle is moving and decent – the carnage is just enough to haunt you but not enough to punish you'.[49] Yet a theme throughout this chapter has been the contemporary text-maker's willingness to confront his viewers with the very worst, the ultimately indescribable nightmare that the war routinely inflicted on its participants; most American film critics, hailing Eastwood's film, seem glad to have been spared the disturbance, an attitude that may call their glowing assessments into question. Both films are haunted by the historical figure of Ralph Ignatowski, an Iwo Jima Marine who was taken prisoner by the Japanese on 4 March 1945 and was discovered dead and maimed three days later. The atrocities he had evidently endured before being killed, involving his tongue, eyes, limbs, and genitalia, were plain upon his discovery, and the incident is remembered as the epitome of Japanese ferocity, and well as for the trauma inflicted on the comrades who found him. Both films draw upon the Ignatowski incident to increase drama, yet maintain a safe visual distance from its horrific details.

Instead, *Flags of our Fathers* reveals the less-than-glorious origins of Associated Press photographer Joe Rosenthal's iconic picture of anonymous but earnest Marines managing heroically to stake their claim on Iwo Jima's Mount Suribachi. While the photograph was not staged (see below), it caught Marines in a rather mundane task, following orders during a lull in battle, instead of marking some clear moment of victory, and the exceedingly successful but emotionally hollowing war-bond drive that exploited both the picture and the flag-raisers is the political focus of the film. The question is whether much or any of this is a revelation to modern audiences who are rarely surprised to learn that their government manipulates the media to touch heart-strings and purse-strings in accordance with its own agenda. Certainly the film does not 'reveal' that these crass manipulations had any other but the noblest ends, nor does it break any rules with respect to the construction and dispatch of its youthful, attractive protagonists. In Owen Gleiberman's helpful assessment,

> The trouble is, [Eastwood is] preaching to the choir – or at least to a culture profoundly influenced by Tom Brokaw's *The Greatest Generation* and Steven Spielberg's *Saving Private Ryan*, that has already absorbed the lesson that 'the Good War,' while it may have been noble, was nevertheless hell. I think it's fair to say that most of us are past the point of thinking of the soldiers who fought in WWII as plaster saints, yet *Flags of our Fathers*, an honorable and rather plodding movie, insists on demythologizing what no longer needs to be demythologized.[50]

Also, Eastwood's film indulges at length in the emotional manipulation triggered by the indeed moving photograph and public reaction to it that it attempts to criticise at the same time. While David Edelstein reads this as a case of inadvertent 'cross-purposes' that the film goes on to correct,[51] the other reading is that the film is entirely aware of its core contradictions but still wants it both ways – saying something new by undermining a cherished American icon, yet wallowing in this iconicity at the same time.

Letters from Iwo Jima did less well at the box office (number 138 for the year at $13 million versus *Flags*' spot as the ninety-fourth highest grossing film at $33 million) for taking a risk with respect to the foreign language dialogue that did not pay off. The story features an almost entirely Japanese cast and settles on the plights of four major characters of divergent ranks who nevertheless share a disregard for the protocol of Japanese bushido – fighting to the death–even if this includes the honourable act of suicide. On the doomed island of Iwo Jima, the Japanese military commander ruffles the feathers of his tradition-minded underlings by refusing to defend the beach (ordering a massive, and at first effective tunnel network to be constructed instead) and questioning core values such as the need to save face at all cost. Significantly, the commander and another positively portrayed high-ranking officer both have had happy experience in the United States before the war and regret now having to fight against it. Another main character, an enlisted man who was a humble baker in civilian life, enters the film grumbling about having to dig so hard and runs from mortal danger throughout the film. While the commander in fact commits suicide before being taken prisoner, the fate of the enlisted man is ambiguous – he is wounded but in American care – at film's end.

The film opened first, and had good receipts, in Japan yet not surprisingly, it was criticised by Japanese and other international audiences for valorising only those characters that espoused an American-style ethos of anti-fanaticism and looking out for number one. It is striking how often American critics of this film who once more overwhelmingly embraced it read this regrettable Americanisation as 'humanisation', since, as each positive review implied, anyone in his right mind must hate the thought of self-sacrifice as avidly as do self-serving Americans. Frequently critics credited Eastwood with showing the real Japanese soldier and, by extension, the real Japanese national mindset, never mind his utter lack of credentials as a sociologist of that culture. In Stephen Hunter's representative mis-reaction,

> . . . the movie makes the point, over and over again, that this self-extinction was enforced from above, a brutal dictate of the Japanese warlord class who had taken over the government. The poor regular guys: Their attitude toward pulling the pin and holding the little crenellated cylinder to their chest was no different than yours or mine, as in: No thanks, I'll skip this grenade stuff if it's all the same to you.[52]

One has only to recall the striking scene from John Hersey's *Hiroshima* (see the case study in Chapter 1), during which a German missionary comes upon thousands of bomb-injured citizens in a city park and is awestruck by their stoic, utter silence, to realise how entirely – and respectably – *other* to the typical American reaction is the Japanese cultural response to mass disaster. Yet the film claimed for itself reliable and groundbreaking familiarity with the 'real' Japanese mindset, and the critical consensus mindlessly ratified this. The script of *Letters from Iwo Jima*, while loosely based on two Japanese-authored texts, is the product of Eastwood's frequent screenwriter, Paul Haggis, again whose credentials as a certificated scholar of Japanese culture are surely non-existent. Eastwood's thesis, that the Japanese are okay after all because their outlook is 'no different than [*sic*] yours or mine', epitomises the cultural imperialism that should have turned reviewers against his film; instead it was both unremarked and un-critiqued by the vast majority of the critical audience, as was the egregious ableism of Eastwood's wildly popular, Oscar-winning *Million Dollar Baby* (2005).[53]

Public Monuments Commemorating the War

As mentioned above, *Flags of Our Fathers* touched upon a controversy surrounding the origins of Associated Press photographer Joe Rosenthal's 'Mount Suribachi' photograph of 1945. Almost immediately after its release, a rumour circulated that not only did the flag-planting not reflect any identifiable turn in the battle of Iwo Jima but that, in fact, Rosenthal had taken a group of Marines with him to the top of the mountain and staged the entire shot.[54] Rosenthal defended himself against the false second half of this allegation the rest of his long life (he died in 2006 at ninety-four) and, interestingly, debate has surrounded several more recent World War II memorials indicating that, since the final days of the war itself, the very attempt to capture and interpret so profound, individual and yet ineffable an experience has been fraught with controversy. The mid-1990s Enola Gay exhibit at the Smithsonian Institute's National Air and Space Museum and the now completed FDR and World War II Memorials on the Mall in Washington DC have each inspired interest groups to protest about the politics and aesthetics of the monument in question. The Enola Gay exhibition, planned to mark the fiftieth anniversary of the Hiroshima and Nagasaki bombings that ended the war, became so controversial that it was finally cancelled before its opening; a major alteration was made to the FDR monument, and the World War II Memorial has been decried by preservationists and art critics.

In 1994, the American Legion and the Air Force Association (AFA) came out in force against a planned exhibit at the National Air and Space Museum (NASM) on the historical significance of the Enola

Gay, the B-29 that dropped the atomic bomb on Hiroshima. Since its decommissioning, the Enola Gay had been an 'uncomfortable presence' among the artefacts of World War II;[55] it was shuttled from one holding facility to another, exposed to weather and vandals, dismantled and finally mothballed, because of a widely felt but unspoken shame attached to its record of service. Veterans had sought the plane's reconstruction and display although exhibitors at the Smithsonian wrestled with the proper context. One Advisory Committee member, a retired Navy admiral, called the atomic bombings 'genocide' and worried that, no matter how sober the exhibit, 'the impression cannot be avoided that we are celebrating the first and so far only use of nuclear weapons against human beings'.[56] Still, responding to veterans, Smithsonian Secretary Robert McCormick Adams and NASM Director Martin Harwit planned an exhibit that would emphasise the damage done to both land and people by the atom bomb.

When they learned of this intended narrative slant, the veterans groups felt that the museum was attempting to apologise for action that many in 1945 – and since then – have hailed as essential to ending the war. AFA spokesman John T. Correll described the NASM as intending 'to use the Enola Gay as a prop in a political horror show'.[57] Intense debate surrounded the projected number of American lives saved by the war's abrupt conclusion – as many as a million and as few as 63,000 – and protest groups objected to what they felt was the museum's failure to emphasise the support the bomb had back in 1945. Meanwhile, the Smithsonian administrators defended their exhibit as a cautionary account, necessary to counterbalance the many pro-military galleries elsewhere in the museum. Following vociferous reaction from the AFA, Congress looked into the matter, and Harwit was dismissed. The exhibit was cancelled on 30 January 1995, and the Enola Gay moved, with a briefer accompanying narrative, to an NASM centre near Dulles International Airport just outside Washington. While this attempt to interrogate the wisdom of atomic warfare failed to reach the public domain, Jayne Loader and Keith and Pierce Rafferty's 1982 cult classic *The Atomic Café* continues to find new audiences (see the case study below).

The Atomic Café (1982)

Created during an era of renewed concern for nuclear safety and disarmament, Kevin Rafferty, Jayne Loader, and Pierce Rafferty's *The Atomic Café* is a cult favourite among students of the early cold war period. Compiled from copious archival footage from the commercial and military sectors – presidential speeches, television interviews, public service announcements, military training films and stock footage from news syndication services – the film juxtaposes the sublime and ridiculous of atomic politics, technology and popular culture (atomic cocktails, atomic love songs, an actual 'Atomic Café') to create a searing anti-nuclear statement. As these archival materials speak persuasively – and to the modern viewer with consummate irony – on their own, the filmmakers forewent pundit commentary and a synthesising narrative voiceover for a soundtrack of stirring (often menacing) orchestral music and atomic-themed novelty tunes from the late 1940s and 1950s. Occasionally subtitles occur, indicating a speaker or date of occurrence, but even many of these belong to the archival footage. Instead it is the jarring juxtaposition of peppy, inane folk songs or patently false official reassurances with images of cultural imperialism and massive post-nuclear destruction that provide the filmmakers' implicit thesis: Americans, clueless as to the seriousness of the bomb's effects, lulled themselves into indifference through sanitised representation thereof. Not surprisingly, the government and the media are indicted for hiding – or joking away – the ramifications of atomic weaponry; the endangering of soldiers and civilians due to official ignorance and malfeasance is a recurring theme.

The film moves for the most part chronologically through the atomic (and wider social) timeline of the immediate post-war period; footage includes anti-Russian propaganda films, accused communist spies Julius and Ethel Rosenberg being led to trial and to death, Eisenhower's first presidential campaign, arguments between Vice-President Nixon and Soviet Premier Khrushchev, integrated military ranks, and scenes from the earliest suburbs in their treeless, desolate, oddly post-apocalyptic configuration. The first third of the film presents archival footage from the mid- to late 1940s, including military preparation for the Hiroshima and Nagasaki bombings, Truman's solemn assessment of the aftermath (undermined by his smug chuckling moments before his official announcement begins) and grim footage of the empty wasteland that was once Hiroshima and its burned and scarred survivors. Regarding the United States military's atomic testing programme, inaugurated with Operation Crossroads on Bikini Atoll in 1946, scenes are shown of friendly, South Pacific islanders unilaterally removed (yet showing signs of radiation poisoning later in the film), soldiers misled as to the long-term effects of radiation exposure, and the televised surprise announcement that the Soviets had exploded their first fission bomb on 29 August 1949.

The late 1940s footage emphasises marked ignorance, with respect to the bomb's harmful effects and thus the egregious lack of necessary precautions, that characterised early atomic tests. Yet clips from the 1950s – at which time we had begun to learn better – whose messages continued to understate the dangers of atomic explosion and post-atomic survival prospects take on a deliberate, insidious, culpable cast. Soldiers are featured players in the earlier segments, yet women at home with their babies and radios, and children diving under their desks at school appear throughout the later scenes. By the 1950s, when our understanding of atomic devastation was clearer than ever, the atomic threat moved inland, from a military exercise to a national threat. The film presents the United States government's preparedness icon, Bert the Turtle, a charming cartoon character who taught children how to Duck and Cover by leaping at the first flash of nuclear Armageddon, into his shell. That safety was located by the Duck and Cover film-strip campaign under wooden desks, picnic blankets and raincoats is as comical as it is grim; the US's craze for bomb shelters – fraught with their own ethical and physical hazards – is also documented by the archival footage.

The Atomic Café was part of a boom in anti-nuclear textual production that occurred in response to the speech-making and policy-setting of two conservative world leaders, US President Ronald Reagan and British Prime Minister Margaret Thatcher, in the early 1980s. Following a decade of relaxed relations between the West and its communist adversaries, it was especially Reagan's antagonism to the Soviet Union, accompanied by two frightening near misses at nuclear power plants, at Pennsylvania's Three-Mile Island in 1979 and the USSR's Chernobyl facility in 1986, that spurred anti-nuclear writers and film-makers to issue cautionary tales. In film, *The Atomic Café* was accompanied by Hollywood productions including *The China Syndrome* (1979) and *Silkwood* (1983), about the hazards of nuclear-energy generation, as well as the post-apocalyptic *Mad Max* series starring Mel Gibson (begun in 1979). More serious and challenging films from the era include Lynne Littman's *Testament* (1983), for which Jane Alexander received a Best Actress Oscar nomination, and the made-for-television *The Day After* (1983). Both films presented the realised nightmare of total nuclear war and its bitter aftermath. In the arena of scholarship, a special issue called 'Nuclear Criticism' was published in the prestigious journal *Diacritics* in the summer of 1984, and Paul Boyer's *By the Bomb's Early Light* in 1985. Boyer's work is especially valuable for its close focus on official, artistic and popular reaction to the bomb in the immediate post-war period, that is 1946–9.

The FDR Memorial is located along the Cherry Tree Walk near the National Mall and consists of four outdoor rooms, one for each of Roosevelt's four terms in office. Representative sculptures (for example, men in a bread line in the Depression-era room) and themed waterfalls feature in each; as the exhibit progresses, the waterfalls increase in architectural complexity to indicate the growing challenges to Roosevelt throughout his presidential career. The monument drew criticism from disability rights groups who objected to the designers' attempt to obscure the fact that Roosevelt had spent most of his adult

Figure C.3 This World War II Memorial caused controversy with respect to both its location and its construction. © Martin Halliwell, 2007.

life in a wheelchair. While a prominent sculpture of FDR shows him seated, there is no display of wheels on a chair or braces on legs, since the figure is draped in Roosevelt's signature cape – a voluminous item of clothing he adopted expressly to hide his disability. In a gesture of shame that represented the crowning insult to disability advocates, small casters were sculpted on to the back of chair, hidden from view unless one stepped behind the statue. Three-and-a-half years after its dedication in 1997, a disability rights group was instrumental in adding a 'Prologue Room', which houses a sculpture of Roosevelt seated not in a wheelchair but in an ordinary dining chair with wheels similar to the one he had had constructed for himself.

The World War II Memorial pleased the veterans it was intended to honour, except that its exceptionally late date of establishment – almost sixty years after war's end in 2004 – meant that Congress had to work rapidly to approve a design and select a location while World War II veterans themselves were still alive to enjoy the recognition. The speeded-up development process angered Mall preservation groups and art critics who disagreed with both the artistic and political prospects represented by the monument's location: causing the removal of the Rainbow Pool, an oval body of water that adjoined the Reflecting Pool of the Lincoln Memorial, the World War II Memorial both encroached illegally upon the space of an already established monument and spoiled what since inception had been intended as an uninterrupted vista between the Lincoln Memorial and Washington Monument. Mall preservationists also noted that the World War II Memorial cuts down on the space for public assembly along the historic site, where protesters and activists have gathered for decades. Art critic Christopher Knight critiqued the monument's over-flocked columns, cacophonous water exhibits, and misnumbered stars: oddly, there are 4,048 gold stars worked on to sixteen bronze panels on the monument's Freedom Wall, one for roughly every hundred service members killed in action. Says Knight, 'But the arbitrariness of this assignment of multiplication renders it meaningless. Worse, it vitiates the memorial's most profound purpose.'[58] Knight noted that, in fact, almost 406,000 Americans were killed during the war, meaning that about 1,000 are not represented in the '100 per' figure intended by the designer. The discrepancy indicates that the number of stars was selected for its pleasing aesthetics, with historical significance attached after the fact, perhaps the most regrettable feature of what for some is a memorial so busily designed as to lack the necessary focus and respect.

Conclusion

Thus the Great SNAFU (situation normal: all fouled up) tradition that waned twenty-five years ago in war-related fiction and non-fiction has found new life in the monument construction designed to remember World War II in national public space. Probably, hazards were inevitable as soon as more than one individual came together in such a project, so complex and diverse are the memories, meanings and interpretive occasions offered by the momentous event of the war. These 'monumental' debates and debacles themselves become part of the World War II archive, the important act of remembering and refining understanding that Studs Terkel called for in his groundbreaking work of the mid-1980s. Part documentary, part public monument, part all-media package (with companion book, DVD, and CD for sale), Ken Burns's *The War* aired as a seven-part PBS series in September 2007. Burns is an award-winning documentarian whose multi-hour films present archival materials – photographs, documents, and letters and diaries read by actors in the guise of their authors – and an evocative soundtrack. Because the war depicted here is recent enough (as opposed to, for instance, the Civil War, which was a previous Burns subject), Burns has not only photographs but film (even rare colour footage) to share with his audience; likewise, actual participants in World War II are still around to be interviewed, so Burns turns to them instead of re-enacters for the running commentary, selecting veterans and home-fronters from four widely spaced American cities.

Yet the film's larger context – a partnership with a hundred PBS affiliates and the Library of Congress's Veteran's History Project, whose mission is to preserve the testimonies of World War II veterans – conveys the urgent need to speak with those who remember while they are still with us. While the World War II memorial industry – as industry – will always be in danger of sacrificing the true import of the war's events for the narrative formulas and dramatic pay-offs that simply sell more books or tickets, the very act of remembering keeps alive an era whose participants are rapidly disappearing, as it deepens collective understanding of an experience that is ultimately unrecreatable, unrepresentable. If finally 'the 1940s' are remembered as only 'the Good War' of that decade's first half, at least these years are remembered well (even if never remembered correctly) – as a revelatory, instructive index of America's ever-changing estimation of itself as a young nation with a complex past and as an actor on the world stage.

Notes

Introduction

1. Norman Cousins, *Modern Man is Obsolete* (New York: Viking, 1945), p. 41.
2. John Hersey, 'Hiroshima', *The New Yorker* (31 August 1946), p. 15.
3. Paul Sothe Holbo, ed., *Isolationism and Interventionism, 1932–1941* (Chicago: Rand McNally, 1967), p. 46.
4. Ibid., p. 26.
5. Ibid., pp. 42–3.
6. Manfred Jonas, *Isolationism in America, 1935–1941* (Ithaca: Cornell University Press, 1966), pp. 33–4. See also Emily Rosenberg, *A Date Which Will Live: Pearl Harbor in American Memory* (Durham, NC: Duke University Press, 2003), pp. 41–2.
7. Gunnar Myrdal, *An American Dilemma: The Negro Problem and Modern Democracy* (New York: Harper and Brothers Publishers, 1944), p. 1004.
8. See also Ole R. Holsti, *Public Opinion and American Foreign Policy* (Ann Arbor: University of Michigan Press, 2004), pp. 17–18.
9. Holbo, ed., *Isolationism and Interventionism*, p. 23.
10. Holbo, ed., *Isolationism and Interventionism*, p. 10.
11. Lewis Mumford, *Faith for Living* (New York: Harcourt, Brace, and Company, 1940), p. 12.
12. Ibid., p. 23.
13. Ibid., p. 11.
14. Ibid., pp. 36–7.
15. Ibid., p. 117.
16. Erich Fromm, *Escape from Freedom* (New York: Rinehart and Company, 1941), p. 232.
17. Mumford, *Faith for Living*, p. 38.
18. Fromm, *Escape from Freedom*, p. 237.
19. Eric Matthews, *Twentieth-Century French Philosophy* (Oxford: Oxford University Press), p. 67.
20. Arendt 'German Guilt', *Essays in Understanding: 1930–1954*, ed. Jerome Kohn (New York: Harcourt, Brace, and Company, [1945] 1994), pp. 128–9.
21. Ibid., pp. 123–4.
22. Richard H. Pells finds the continuation of this argument in Arendt's masterwork,

The Origins of Totalitarianism, an analysis of Hitler's and of Stalin's regimes. In this work, says Pells, 'Arendt characterised the archetypal totalitarian bureaucrat . . . as the impersonal bearer of truth, the incarnation of latent trends, the anonymous agent of historical forces . . . Above all, he was a servant of the Leader . . . [who] assumed complete responsibility for everything done in their names by the bureaucracy.' Richard H. Pells, *The Liberal Mind in a Conservative Age: American Intellectuals in the 1940s and 1950s* (New York: Harper and Row, 1985), p. 92; Arendt, 'The Concentration Camps', *Partisan Review*, 15 (7) (July 1948), p. 760; Arendt, 'German Guilt', p. 130.

23. These theories are helpfully surveyed by Rosenberg, *A Date Which Will Live*, pp. 40–6.

24. Cited in Holsti, *Public Opinion and American Foreign Policy*, p. 19.

25. Pells, *The Liberal Mind in a Conservative Age: American Intellectuals in the 1940s and 1950s*, p. 8.

26. Richard H. Minear, *Dr. Seuss Goes to War: The World War II Editorial Cartoons of Theodore Seuss Geisel* (New York: W. W. Norton and Company, 1999), p. 25.

27. 'About Dr. Seuss', *Independent Lens – The Political Dr. Seuss*, PBS, http://www.pbs.org/independentlens/politicaldrseuss/dr.html#.

28. Ibid.

29. Hayley Wood, 'The Political Dr. Seuss', *Mass Humanities* (Fall 2004), http://www.mfh.org/newsandevents/newsletter/MassHumanities/Fall2004/political.html.

30. 'About Dr. Seuss', http://www.pbs.org/independentlens/politicaldrseuss/dr.html#.

31. Philip Nel, *Dr. Seuss: American Icon* (New York: Continuum, 2004), p. 44.

32. Arthur Verge, 'Daily Life in Wartime California', *The Way We Really Were: The Golden State in the Second Great War*, ed. Roger W. Lotchin (Urbana: University of Illinois Press, 2000), p. 20.

33. K. Scott Wong, 'War Comes to Chinatown: Social Transformation and the Chinese of California', *The Way We Really Were*, ed. Lotchin, p. 171.

34. Kevin Allen Leonard, 'Brothers under the Skin?: African Americans, Mexican Americans, and World War II in California', *The Way We Really Were: The Golden State in the Second Great War*, ed. Roger W. Lotchin (Urbana: University of Illinois Press, 2000), pp. 198–200.

35. Francis E. Merrill, *Social Problems and the Homefront: A Study of War-time Influences* (New York: Harper and Brothers Publishers, 1948), pp. 202–3.

36. A. Philip Randolph cited in Myrdal, *An American Dilemma*, p. 414.

37. Earl Brown, 'American Negroes and the War', *Harpers* (April, 1942), p. 549.

38. Ibid., pp. 550–1.

39. See also Richard R. Lingeman, *Don't You Know there's a War On?: The American Home Front, 1941–1945* (New York: Putnam/Perigee, 1970), Chapter IX.

40. Myrdal, *An American Dilemma*, p. 409.

41. St Clair Drake and Horace R. Cayton, *Black Metropolis: A Study of Negro Life in a Northern City* (New York: Harcourt, Brace, and Company, 1945), p. 31.

42. Ibid., p. 748. Meanwhile, Cayton, writing for *The Nation* in 1942, reported widespread antipathy to war within the 'alienated' black community: 'Having been

denied many of the rights and privileges of US citizenship, Negroes are not now psychologically prepared to accept responsibility for the acts of the collective society from which they have always felt isolated,' 'Fighting for White Folks?', *The Nation* (26 September 1942), p. 267. Referring to a propaganda film issued by the Office of Facts and Figures, 'showing a Negro labor [instead of combat] battalion singing while they marched and worked', Cayton observed that 'the film simply antagonised Negroes, since it . . . conformed to the stereotype of singing Negroes, and emphasized their Jim Crow position in the army. It would have been much better for Negro morale if the film had not been made,' 'Fighting for White Folks?', p. 269.

43. Drake and Cayton, *Black Metropolis*, p. 747.
44. Myrdal, *An American Dilemma*, p. 426.
45. Walter White, *A Rising Wind* (Garden City, NY: Doubleday, Doran, and Company, 1945), p. 13.
46. White, *A Rising Wind*, p. 144.
47. Myrdal, *American Dilemma*, p. 1016; see also White, *A Rising Wind*, p. 153.
48. W. E. B. Du Bois, *Dusk of Dawn: An Essay toward an Autobiography of a Race Concept*, intro. Irene Diggs (New Brunswick, NJ: Transaction Publishers, [1940] 1997), p. 221.
49. W. E. B. Du Bois, *Color and Democracy: Colonies and Peace* (New York: Harcourt, Brace, and Company, 1945), p. 119.
50. Steven Mintz and Susan Kellogg. *Domestic Revolutions: A Social History of American Family Life* (New York: Free Press, 1988) p. 168.
51. Roosevelt cited in Verge, 'Daily Life in Wartime California' in *The Way We Really Were: The Golden State in the Second Great War*, ed. Lotchin, p. 17.
52. Pells, *The Liberal Mind in a Conservative Age: American Intellectuals in the 1940s and 1950s*, p. 30.
53. Ibid., pp. 114–15.
54. See Paul Boyer's excellent survey of positive, negative and ambivalent reactions to Hiroshima, Nagasaki, and the bomb, especially Chapters 1 and 16. Paul Boyer, *By the Bomb's Early Light: American Thought and Culture at the Dawn of the Atomic Age* (New York: Pantheon, 1985).
55. See Alperovitz, 'Introduction', *Atomic Diplomacy: Hiroshima and Potsdam*, (New York: Penguin, [1965] 1985).
56. Truman cited in Donald Porter Geddes, ed., *The Atomic Age Opens* (Cleveland, OH: Forum/World Publishing, 1945), p. 42.
57. Henry L. Stimson, 'The Decision to Use the Atom Bomb', *Harpers* (February 1947), p. 101.
58. Ibid., p. 102.
59. Ibid., p. 98.
60. Ibid., p. 105.
61. Alice Kimball Smith, *A Peril and a Hope: The Scientists' Movement in America, 1945–47* (Chicago: University of Chicago Press 1965), p. 78.
62. Ibid., p. 80.
63. Jessica Wang, *American Science in an Age of Anxiety: Scientists, Anticommunism, and the Cold War* (Durham: University of North Carolina Press, 1999), p. 13.
64. Alperovitz, *Atomic Diplomacy*, p. 14.
65. Ibid., pp. 26–7; see also Boyer, *By the Bomb's Early Light*, pp. 191–2.

66. W. E. B. Du Bois, *Newspaper Columns: Vol. 2, 1945–61*, ed. Herbert Aphtheker (White Plains, NY: Kraus-Thomson Organization Limited, 1986), p. 670.
67. Cited in Alperovitz, *Atomic Diplomacy*, p. 15.
68. Ibid., p. 16.
69. Ibid., p. 60.
70. Cousins, *Modern Man is Obsolete*, p. 23.
71. While Cousins seems to regard this reduced-work week as primarily an atomic boon, Paul Boyer surveys social critics who feared the chaos and disorder such mass leisure – for James Reston of the *New York Times*, 'simply a euphemism for unemployment' – would bring. Speculators upon the atom's peacetime payoffs worried over widespread moral laxity, de-individualisation, boredom, economic downturn, and a centralising of power. See also Boyer, *By the Bomb's Early Light*, pp. 141–3.
72. Geoffrey Perrett, *Days of Sadness, Years of Triumph: The American People 1939–1945* (New York: Coward, McCann, and Geoghegan, Inc., 1973), p. 281.
73. Ibid., pp. 281–2.
74. See Richard H. Polenberg, *War and Society: The United States 1914–1945* (Philadelphia: J. B. Lippincott, 1972), pp. 46–7.
75. Reinhold Niebuhr, *The Children of Light and the Children of Darkness* (New York: Scribner's, [1944] 1960), p. 174.
76. Ibid., p. 178.
77. Steve Rothman, 'The Publication of *Hiroshima* in *The New Yorker*', 8 January 1997, http://www.herseyhiroshima.com/hiro.php.
78. David Sanders, *John Hersey* (New York: Twayne, 1967), p. 41.
79. Hersey, 'Hiroshima', p. 28.
80. Ibid., p. 66.
81. Ibid., p. 25.
82. Ibid., p. 33.
83. Ibid., p. 46.
84. Ibid., p. 25.
85. Cited in Sanders, *John Hersey*, p. 39.
86. Robert J. Lifton, *Death in Life: Survivors of Hiroshima* (New York: Basic Books, 1967), p. 474.
87. See Sanders, *John Hersey*, pp. 49–50.
88. Lifton, *Death in Life*, pp. 331, 337.
89. Lewis Mumford, *The Myth of the Machine: Technics and Human Development* (New York: Harcourt, Brace, and World, 1966), p. 222.
90. John C. Chalberg, *Isolationism: Opposing Viewpoints* (San Diego, CA: Greenhaven Press, 1995), p. 245; see also Michael S. Sherry 'Epilogue', *Preparing for the Next War: American Plans for Postwar Defense, 1941–45* (New Haven: Yale University Press, 1977).
91. T. G. Fraser and Donette Murray, *America and the World since 1945*, (Houndmills, Basingstoke, Hampshire: Palgrave Macmillan, 2002), p. 28.
92. Ibid., p. 25; see also Sherry, *Isolationism*, Chapter 6.
93. Walter Lippmann, *The Cold War: A Study in US Foreign Policy* (New York: Harper and Brothers, 1947), p. 53.
94. Erich Fromm, *Man for Himself: An Inquiry into the Psychology of Ethics* (New York: Rinehart and Company, 1947), p. 247.

95. Ibid., p. 248; see also Mumford, *Condition of Man* (New York: Harcourt, Brace, and Company, 1944), p. 308.

96. Rosie the Riveter was a wartime icon, usually depicted as a fetching but well-muscled woman war-worker dressed in industrial uniform. She inspired women to do their part to win the war, as well as help themselves to their first measure of physical and financial independence.

97. Hoover cited in Elaine Tyler May, *Homeward Bound: American Families in the Cold War Era* (New York: Basic Books, 1988), p. 74.

98. D'Ann Campbell, *Women at War with America: Private Lives in a Patriotic Era* (Cambridge, MA: Harvard University Press, 1984), p. 221.

99. Sherna Berger Gluck 'Introduction', *Rosie the Riveter Revisited: Women, the War, and Social Change* (Boston: Twayne, 1987); see also Karen Anderson, *Wartime Women: Sex Roles, Family Relations, and the Status of Women During World War II* (Westport, CT: Greenwood Press, 1981); Maureen Honey, *Creating Rosie the Riveter: Class, Gender, and Propaganda during World War II* (Amherst: University of Massachusetts Press, 1984); and Elaine Tyler May, *Homeward Bound*, Chapter 3.

100. Gluck, *Rosie the Riveter Revisited*, p. 16.

101. Elaine Tyler May, *Homeward Bound*, p. 73.

102. Ferdinand Lundberg and Marynia F. Farnham, *Modern Woman: The Lost Sex* (New York: Harper and Brothers, 1947), p. 218.

103. Ibid., p. 207.

104. Ibid., pp. 209–13.

105. Ibid., p. 214.

106. Ibid., p. 215.

107. Ibid., p. 237.

108. Ibid., p. 266.

109. Ibid., p. 267.

110. Ibid., pp. 268–9.

111. Ibid., p. 296.

112. Ibid., p. 291.

113. Ibid., p. 289.

114. Ethel Goldwater, ' "Woman's Place": The New Alliance of "Science" and Anti-Feminism', *Commentary* 4.6 (1947), p. 578.

115. Margaret Mead, 'Dilemmas the Modern Woman Faces', *The New York Times Book Review* (26 January 1947), p. 18.

116. Hedda Grant, 'Still a Man's World', *International Socialist Review* 23.2 (1962), p. 58 and Betty Friedan, *The Feminine Mystique*, intro. Anna Quindlen (New York: W. W. Norton and Company, [1963] 2001), p. 42.

117. Friedan, *The Feminine Mystique*, p. 120.

1. Fiction and Journalism

1. Malcolm Bradbury, *The Modern American Novel* (Oxford: Oxford University Press, 1983), p. 128.

2. Ibid., p. 128.

3. Frederick R. Karl, *American Fictions, 1940–1980: A Comprehensive and Critical Evaluation* (New York: Harper and Row, 1983), p. 89.

4. Schwartz cited in Tony Hilfer, *American Fiction since 1940* (London: Longman, 1992), pp. 56–7.
5. William Faulkner, *Selected Letters*, ed. William Blotner (New York: Random House, 1977), p. 262.
6. The entire speech as well as a partial sound recording is available on line: http://nobelprize.org/literature/laureates/1949/faulkner-speech.html.
7. William Moss, 'Not "an american first – he could be an artist first": Faulkner, the Individual Artist Versus the Public Man', American Literature Association, 2005.
8. Joyce Moss and George Wilson, '*The Human Comedy* by William Saroyan', *Literature and Its Times: Profiles of 300 Notable Literary Works and the Historical Events that Influenced Them. Volume Four: World War II to the Affluent Fifties (1940–1950s)* (Detroit, MI: Gale, 1997), p. 200.
9. Karl, *American Fictions, 1940–1980*, p. 83.
10. Elizabeth A. Wheeler, *Uncontained: Urban Fiction in Postwar America* (New Brunswick, NJ: Rutgers University Press, 2001), p. 44.
11. Ibid., p. 40
12. Mickey *Spillane, One Lonely Night*, intro. Lawrence Block (New York: New American Library, [1951] 2001), p. 6.
13. The cult status of Rand's work is indicated by the fact that No. 3 on this Reader's List is L. Ron Hubbard's *Battlefield Earth* and No. 4 is J. R. R. Tolkien's *The Lord of the Rings*.
14. Chester E. Eisinger, *Fiction of the Forties* (Chicago: University of Chicago Press, 1963), p. 101.
15. Hilfer, *American Fiction since 1940*, pp. 47, 48.
16. See also Keith Clark's Darwinian reading of *The Street* versus Marilyn Chandler McEntyre's Thoreauvian take on *Cannery Row*. Keith Clark, 'A Distaff Dream Deferred?: Ann Petry and the Art of Subversion', *African American Review* 26 (1992) pp. 495–505; Marilyn Chandler McEntyre, 'Natural Wisdom: Steinbeck's Men of Nature as Prophets and Peacemakers', *Steinbeck and the Environment: Interdisciplinary Approaches*, ed. Susan F. Beegle, Susan Shillinglaw, and Welsey N. Tiffney Jr (Tuscaloosa, AL: University of Alabama Press, 1997), pp. 113–24.
17. Irving Howe 'Black Boys and Native Sons', *Dissent* 10 (4) (1963), p. 354.
18. Arnold Rampersad, 'Introduction', *Native Son* by Richard Wright (New York: Perennial Classics, 1998), p. xxii.
19. Desmond Harding, 'The Power of Place: Richard Wright's *Native Son*', *CLA Journal* 40 (3) (1997), p. 307.
20. Rampersad, 'Introduction', p. xi.
21. Richard Wright, *Native Son*, intro. Arnold Rampersad (New York: Perennial Classics, [1940] 1998), p. 6.
22. Rampersad, 'Introduction', p. xiii.
23. Trudier Harris, 'Native Sons and Foreign Daughters', *New Essays on* Native Son, ed. Keneth Kinnamon (Cambridge: Cambridge University Press, 1990), p. 66.
24. Rampersad, 'Introduction', p. xxi.
25. James Smethurst, 'Invented by Horror: The Gothic and African American Literary Ideology in *Native Son*', *African American Review* 35 (1) (2001), p. 32.
26. Eisinger, *Fiction of the Forties*, p. 214.
27. Hilfer, *American Fiction since 1940*, pp. 23–5.

28. James H. Justus has pursued the father-son relationships throughout the novel, and Keith Perry argues that Warren's fictionalisation of Long is less faithful yet more profound than several others attempted during that period – perhaps even a better model of the political mastermind than Long ever was himself (p. 221). James H. Justus, 'The Power of Filiation in *All the King's Men*', *Modern American Fiction: Form and Function*, ed. Thomas Daniel Young (Baton Rouge: Louisiana State University Press, 1989), pp. 156–69. Keith Perry, *The Kingfish in Fiction: Huey P. Long and the Modern American Novel* (Baton Rouge: Louisiana State University Press, 2004).

29. Hilfer, *American Fiction since 1940*, p. 56.

30. Matthew Lessig, 'Class, Characters, and Croppers: Faulkner's Snopeses and the Plight of the Sharecropper', *Arizona Quarterly* 55 (4) (Winter 1999), p. 104.

31. Lingeman, *Don't You Know there's a War On?*, p. 275.

32. Donald I. Rogers, *Since You Went Away* (New Rochelle, NY: Arlington House, 1973), p. 156.

33. Lingeman, *Don't You Know there's a War On?*, pp. 278–9.

34. Paul Milkman, *PM: A New Deal in Journalism, 1940–1948* (New Brunswick, NJ: Rutgers University Press, 1997), p. 3.

35. Milkman, *PM: A New Deal in Journalism*, p. 4.

36. Ibid., p. 201.

37. James L. Baughman, *Henry Luce and the Rise of the American News Media* (Boston: Twayne / G.K. Hall, 1987), p. 89.

38. Aurora Wallace, *Newspapers and the Making of Modern America: A History* (Westport, CT: Greenwood Press, 2005), p. 69.

39. Ibid., p. 66.

40. See Jean Folkerts and Dwight L. Teeter, *Voices of a Nation: A History of the Media in the United States* (New York: MacMillan, 1989), p. 462; Wallace, *Newspapers and the Making of Modern America*, pp. 65–7; Patrick Washburn, *A Question of Sedition: The Federal Government's Investigation of the Black Press During World War II* (New York: Oxford University Press, 1986); and William F. Yurasko, 'The Pittsburgh Courier During World War II: An Advocate for Freedom', *VV Campaign.org*, http://www.yurasako.net/vv/courier.html.

41. David Reed, *The Popular Magazine in Britain and the United States 1880–1960*, (London: The British Library, 1997), p. 196.

42. See Ibid., pp. 217–18 and Mary Ellen Zuckerman, *A History of Popular Women's Magazines in the United States, 1792–1995* (Westport, CT: Greenwood Press, 1998), pp. 207–8.

43. Zuckerman, *A History of Popular Women's Magazines in the United States*, p. 205.

44. Ibid., p. 196.

45. Ibid., p. 206.

46. A. F. Whitney, 'Labor Gets No Break in the Press', *Freedom of the Press Today: A Clinical Examination by 28 Specialists*, ed. Harold L. Ickes (New York: The Vanguard Press, 1941), pp. 286–7.

47. Zuckerman, *A History of Popular Women's Magazines in the United States*, p. 196.

48. Reed, *The Popular Magazine in Britain and the United States*, pp. 200–1.

49. Geoffrey Perrett, *Days of Sadness, Years of Triumph: The American People 1939–1945* (New York: Coward, McCann, and Geoghegan, Inc., 1973), p. 310.

50. Reed, *The Popular Magazine in Britain and the United States*, p. 213.
51. Ibid., p. 201.
52. Ibid., p. 212.
53. Ibid., p. 200.
54. Ibid., p. 203.
55. Baughman, *Henry Luce and the Rise of the American News Media*, p. 5.
56. Ibid., p. 6.
57. Ibid., p. 2.
58. Ibid., p. 132.
59. John Morton Blume, *V was for Victory: Politics and American Culture During World War II* (New York: Harcourt, Brace, Jovanovich, 1976), pp. 284–5; see also Baughman, *Henry Luce and the Rise of the American News Media*, p. 134.
60. Henry R. Luce, 'The Day of Wrath', *Life* (22 December 1941), p. 11.
61. *Life* (19 June 1944), p. 67.
62. *Life* (23 April 1945), p. 19.
63. Dwight McDonald, 'A Theory of Mass Culture', *Mass Culture: The Popular Arts in America*, ed. Bernard Rosenberg and David Manning White (Glencoe, IL: Free Press, [1953] 1957), p. 62.
64. George H. Roeder, 'Censoring Disorder: American Visual Imagery of World War II', *The War in American Culture: Society and Consciousness During World War II*, ed. Lewis A. Erenberg and Susan E. Hirsch (Chicago: University of Chicago Press, 1996), p. 56.
65. *Life* (17 June 1940), p. 49.
66. *Life* (26 November 1945), p. 32.
67. *Life* (5 June 1944), p. 78.
68. See Ted Gottfried, *The American Media* (New York: Impact/Franklin Watts, 1992), p. 54.
69. Baughman, *Henry Luce and the Rise of the American News Media*, p. 2.
70. Ken Read-Brown, 'Norman Cousins: Editor and Writer, 1915–1990', *Notable American Unitarian Friends* (2 February 2006), http://www. harvardsquarelibrary.org/unitarians/cousins.html.
71. Kathleen A. Cairns, *Front-Page Women Journalists, 1920–1950* (Lincoln: University of Nebraska Press, 2003), p. 97.
72. Ibid., p. 98.
73. Ibid., p. 97.
74. See Washburn, *A Question of Sedition*, pp. 87–91.
75. Gottfried, *The American Media*, p. 89.
76. Blume, *V was for Victory*, p. 155.
77. See Sam G. Riley, *Biographical Dictionary of American Newspaper Columnists* (Westport, CT: Greenwood Press, 1995), pp. 245–6.
78. Gottfried, *The American Media*, p. 84.
79. Perrett, *Days of Sadness, Years of Triumph*, pp. 219–20.
80. Milkman, *PM: A New Deal in Journalism*, p. 209.
81. Riley, *Biographical Dictionary*, p. 264.
82. Christopher De Santis, ed., 'Adventures of a Social Writer: 1940–1949', *Dictionary of Literary Biography, Vol. 315: Langston Hughes: A Documentary Volume* (Detroit: Thomson-Gale, 2005), p. 164.

83. Cited in De Santis, 'Adventures of a Social Writer: 1940–1949', p. 177.
84. De Santis, 'Adventures of a Social Writer: 1940–1949', p. 164.
85. Cited in Donna Akiba Sullivan Harper, *Not So Simple: The 'Simple' Stories by Langston Hughes* (Columbia, MO: Columbia University Press, 1995), p. 9.
86. Harper, *Not So Simple*, p. 55.
87. Frank Luther Mott, *American Journalism – A History of Newspapers in the United States Through 260 Years: 1690 to 1950*, rev. edn (New York: MacMillan, 1950), p. 741.
88. Riley, *Biographical Dictionary*, p. 325.
89. Samuel Hynes et al., *Reporting World War II: Part I, American Journalism 1938–1944* (New York: The Library of America, 1995), p. 894.
90. Baughman, *Henry Luce and the Rise of the American News Media*, p. 133.
91. Riley, *Biographical Dictionary*, p. 135; Hynes et al., *Reporting World War II: Part II, American Journalism 1944–1946*, p. 917.
92. See Lee G. Miller, *An Ernie Pyle Album: Indiana to Ie Shima* (New York: William Sloane Associates, 1946).
93. Cited in James Tobin, *Ernie Pyle's War: America's Eyewitness to World War II* (New York: The Free Press, 1997), p. 257.
94. Riley, *Biographical Dictionary*, p. 257.
95. Cited in Paul Fussell, *Wartime: Understanding and Behavior in the Second World War* (New York: Oxford University Press, 1989), p. 155.
96. For a discussion of Pyle's and Mauldin's focus on the ordinary soldier, as this was shared by Hersey, Sherrod, and most popular news publications during the war, see Blume, *V Was for Victory*, pp. 53–64.
97. George Roeder, *The Censored War: American Visual Experience During World War II* (New Haven: Yale University Press, 1993), p. 14; see also Perrett, *Days of Sadness, Years of Triumph*, p. 214.
98. Boyer, *By the Bomb's Early Light*, pp. 187–8.

2. Radio and Music

1. See Stanley Cloud and Lynne Olson, *The Murrow Boys: Pioneers on the Front Lines of Broadcast Journalism* (Boston: Houghton Mifflin Company, 1996), pp. 38–40.
2. Irving Fang, *Those Radio Commentators!* (Ames, IA: Iowa State University Press, 1977), p. 36.
3. See Fang, *Those Radio Commentators!*, pp. 30–34.
4. Perrett, p. 277. See also McLeod who calls the Normandy invasion the greatest moment in 'old-time radio' history ('Old Time').
5. Cloud and Olson, p. 227.
6. J. Fred MacDonald, *Don't Touch that Dial: Radio Programming in American Life, 1920–1960* (Chicago: Nelson-Hall, 1979) p. 77.
7. Ibid., p. 83.
8. Cited in Fang, *Those Radio Commentators!*, p. 184.
9. Fang, *Those Radio Commentators!*, p. 162.
10. Ibid., p. 167.
11. Ibid., pp. 77, 300–1.
12. Cited in Fang, *Those Radio Commentators!*, p. 290.

13. Fang, *Those Radio Commentators!*, p. 292.
14. Sherrill cited in Jim Heintze, 'Biography of Drew Pearson', *American University Library Special Collections Unit*, http://www.library.american.edu/pearson/biography.html.
15. See Heintze, 'Biography of Drew Pearson', n.p.
16. Cited in Heintze, 'Biography of Drew Pearson', n.p.
17. Gerald Nachman, *Raised on Radio* (New York: Pantheon Books, 1998), p. 3.
18. Cited in Gottfried, *The American Media*, p. 116.
19. Gottfried, *The American Media*, p. 117.
20. A. M. Sperber, *Murrow: His Life and Times* (New York: Fordham University Press, 1998), p. 179.
21. Ibid., p. 180.
22. Cloud and Olson, *The Murrow Boys*, p. 91.
23. Sperber, *Murrow*, p. 163.
24. Murrow, Edward R. *In Search of Light: The Broadcasts of Edward R. Murrow, 1938–1961*, ed. Edward J. Bliss Jr (New York: Alfred A. Knopf, 1967), p. 358.
25. Sperber, *Murrow*, p. 163.
26. Ibid., p. 182.
27. Ibid., p. 183.
28. Murrow, *In Search of Light*, pp. 146–7.
29. 'Don McNeill', *The Radio Hall of Fame*, http://www.radiohof.org/musicvariety/donmcneill.html.
30. Some of the better websites for listening to archival clips include *Radio News* (http://www.otr.com/news.html), *Radio Hall of Fame Inductees* (http://www.museum.tv/rhofsection.php?page=140), *Rich Samuels/Chicago Radio History* (http://www.richsamuels.com/index1.html), and *Jerry's Vintage Radio Logs/Jerry Haendiges' Vintage Radio* (http://otrsite.com/radiolog).
31. Elizabeth Thomsen, 'Welcome to the Great Gildersleeve Website', http://www.ethomsen.com/gildy/.
32. MacDonald, *Don't Touch that Dial!*, pp. 134–5.
33. Elisabeth McLeod, 'Elisabeth McLeod Posts', http://members.aol.com/jeff1070/amos.html.
34. See MacDonald, *Don't Touch that Dial!*, p. 331; see also Eric Barnouw, *The Golden Web: A History of Broadcasting in the United States, Vol. II – 1933 to 1953* (New York: Oxford University Press, 1968), pp. 110–11.
35. Ibid., 64–5; see also Mary Livingstone Benny and Hilliard Marks with Marcia Borie, *Jack Benny* (Garden City, NY: Doubleday, 1978), p. 78.
36. Margaret T. McFadden, 'America's Boy Friend Who Can't Get a Date: Gender, Race, and the Cultural Work of the Jack Benny Program, 1932–1946', *Journal of American History* 80 (1) (1993), 113–34.
37. Livingstone Benny and Marks, *Jack Benny*, p. 79.
38. Jack Benny and Joan Benny, *Sunday Nights at Seven: The Jack Benny Story* (New York: Warner Books, 1990), p. 103.
39. Ibid., p. 108.
40. Ibid., p. 108.
41. Michelle Hilmes, *Radio Voices: American Broadcasting, 1922–1952* (Minneapolis: University of Minnesota Press, 1997), p. 196.
42. Nachman, *Raised on Radio*, p. 62–3.

43. See Allison McCracken, 'Scary Women and Scarred Men: *Suspense*, Gender Trouble, and Postwar Change, 1942–1950', *Radio Reader: Essays in the Cultural History of Radio*, ed. Michele Hilmes and Jason Loviglio (New York: Routledge, 2002), pp. 183–207.

44. The recording is currently available for listening at http://www. otrcat.com/suspense.htm.

45. See Hilmes, *Radio Voices*, 'Conclusion'.

46. MacDonald, *Don't Touch that Dial!*, p. 61.

47. Ibid., p. 61.

48. George T. Simon, *The Big Bands*, 4th edn (New York: Schirmer Books, 1981), p. 56.

49. Piano historian, Peter J. Silvester, tells the story of Café Society's instrumental role in the re-emergence of boogie-woogie as a popular musical style during this period. In its close lower Manhattan quarters, two and sometimes three pianos were wheeled into the small performance area to accommodate the boogie-woogie greats of this period, Albert Ammons, Pete Johnson, and Meade Lux Lewis, as well as their large-framed vocalist, Joe Turner. Silvester notes that, following the four performers' scene-stealing performance in John Hammond's two 'Spirituals to Swing' concerts at Carnegie Hall in the late 1930s, 'by 1940 it could be said with some authority that boogie-woogie had finally arrived in the world'. Silvester, *A Left Hand Like God: A History of Boogie-Woogie Piano* (New York: Da Capo Press, 1988), p. 144.

50. Lewis A. Erenberg, *Swingin' the Dream: Big Band Jazz and the Rebirth of American Culture* (Chicago: University of Chicago Press, 1998), p. 205.

51. Kathleen E. R. Smith, *God Bless America: Tin Pan Alley Goes to War* (Lexington: University Press of Kentucky, 2003), p. 10.

52. Ibid., p. 8.

53. Lawrence McClellan Jr, *The Later Swing Era: 1942 to 1955* (Westport, CT: Greenwood Press, 2004), p. 53.

54. Sherrie Tucker, *Swing Shift: 'All-Girl' Bands of the 1940s* (Durham, NC: Duke University Press, 2000), p. 165.

55. McClellan, *The Later Swing Era*, p. 54.

56. Ibid., p. 54.

57. Simon, *The Big Bands*, p. 187.

58. Ibid., p. 187.

59. See Simon, *The Big Bands*, p. 176

60. Erenberg, *Swingin' the Dream*, p. 170.

61. Ibid., p. 128.

62. Holiday cited in Henry Pleasants, *The Great American Popular Singers* (New York: Simon and Schuster, 1974), p. 161.

63. Erenberg, *Swingin' the Dream*, p. 98.

64. Paul Oliver, *The Story of the Blues* (Boston: Northeastern University Press, [1969] 1997), p. 74.

65. Simon, *The Big Bands*, p. 85.

66. Ibid., p. 87.

67. Erenberg, *Swingin' the Dream*, p. 186.

68. Ibid., p. 209.

69. Ibid., p. 196.

70. See McClellan, *The Later Swing Era*, Chapter 1.
71. Michael Pitts and Frank Hoffmann, assisted by Dick Carty and Jim Bedoian, *The Rise of the Crooners* (Lanham, MD: Scarecrow Press, 2002), p. 113.
72. See McClellan, *The Later Swing Era*, pp. 104–6.
73. Pleasants, *The Great American Popular Singers*, p. 185.
74. Kathleen Smith, *God Bless America*, p. 21.
75. Cited in McClellan, *The Later Swing Era*, p. 109.
76. Frank Buxton, 'This is Bob "Camp Roberts" Hope . . .: Bob Hope on the Radio', *Bob Hope: A Half Century of Radio and Television* (N.P.: Museum of Broadcasting, 1986), p. 20.
77. Ibid., p. 20.
78. Peter W. Kaplan, 'Hey, How About that Bob Hope?', *Bob Hope: A Half Century of Radio and Television*, p. 25.
79. Simon, *The Big Bands*, pp. 174–5.
80. Thelonius Monk cited in William B. Scott and Peter M. Rutkoff, *New York Modern: The Arts and the City* (Baltimore: Johns Hopkins University Press, 1999), p. 275.
81. See Erenberg, *Swingin' the Dream*, p. 230.
82. 'Jack Kerouac – On the Road', *C-SPAN American Writers II: The Twentieth Century* http://www.americanwriters.org/writers/kerouac.asp; see also David Hopkins, 'To Be or Not to Bop: Jack Kerouac's *On the Road* and the Culture of Bebop and Rhythm 'n' Blues', *Popular Music* 24 (2) (2005), p. 279.
83. Pleasants, *The Great American Popular Singers*, p. 207.
84. Ibid., p. 209.
85. Charles K. Wolfe, ' "Jesus Hits Like an Atom Bomb": Nuclear Warfare in Country Music, 1944–56', *Country Music Goes to War*, ed. Charles K. Wolfe and James E. Akenson (Lexington: University Press of Kentucky, 2005), p. 105.
86. Wayne W. Daniel, 'Hayloft Patriotism: The *National Barn Dance* during World War II', *Country Music Goes to War*, ed. Charles K. Wolfe and James E. Akenson (Lexington: University Press of Kentucky, 2005), pp. 93–4.
87. Boyer, *By the Bomb's Early Light*, p. 25.
88. Ibid., pp. 25, 340.
89. Ibid., p. 25.
90. Ibid., p. 371.
91. Ibid., p. 68. Country musicians were not the only ones to capitalise on atomic novelty songs; the Slim Gaillard Quartette recorded 'Atomic Cocktail' in 1946, and Bill Haley and the Comets' hit 'Thirteen Women (And Only One Man in Town)' was first heard in public in 1954. Many of these cold war classics have been collected into *Atomic Platters* (2005), a boxed set issued by Bear Family records. An excellent website devoted to cold war/atomic culture is Conelrad, www.conelrad.com.
92. Ronald D. Cohen, 'Music Goes to War: California, 1940–45', *The Way We Really Were: The Golden State in the Second World War*, ed. Roger W. Lotchin (Urbana: University of Illinois Press, 2000), p. 48.
93. Daniel, 'Hayloft Patriotism', p. 85.
94. Don Cusic, 'Gene Autry in World War II', *Country Music Goes to War*, ed. Charles K. Wolfe and James E. Akenson (Lexington: University Press of Kentucky, 2005), p. 55.

95. Ibid., p. 52.
96. Wolfe, ' "Jesus Hits Like an Atom Bomb" ', p. 108.
97. Daniel, 'Hayloft Patriotism', p. 94.
98. Cusic, 'Gene Autry in World War II', p. 55.
99. 'Woody Guthrie Biography', *Woody Guthrie: This Land Was Made for You and Me*, www.woodyguthrie.org/biography/biography4.htm.

3. Theatre and Film

1. 'American Theatre Wing History', *American Theatre Wing*, http://americantheatrewing.org/about/history_of_atw.php
2. Van Vechten cited in James V. Hatch, 'Chapter 11 – Creeping Toward Integration', *A History of African American Theatre* by Errol G. Hill and James V. Hatch, Cambridge Studies in American Theatre and Drama (Cambridge: Cambridge University Press, 2003), p. 336.
3. 'Past Winners of Tony Awards', *The Tony Awards*, http://www.tonyawards.com/p/tonys_search.
4. Not so funny was the lawsuit brought against the show's producers by Max Sennett, creator of the silent-era Keystone comedies, in the amount of $250,000. Sennett was eventually awarded an undisclosed amount, and the show was evidently altered to limit the direct references to Sennett. See Abe Laufe, *Broadway's Greatest Musicals* (New York: Funk and Wagnalls, 1969), p. 108.
5. Ethan Mordden, *Beautiful Mornin'*, p. 113; see also Stanley Green, *The World of Musical Comedy* (New York: Ziff-Davis Publishing Company, 1960), p. 204.
6. Green, *The World of Musical Comedy*, p. 72.
7. Ibid., p. 245.
8. Mordden, *Beautiful Mornin': The Broadway Musical in the 1940s* (New York: Oxford University Press, 1999), p. 77.
9. Green, *The World of Musical Comedy*, p. 245.
10. Ibid., p. 244.
11. Porter cited in Green, *The World of Musical Comedy*, p. 177.
12. Laufe, *Broadway's Greatest Musicals*, p. 69.
13. Ibid., p. 72.
14. Mordden, *Beautiful Mornin'*, p. 200.
15. Merman cited in Green, *The World of Musical Comedy*, p. 101.
16. Mordden, *Beautiful Mornin'*, p. 199.
17. Green, *The World of Musical Comedy*, p. 207.
18. See Green, *The World of Musical Comedy*, pp. 218–19 and Mordden, *Beautiful Mornin'*, pp. 108–11.
19. Green, *The World of Musical Comedy*, p. 214.
20. Allen Woll, *Black Musical Theatre: From* Coontown *to* Dreamgirls (Baton Rouge: Louisiana State University Press, 1989), p. 207.
21. Ibid., p. 211
22. Lewis Erenberg reports that Ellington and his orchestra appeared on stage often in the late 1930s and early 1940s, as in the revue 'Bourbon's Got the Blues', which satirised southern segregation. The first musical he himself composed, *Jump for Joy* (1941), was another revue-style critique of segregation and stereotypes; it

opened at the Mayan Theatre in Los Angeles but was prevented from moving east owing to the United States' entry into war. Erenberg, *Swingin' the Dream*, pp. 147–8.

23. Woll, *Black Musical Theatre*, pp. 213–15.
24. Laufe, *Broadway's Greatest Musicals*, p. 130.
25. Mordden, *Beautiful Mornin'*, pp. 263–4.
26. Woll, *Black Musical Theatre*, p. 218; see also Hilland and Hatch, *A History of African American Theatre*, p. 367.
27. Mordden, *The American Theatre* (New York: Oxford University Press, 1981), pp. 198–9.
28. Hatch, 'Chapter 11 – Creeping Toward Integration', p. 338.
29. '*Anna Lucasta* Opens on Broadway', *African American Registry*, http://www.aaregistry.com/african_american_history/1809/Anna_Lucasta_ope ns_on_Broadway.
30. Hatch, 'Chapter 11 – Creeping Toward Integration', p. 353.
31. See Martin Halliwell, *American Culture in the 1950s* (Edinburgh: Edinburgh University Press, 2007), pp. 111–12.
32. Wolcott Gibbs, 'Bad Girl', *The New Yorker* (9 September 1944), p. 40.
33. Lewis Nichols, 'The Play', *New York Times* (3 August 1944), p. 15.
34. 'American Negro Theatre formed', *African American Registry*, n.p., http://www.aaregistry.com/african_american_history/223/American_Negro_Theater_ formed.
35. Ibid., see also Hatch, 'Chapter 11 – Creeping Toward Integration', p. 354.
36. 'American Negro Theatre formed', n.p.
37. Hatch, 'Chapter 11 – Creeping Toward Integration', p. 352.
38. 'American Negro Theatre formed', n.p., see also Langston Hughes, Milton Meltzer, and L. Eric Lincoln, *A Pictorial History of Black Americans* (New York: Crown, 1956).
39. Hill cited in Hilland and Hatch, *A History of African American Theatre*, p. 356.
40. Gerald M. Berkowitz, *American Drama of the 20th Century* (London: Longman, 1992), p. 64.
41. Ibid., p. 65.
42. Ibid., p. 109.
43. Thomas P. Adler, *American Drama, 1940–1960: A Critical History* (New York: Twayne, 1994), p. 140 and Mordden, *The American Theatre*, p. 211.
44. Despite his ultra-left beginnings, Kazan is a controversial figure because of his 'friendly' testimony before the House Un-American Activities Committee in 1952. See the Case Study on 'HUAC in Hollywood'.
45. See Ethan Mordden, *The Hollywood Studios: House Style in the Golden Age of the Movies* (New York: Knopf, 1988) and Thomas Schatz, *The Genius of the System: Hollywood Filmmaking in the Studio Era* (New York: Metro/Henry Holt, 1988).
46. Peter Roffman and Jim Purdy, *The Hollywood Social Problem Film: Madness, Despair, and Politics from the Depression to the Fifties* (Bloomington: Indiana University Press, 1981), pp. 125–6.
47. Another comic convention that ended early in the decade was the screwball comedy, perfected, often under the direction of Howard Hawks or Preston Sturges, by the likes of Katherine Hepburn, Carole Lombard, Fredric March,

Rosalind Russell, Barbara Stanwyck, and Cary Grant. In such comedies, lovers locked in sexually tensioned battles of verbal wit (and sometimes flying fists) entertained moviegoers in the late 1930s and into the turn of the next decade. In 1940, two Grant classics, *His Girl Friday* and *The Philadelphia Story*, appeared; shortly thereafter, the war soured the atmosphere for such sophisticated foolishness, engendering other cinematic tastes and avenues of escape. Wheeler Winston Dixon observes: 'One need only survey the films made in 1940 and early 1941, as opposed to films made after the United States entered the war, to see the stark contrast.' For Dixon, film output of the earliest years of the decade consisted of 'escapist musicals' and 'memorable classics [that] nevertheless remained oddly insular in a world that was tottering on the brink of destruction'. 'Introduction: Movies and the 1940s', *American Cinema of the 1940s: Themes and Variations*, ed. Wheeler Winston Dixon (New Brunswick, NJ: Rutgers University Press, 2006), p. 3.

48. Thomas Doherty, *Projections of War: Hollywood, American Culture, and World War II* (New York: Columbia University Press, 1993), p. 182; Roeder, *The Censored War*, p. 102.

49. 'The Battle over *Citizen Kane*', *The American Experience*, PBS, http://www.pbs.org/wgbh/amex/kane2/.

50. Cited in R. Barton Palmer, *Hollywood's Dark Cinema: The American Film Noir* (New York: Twayne, 1994), p. 18.

51. See Walker, 'Film Noir: Introduction', *The Movie Book of Film Noir*, ed. Ian Cameron (London: Studio Vista, 1992), p. 33.

52. Palmer, *Hollywood's Dark Cinema*, p. 117.

53. Gerald Mast, *A Short History of the Movies* (Indianapolis, IN: Pegasus/Bobbs Merrill, 1971), pp. 306–7.

54. Mast, *A Short History of the Movies*, p. 309. Radio historian Gerald Nachman notes that 'Billy Wilder admits that he stole such common radio devices as the interior voiceover for movies like *Double Indemnity* and *Sunset Boulevard*'. *Raised on Radio*, p. 299. Although Walker argues that *Citizen Kane* does not technically qualify as film noir, it is readable as an influence on the genre and also uses – among its other sound features – voiceover narration. 'Film Noir: Introduction', p. 33.

55. Robert Sklar, *Movie-Made America: A Cultural History of American Movies*, rev. edn (New York: Random House, [1975] 1994), p. 194.

56. Sarah Kozloff, '1941 – Movies on the Edge of War', *American Cinema of the 1940s: Themes and Variations*, ed. Wheeler Winston Dixon (New Brunswick, NJ: Rutgers University Press, 2006), p. 62.

57. See Harry Benshoff and Sean Griffin, *America on Film: Representing Race, Class, Gender, and Sexuality at the Movies* (Malden, MA: Blackwell Publishing, 2004), p. 260, and Doherty, *Projections of War*, p. 111.

58. It was a great decade all around for animated features. Walt Disney succeeded with *Fantasia* (1940), *Pinocchio* (1940), *Dumbo* (1941), *Bambi* (1942) and *Cinderella* (1949). The *Tom and Jerry* films began in 1947 and Terrytoon's *Mighty Mouse* in 1949.

59. Bernard F. Dick, *The Star-Spangled Screen: The American World War II Film* (Lexington: The University Press of Kentucky, 1985), p. 166.

60. Ibid., p. 167.

61. Clayton R. Koppes and Gregory D. Black, *Hollywood Goes to War: How Politics, Profits, and Propaganda Shaped World War II Movies* (New York: Free Press, 1987), p. 290.
62. Lawrence J. Quirk, *The Great War Films: From* The Birth of a Nation *to Today* (New York: Citadel Press, 1994), pp. 112–13.
63. Dick, *The Star-Spangled Screen*, p. 215.
64. Benshoff and Griffin, *America on Film*, p. 83.
65. Doherty, *Projections of War*, p. 213.
66. Benshoff and Griffin, *America on Film*, p. 82.
67. Doherty, *Projections of War*, pp. 215–16.
68. Ibid., p. 144.
69. Ibid., p. 144.
70. Ibid., p. 246.
71. Koppes and Black, *Hollywood Goes to War*, p. 271.
72. Joe Morella, Edward Z. Epstein, and John Griggs, *The Films of World War II* (Secaucus, NJ: Citadel Press, 1973), p. 6.
73. See Koppes and Black, *Hollywood Goes to War*, p. 161.
74. Cited in Morella, Epstein, and Griggs, *The Films of World War II*, p. 150.
75. Cited in Morella, Epstein, and Griggs, *The Films of World War II*, p. 161.
76. Larry Ceplair and Steven Englund, *The Inquisition in Hollywood: Politics in the Film Community, 1930–1960* (Urbana, IL: University of Illinois Press, [1979] 2003), p. 254.
77. Ayn Rand, 'Ayn Rand's HUAC Testimony: Sunday, October 19, 1947', Ayn Rand Institute http://www.aynrand.org/site/News2?news_iv_ ctrl=-1&page= NewsArticle&id=6125.
78. Sklar, *Movie-Made America*, p. 260
79. Bernard F. Dick, *Radical Innocence: A Critical Study of the Hollywood Ten* (Lexington: The University Press of Kentucky, 1989), p. 3.
80. Sklar, *Movie-Made America*, p. 264.
81. Paul Buhle and David Wagner, *Hide in Plain Sight: The Hollywood Blacklistees in Film and Television, 1950–2002* (New York: Palgrave Macmillan, 2003), p. 250.
82. See Buhle and Wagner, *Hide in Plain Sight*, p. 251–2.
83. Roffman and Purdy, *The Hollywood Social Problem Film*, p. 147.
84. James Naremore, *More than Night: Film Noir and its Contexts* (Berkeley: University of California Press, 1998), p. 125.
85. Buhle and Wagner, *Hide in Plain Sight*, p. 2.
86. Koppes and Black, *Hollywood Goes to War*, p. 122.
87. Farber cited in Allen Woll, *The Hollywood Musical Goes to War* (Chicago: Nelson-Hall, 1983), p. 125.
88. Ibid., p. 123.
89. Ibid., p. 124.
90. Koppes and Black, *Hollywood Goes to War*, p. 179; see also Doherty, *Projections of War*, Chapter 9.
91. See Woll, *The Hollywood Musical Goes to War*, Chapter 9, and Benshoff and Griffin, *America on Film*, p. 142.
92. Mast, *A Short History of the Movies*, p. 302.
93. Cited in Lary May, 'Making the American Consensus: The Narrative of Conversion and Subversion in World War II Films', *The War in American*

Culture: Society and Consciousness During World War II, ed. Lewis A. Erenberg and Susan E. Hirsch (Chicago: University of Chicago Press, 1996), p. 77.

94. Sam P. Simone, *Hitchcock as Activist: Politics and the War Films* (Ann Arbor, MI: UMI Research Press, 1985), p. 87.
95. Ibid., p. 62.
96. Benshoff and Griffin, *America on Film*, p. 40.
97. Ibid., p. 41.
98. Roffman and Purdy, *The Hollywood Social Problem Film*, p. 245.
99. Ibid., p. 250.
100. Ibid., pp. 250–1.
101. Cited in Roffman and Purdy, *The Hollywood Social Problem Film*, p. 258.
102. Roffman and Purdy, *The Hollywood Social Problem Film*, p. 257.
103. Ibid., p. 227.
104. Leighton Grist, 'Moving Targets and Black Widows: Film Noir in Modern Hollywood', *The Movie Book of Film Noir*, ed. Ian Cameron (London: Studio Vista, 1992), p. 212.
105. See also Palmer, *Hollywood's Dark Cinema*, p. 46.
106. Ibid., p. 41.
107. Ibid., p. 41; see also Walker 'Film Noir: Introduction', p. 38.
108. Palmer, *Hollywood's Dark Cinema*, pp. 49–50.
109. Ibid., p. 51.

4. Visual Art, Serious and Popular

1. John I. H. Baur, 'Part Two: 1940–1960', *American Art of Our Century* by Lloyd Goodrich and John I. H. Baur (New York: Praeger, 1961), p. 90; see also Anthony Everitt, *Abstract Expressionism* (Woodbury, NY: Barron's, [1975] 1978), p. 9.
2. Everitt, *Abstract Expressionism*, p. 3.
3. Ibid., p. 4.
4. Ibid., p. 3.
5. Rosenberg cited in Loredana Parmesani, *Art of the Twentieth Century: Movements, Theories, Schools, and Tendencies 1900–2000* (Milan: Skira Editore, 1998), p. 51.
6. Everitt, *Abstract Expressionism*, p. 25.
7. Edward Lucie-Smith, *Visual Arts in the Twentieth Century* (New York: Harry N. Abrams, [1996] 1997), p. 190.
8. Ibid., p. 190.
9. Schwabacher cited in Baur, 'Part Two: 1940–1960', p. 197.
10. The lives of married women artists of this period were fraught with professional dilemmas. In her helpful study, Eleanor Munro reports, 'it was after meeting Pollock that Krasner made what was, she later felt, a mistaken decision to abandon working from nature as [Hans] Hofmann taught, in order to take on the canvas as a "thing in itself", to "work it up" in Surreal automatic gestures.' Adopting the action-style of her renowned husband, 'she seems to have short-circuited her gift. Her attempts to create an "all-over" image out of random upsurges from the unconscious led only to an accumulation of thick, granular impasto with a nervous, vibrating intensity . . .', p. 113. French sculptor Louise

Bourgeois, who worked provocatively in wood throughout the 1940s, married an American art historian and emigrated to the United States in 1938. She 'did not promote her work publicly until the Feminist Movement gave her what felt like a mandate to do so', p. 156. Eleanor Munro, *Originals: American Women Artists*, new ed. (New York: Da Capo Press, 2000).

11. Everitt, *Abstract Expressionism*, p. 25.
12. Parmesani, *Art of the Twentieth Century*, p. 51.
13. Cooper cited in 'Adolph Gottlieb: Pictographs, 1941–1951 / First Exhibition in a Decade of Gottlieb's Pictographs', 19 October 2004, *PaceWildenstein* http://www.pacewildenstein.com/Exhibitions/ViewExhibition.aspx?artist=Adolph Gottlieb&title=Pictographs1941-1951&type=Exhbition&guid=b220f675–3036-4831–9e0f-8a16bd1a58af.
14. Everitt, *Abstract Expressionism*, p. 30.
15. Nancy Spector, 'Robert Motherwell', *Guggenheim Museum / The Collection* http://www.guggenheimcollection.org/site/artist_work_md_116_1.html.
16. Ibid.
17. Nancy Spector, 'Ad Reinhardt', *Guggenheim Museum / The Collection* http://www.guggenheimcollection.org/site/date_work_md_133A_1.html.
18. Everitt, *Abstract Expressionism*, p. 32.
19. Ibid., p. 29.
20. Edward Lucie Smith, *Visual Arts in the Twentieth Century*, p. 185.
21. Jean-Paul Sartre, 'The Mobiles of Calder', *Alexander Calder, Exhibition Held 9–27 December 1947, Calder Foundation* www.calder.org/SETS/life_biogr_set.html.
22. Karol Vail, *Peggy Guggenheim: A Celebration* (New York: Guggenheim Museum, 1998), p. 44
23. Ibid., p. 41.
24. Ibid., p. 44.
25. Ibid., p. 56.
26. Jacqueline Bograd Weld, *Peggy: The Wayward Guggenheim* (New York: E. P. Dutton, 1986), p. xii.
27. Ibid., p. xi.
28. Mary Dearborn, *Mistress of Modernism: The Life of Peggy Guggenheim* (Boston: Houghton Mifflin, 2004), p. 200; see also Anton Gill, *Art Lover: A Biography of Peggy Guggenheim* (New York: HarperCollins, 2002), p. 304.
29. Laurence Tacou-Rumney, *Peggy Guggenheim: A Collector's Album* (Paris: Flammarion, 1996), p. 135.
30. Greenberg cited in Tacou-Rumney, *Peggy Guggenheim*, p. 134.
31. Vail, *Peggy Guggenheim*, p. 81.
32. Ibid., p. 112.
33. See Wanda M. Corn, 'Ways of Seeing', *Norman Rockwell: Pictures for the American People*, ed. Maureen Hart Hennessey and Anne Knutson (New York: Harry N. Abrams, Inc., 1999), pp. 91–2.
34. Steven Heller and Louise Fili, *Cover Story: The Art of American Magazine Covers, 1900–1950* (San Francisco: Chronicle Books, 1996), p. 8.
35. Baur, 'Part Two: 1940–1960', p. 163.
36. Catlett cited in Cedric Dover, *American Negro Art* (Greenwich, CT: New York Graphic Society, [1960] 1969), p. 54. Writing in *New Masses* in 1946, Catlett lashed

out at the American Federation of Arts' second 'all-Negro' exhibition, entitled 'The Negro Artist Comes of Age': 'The title itself is an insult. Negro artists have contributed to American culture since the late eighteenth century . . . And there seems to be little purpose in such a separate exhibit . . . Such a show as this one adds to the cultural restrictions and lessens to an extent cultural equality of opportunity.' Cited in Patricia Hills, *Modern Art in the USA: Issues and Controversies of the 20th Century* (Upper Saddle River, NJ: Prentice Hall, 2001), pp. 180–1.

37. Dover, *American Negro Art*, p. 55.
38. Ibid., p. 52.
39. 'Timeline: Romare Bearden', *Romare Bearden Foundation*. http://www.beardenfoundation.org/artlife/timeline/timeline.shtml.
40. Dover, *American Negro Art*, p. 32.
41. Ibid., p. 42.
42. Ibid., pp. 37–8.
43. Ibid., p. 46.
44. Henry Louis Gates Jr, and Cornel West, *The African American Century: How Black Americans Have Shaped Our Country* (New York: Free Press, 2000), p. 173.
45. Lawrence cited in Ellen Harkins Wheat, *Jacob Lawrence: American Painter* (Seattle: University of Washington Press, 1986), p. 69.
46. Ibid., p. 68.
47. Edward Lucie-Smith, *Lives of the Great 20th-Century Artists* (London: Thames and Hudson, 1999), p. 213.
48. Michael R. Taylor, 'Between Realism and Surrealism: The Early Work of Andrew Wyeth', *Andrew Wyeth: Memory and Magic* (Atlanta: High Museum of Art, 2005), p. 27.
49. Wyeth critic John Wilmerding notes that 'the different colouration [*sic*] of each [location] condition[s] his palette: Chadds Ford is often seen in monochromatic tans, browns, and whites; Maine in brighter greens and blues', p. 19. Like Lawrence, Wyeth worked with the difficult medium of egg tempera. 'Introduction', *Andrew Wyeth: Memory and Magic* (Atlanta: High Museum of Art, 2005).
50. Anne Classen Knutson, 'Andrew Wyeth's Language of Things', *Andrew Wyeth: Memory and Magic* (Atlanta: High Museum of Art, 2005), p. 58.
51. Ibid., p. 58.
52. Wilmerding, 'Introduction', p. 19.
53. Knutson, 'Andrew Wyeth's Language of Things', p. 76.
54. Artists for Victory was both the name of an official volunteer organisation, comprised eventually of some 10,000 artists and graphic designers pledged to support the war effort with their work, and the name of various art exhibitions staged by major museums throughout the war. Most prominent were the exhibitions held at the Metropolitan Museum of Art in New York, whose first one (1942–43) included prize-winning work by Jacob Lawrence and the illustrator John (Jack) Atherton. See also Barbara McCloskey, *Artists of World War II*, Artists of an Era series (Westport, CT: Greenwood Press, 2005), pp. 174–5.
55. As Dover notes of such cultural phenomena, 'it is clear that the remarkable germination of interest in Negro achievements between 1940 and 1945 was accelerated by the domestic situation and the importance of creating good impressions abroad'. *American Negro Art*, p. 42.
56. Ibid., p. 142.

57. 'Richmond Barthé's *The Negro Looks Ahead* Acquired by The Amon Carter Museum', *Amon Carter Museum*, http://www.cartermuseum.org/Press/releases/january-31–2007

58. Dover, *American Negro Art*, p. 46.

59. Lowery Stokes Sims, 'Bill Traylor and William Edmondson and the Challenges to African American Artists Between the World Wars', *Bill Traylor, William Edmondson, and the Modernist Impulse*, ed. Josef Helfenstein and Roxanne Stanulis (Champaign: University of Illinois Press, 2004), p. 38.

60. Jane Livingston and John Beardsley, *Black Folk Art in America, 1930–1980* (Jackson: University of Mississippi Press, 1982), p. 72.

61. Sims, 'Bill Traylor and William Edmondson', p. 40.

62. Allen Rankin, 'He Lost 10,000 Years', *Collier's* (22 June 1946), n.p.

63. Livingston and Beardsley, *Black Folk Art in America*, p. 87; Helfenstein, *Bill Traylor, William Edmonson, and the Modernist Impulse*, p. 8.

64. Jane Kallir, *The World of Grandma Moses* (Baltimore: Garamond Pridemark, 1984), pp. 15–16.

65. Ibid., p. 11.

66. Ibid., p. 13.

67. Ibid., p. 14.

68. Romare Bearden and Harry Henderson, *A History of African-American Artists, from 1792 to the Present* (New York: Pantheon, 1993), p. 369.

69. Pippin cited in Judith E. Stein, *I Tell My Heart: The Art of Horace Pippin* (Philadelphia: Pennsylvania Academy of the Fine Arts, 1993), p. 3.

70. 'Meet Horace Pippin (1888–1946) / Counting on Art', *NGA Classroom – National Gallery of Art* http://www.nga.gov/education/classroom/ counting_on_art/bio_pippin.shtm.

71. Judith Zilczer, '*Holy Mountain III*', *Hirshhorn Museum and Sculpture Garden* http://hirshhorn.si.edu/collection/record.asp?Artist=Pippin&hasImage=1&ViewMode=&Record=4.

72. Stein, *I Tell My Heart*, p. 13.

73. Ibid., p. 32.

74. Clark cited in Stein, *I Tell My Heart*, p. 32.

75. Rodman cited Dover, *American Negro Art*, p. 45.

76. Bearden and Henderson, *A History of African-American Artists*, p. 356.

77. Susan E. Meyer, *America's Great Illustrators* (New York: Harry N. Abrams, 1978), p. 167.

78. Ibid., p. 167.

79. Ernest W. Watson, *Forty Illustrators and How They Work* (New York: Watson-Guptill Publications, Inc., [1946] 1953), p. 255.

80. Laura Claridge, *Norman Rockwell: A Life* (New York: Random House, 2001), p. 299.

81. See Claridge, *Norman Rockwell*, p. 9 and Meyer, *America's Great Illustrators*, p. 169.

82. Claridge, *Norman Rockwell*, p. 313.

83. Ibid., p. 299.

84. Ibid., p. 23.

85. See Maureen Hart Hennessey, 'The Four Freedoms', *Norman Rockwell: Pictures for the American People*, ed. Maureen Hart Hennessey and Anne Knutson (New

York: Harry N. Abrams, Inc., 1999), pp. 96–100, and McCloskey, *Artists of World War II*, pp. 177–9.

86. Clement Greenberg, 'Avant-Garde and Kitsch', *Mass Culture: The Popular Arts in America*, ed. Bernard Rosenberg and David Manning White (Glencoe, IL: Free Press, [1946] 1957), p. 103.

87. Ned Rifkin, 'Why Norman Rockwell, Why Now?', *Norman Rockwell: Pictures for the American People*, ed. Maureen Hart Hennessey and Anne Knutson (New York: Harry N. Abrams, Inc., 1999), p. 19.

88. Holland cited in Steven Heller, 'Rebelling Against Rockwell', *Norman Rockwell: Pictures for the American People*, ed. Maureen Hart Hennessey and Anne Knutson (New York: Harry N. Abrams, Inc., 1999), p. 170.

89. Laurie Norton Moffatt, 'The People's Painter', *Norman Rockwell: Pictures for the American People*, ed. Maureen Hart Hennessey and Anne Knutson (New York: Harry N. Abrams, Inc., 1999), p. 23.

90. Heller, 'Rebelling Against Rockwell', p. 169.

91. Holland cited in Heller, 'Rebelling Against Rockwell', p. 170.

92. Johnson cited in Moffatt, 'The People's Painter', p. 27.

93. Corn, 'Ways of Seeing', p. 93.

94. McCloskey, *Artists of World War II*, p. 176.

95. Reed, *The Popular Magazine in Britain and the United States*, p. 172.

96. Watson, *Forty Illustrators and How They Work*, p. 272.

97. Catherine Gudis, *Buyways: Billboards, Automobiles, and the American Landscape* (New York: Routledge, 2004), p. 93.

98. Bill Vossler, *Burma-Shave: The Rhymes, the Signs, the Times* (St Cloud, MN: North Star Press, 1997), p. 75.

99. Cited in Vossler, *Burma-Shave*, p. 105.

100. Vossler, *Burma-Shave*, pp. 75, 16.

101. Kirk Varnedoe and Adam Gopnik, *High and Low: Modern and Popular Culture* (New York: Harry N. Abrams, Inc., 1990), p. 182.

102. Reinhold Reitberger and Wolfgang Fuchs, *Comics: Anatomy of a Mass Medium* (Boston: Little Brown, 1970), p. 11.

103. Bradford W. Wright, *Comic Book Nation: The Transformation of Youth Culture in America* (Baltimore: Johns Hopkins University Press, 2001), p. 31.

104. Ibid., p. 57.

105. Ibid., p. 96.

106. Ibid., p. 10.

107. Robert C. Harvey, *The Art of the Comic Book: An Aesthetic History* (Jackson: University Press of Mississippi, 1996), p. 35.

108. Wright, *Comic Book Nation*, p. 21.

109. See also Mitra C. Emad, 'Reading Wonder Woman's Body: Mythologies of Gender and Nation', *The Journal of Popular Culture* 39 (6) (2006). As comic book historian William W. Savage Jr, notes: 'Only [comic strip character] Little Lulu, in comic books since 1945, seemed consistently and assertively feminist in the postwar decade. She was a frumpy woman-child in a man's world . . .; a Rosie the Riveter grown down . . . Little Lulu was tough and resilient, unlike most of her bigger sisters in the chauvinistic medium of comic books; and in consequence of those qualities – and the strength of her personality generally – she taught valuable lessons to the children (of both sexes) who followed her rather ordinary

adventures.' *Comic Books and America, 1945–1954* (Norman, OK: University of Oklahoma Press, 1990), p. 79.

110. Reitberger and Fuchs, *Comics*, p. 251.
111. Harvey, *The Art of the Comic Book*, p. 16.
112. Wright, *Comic Book Nation*, p. 43.
113. Harvey, *The Art of the Comic Book*, p. 35.
114. Wright, *Comic Book Nation*, p. 59
115. Reitberger and Fuchs, *Comics*, p. 19.
116. Savage, *Comic Books and America*, pp. 16–17.
117. Wright, *Comic Book Nation*, pp. 114, 125.
118. Savage, *Comic Books and America*, pp. 67–8.
119. Wright, *Comic Book Nation*, pp. 72, 73.
120. Robert Shaffer, 'Pearl S. Buck and the East and West Association: The Trajectory and Fate of "Critical Internationalism", 1940–1950', *Peace & Change* 28 (1) (2003), p. 12.
121. See Wright, *Comic Book Nation*, p. 62.
122. Ibid., p. 63.
123. Shaffer, 'Pearl S. Buck and the East and West Association', p. 1.
124. Wright, *Comic Book Nation*, p. 63.
125. Shaffer, 'Pearl S. Buck and the East and West Association', p. 11.
126. Buck cited in Shaffer, 'Pearl S. Buck and the East and West Association', pp. 11–12.
127. Cited in Shaffer, 'Pearl S. Buck and the East and West Association', p. 12.
128. 'Comic Culture', *Time* (18 December 1944), *Time Archive* http://www.time.com/time/magazine/article/0,9171,778319,00.html.

5. The Arts of Sacrifice and Consumption

1. See, for instance, Roeder, *The Censored War*, pp. 69, 83.
2. Perry R. Duis, 'No Time for Privacy: World War II and Chicago's Families', *The War in American Culture: Society and Consciousness During World War II*, ed. Lewis A. Erenberg and Susan E. Hirsch (Chicago: University of Chicago Press, 1996), p. 20.
3. Roeder, *The Censored War*, p. 82.
4. Allan M. Winkler, *The Politics of Propaganda: The Office of War Information, 1942–1945* (New Haven: Yale University Press, 1978), p. 4.
5. Ibid., p. 4.
6. Ibid., p. 64.
7. Ibid., p. 63.
8. Cited in Roeder, *The Censored War*, p. 14.
9. Fussell, *Wartime*, p. 7
10. Ibid., p. 8.
11. This image is viewable online at the Prints and Photographs Reading Room website of the Library of Congress, www.loc.gov/rr/print. Path: Prints and Photographs Online Catalogue, Search: War Posters American 1940 1950, Select: 11 of 436.
12. This image is viewable online at the Prints and Photographs Reading Room website of the Library of Congress, www.loc.gov/rr/print. Path: Prints and Photographs Online Catalogue, Search: War Posters American 1940 1950, Select: 149 of 436.

13. This image is viewable online at the Prints and Photographs Reading Room website of the Library of Congress, www.loc.gov/rr/print. Path: Prints and Photographs Online Catalogue, Search: War Posters American 1940 1950, Select: 16 of 436

14. Geoffrey Perrett notes that aluminum sought after in 1941 and rubber salvaged in 1942 both proved to be 'militarily useless'. When it was determined that 'paper will win the war . . . "waste paper piled up in the greater cities until, attracting rats, it became a menace to public health and was burned" '. *Days of Sadness, Years of Triumph*, p. 234. Also, Roeder found that 'the War Production Board used high fences to hide piles of rusting scrap metal, patriotically donated but never used, which might have cast doubt on the urgency of government collection campaigns'. *The Censored War*, p. 58.

15. Roeder, *The Censored War*, p. 61.

16. Judith A. Bellafaire's excellent online history of the Women's Army Auxiliary Corps dispels this and many other rumours. 'The Women's Army Corps: A Commemoration of World War II Service', CMH Publication 72–15. CMH Online. *U.S. Army Center for Military History*. 17 February 2005. http://www.army.mil/cmh-pg/brochures/ wac/wac.htm.

17. Roeder, *The Censored War*, p. 60.

18. Ibid., p. 72.

19. Fussell, *Wartime*, p. 141.

20. Duis, 'No Time for Privacy', p. 28.

21. Daniel, 'Hayloft Patriotism', p. 89.

22. Ibid., p. 91.

23. Doherty, *Projections of War*, p. 82.

24. Lingeman, *Don't You Know there's a War On?*, p. 306.

25. See Duis, 'No Time for Privacy', p. 21; Doherty *Projections of War*, p. 83; and Roeder, *The Censored War*, p. 72.

26. Lingeman, *Don't You Know there's a War On?*, p. 305.

27. See Perrett, *Days of Sadness, Years of Triumph*, p. 234.

28. Rogers, *Since You Went Away*, p. 148.

29. See Fussell, *Wartime*, p. 149.

30. Editors of *Consumer Reports*, *I'll Buy That!: 50 Small Wonders and Big Deals that Revolutionized the Lives of Consumers – A Fifty-Year Retrospective* (Mount Vernon, NY: Consumers Union, 1986), p. 216.

31. Ibid., p. 216.

32. Ibid., p. 88. According to Rogers, GM produced $12.5 billion worth of military equipment during the war; Ford made B-29 bombers so quickly that they were stacked in long lines before being fuelled and flown off to battle: *Since You Went Away*, p. 171. Henry J. Kaiser increased efficiency in battleship production, 'building a fleet of ships practically overnight': ibid. p. 169.

33. See Duis, 'No Time for Privacy', p. 17.

34. Ibid., p. 20.

35. Ibid., p. 22.

36. Ibid., p. 22.

37. Ibid., p. 23.

38. Rogers, *Since You Went Away*, p. 172.

39. Duis, 'No Time for Privacy', p. 34.

40. Charles C. Alexander, *Breaking the Slump: Baseball in the DePression Era* (New York: Columbia University Press, 2002), p. 264.

41. Lewis A. Erenberg, *The Greatest Fight of Our Generation: Louis vs. Schmeling* (New York: Oxford University Press , 2005), p. 183.

42. Jeffrey F. Liss, 'More to this Card Than Season's Greetings', *The Washington Post* (28 December 2003), B4. *washingtonpost.com* http://www.washington-post.com/ac2/wp-dyn/A33490-2003Dec26? language=printer.

43. Elisabeth Blackmar, 'Interview with NYC Reads Book Club, sponsored by *The Gotham Gazette*', *The Park and the People*, n.p. www. gothamgazette.com/article/20040713/202/1031.

44. Richard M. Fried, *The Russians Are Coming! The Russians Are Coming!: Pageantry and Patriotism in Cold-War America* (New York: Oxford University Press, 1998), p. 16.

45. Nicholas M. Prevas, 'Church History', *Greek Orthodox Church of the Annunciation* http://www.goannun.org/church/history.asp.

46. Michael Olesker, *Journeys to the Heart of Baltimore* (Baltimore: Johns Hopkins University Press, 2001), p. 68.

47. Wong, 'War Comes to Chinatown', p. 180.

48. Fried, *The Russians Are Coming!*, p. 14.

49. Ibid., p. 17.

50. Lingeman, *Don't You Know there's a War On?*, p. 316.

51. Lingeman provides a detailed account of the Detroit riots of 1943, as well as overviews of Los Angeles's Zoot Suit conflicts and anti-Japanese American policies that adversely affected Californians of Japanese descent. *Don't You Know there's a War On?*, Chapter 9.

52. Duis, 'No Time for Privacy', pp. 32–3.

53. Jeffrey Meikle, 'Into the Fourth Kingdom: Representations of Plastic Materiality, 1920–1950', *Journal of Design History* 5 (3) (1992), p. 180. JSTOR http://links.jstor.org/sici?sici=0952-4649(1992)5%3A3%3C173%3AITFKRO%3E2.0.CO%3B2-6.

54. Peter Dormer, *Design Since 1945* (London: Thames and Hudson, 1993), p. 7.

55. Generations of postwar parents turned to Dr Benjamin Spock, whose *Common Sense Book of Baby and Child Care* appeared in 1946, as did the paperback version, *The Pocket Book of Baby and Child Care*. Readers embraced his relaxed, flexible approach to parenting and the confidence inspired by his most famous admonition to parents, 'Trust yourself. You know more than you think you do.' Spock cited in Editors of *Consumer Reports*, *I'll Buy That!*, p. 174. 'Within [its first] ten years, the paperback had gone through fifty-nine paperback printings and sold about a million copies per year . . .' Editors of *Consumer Reports*, *I'll Buy That!*, p. 175. By the late 1990s it would sell more than fifty million copies and be translated into almost forty languages.

56. David Gelernter, *1939: The Lost World of the Fair* (New York: Avon Books, 1995), p. 352.

57. 'Touring the Future', *The Iconography of Hope: The 1939–1940 New York World's Fair*, American Studies Program, University of Virginia, *America in the 1930s* series http://xroads.virginia.edu/~1930s/DISPLAY/39wf/taketour.htm.

58. 'History of the Fair: The Design and Marketing of the Future', *The Iconography of Hope: The 1939–1940 New York World's Fair*, American Studies Program, University of Virginia, *America in the 1930s* series.

59. 'Welcome to Tomorrow', *The Iconography of Hope: The 1939–1940 New York World's Fair*, American Studies Program, University of Virginia, ibid.

60. 'History of the Fair: The Design and Marketing of the Future', *The Iconography of Hope: The 1939–1940 New York World's Fair*, American Studies Program, University of Virginia, *America in the 1930s* series, ibid.

61. 'Welcome to Tomorrow'. While the Fair's scale and significance, both physically and historically, remain difficult to comprehend, there exist two excellent websites devoted to providing modern students of this period with some sense of it all. One is the University of Virginia site, referred to throughout out this discussion, and the other is Paul M. Van Dort's *1939 New York World's Fair*, both of which contain virtual tours.

62. Stephen van Dulken, *Inventing the 20th Century: 100 Inventions that Shaped the World from the Airplane to the Zipper* (Washington Square, NY: New York University Press, 2000), p. 124.

63. 'The Rise of American Consumerism', *American Experience: Tupperware!* PBS http://www.pbs.org/wgbh/amex/tupperware/peopleevents/e_consumer.html.

64. 'The "Future" in the 1950s', *The American Experience: Tupperware!* PBS http://www.pbs.org.wgbh/amex/tupperware/timeline/index.html.

65. Editors of *Consumer Reports*, *I'll Buy That!*, p. 186.

66. Ibid., p. 187. Sheehy notes that, mid-century, flamingos were adopted by the middlebrow as well; their vibrant colours and sensuous curves were popular in art deco designs of the 1930s. 'By the 1940s, the flamingo appeared even more widely in interior design.' Fuelled by that era's rage for all things pink, the flamingo's image 'adorned numerous household items: drinking glasses, serving trays, metal boxes, and ashtrays'. The first plastic lawn-ornament flamingo was not created until 1957; before then, many garden flamingos were made of cement. Colleen J. Sheehy, *The Flamingo in the Garden: American Yard Art and the Vernacular Landscape* (New York: Garland, 1998), pp. 90–2.

67. Catherine McDermott, *Designmuseum: 20th-Century Design* (Woodstock, NY: Overlook Press, 2000), p. 178.

68. William J. Hennessey, *Russel Wright: American Designer* (Cambridge, MA: MIT Press, 1983), p. 16.

69. Ibid., p. 16.

70. Ibid., pp. 43–4.

71. Hennessey reports that in the late 1940s 'Emily Post attacked the very idea of informal service – in several letters to *Time*, which Wright answered with great gusto'. *Russel Wright*, p. 43.

72. Mary Wright and Russel Wright, *Mary and Russel Wright's Guide to Easier Living* (New York: Simon and Schuster, 1951), p. 67.

73. Donald Albrecht and Robert Schonfeld, 'Russel Wright: Creating American Style', *Manitoga / The Russel Wright Design Center* http:// www.russelwrightcenter/org./russelwright.html.

74. McDermott, *Designmuseum*, p. 178.

75. Albrecht and Schonfeld, 'Russel Wright: Creating American Style'.
76. Historian Stephen van Dulken reports that, during the war, scientists for Corning Glass and General Electric were looking for silicon-derived rubber substitutes and also arrived separately at the otherwise useless toy putty. Only when it was packaged in egg-shaped containers and marketed to children did the bouncy, somewhat sticky substance, now known as Silly Putty, take off, which it has by the hundred millions since 1950: *Inventing the 20th Century*, p. 118. Also according to van Dulken, the Slinky toy was invented by Richard James, a mechanical engineer who, while testing ships for the US Navy during the war, noticed the way torsion springs jumped from table to floor: ibid., p. 120.
77. 'Timeline: Women, Work, and Plastics History', *The American Experience: Tupperware!* PBS http://www.pbs.org.wgbh/amex/tupperware/timeline/index.html.
78. Editors of *Consumer Reports*, *I'll Buy That!*, p. 70.
79. Ibid., p. 13.
80. Ibid., p. 58.
81. Ibid., pp. 59–60.
82. David J. Cole, Eve Browning, and Fred E. H. Schroeder, *Encyclopedia of Modern Everyday Inventions* (Westport, CT: Greenwood Press, 2003), p. 173.
83. Ibid., p. 174.
84. Ibid., p. 64.
85. Editors of *Consumer Reports*, *I'll Buy That!*, p. 233.
86. Ibid., p. 46.
87. Ibid., p. 196.
88. 'A Short History of Manufactured Fibers', *Fibersource – Carpet and Rug Institute* http://www.fibersource.com/f-tutor/history.htm.
89. McDermott, *Designmuseum*, p. 19.
90. Editors of *Consumer Reports*, *I'll Buy That!*, pp. 198, 199.
91. 'Our History: The Rayon Years', *Dupont Old Hickory Community/ Our Old Hickory Heritage*, Dupont Old Hickory Site (1982) http://www.oldhickoryrecord.com/history/htm.
92. Ibid.
93. Editors of *Consumer Reports*, *I'll Buy That!*, p. 200.
94. van Dulken, *Inventing the 20th Century*, p. 40.
95. See van Dulken, *Inventing the 20th Century*, p. 124.
96. 'Brownie Wise, 1913–1992', *The American Experience: Tupperware!* PBS http://www.pbs.org.wgbh/amex/tupperware/p_wise.html.
97. 'Earl J. Tupper, 1907–1983', *The American Experience: Tupperware!* PBS http://www.pbs.org.wgbh/amex/tupperware/p_tupper.html.
98. Dormer, *Design Since 1945*, p. 123.
99. Ibid., p. 123.
100. See Pat Kirkham, *Charles and Ray Eames: Designers of the 20th Century* (Cambridge, MA: MIT Press, 1995), pp. 212–14.
101. McDermott, *Designmuseum*, p. 125.
102. Cited in Kirkham, p. 223.
103. Ibid., p. 223.
104. Ibid., p. 219.

105. Ibid., p. 221.

106. Raymond Loewy, *Never Leave Well Enough Alone* (New York: Simon and Schuster, 1951), pp. 168–9.

107. In an unpaginated photoessay between pages 146 and 147 of his autobiography, Loewy describes and depicts this assembly-line process for the massive GG-I electric locomotive, designed for the Pennsylvania Railroad in the late 1930s. *Never Leave Well Enough Alone.*

108. McDermott, *Designmuseum*, p. 202.

109. Loewy, *Never Leave Well Enough Alone*, p. 291.

110. Penny Sparke, *An Introduction to Design and Culture in the 20th Century* (London: Routledge, 1986), p. 132.

111. Ibid., p. 135.

112. Ibid., p. 129.

Conclusion

1. A helpful exception to this rule is William S. Graebner's *The Age of Doubt: American Thought and Culture in the 1940s* (Boston: Twayne, 1991). Here, the author is so well focused on the intellectual trends and resultant cultural phenomena of the late 1940s that, according to Kleinegger, he actually slights the war years. 'Moody Decade: The 1940s Revisisted', *American Quarterly* 1 (March 1992), p. 135. Such a slant makes Graebner's book exceptional yet again compared with most contemporary historicising of the period.

2. Philip D. Beidler, *The Good War's Greatest Hits: World War II and American Remembering* (Athens, GA: University of Georgia Press, 1998), p. 151.

3. Ibid., p. 164.

4. Fussell, *Wartime*, p. 290.

5. Lingeman undermines the forthrightness of his overview by chalking up these egregious misbehaviours to 'War Nerves', the title of the chapter in question: Chapter 9, *Don't You Know there's a War On?*

6. Ibid., p. 258.

7. Ibid., p. 269.

8. Ibid., p. 267.

9. Ibid., p. 254.

10. Ibid., p. 259.

11. Ibid., p. 270.

12. John Ospital, *We Wore Jump Boots and Baggy Pants* (Aptos, CA: Willow House, 1977), p. v.

13. Ibid., p. 39.

14. Ibid., p. 75.

15. Fussell, *Wartime*, pp. 164–80.

16. Ibid., p. 268.

17. Ibid., p. 270.

18. Ibid., p. 269.

19. Studs Terkel, *'The Good War': An Oral History of World War II* (New York: Pantheon, 1984), p. 8.

20. Ibid., p. 3.

21. '*My War*, Andy Rooney', *Public Affairs: Good Books about Things*

that Matter http://www.publicaffairsbooks.com/publicaffairsbooks-cgi-bin/
display?book=9781586481599.

22. Andy Rooney, *My War* (New York: Public Affairs, [1995] 2000), p. 127.
23. Ibid., p. 40.
24. Ibid., p. 125.
25. Ibid., p. 270.
26. Ibid., p. 4.
27. Ibid., p. 245.
28. Ibid., p. 230.
29. Ibid., p. 205.
30. Ibid., p. 312.
31. Ibid., p. 310.
32. Ibid., p. 313.
33. Paul Fussell, 'Uneasy Company: *Band of Brothers* is *Private Ryan* for Grown-Ups', *Slate* (7 September 2001) http://www.slate.com/id/ 114810/.
34. David Plotz, 'Should Stephen Ambrose be Pardoned?: The Patriot as Prose-Thief', *Slate* (14 October 2002) http://www.slate.com/id/ 2072336/.
35. David Plotz, 'The Plagiarist: Why Stephen Ambrose is a Vampire', *Slate* (11 January 2002) http://www.slate.com/?id=2060618.
36. See Plotz, 'Should Stephen Ambrose be Pardoned?' and 'The Plagiarist'; Fred Barnes, 'Ambrose Apologizes', *The Weekly Standard* (7 January 2002), *The Daily Standard* http://www.weeklystandard.com/ Content/Public/Articles/ 000/000/000/752brzuv.asp and 'Stephen Ambrose, Copycat', *The Weekly Standard* (14 January 2007), *The Daily Standard* (4 January 2007) http:// www.weeklystandard.com/ Content/Public/Articles/000/000/000/738lfddv. asp?pg=2; and Mark Lewis, 'Ambrose Has Done It Before', *Forbes* (7 January 2002), *Forbes.com* http://www.forbes.com/2002/01/07/0107ambrose.html. and 'More Controversy for Stephen Ambrose', *Forbes* (9 January 2002), *Forbes.com* http://www.forbes.com/2002/01/09/0109ambrose.html.
37. See also Robert G. Theobaben, ed., *For Comrade and Country: Oral Histories of World War II Veterans* (Jefferson, NC: McFarland and Company, 2003), p. 4.
38. See Clint Willis, ed., *The War: Stories of Life and Death from World War II* (New York: Thunder's Mouth Press, 1999), p. 314. Perhaps drawing Fussell to Sledge's book was its literally and metaphorically dark cover: a difficult-to-discern mound of clothing (containing a crumpled body or not) topped by a military helmet seems to have been abandoned in the desert on an otherwise starry, peaceful night. Fussell's cover echoes that same dark vision, featuring a black-and-white photograph of a serviceman in terrified foetal position; whether the man pictured is 'merely' traumatised, wounded, or dead is impossible to tell.
39. For example, Theobaben, *For Comrade and Country*, p. 12, but see Fussell, *Wartime*, p. 287.
40. Even an editor like Willis, inspired by Fussell's cynical assessment, dismisses the attempt to glorify war yet wrestles with the prospect of denying it all meaning: despite its inherent ideological tendencies, war writing can teach its readers compassion; regarding the war itself, 'meaning exists for us whether we identify it or not'. *The War*, pp. 4–5.
41. Fussell, 'Uneasy Company'.
42. In fact, HBO's *Band of Brothers* appears to borrow liberally from the record of

the 411th, an infantry regiment with the 103rd Infantry Division. In a late episode, entitled 'Why We Fight', members of Easy Company come upon one of the Landsberg concentration camps and discover for themselves the depths of Nazi depravity; the scene is moving and graphic: corpse-like figures in various stages of dying and decay assault the paratroops' visual, olfactory, and moral senses; later, German civilians are pressed into the punishing task of gathering and burying the bodies, by way of atoning for the crime they surely knew about. Yet in their history of the 103rd Mueller and Turk observe, 'At Landsberg, the men of the 103d Infantry Division discovered what they had been fighting against. They found six concentration camps where victims of the super-race had died by the thousands of atrocities, starvation and exposure. The grounds of the camp were littered with the skeletonised bodies of Jews, Poles, Russians, French, and un-Nazified German . . . German civilians who were forced by 411th guards to pick up these wasted bodies for decent burial sniveled that they had not known such things existed. Ralph Meuller and Jerry Turk, *Report After Action: The Story of the 103rd Infantry Division* (Headquarters, 103rd Infantry Division, US Army, 1945), p. 131. Ambrose comments only that the 506 'saw' Landsberg: *Band of Brothers*, p. 262. In his autobiography, Major Winters does not mention Landsberg at all.

43. See Mark Bando, 'Episode 2 – Day of Days', *Trigger Time: Mark Bando's Website* http://www.101airborneww2.com/bandofbrothers4. html.

44. Fussell, *Wartime*, pp. 268–9.

45. Fussell, 'Uneasy Company'.

46. See Jonathan Rosenbaum, 'Saving Private Ryan', *The Chicago Reader* http://onfilm.chicagoreader.com/movies/capsules/16665_SAVING_PRIVATE _RYAN.html; Kenneth Turan, 'Soldiers of Misfortune', *The Los Angeles Times. Calendarlive.com* (23 July 1998) http://www.calendarlive.com/movies/ reviews/cl-movie980723-5,0,6595970.story; and Roger Ebert, 'Saving Private Ryan', *RogerEbert.com* (24 July 1998) http://rogerebert.suntimes.com/apps/ pbcs.dll/article?AID=%2F19980724%2FREVIEWS%2F807240304%2F1023 &AID1=%2F19980724%2FREVIEWS%2F807240304%2F1023&AID2=.

47. Rod Dreher (review segment), *Metacritic.com* http://www.metacritic.com/ video/titles/savingprivateryan.

48. David Edelstein, 'Apocalypse Then: The Viscera of War', *Slate* (24 July 1998) http://www.slate.com/id/3259/.

49. David Edelstein, 'Mommy Weirdest', *New York* (30 October 2006) http:// nymag.com/movies/reviews/23143/index1.html.

50. Owen Gleiberman, 'Flags of Our Fathers', *Entertainment Weekly, EW.com* (18 October 2007) http://www.ew.com/ew/article/ 0,,1547538,00.html.

51. Edelstein, 'Mommy Weirdest'.

52. Stephen Hunter, 'Under the Sands of Iwo Jima', *The Washington Post, washing-tonpost.com* (12 January 2007) http://www.washingtonpost.com/wp-dyn/con-tent/article/2007/01/11/AR2007011102203.html. See also A. O. Scott, 'Blurring the Line in the Bleak Sands of Iwo Jima', *New York Times, nytimes.com* (20 December 2006) http://movies2.nytimes.com/2006/12/20/movies/20lett.html? ref= movies para. 6.

53. Ableism, like racism, sexism, and classism, is an unfounded, harmful prejudice – in this case against persons with physical or mental impairments or any non-normative bodily condition. *Million Dollar Baby* (2004) deals with the issue of

serious physical impairment only from an able-bodied perspective, as do most Hollywood films: its final action reinforces the typical able-bodied attitude toward major impairment – 'if that happened to me, I'd kill myself', – and releases the protagonist from the burden of having to care long-term for a seriously disabled young woman. Likewise he is spared the morally unsavoury position of leaving her behind, as the film emphatically allocates the decision to end her life to the young woman herself. Again, this is a classic Hollywood formula that outrages persons with severe impairments – the vast majority of whom choose to continue life and expect full acceptance in the social realm.

54. See Mitchell Landsberg, 'Fifty Years Later, Iwo Jima Photographer Fights His Own Battle', *Associated Press* http://www.ap.org/pages/ about/pulitzer/ rosenthal.html.
55. Edward T. Linenthal, 'Anatomy of a Controversy', *History Wars: The Enola Gay and Other Battles for the American Past*, ed. Edward T. Linenthal and Tom Engelhardt (New York: Henry Holt, 1996), p. 11.
56. Cited in Linenthal, 'Anatomy of a Controversy', p. 16.
57. John T. Correll, 'The Smithsonian and the Enola Gay: A Retrospective on the Controversy 10 Years Later', *Enola Gay: An Air Force Association Special Page* (April 2004) http://www.afa.org/new_root/ EnolaGay/theReport.asp.
58. Christopher Knight, 'A Memorial to Forget', *Los Angeles Times*, *National Coalition to Save Our Mall* (23 May 2004) http://www. savethemall.org/ updates/20040624.html.

Bibliography

General

Gar Alperovitz, *Atomic Diplomacy: Hiroshima and Potsdam* (New York: Penguin, [1965] 1985).

Stephen E. Ambrose, *Band of Brothers: E Company, 506th Regiment, 101st Airborne from Normandy to Hitler's Eagle's Nest* (New York: Simon and Schuster, [1992] 2001).

Stephen E. Ambrose, *D-Day: June 6, 1944: The Climactic Battle of World War II* (New York: Simon and Schuster, 1995).

Stephen E. Ambrose, *The Wild Blue: The Men and Boys Who Flew the B-24s over Germany, 1944–1945* (New York: Simon and Schuster, 2001).

Karen Anderson, *Wartime Women: Sex Roles, Family Relations, and the Status of Women During World War II* (Westport, CT: Greenwood Press, 1981).

Hannah Arendt, 'The Concentration Camps', *Partisan Review* 15 (7) (July 1948), pp. 743–63.

Hannah Arendt, 'German Guilt', *Essays in Understanding: 1930–1954*, ed. Jerome Kohn (New York: Harcourt, Brace, and Company, [1945] 1994), pp. 121–32.

Philip D. Beidler, *The Good War's Greatest Hits: World War II and American Remembering* (Athens, GA: University of Georgia Press, 1998).

Judith A. Bellafaire, 'The Women's Army Corps: A Commemoration of World War II Service', CMH Publication 72-15, CMH Online, *U.S. Army Center for Military History* (17 February 2005) http://www.army.mil/cmh-pg/brochures/wac/wac.htm

John Morton Blume, *V was for Victory: Politics and American Culture During World War II* (New York: Harcourt, Brace, Jovanovich, 1976).

Paul Boyer, *By the Bomb's Early Light: American Thought and Culture at the Dawn of the Atomic Age* (New York: Pantheon, 1985).

Tom Brokaw, *The Greatest Generation* (New York: Random House, 1998).

Tom Brokaw, *The Greatest Generation Speaks: Letters and Reflections* (New York: Random House, 1999).

Earl Brown, 'American Negroes and the War', *Harpers* (April 1942), pp. 545–52.

D'Ann Campbell, *Women at War with America: Private Lives in a Patriotic Era* (Cambridge, MA: Harvard University Press, 1984).

Horace R. Cayton, 'Fighting for White Folks?', *The Nation* (26 September 1942), pp. 267–70.

John C. Chalberg, *Isolationism: Opposing Viewpoints* (San Diego, CA: Greenhaven Press, 1995).

John T. Correll, 'The Smithsonian and the Enola Gay: A Retrospective on the Controversy 10 Years Later', *Enola Gay: An Air Force Association Special Page* (April 2004) http://www.afa.org/new_root/EnolaGay/theReport. asp

Norman Cousins, *Modern Man is Obsolete* (New York: The Viking Press, 1945).

St Clair Drake and Horace R. Cayton, *Black Metropolis: A Study of Negro Life in a Northern City* (New York: Harcourt, Brace, and Company, 1945).

W. E. B. Du Bois, *Color and Democracy: Colonies and Peace* (New York: Harcourt, Brace, and Company, 1945).

W. E. B. Du Bois, *Dusk of Dawn: An Essay toward an Autobiography of a Race Concept*, intro. Irene Diggs (New Brunswick: Transaction Publishers, [1940] 1997).

T. G. Fraser, and Donette Murray, *America and the World Since 1945* (Basingstoke: Palgrave Macmillan, 2002).

Erich Fromm, *Escape from Freedom* (New York: Rinehart and Company, 1941).

Erich Fromm, *Man for Himself: An Inquiry into the Psychology of Ethics* (New York: Rinehart and Company, 1947).

Paul Fussell, *Wartime: Understanding and Behavior in the Second World War* (New York: Oxford University Press, 1989).

Henry Louis Gates Jr, and Cornel West, *The African American Century: How Black Americans Have Shaped Our Country* (New York: Free Press, 2000).

Donald Porter Geddes (ed.), *The Atomic Age Opens* (Cleveland: Forum/World Publishing, 1945).

David Gelernter, *1939: The Lost World of the Fair* (New York: Avon Books, 1995).

Sherna Berger Gluck, *Rosie the Riveter Revisited: Women, the War, and Social Change* (Boston: Twayne, 1987).

William S. Graebner, *The Age of Doubt: American Thought and Culture in the 1940s* (Boston: Twayne, 1991).

John Hersey, 'Hiroshima', *The New Yorker* (31 August 1946), pp. 15–68.

Paul Sothe Holbo (ed.), *Isolationism and Interventionism, 1932–1941* (Chicago: Rand McNally, 1967).

Maureen Honey, *Creating Rosie the Riveter: Class, Gender, and Propaganda during World War II* (Amherst: University of Massachusetts Press, 1984).

Langston Hughes, Milton Meltzer, and L. Eric Lincoln, *A Pictorial History of Black Americans* (New York: Crown, 1956).

Manfred Jonas, *Isolationism in America, 1935–1941* (Ithaca, NY: Cornell University Press, 1966).

Kevin Allen Leonard, ' "Brothers under the Skin?": African Americans, Mexican Americans, and World War II in California' in *The Way We Really Were: The Golden State in the Second Great War*, ed. Roger W. Lotchin (Urbana: University of Illinois Press, 2000), pp. 187–214.

Robert J. Lifton, *Death in Life: Survivors of Hiroshima* (New York: Basic Books, 1967).

Edward T. Linenthal, 'Anatomy of a Controversy' in *History Wars: The Enola Gay and Other Battles for the American Past*, ed. Edward T. Linenthal and Tom Engelhardt (New York: Henry Holt, 1996), pp. 9–62.

Richard R. Lingeman, *Don't You Know there's a War On?: The American Home Front, 1941–1945* (New York: Putnam/Perigee, 1970).

Walter Lippmann, *The Cold War: A Study in US Foreign Policy* (New York: Harper and Brothers, 1947).

Henry R. Luce, 'The American Century', *Life* (17 February 1941), pp. 61–5.

Henry R. Luce, 'The Day of Wrath', *Life* (22 December 1941), pp. 11–12.

Ferdinand Lundberg and Marynia F. Farnham, *Modern Woman: The Lost Sex* (New York: Harper and Brothers, 1947).

Dwight McDonald, 'A Theory of Mass Culture' in *Mass Culture: The Popular Arts in America*, ed. Bernard Rosenberg and David Manning White (Glencoe, IL: Free Press, [1953] 1957).

Eric Matthews, *Twentieth-Century French Philosophy* (Oxford: Oxford University Press, 1996).

Elaine Tyler May, *Homeward Bound: American Families in the Cold War Era* (New York: Basic Books, 1988).

Francis E. Merrill, *Social Problems and the Homefront: A Study of War-time Influences* (New York: Harper and Brothers, 1948).

Steven Mintz and Susan Kellogg, *Domestic Revolutions: A Social History of American Family Life* (New York: Free Press, 1988).

Lewis Mumford, *The Condition of Man* (New York: Harcourt, Brace, and Company, 1944).

Lewis Mumford, *Faith for Living* (New York: Harcourt, Brace, and Company, 1940).

Gunnar Myrdal, *An American Dilemma: The Negro Problem and Modern Democracy* (New York: Harper and Brothers Publishers, 1944).

John Ospital, *We Wore Jump Boots and Baggy Pants* (Aptos, CA: Willow House, 1977).

Richard H. Pells, *The Liberal Mind in a Conservative Age: American Intellectuals in the 1940s and 1950s* (New York: Harper and Row, 1985).

Geoffrey Perrett, *Days of Sadness, Years of Triumph: The American People 1939–1945* (New York: Coward, McCann, and Geoghegan, Inc., 1973).

Richard H. Polenberg, *War and Society: The United States 1914–1945* (Philadelphia: J. B. Lippincott, 1972).

George H. Roeder Jr, *The Censored War: American Visual Experience During World War II* (New Haven, Yale University Press, 1993).

George H. Roeder Jr, 'Censoring Disorder: American Visual Imagery of World War II' in *The War in American Culture: Society and Consciousness During World War II*, ed. Lewis A. Erenberg and Susan E. Hirsch (Chicago: University of Chicago Press, 1996), pp. 46–70.

Donald I. Rogers, *Since You Went Away* (New Rochelle, NY: Arlington House, 1973).

Andy Rooney, *My War* (New York: Public Affairs, [1995] 2000).

Emily Rosenberg, *A Date Which Will Live: Pearl Harbor in American Memory* (Durham, NC: Duke University Press, 2003).

Robert Shaffer, 'Pearl S. Buck and the East and West Association: The Trajectory and Fate of "Critical Internationalism", 1940–1950', *Peace & Change* 28 (1) (2003), pp. 1–36.

Michael S. Sherry, *Preparing for the Next War: American Plans for Postwar Defense, 1941–45* (New Haven: Yale University Press, 1977).

Alice Kimball Smith, *A Peril and a Hope: The Scientists' Movement in America, 1945–47* (Chicago: University of Chicago Press, 1965).

Henry L. Stimson, 'The Decision to Use the Atom Bomb', *Harpers* 194 (February, 1947), pp. 97–107.

I. F. Stone, *Underground to Palestine* (New York: Pantheon Books, [1946] 1978).

Studs Terkel, *The 'Good War': An Oral History of World War II* (New York: Pantheon, 1984).

Arthur Verge, 'Daily Life in Wartime California' in *The Way We Really Were: The Golden State in the Second Great War*, ed. Roger W. Lotchin (Urbana: University of Illinois Press, 2000), pp. 13–29.

Jessica Wang, *American Science in an Age of Anxiety: Scientists, Anticommunism, and the Cold War* (Durham: University of North Carolina Press, 1999).

Walter White, *A Rising Wind* (Garden City, NY: Doubleday, Doran, and Company, 1945).

Walter White, *A Man Called White: The Autobiography of Walter White* (New York: The Viking Press, 1948).

Wendell Willkie, *One World* (New York: Simon and Schuster, 1943).

Allan M. Winkler, *The Politics of Propaganda: The Office of War Information, 1942–1945* (New Haven: Yale University Press, 1978).

Scott K. Wong, 'War Comes to Chinatown: Social Transformation and the Chinese of California' in *The Way We Really Were: The Golden State in the Second Great War*, ed. Roger W. Lotchin (Urbana: University of Illinois Press, 2000), pp. 164–86.

Philip Wylie, *A Generation of Vipers* (New York: Dalkey Archive Press, [1942] 1996).

Fiction and Journalism

James L. Baughman, *Henry Luce and the Rise of the American News Media* (Boston: Twayne / G. K. Hall, 1987).

Malcolm Bradbury, *The Modern American Novel* (Oxford: Oxford University Press, 1983).

Cleanth Brooks, *The Well-Wrought Urn: Studies in the Structure of Poetry* (New York: Reynal and Hitchcock, 1947).

Cleanth Brooks and Robert Penn Warren, *Understanding Fiction* (New York: F. S. Crofts and Company, [1943] 1946).

Kathleen A. Cairns, *Front-Page Women Journalists, 1920–1950* (Lincoln: University of Nebraska Press, 2003).

Keith Clark, 'A Distaff Dream Deferred?: Ann Petry and the Art of Subversion', *African American Review* 26 (1992), pp. 495–505.

Malcolm Cowley, *The Portable Faulkner* (New York: The Viking Press [1946], 1954).

Christopher C. De Santis (ed.), 'Adventures of a Social Writer: 1940–1949', *Dictionary of Literary Biography, Vol. 315: Langston Hughes: A Documentary Volume* (Detroit: Thomson-Gale, 2005), pp. 162–212.

W. E. B. Du Bois, *Newspaper Columns: Vol. 2, 1945–61*, ed. Herbert Aptheker (White Plains, NY: Kraus-Thomson Organization Limited, 1986), p. 670.

Chester E. Eisinger, *Fiction of the Forties* (Chicago: University of Chicago Press, 1963).

William Faulkner, *Selected Letters*, ed. William Blotner (New York: Random House, 1977).

Desmond Harding, 'The Power of Place: Richard Wright's *Native Son*', *CLA Journal* 40 (3) (1997), pp. 367–79.

Trudier Harris, 'Native Sons and Foreign Daughters', *New Essays on* Native Son, ed. Keneth Kinnamon (Cambridge: Cambridge University Press, 1990), pp. 63–84.

Donna Akiba Sullivan Harper, *Not So Simple: The 'Simple' Stories by Langston Hughes* (Columbia, MO: Columbia University Press, 1995).

Tony Hilfer, *American Fiction since 1940* (London: Longman, 1992).

Irving Howe, 'Black Boys and Native Sons', *Dissent* 10 (4) (1963), pp. 353–68.

Samuel Hynes, et al., *Reporting World War II: Part I, American Journalism 1938–1944* (New York: The Library of America, 1995).

Samuel Hynes, et al., *Reporting World War II: Part II, American Journalism 1944–1946* (New York: The Library of America, 1995).

Frederick R. Karl, *American Fictions, 1940–1980: A Comprehensive and Critical Evaluation* (New York: Harper and Row, 1983).

Harry L. Katz, 'About Herblock', *Herblock's History: Political Cartoons from the Crash to the Millennium* http://www.loc.gov/rr/print/swann/ herblock/about. html.

Matthew Lessig, 'Class, Characters, and Croppers: Faulkner's Snopeses and the Plight of the Sharecropper', *Arizona Quarterly* 55 (5) (Winter 1999), pp. 79–113.

Bill Mauldin, *Up Front* (New York: Henry Holt and Company, 1944).

Bill Mauldin, *This Damn Tree Leaks: A Collection of War Cartoons* (Italy: Rpt from *The Stars and Stripes – Mediterranean*, 1945).

Paul Milkman, *PM: A New Deal in Journalism, 1940–1948* (New Brunswick, NJ: Rutgers University Press, 1997).

Lee G. Miller, *An Ernie Pyle Album: Indiana to Ie Shima* (New York: William Sloane Associates, 1946).

Richard H. Minear, *Dr. Seuss Goes to War: The World War II Editorial Cartoons of Theodore Seuss Geisel* (New York: W. W. Norton and Company, 1999).

Frank Luther Mott, *American Journalism – A History of Newspapers in the United States Through 260 Years: 1690 to 1950*, rev. edn (New York: MacMillan, 1950).

Philip Nel, *Dr. Seuss: American Icon* (New York: Continuum, 2004).

The New Yorker Book of War Pieces (New York: Reynal and Hitchcock, 1947).

Arnold Rampersad, 'Introduction', *Native Son* by Richard Wright (New York: Perennial Classics, 1998).

John Crowe Ransom, *The New Criticism* (Norfolk, CT: New Directions, 1941).

David Reed, *The Popular Magazine in Britain and the United States 1880–1960* (London: The British Library, 1997).

Sam G. Riley, *Biographical Dictionary of American Newspaper Columnists* (Westport, CT: Greenwood Press, 1995).

Steve Rothman, 'The Publication of "Hiroshima" in *The New Yorker*' (8 January 1997) http://www.herseyhiroshima.com/hiro.php.

James Smethurst, 'Invented by Horror: The Gothic and African American Literary Ideology in *Native Son*', *African American Review* 35 (1) (2001), pp. 29–40.

A. M. Sperber, *Murrow: His Life and Times* (New York: Fordham University Press, 1998).

Roger Starr, '*PM*: New York's Highbrow Tabloid', *City Journal* 3 (3) (1993) http://city-journal.org/article02.php?aid=1480.

James Tobin, *Ernie Pyle's War: America's Eyewitness to World War II* (New York: The Free Press, 1997).

Aurora Wallace, *Newspapers and the Making of Modern America: A History* (Westport, CT: Greenwood Press, 2005).

Patrick Washburn, *A Question of Sedition: The Federal Government's Investigation of the Black Press During World War II* (New York: Oxford University Press, 1986).

Elizabeth A. Wheeler, *Uncontained: Urban Fiction in Postwar America* (New Brunswick, NJ: Rutgers University Press, 2001).

William F. Yurasako, 'The Pittsburgh Courier During World War II: An Advocate for Freedom', *VV Campaign.org* http://www.yurasako.net/ vv/courier.html.

Mary Ellen Zuckerman, *A History of Popular Women's Magazines in the United States, 1792–1995* (Westport, CT: Greenwood Press, 1998).

Radio and Music

Eric Barnouw, *The Golden Web: A History of Broadcasting in the United States, Vol. II – 1933 to 1953* (New York: Oxford University Press, 1968).

Jack Benny and Joan Benny, *Sunday Nights at Seven: The Jack Benny Story* (New York: Warner Books, 1990).

Mary Livingstone Benny and Hilliard Marks with Marcia Borie, *Jack Benny* (Garden City, NY: Doubleday, 1978).

Frank Buxton, 'This is Bob "Camp Roberts' Hope". . .: Bob Hope on the Radio', *Bob Hope: A Half Century of Radio and Television* (N.P.: Museum of Broadcasting, 1986), pp. 9–21.

Stanley Cloud and Lynne Olson, *The Murrow Boys: Pioneers on the Front Lines of Broadcast Journalism* (Boston: Houghton Mifflin Company, 1996).

Ronald D. Cohen, 'Music Goes to War: California, 1940–45', *The Way We Really Were: The Golden State in the Second World War*, ed. Roger W. Lotchin (Urbana: University of Illinois Press, 2000), pp. 47–67.

Don Cusic, 'Gene Autry in World War II', *Country Music Goes to War*, ed. Charles K. Wolfe and James E. Akenson (Lexington: University Press of Kentucky, 2005), pp. 43–57.

Wayne W. Daniel, 'Hayloft Patriotism: The *National Barn Dance* during World War II', *Country Music Goes to War*, ed. Charles K. Wolfe and James E. Akenson (Lexington: University Press of Kentucky, 2005), pp. 81–101.

Lewis A. Erenberg, *Swingin' the Dream: Big Band Jazz and the Rebirth of American Culture* (Chicago: University of Chicago Press, 1998).

Irving Fang, *Those Radio Commentators!* (Ames, IA: Iowa State University Press, 1977).

Jean Folkerts and Dwight L. Teeter, *Voices of a Nation: A History of the Media in the United States* (New York: MacMillan, 1989).

Ted Gottfried, *The American Media* (New York: Impact/Franklin Watts, 1992).

Jim Heintze, 'Biography of Drew Pearson', *American University Library Special Collections Unit* http://www.library.american.edu/pearson/biography.html.

Michele Hilmes, *Radio Voices: American Broadcasting, 1922–1952* (Minneapolis: University of Minnesota Press, 1997).

Bob Hope, *I Never Left Home* (New York: Simon and Schuster, 1944).

David Hopkins, 'To Be or Not to Bop: Jack Kerouac's *On the Road* and the Culture of Bebop and Rhythm 'n' Blues', *Popular Music* 24 (2) (2005), pp 279–86.

Peter W. Kaplan, 'Hey, How About that Bob Hope?' in *Bob Hope: A Half Century of Radio and Television* (N.P.: Museum of Broadcasting, 1986), pp. 23–32.

Lawrence McClellan Jr, *The Later Swing Era: 1942 to 1955* (Westport, CT: Greenwood Press, 2004).

Allison McCracken, 'Scary Women and Scarred Men: *Suspense*, Gender Trouble, and Postwar Change, 1942–1950 in *Radio Reader: Essays in the Cultural History of*

Radio, ed. Michele Hilmes and Jason Loviglio (New York: Routledge, 2002), pp. 183–207.

J. Fred MacDonald, *Don't Touch that Dial!: Radio Programming in American Life, 1920–1960* (Chicago: Nelson-Hall, 1979).

Margaret T. McFadden, 'America's Boy Friend Who Can't Get a Date: Gender, Race, and the Cultural Work of the Jack Benny Program, 1932–1946', *Journal of American History* 80 (1) (1993), pp. 113–34.

Elizabeth McLeod, *The Original Amos 'n' Andy: Freeman Gosden, Charles Correll, and the 1928–43 Radio Serial* (Jefferson, NC: McFarland and Company, 2005).

Edward R. Murrow, *In Search of Light: The Broadcasts of Edward R. Murrow, 1938–1961*, ed. Edward J. Bliss Jr (New York: Alfred A. Knopf, 1967).

Gerald Nachman, *Raised on Radio* (New York: Pantheon Books, 1998).

Paul Oliver, *The Story of the Blues* (Boston: Northeastern University Press, [1969] 1997).

Michael Pitts and Frank Hoffmann, assisted by Dick Carty and Jim Bedoian, *The Rise of the Crooners* (Lanham, MD: Scarecrow Press, 2002).

Henry Pleasants, *The Great American Popular Singers* (New York: Simon and Schuster, 1974).

Peter J. Silvester, *A Left Hand Like God: A History of Boogie-Woogie Piano* (New York: Da Capo Press, 1988).

George T. Simon, *The Big Bands* 4th edn (New York: Schirmer Books, 1981).

Kathleen E. R. Smith, *God Bless America: Tin Pan Alley Goes to War* (Lexington: University Press of Kentucky, 2003).

Sherry Tucker, *Swing Shift: 'All-Girl' Bands of the 1940s* (Durham, NC: Duke University Press, 2000).

Charles K. Wolfe, '"Jesus Hits Like an Atom Bomb": Nuclear Warfare in Country Music, 1944–56' in *Country Music Goes to War*, ed. Charles K. Wolfe and James E. Akenson (Lexington: University Press of Kentucky, 2005), pp. 102–25.

Scott Yanow, *Bebop* (San Francisco: Miller Freeman Books, 2000).

Drama and Film

Thomas P. Adler, *American Drama, 1940–1960: A Critical History* (New York: Twayne, 1994).

'American Negro Theater formed', *African American Registry* http://www.aaregistry. com/african_american_history/223/American_Negro_ Theater_formed.

'American Theatre Wing History', *American Theatre Wing* http://americantheatrew-ing.org/about/history_of_atw.php.

'Anna Lucasta Opens on Broadway', *African American Registry* http://www.aareg-istry.com/african_american_history/1809/Anna_Lucasta_opens_on_Broadway.

Harry Benshoff and Sean Griffin, *America on Film: Representing Race, Class, Gender, and Sexuality at the Movies* (Malden, MA: Blackwell Publishing, 2004).

Gerald M. Berkowitz, *American Drama of the 20th Century* (London: Longman, 1992).

Andrew Britton, '*The Lady from Shanghai*: Betrayed by Rita Hayworth', *The Movie Book of Film Noir*, ed. Ian Cameron (London: Studio Vista, 1992), pp. 213–21.

Paul Buhle and Dave Wagner, *Hide in Plain Sight: The Hollywood Blacklistees in Film and Television, 1950–2002* (New York: Palgrave Macmillan, 2003).

Larry Ceplair and Steven Englund, *The Inquisition in Hollywood: Politics in the Film Community, 1930–1960* (Urbana, IL: University of Illinois Press, [1979] 2003).

'Comic Culture', *Time* 18 December 1944. *Time Archive* http://www. time.com/ time/magazine/article/0,9171,778319,00.html.

Bernard F. Dick, *The Star-Spangled Screen: The American World War II Film* (Lexington: The University Press of Kentucky, 1985).

Bernard F. Dick, *Radical Innocence: A Critical Study of the Hollywood Ten* (Lexington: The University Press of Kentucky, 1989).

Winston Wheeler Dixon, 'Introduction: Movies and the 1940s' in *American Cinema of the 1940s: Themes and Variations*, ed. Wheeler Winston Dixon (New Brunswick, NJ: Rutgers University Press, 2006), pp. 1–21.

Thomas Doherty, *Projections of War: Hollywood, American Culture, and World War II* (New York: Columbia University Press, 1993).

Stanley Green, *The World of Musical Comedy* (New York: Ziff-Davis Publishing Company, 1960).

Leighton Grist, 'Moving Targets and Black Widows: Film Noir in Modern Hollywood', *The Movie Book of Film Noir*, ed. Ian Cameron (London: Studio Vista, 1992). 267–85.

James V. Hatch, 'Chapter 11 – Creeping Toward Integration' in *A History of African American Theatre* by Errol G. Hill and James V. Hatch, Cambridge Studies in American Theatre and Drama (Cambridge: Cambridge University Press, 2003), pp. 335–74.

Clayton R. Koppes and Gregory D. Black, *Hollywood Goes to War: How Politics, Profits, and Propaganda Shaped World War II Movies* (New York: Free Press, 1987).

Sarah Kozloff, '1941- Movies on the Edge of War' in *American Cinema of the 1940s: Themes and Variations*, ed. Wheeler Winston Dixon (New Brunswick, NJ: Rutgers University Press, 2006), pp. 48–73.

Abe Laufe, *Broadway's Greatest Musicals* (New York: Funk and Wagnalls, 1969).

Gerald Mast, *A Short History of the Movies* (Indianapolis: Pegasus/Bobbs Merrill, 1971).

Gerald Mast, *Can't Help Singin': The American Musical on Stage and Screen* (Woodstock, NY: Overlook Press, 1987).

Lary May, 'Making the American Consensus: The Narrative of Conversion and Subversion in World War II Films' in *The War in American Culture: Society and Consciousness During World War II*, ed. Lewis A. Erenberg and Susan E. Hirsch (Chicago: University of Chicago Press, 1996), pp. 71–102.

Ethan Mordden, *The American Theatre* (New York: Oxford University Press, 1981).

Ethan Mordden, *The Hollywood Studios: House Style in the Golden Age of the Movies* (New York: Knopf, 1988).

Ethan Mordden, *Beautiful Mornin': The Broadway Musical in the 1940s* (New York: Oxford University Press, 1999).

Joe Morella, Edward Z. Epstein, and John Griggs, *The Films of World War II* (Secaucus, NJ: Citadel Press, 1973).

James Naremore, *More than Night: Film Noir and its Contexts* (Berkeley: University of California Press, 1998).

R. Barton Palmer, *Hollywood's Dark Cinema: The American Film Noir* (New York: Twayne, 1994).

Lawrence J. Quirk, *The Great War Films: From* The Birth of a Nation *to Today* (New York: Citadel Press, 1994).

Peter Roffman and Jim Purdy, *The Hollywood Social Problem Film: Madness, Despair, and Politics from the Depression to the Fifties* (Bloomington: Indiana University Press, 1981).

Thomas Schatz, *The Genius of the System: Hollywood Filmmaking in the Studio Era* (New York: Metro/Henry Holt, 1988).

Thomas Schatz, *Boom and Bust: American Cinema in the 1940s* (Berkeley: University of California Press, 1999).

Sam P. Simone, *Hitchcock as Activist: Politics and the War Films* (Ann Arbor: UMI Research Press, 1985).

Robert Sklar, *Movie-Made America: A Cultural History of American Movies* rev. edn (New York: Random House, [1975] 1994).

Michael Walker, 'Film Noir: Introduction', *The Movie Book of Film Noir*, ed. Ian Cameron (London: Studio Vista, 1992), pp. 8–38.

Allen Woll, *The Hollywood Musical Goes to War* (Chicago: Nelson-Hall, 1983).

Allen Woll, *Black Musical Theatre: From* Coontown *to* Dreamgirls (Baton Rouge: Louisiana State University Press, 1989).

Visual Arts

John I. H. Baur, 'Part Two: 1940–1960' in *American Art of Our Century* by Lloyd Goodrich and John I.H. Baur (New York: Praeger, 1961).

Romare Bearden and Harry Henderson, *A History of African-American Artists, from 1792 to the Present* (New York: Pantheon, 1993).

Laura Claridge, *Norman Rockwell: A Life* (New York: Random House, 2001).

Wanda M. Corn, 'Ways of Seeing' in *Norman Rockwell: Pictures for the American People,* ed. Maureen Hart Hennessey and Anne Knutson (New York: Harry N. Abrams, Inc., 1999), pp. 81–94.

Mary Dearborn, *Mistress of Modernism: The Life of Peggy Guggenheim* (Boston: Houghton Mifflin, 2004).

Cedric Dover, *American Negro Art* (Greenwich, CT: New York Graphic Society, [1960] 1969).

Mitra C. Emad, 'Reading Wonder Woman's Body: Mythologies of Gender and Nation', *The Journal of Popular Culture* 39 (6) (2006), pp. 954–84.

Anthony Everitt, *Abstract Expressionism* (Woodbury, NY: Barron's, [1975] 1978).

Anton Gill, *Art Lover: A Biography of Peggy Guggenheim* (New York: HarperCollins, 2002).

Clement Greenberg, 'Avant-Garde and Kitsch', *Mass Culture: The Popular Arts in America*, ed. Bernard Rosenberg and David Manning White (Glencoe, IL: Free Press, [1946] 1957).

Robert C. Harvey, *The Art of the Comic Book: An Aesthetic History* (Jackson: University Press of Mississippi, 1996).

Josef Helfenstein, 'Preface' in *Bill Traylor, William Edmondson, and the Modernist*

Impulse, ed. Josef Helfenstein and Roxanne Stanulis (Champaign: University of Illinois Press, 2004), pp. 7–9.

Steven Heller, 'Rebelling Against Rockwell' in *Norman Rockwell: Pictures for the American People*, ed. Maureen Hart Hennessey and Anne Knutson (New York: Harry N. Abrams, Inc., 1999), pp. 169–83.

Steven Heller and Louise Fili, *Cover Story: The Art of American Magazine Covers, 1900–1950* (San Francisco: Chronicle Books, 1996).

Maureen Hart Hennessey, 'The Four Freedoms' in *Norman Rockwell: Pictures for the American People*, ed. Maureen Hart Hennessey and Anne Knutson (New York: Harry N. Abrams, Inc., 1999), pp. 95–104.

Patricia Hills, *Modern Art in the USA: Issues and Controversies of the 20th Century* (Upper Saddle River, NJ: Prentice Hall, 2001).

Jane Kallir, *The World of Grandma Moses* (Baltimore: Garamond Pridemark, 1984).

Anne Classen Knutson, 'Andrew Wyeth's Language of Things' in *Andrew Wyeth: Memory and Magic* (Atlanta: High Museum of Art, 2005), pp. 45–83.

Jane Livingston and John Beardsley, *Black Folk Art in America, 1930–1980* (Jackson: University Press of Mississippi, 1982).

Alaine Locke, *The Negro in Art: A Pictorial Record of the Negro Artist and of the Negro Theme in Art* (New York: Hacker Art Books, [1940] 1979).

Edward Lucie-Smith, *Visual Arts in the Twentieth Century* (New York: Harry N. Abrams, [1996] 1997).

Edward Lucie-Smith, *Lives of the Great 20th-Century Artists* (London: Thames and Hudson, 1999).

Edward Lucie-Smith, *Movements in Art Since 1945* (London: Thames and Hudson, [1969] 2001).

Barbara McCloskey, *Artists of World War II*, Artists of an Era series (Westport, CT: Greenwood Press, 2005).

Susan E. Meyer, *America's Great Illustrators* (New York: Harry N. Abrams, 1978).

Laurie Norton Moffatt, 'The People's Painter' in *Norman Rockwell: Pictures for the American People*, ed. Maureen Hart Hennessey and Anne Knutson (New York: Harry N. Abrams, Inc., 1999), pp. 23–8.

Eleanor Munro, *Originals: American Women Artists*, new edn (New York: Da Capo Press, 2000).

Loredana Parmesani, *Art of the Twentieth Century: Movements, Theories, Schools, and Tendencies 1900–2000* (Milan: Skira Editore, 1998).

Phil Patton, 'High Singing Blue: Bill Traylor', Catalogue Essay, Hirshl and Adler Modern (1996), *Phil Patton* http://www.philpatton.com/traylor. html.

James A. Porter, *Modern Negro Art* (New York: Arno Press, [1943] 1969).

Allen Rankin, 'He Lost 10,000 Years', *Collier's* (22 June 1946), n.p.

Walt Reed, *The Illustrator in America, 1900–1960s* (New York: Reinhold, 1966).

Reinhold Reitberger and Wolfgang Fuchs, *Comics: Anatomy of a Mass Medium* (Boston: Little Brown, 1970).

Ned Rifkin, 'Why Norman Rockwell, Why Now?' in *Norman Rockwell: Pictures for the American People*, ed. Maureen Hart Hennessey and Anne Knutson (New York: Harry N. Abrams, Inc., 1999), pp. 11–16.

William W. Savage Jr, *Comic Books and America, 1945–1954* (Norman, OK: University of Oklahoma Press, 1990).

Lowery Stokes Sims, 'Bill Traylor and William Edmondson and the Challenges to African American Artists Between the World Wars' in *Bill Traylor, William Edmondson, and the Modernist Impulse*, ed. Josef Helfenstein and Roxanne Stanulis (Champaign: University of Illinois Press, 2004), pp. 35–43.

Judith E. Stein, *I Tell My Heart: The Art of Horace Pippin* (Philadelphia: Pennsylvania Academy of the Fine Arts, 1993).

Laurence Tacou-Rumney, *Peggy Guggenheim: A Collector's Album* (Paris: Flammarion, 1996).

Michael R. Taylor, 'Between Realism and Surrealism: The Early Work of Andrew Wyeth' in *Andrew Wyeth: Memory and Magic* (Atlanta: High Museum of Art, 2005), pp. 27–43.

Karole Vail, *Peggy Guggenheim: A Celebration* (New York: Guggenheim Museum, 1998).

Kirk Varnedoe and Adam Gopnik, *High and Low: Modern and Popular Culture* (New York: Harry N. Abrams, Inc., 1990).

Bill Vossler, *Burma-Shave: The Rhymes, the Signs, the Times* (St Cloud, MN: North Star Press, 1997).

Ernest W. Watson, *Forty Illustrators and How They Work* (New York: Watson-Guptill Publications, Inc., [1946] 1953).

Jacqueline Bograd Weld, *Peggy: The Wayward Guggenheim* (New York: E. P. Dutton, 1986).

Ellen Harkins Wheat, *Jacob Lawrence: American Painter* (Seattle: University of Washington Press, 1986).

John Wilmerding, 'Introduction' in *Andrew Wyeth: Memory and Magic* (Atlanta: High Museum of Art, 2005), pp. 15–25.

Bradford W. Wright, *Comic Book Nation: The Transformation of Youth Culture in America* (Baltimore: Johns Hopkins University Press, 2001).

1940s Design and Lifestyle

David J. Cole, Eve Browning, and Fred E. H. Schroeder, *Encyclopedia of Modern Everyday Inventions* (Westport, CT: Greenwood Press, 2003).

Peter Dormer, *Design Since 1945* (London: Thames and Hudson, 1993).

Perry R. Duis, 'No Time for Privacy: World War II and Chicago's Families' in *The War in American Culture: Society and Consciousness During World War II*, ed. Lewis A. Erenberg and Susan E. Hirsch (Chicago: University of Chicago Press, 1996).

Editors of *Consumer Reports*, *I'll Buy That!: 50 Small Wonders and Big Deals that Revolutionized the Lives of Consumers – A Fifty-Year Retrospective* (Mount Vernon, NY: Consumers Union, 1986).

Richard M. Fried, *The Russians Are Coming! The Russians Are Coming!: Pageantry and Patriotism in Cold-War America* (New York: Oxford University Press, 1998).

Catherine Gudis, *Buyways: Billboards, Automobiles, and the American Landscape* (New York: Routledge, 2004).

William J. Hennessey, *Russel Wright: American Designer* (Cambridge, MA: MIT Press, 1983).

Pat Kirkham, *Charles and Ray Eames: Designers of the Twentieth Century* (Cambridge, MA: MIT Press, 1995).

Raymond Loewy, *Never Leave Well Enough Alone* (New York: Simon and Schuster, 1951).

Catherine McDermott, *Designmuseum: 20th-Century Design* (Woodstock, NY: Overlook Press, 2000).

Jeffrey Meilke, 'Into the Fourth Kingdom: Representations of Plastic Materiality, 1920–1950', *Journal of Design History* 5 (3) (1992), pp. 173–82 JSTOR http://links.jstor.org/sici?sici=0952-4649(1992)5%3A3%3C173%3AITFKRO%3E2.0.CO%3B2-6.

Colleen J. Sheehy, *The Flamingo in the Garden: American Yard Art and the Vernacular Landscape* (New York: Garland, 1998).

Penny Sparke, *An Introduction to Design and Culture in the 20th Century* (London: Routledge, 1986).

Stephen van Dulken, *Inventing the 20th Century: 100 Inventions that Shaped the World from the Airplane to the Zipper* (Washington Square, NY: New York University Press, 2000).

Mary Wright and Russel Wright, *Mary and Russel Wright's Guide to Easier Living* (New York: Simon and Schuster, 1951).

Websites of Interest

'The Battle Over *Citizen Kane*', *American Experience*. PBS http://www.pbs.org/wgbh/amex/kane2/.

Faulkner, William. 'Banquet Speech, 1949 Nobel Prize in Literature', *Nobelprize.org*. 17 May 2006 http://nobelprize.org/literature/laureates/1949/faulkner-speech.html.

'History of the Fair: The Design and Marketing of the Future', *The Iconography of Hope: The 1939–1940 New York World's Fair* American Studies Program, University of Virginia, *America in the 1930s* series http://xroads.virginia.edu/~1930s/DISPLAY/39wf/history.htm.

Elizabeth McLeod, 'Old Time Radio's Moments of the Century' http:// www.mid-coast.com/~lizmcl/moments.html

The Radio Hall of Fame http://www.radiohof.org.

'Touring the Future', *The Iconography of Hope: The 1939–1940 New York World's Fair*, American Studies Program, University of Virginia, *America in the 1930s* series http://xroads.virginia.edu/~1930s/DISPLAY/39wf/ taketour.htm.

'Tupperware!' *American Experience* PBS http://www.pbs.org.wgbh/amex/tupper-ware/.

Paul M. Van Dort, 'World's Fair Tour Home Page', *1939 New York World's Fair* http://www.pmphoto.to/WorldsFairTour/home.htm.

'Welcome to Tomorrow', *The Iconography of Hope: The 1939–1940 New York World's Fair*, American Studies Program, University of Virginia, *America in the 1930s* series http://xroads.virginia.edu/~1930s/DISPLAY/ 39wf/welcome.htm.

Index

Abe Lincoln, 152
ableism, 256 n.53
Abbott (Bud) and Costello (Lou) 117
abstract expressionism, 136
Ace, Goodman, 74
Ace, Jane, 74
action painting, 138
Actor's Studio, 110
Adams, Robert McCormick, 221
Ahn, Philip, 119
Air Force, 117
Albers, Josef, 148
The Aldrich Family (aka *Henry Aldrich*), 74,
    76
Alexander, Jane, 223
Algren, Nelson, 37
Allen, Fred, 73, 76
Allen, Gracie, 74, 76
All My Sons, 99, 111–12
All the King's Men (novel), 41–3, 233 n.28
    (film), 43
Almanac Singers (aka The Weavers), 95
'Ambitious Ambrose', 49
Ambrose, Stephen E., 210–11, 213
America First movement, 4, 9, 181
An American Dilemma 13–14
American Modern, 189–91
American Negro Exposition (aka Diamond
    Jubilee Exposition), 147
American Negro Theater, 106–7
'American scene', 136
American Theater Wing, 98–9
Ammons, Albert, 237 n.49
Amos 'n' Andy, 76
Anna's Light, 137
Anderson, Eddie (aka Rochester), 77, 78–9
Anderson, Maxwell, 104

Andrews, Dana, 127
Andrews Sisters, 89
Anna Lucasta, 106–7
Annie Get Your Gun, 103
anti-Semitism, 8, 59, 66, 128
Apocalypse Now, 214
Appalachian Spring, 95
appeasement, 6
Archie comics series, 165–6
Arden, Eve, 73
Arendt, Hannah, 7, 227–8 n.22
Arlen, Harold, 103–4
Armed Service Editions, 45
Armstrong, Louis, 89, 91
Army Signal Corps, 171
Arnaz, Desi, 126
Arnold, Eddie, 94–5
Arsenic and Old Lace, 108
Artists for Victory, 150, 161, 245 n.54
Art of This Century gallery, 142
Artzybasheff, Boris, 161
Ashby, Hal, 214
Asch, Moses, 95
Astaire, Fred, 117, 125, 215
Atherton, Jack, 161, 245 n.54
Atom Man, 165
atomic age, 20–1, 162, 165, 201, 222–3
atomic bombing of Japan, 1, 8, 17–21, 33, 162,
    229 n.54
Atomic Café, 221–3
Atomic Energy Commission, 20
Autry, Gene, 94, 165

Baby Snooks, 74
Bailey, Pearl, 104
Baker, Ernest Hamlin, 161
Baldwin, James, 41

The Baltimore Afro-American, 48
Band of Brothers, 210, 211–14, 215, 255
    n. 42
Barclay, McClelland, 161
The Barracks, 155
Barthé, Richmond, 150–1, 152
Basie, Count, 82, 86–7, 88
Bass, Charlotta, 54
Bataan, 118, 119
Bataán Death March, 211
Batman, 164
Battle of the Bulge (Battle of Bastogne), 59,
    209
Bauhaus school of design, 140, 197
Bay, Michael, 214
Black Mountain College, 148
Bearden, Romare, 145, 146, 168
Beavers, Louise, 125
Beggar's Holiday, 104, 105
Behind the Rising Sun, 119, 120
Being and Nothingness, 6
Belafonte, Harry, 107
Bel Geddes, Norman, 186–7
A Bell for Adano, 38
The Bells of St. Mary's, 124
Bellson, Louie, 85
Bellow, Saul, 34
Bendix, William, 77
Benny, Jack, 73, 76, 77, 78–9, 180
Bergen, Edgar, 73
Bergman, Ingrid, 118
Berlin Airlift, 25, 90
Berlin, Irving, 89, 89, 95, 100, 102, 103, 105,
    180
Bernstein, Leonard, 96, 105, 123
Bertoia, Harry, 196, 197
Bert the Turtle, 223
Bessie, Alvah, 122
The Best Years of Our Lives, 127–8, 129
The Betrothal II, 138
Beulah, 76, 77, 78
Beulah (character), 77
Biberman, Herbert, 122
Bickersons, 74
Biddle, Francis 54
Bienfait, Jean, 198
Biggers, John, 147
Bikini Atoll, 222
Bilbo, Senator Theodore, 58, 78
Bill Haley and the Comets, 238 n.91
biomorphisms, 137
Black Metropolis, 14
Blitz of London, 64, 69–71

Black, Brown, and Beige, 81
The Black Horse, 161
black market, 175, 177, 194, 204–5
Black on Grey, 140
Blanton, Jimmy, 85
Block, Martin, 81
Blood on the Sun, 119
Bloomer Girl, 103, 104
Blue Grass Boys, 93
Blue Poles, 139
Bogart, Humphrey, 118, 125
Bolger, Ray, 100
Booth, Ellen, 197
Booth, George, 197
Born on the Fourth of July, 215
Born Yesterday, 108
Bourgeois, Louise, 243–4 n.10
Bourke-White, Margaret, 59
The Boxer, 150
Boy with Tire, 149
Bracken, Eddie, 117
Bradley, General Omar, 59
Braids, 149
Brando, Marlon, 110, 122
The Breakfast Club, 74, 77
Bridges, Lloyd, 119
Brink, 139
Broadway, 97–8
Brokaw, Tom, 208, 210, 211, 215, 218
Brooks, Cleanth, 35
Brown, Cecil, 64
Brown, Earl, 53
Brown, Les, 82
Bruckheimer, Jerry, 214
Buck, Pearl S., 15, 167
Bulletin of the Atomic Scientists, 20
Bundy, Gilbert, 161
Burma-Shave billboards, 162
Bureau of Motion Pictures, 171
Burns, George, 74, 76
Burst, 139
Buxton, Frank, 89
By Jupiter, 100, 102

Cabin in the Sky (musical play) 102, 103
    (film), 125
Cadmus, Paul, 144
Café Society, 81, 237 n.49
Cagney, James, 116
Cahn, Sammy, 100
Calder, Alexander, 142, 143, 197
The California Eagle, 48, 54
Call Me Mister, 104

Calloway, Cab
Camus, Albert, 7
Cannery Row, 39–40, 232 n.16
Capote, Truman, 45
Capra, Frank, 119, 124, 160
Captain America, 2, 135, 164–5
Captain Marvel, 165
Captain Marvel (character), 164
Captain Waskow, 211
Carmen Jones, 104
Carnegie Hall, 81, 92, 237 n.49
Carothers, Wallace, 187
Carousel, 102
Carter Family, 93
Carver, George Washington, 180
Casablanca, 118, 125
Cassidy, Hopalong, 165
Catlett, Elizabeth, 145, 244–5 n.36
Cat on a Hot Tin Roof, 110
Catch 22, 203–4
Catching the Thanksgiving Turkey, 154
Cathedral, 139
Caught in the Draft, 117
Cayton, Horace R., 14, 228–9 n.42
'Chamber of Horrors', 61, 171
Chamberlain, Neville, 6
Chandler, Raymond, 37
Channing, Carol, 100
Chaplin, Charles, 2, 113, 123
Charwomen in the Theater, 160
Chase, Ilka, 45
Chase, Mary, 108
Chernobyl nuclear power plant, 223
The Chicago Defender, 48, 54–5, 57, 76
Childress, Alice, 107
China, 118
China Marine, 211
The China Syndrome, 223
Christian, Charlie, 86
Christina's World, 149–50
Churchill, Winston, 25–6, 211
Cimino, Michael, 214
Cisco Kid, 80
Citizen Kane, 53, 114–16, 241 n.54
Clara Ward Singers, 93
Clark, Bobby, 100, 102
Clooney, Rosemary, 89
Close, Upton, 66
Coates, Robert, 136
Cobb, Lee J., 112
Colbert, Claudette, 120, 121
cold war, 1, 24–8, 61
The Cold War, 26–8

Cole, Lester, 122
Colonna, Jerry, 90
Color and Democracy, 15
Comden, Betty, 96, 100
Coming Home, 214
Command Decision, 118
Commonweal, 21, 120
*The Communist Conspiracy Against the
    Negroes*, 57
Como, Perry, 89
'Concentration Camps', 7, 227–8 n.22
Coney Island, 187
The Connoisseur, 160
Cooper, Gary, 117, 121, 124
Copland, Aaron, 95–6
Coppola, Francis Ford, 214
Cornell, Katherine, 99, 150
Correll, Charles, 76
Correll, John T., 221
Counterattack, 123
Cousins, Norman, 1, 21–2, 53–4, 230 n.71
Cowley, Malcolm, 36, 43
Crain, Jeanne, 129
Cranbrook Academy of Art, 197
Crawford, Broderick, 107
Crime Does Not Pay, 166
Crosby, Bing, 88, 124, 125
Crosby, Bob, 81
Cross Creek, 45
Crossfire, 128
Crucifixion, 152
Cry Havoc, 121
Cry, the Beloved Country, 104
Cunningham, Sis, 95

Daffy Duck, 118
Dahanos, Steven, 172
Damon, Matt, 215, 216
Dandridge, Dorothy, 54
Dangling Man, 34
Davies, Marion, 115
Davis, Bette, 123–4
Davis, Elmer, 65, 66, 171
Davis, Ossie
Davis, Sammy, 89, 107
Davis, Ulysses, 152
The Day After, 223
Day, Doris, 89, 90
The Day the Earth Stood Still, 67
Death of a Salesman, 111, 112
Death of the Bullfighter, 146
Deception, 124
Deep are the Roots, 106

The Deer Hunter, 214
Dee, Ruby, 107
de Kooning Elaine (née Fried), 138
de Kooning, Willem, 136, 138, 139, 143
Delta Wedding, 44
DeMille, Agnes, 101
Dewey, Thomas, 16–17, 201
Diddley, Bo, 92
Dietrich, Marlene, 99
Disney, Walt, 121, 122, 185
Dogfight Over the Trenches, 155
Domino Players, 155
Don't You Know there's a War On?, 204–5
Doomsday Clock, 20
Dorne, Albert, 160, 161
Dorsey Brothers, 82
Dorsey, Jimmy, 85–6
Dorsey, Rev. Thomas A., 92
Dorsey, Tommy, 84–6, 88
Double V Campaign, 48
Double Indemnity, 131–3, 241 n.54
Douglas, Aaron, 146, 147, 152
Down Argentine Way, 126
Downs, Bill, 65
Draftee Daffy, 118
Drake, St Clair, 14
Dreyfuss, Henry, 186–87, 196
Dr Seuss (aka Theodore Geisel), 4, 9–10
Du Bois, W. E. B. (William Edward
    Burghardt), 15, 17, 21, 24
Duchamp, Marcel, 143
Duck and Cover campaign, 223
Duke, Vernon, 102
Dunham, Katherine, 103
Durham, Eddie, 83
Dusk of Dawn, 15
Dmytryk, Edward, 120, 122

Eames, Charles, 187–8, 196–8
Eames, Ray, 187, 196–8
Eastwood, Clint, 202, 216–20
Edmondson, William, 144, 152, 153–4
Edwards, James, 119
Eichmann in Jerusalem, 7
Einstein, Albert, 19, 24, 185
Elegies to the Spanish Republic, 139
Ellington, Duke, 81, 82, 84–5, 86–7, 104,
    239–40 n.22
Ellison, Ralph, 41
The End of War: Starting Home, 155
Enola Gay exhibit, 220–1
'Everybody's Protest Novel', 41

Executive Order 8802, 10, 12, 48
existentialism, 6–7, 33–4, 37–9, 137

Fabray, Nanette, 100, 103–4
Factory Workers, 146
Fair Deal Program, 17
Faith for Living, 5
Famous Artists correspondence school, 160
Farber, Manny, 125
Farewell, My Lovely, 37
Farmhouse with Airplanes, 152
Farnham, Marynia F., 30–1
Farnsworth House, 142
Father Coughlin, 3, 11, 66
Faulkner, William, 35, 36, 41, 43–4
Fayard Brothers, 104
Federal Arts Project, 136
Feller, Arthur (aka Weegee), 47
Ferrer, Mel, 129
Fibber McGee and Molly, 74–6, 77
The Fighting 69th, 117
film noir, 130–3, 241 n.54
Finnian's Rainbow, 104, 105
Fitzgerald, Ella, 86, 89
Flags of Our Fathers, 202, 216–20
Flatt, Lester, 93
Flynn, Errol, 118
Foggy Mountain Boys, 93
Foley, Red, 94
Follow the Girls, 100, 102
Ford, John, 113
Ford Motor Company, 249 n.32
Foreign Correspondent, 126, 127
For Me and My Gal, 117
For Whom the Bell Tolls, 37
The Fountainhead, 39
Four Freedoms poster series, 135, 158–9, 171
Friedan, Betty, 31
'From Spirituals to Swing', 81, 237 n.49
From this Day Forward, 128
Fromm, Erich, 5, 28
Frozen Sounds No. 1, 139
Fuchs, Klaus, 19
Fugitive Poets, 35
Full Metal Jacket, 215
Fussell, Paul, 172, 202, 204, 206–7, 211, 212,
    214, 215

Gable, Clark, 118
The Gang's All Here, 126
Gardella, Tess 77
Garden in Sochi, 138
Garfield, John, 116, 123–4, 129, 156

Garland, Judy, 125, 215
Garner, James, 151
Gas, 149
Geisel, Theodore (aka Dr Seuss), 4, 9–10
Gelhorn, Martha, 59
A Generation of Vipers, 29
Gentlemen Prefer Blondes, 100
Gentlemen's Agreement, 128
GI Bill of Rights, 28, 184
Gielgud, John, 150
Gilliespie, Dizzy, 92
'Glass House', 142
The Glass Menagerie, 109–10
GM (General Motors), 249 n.32
'God Bless America', 95, 180
Goddard, Paulette, 107, 121
Godfrey, Arthur, 69
Go Down, Moses and Other Stories, 43–4
Going My Way, 124
The Goldbergs, 79
The Golden Apples (1949), 44
Goldwater, Ethel, 31
Gone with the Wind, 113
Goodman, Benny, 81, 82, 84–5, 86–7
Good Neighbor Policy, 114, 126
'The Good War', 202, 226
'*The Good War*' (book), 207–9
Gordon, Dexter, 92
Gorky, Arshile, 136, 137–8, 160
Gosden, Freeman, 76
Gottlieb, Adolph, 139, 146
Gould, Beatrice, 48–9
Gould, Bruce, 48–9
Grable, Betty, 88
Grandma Moses, 144, 154
Grand Ol' Opry, 93
Grant, Cary, 67, 117, 240–1 n.47
Grant, Hedda, 31
The Grapes of Wrath, 113
Grease, 202
Great Britain, 3, 19, 120
The Great Dictator, 2, 113
Great Gildersleeve, 74
The Greatest Generation, 208, 218
Green, Adolph, 96, 100
Greenberg, Clement, 143, 159
Green Grow the Lilacs, 101
Green Hornet, 80
Green Lantern, 165, 166
Gropius, Walter, 140
Grynszpan, Herschel, 65
Guadalcanal Diary (memoir), 45
   (film), 118

Guggenheim, Peggy, 142, 143–4
Guggenheim Museum, 140
Guide to Easier Living, 190–1
Gulf War, 89
Gung Ho, 119
Guthrie, Woody, 95

Hail the Conquering Hero, 117
Hairpin Harmony, 102
Hall, Juanita, 105
Hall, Theodore, 19
Halpert, Edith, 147
The Hamlet, 43
Hammerstein, II, Oscar, 97, 100, 100–2, 104,
   112, 122
Hammett, Dashiell, 123
Hammond, John, 81, 237 n.49
Hampton, Lionel, 82, 86
Hand, Learned, 180
Hanks, Tom, 210, 215, 216
Happy Days, 202
Harburg, Yip, 103–4
Hargrove, Marion, 45
Harmon Foundation, 146, 147
Harmonizing, 155
Hart, Lorenz, 100, 102
Hartung, Philip, 120
Harvey, 108
Harwit, Martin, 221
Hawks, Howard, 240–1 n.47
Hayden, Sterling, 123
Hayworth, Rita, 52, 90, 115
The Heart is a Lonely Hunter, 44–5
Hearst, William Randolph, 53, 55, 114, 115
Heatter, Gabriel, 66, 67–8, 70
Heggen, Thomas, 106
Heller, Joseph, 203–4
Hellman, Lillian, 106, 123
Hemingway, Ernest, 37, 210
Henderson, Fletcher, 83, 86
Henry J. Kaiser, 249 n.32
Hepburn, Katharine, 240–1 n.47
Herblock (aka Herb Block), 58
Herman Miller Furniture Company, 197
Herman, Woody, 82
Hersey, John, 23–4, 38, 219, 235 n.96
Hickey, Margaret, 49
Hicks, Edward, 155
Higgins, Marguerite, 59
High Button Shoes, 100
Hill, Abram, 107
Himes, Chester, 37, 38
Hines, Earl, 82

Hiroshima, 1, 17–19
Hiroshima, 23–4, 219
His Girl Friday, 240–1 n.47
Hitchcock, Alfred, 126–7, 130, 133
Hitler, Adolph, 1, 3, 5–6, 8, 16, 59, 64, 65,
      135, 161, 162, 164, 171, 172, 182, 227–8
      n.22
    annexation of Austria, 3, 64
    annexation of Czechoslovakia, 3, 6, 64, 186
    invasion of Poland, 1, 3, 185–6
Hoffman, Abby, 123
Hoffman, Hans, 197
Holiday, Billie, 86, 89
Holiday Inn, 124, 125
Hollywood Canteen, 123–24
Hollywood Ten, 122
Holme, Celeste, 103
Holy Mountain series, 155–6
Homecoming, 159
Home of the Brave, 119, 128–9
Hooker, Richard, 203
Hoosick Valley, 154
Hoosier Hotshots, 94
Hoover, J. Edgar, 29, 55
Hope, Bob, 73, 74, 76, 88, 89–90, 117
Hopper, Edward, 144, 145, 146, 149, 150
Hopper, Hedda, 55
Horne, Lena, 103, 123
Hospital, 148
Hottlet, Richard C., 64
Houston, Cisco, 95
Howe, Irving, 40
How Green Was My Valley, 114
Howlin' Wolf, 92
HUAC (House Un-American Activities
      Committee), 20, 112, 120, 121–3, 133,
      240 n.44
Hughes, Howard, 185
Hughes, Langston, 57–8, 123
The Human Comedy, 38
Human Torch, 164
Huston, John, 130
Hutchins, Robert M., 4

I am an American Day, 179, 180–1
The Iceman Cometh, 108–9, 110, 111
If He Hollers, Let Him Go, 37
Ignatowski, Ralph, 217
Impedimenta, 149
Ingersoll, Ralph, 46–7, 51
Ingram, Rex, 118
Inner Sanctum, 80
Interior, 155

International Policeman, 165
International Sweethearts of Rhythm, 82–3
Intruder in the Dust (novel), 35, 43–4
      (film), 44, 128–9
Invisible Man, 41
Ireland, John, 107
'Iron Curtain' speech, 25–6
isolationism, 3–8, 58, 65
I, The Jury, 37, 38–9
It's All True, 114
It's a Wonderful Life, 124
Ives, Burl, 95
Iwo Jima, 64

Jackson, Mahalia, 92–3
Jacquet, Illinois, 87
James, Harry, 88
Japan, 17, 19, 21, 61, 120, 174
    racist stereotypes, 8, 77, 119, 133, 162,
      183
Japanese Americans, 16, 17, 55, 56, 119, 181–2
    racist stereotypes, 8
Jarvis, Al, 81
Jesse B. Semple (aka Simple), 57–8
Jesus on the Cross, 152
Jewish state, 25
Joffe, Roland, 214
Johnny Everyman, 165, 166–7
Johnson, Pete, 237 n.49
Johnson, Philip, 142
Johnson Sargent, 152
Johnson, Senator Lyndon, 69
Johnson, William H., 152
John Wayne Adventure Series, 165
Jones, James, 204, 216
Jones, Jennifer, 120
Jones, Louise Mailou, 147
Jordan, Jim (aka Fibber McGee), 76
Jordan, Marion (aka Mollie McGee), 76
Josephson, Barney, 81
Jubilee, 83
Julius Rosenwald Fellowships, 147
Jump for Joy, 239–40 n.22

Kaltenborn, H. V., 64, 66
Kamen, Michael, 214
Kandinsky, Wassily, 137
Kane, Bob, 164
Kanin, Garson, 108
Karamu House, 147
Kaye, Danny, 102
Kazan, Elia, 99, 110, 111, 121–2, 123, 128, 240
      n.44

Kelly, Gene, 117, 125
Kennan, George F., 25–6
Kenton, Stan, 82
Kesselring, Joseph, 108
The Killing Fields, 214
King Biscuit Time, 92
Kirk, Andy, 82
Kiss Me, Kate, 103, 104
kitsch, 159
Kitt, Eartha, 107
Klee, Paul, 137, 143
Knoll, Florence, 196, 197
Knoll, Hans, 196
Kootz collective, 146
Korean War, 1, 61, 89, 165
Krasner, Lee, 243–4 n.10
Krushchev, Nikita, 222
Krupa, Gene, 82, 86, 88
Krystallnacht, 59
Kubrick, Stanley, 215

Ladd, Alan, 117
Ladies Home Journal, 46, 48–9, 50, 59
The Lady From Shanghai, 115
Lady in the Dark, 102
Lake, Veronica, 121
Lancaster, Burt, 123
Landsberg concentration camps, 255 n. 42
Lane, Burton, 104
Langford, Frances, 90
The Last Time I Saw Paris, 45
Lardner, Jr, Ring, 121, 122
Latouche, John, 102
Laughton, Charles, 156
Laurents, Arthur, 119
Lawrence, Jacob, 144, 145, 146, 147–8, 152,
     155, 168, 245 n.49, 245 n.54
Lawson, John Howard, 122, 123
Lead Belly, 95
Leahy, William D., 21
Lee, Canada, 106, 107, 127
Lee, Gypsy Rose, 100
Lee, Peggy, 89
Lee-Smith, Hughie, 149
Lerner, Max, 47, 56
LeSeuer, Larry, 65, 70
Let's Face It!, 102
Letters from Iwo Jima, 202, 216–20
Levitt, William, 188
Levittown, 188–89
Lewis, Jr, Fulton, 66
Lewis, Ira, 55
Lewis, Meade Lux, 237 n.49

Life, 46, 47, 48, 49, 50–3, 139, 142, 161
Lifeboat, 127
Life Goes to War, 207, 214
The Life of Riley, 77
Life With Luigi, 74, 77, 118
Lift Every Voice and Sing, 147
Lifton, Robert J., 24
Lights Out!, 80
Lindbergh, Charles, 4, 9–10
Lingeman, Richard R., 45, 175, 204–6
Lippmann, Walter, 26–8, 51, 56
'Little Boy', 17
Little Lulu, 247 n.109
Loader, Jayne, 221, 222
Locke, Alain, 147
Loesser, Frank, 100
Loewy, Raymond, 188, 198–9
Logan, Joshua, 106
Lomax, Alan, 95
Lombard, Carole, 240–1 n.47
Lone Ranger, 80
Long Day's Journey Into Night, 108, 109
'long telegram', 25–6
Look, 50
Loo, Richard, 119
Lost Boundaries, 128–9
Lost in the Stars, 104
The Lost Weekend, 129
Louis, Joe, 53, 172, 180
Luce, Henry R., 4, 47, 50–3
Lucky Jordan, 117–18
Lucky Strike's Hit Parade, 81
The Lucky Strike Program, 73
     Luke, Keye, 119
Lunceford, Jimmie, 82, 83, 87
Lundberg, Ferdinand, 30–1
Lux Radio Theater, 72–3
Lynes, Russell, 144

MacArthur, General Douglas, 24, 121, 211
Mad Max, 223
The Magnificent Ambersons, 114
Mailer, Norman, 37, 204
Make Believe Ballroom, 80–1
The Maltese Falcon, 114, 130
Maltz, Albert, 122
A Man Called White, 13
Manhattan Project, 18, 20, 21
The Man with the Golden Arm, 37
Ma Perkins, 79
March, Fredric, 127, 240–1 n.47
The March of Time, 72
Marks, Doris, 196

Marshall, General George C., 161
Marshall Plan, 25
Marston, William Moulton, 164
Martin, Mary, 102
Martin, Roberta, 93
Marx, Groucho, 73
M*A*S*H, 203, 205
Mayer, Louis B., 121, 122
Mauldin, Bill, 45, 59–61, 235 n.96
MacLeish, Archibald, 171
McBride, Mary Margaret, 80
McCarthy, Senator Joseph, 26, 49, 55, 64
McCullers, Carson, 35, 44–5
McDaniel, Hattie, 54, 77, 78, 113
McDonald, Dwight, 52
McGovern, George, 210
McMurray, Fred, 132–3
McNeill, Don, 74
The Meeting, 160
Meet John Doe, 124
Meet Me in St. Louis, 125
The Member of the Wedding, 44–5
Mencken, H. L., 57
Mercer, Johnny, 104
Mercury Radio Theater, 115
Merman, Ethel, 101, 102, 103
Merrill, Francis E., 12
Method Acting, 110
Mexican Hayride, 102
Migration series, 147
Milland, Ray, 129
Miller, Arthur, 99, 100, 109, 111–12
Miller, Glenn, 82, 87
Million Dollar Baby, 220
Minnelli, Vincente, 125
Miranda, Carmen, 126
Miró, Joan, 137, 197
Miss Liberty, 103
Mister Roberts, 106
Mix, Tom, 80, 165
mobiles, 142
Molotov–Ribbentrop Pact of 1939, 16
'Modern Man is Obsolete', 21, 54
Modern Negro Art, 147, 152
Modern Woman:, The Lost Sex, 30–1
Monk, Thelonius, 92
Monroe, Bill, 93
Monroe, Marilyn, 100
Montana, Patsy, 94
A Moon For the Misbegotten, 108, 109
Moorehead, Agnes, 80, 115, 120
Motherwell, Robert, 139, 146
Motley, Archibald, 144

Mr. Lucky, 117
Mrs. Miniver, 120
Mt Suribachi, 218
Mueller, Ralph, 255 n. 42
Mumford, Lewis, 5, 28
Munich Agreement/Crisis, 6, 64
Murrow, Edward R., 2, 64, 66, 69–71, 154
Murrow's boys, 64–5
Mussolini, Benito, 8
My Friend Irma, 74
Myrdal, Gunnar, 4, 13–15
The Myth of the Machine, 25
My War, 208–10

NAACP (National Association for the
　Advancement of Colored People), 13, 57
NATO (North Atlantic Treaty
　Organization), 25
Nagasaki, 1, 17–19
Naish, J. Carroll, 77, 118
The Naked and the Dead, 37, 204
National Barn Dance, 93, 94, 174–5
Native Son (novel), 37, 40–1
　(drama), 106
naturalism, 37, 39–40
'The Negro Artist Comes of Age', 244–5 n.36
The Negro in Art, 147
The Negro Looks Ahead, 151
The Negro Soldier, 119, 124
Neel, Alice, 136
Nelson, George, 197
New Criticism, 33, 34–5
The New Criticism, 35
Newman, Barnett, 137, 139, 146
New York World's Fair (1939–40), 147, 184,
　185–7, 251 n.61
Nichols, Leslie, 64
Niebuhr, Reinhold, 22
Nighthawks, 149
Nixon, Richard, 222
Nobel Prize (William Faulkner), 35, 36
　(Eugene O'Neill), 109
Noguchi, Isamu, 197
Normandy (D-Day) invasion, 55, 64, 215–16
Notorious, 127
Now Voyager, 124
Nuremberg Trials, 52

Objective Burma!, 118, 119
Odets, Clifford, 156
Off-Broadway, 98
Office of Facts and Figures, 171, 228–9 n.42
O'Keeffe, Georgia, 144, 145, 146, 148–9

Oklahoma!, 97, 101–2
O'Neal, Frederick, 107
O'Neill, Eugene, 100, 108–9, 110, 111
One Lonely Night, 39
One Man's Family, 79
Onement series, 139
One Out of Seven, 72, 77–8
One Touch of Venus, 102
One World, 22, 45
On the Town, 96, 100
On Whitman Avenue, 106
Operation Crossroads, 222
Oppenheimer, J. Robert, 18, 19
'Orchestrated Hell', 70
Origins of Totalitarianism, 227–8 n.22
Ornitz, Samuel, 122
Orozco, José Clemente, 148
Oscars (Academy Awards), 43, 78, 113, 114,
   118, 120, 123, 128, 129, 216, 223
Ospital, John, 204, 205–6, 207
Other Voices, Other Rooms, 45
Our Lan', 106
Our Miss Brooks, 73–4
Our Town, 108
OWI (Office of War Information), 61, 65,
   118, 119, 125, 150, 170–3

Painting 1948-D, 140
Pal Joey, 102
Panama Hattie, 102
Paramount Consent Decrees, 112–13
Parker, Charlie, 92
Parsons, Louella, 55
partitioning of India and Pakistan, 52
The Passion of Christ, 146
The Passion of Sacco and Vanzetti, 136
Past Imperfect, 45
Patton, General George S., 68, 211
Paul, Eliot, 45
Pearl Harbor, 1, 10, 16, 51, 147, 165
Pearl Harbor, 214
Pearl Harbor and the African Queen, 152
Pearson, Drew, 66, 68
Peck, Gregory, 128
Pegler, Westbrook, 55–6
Pelvis series, 149
The Pepsodent Show, 73
performance art, 169–70
Petry, Ann, 39–40
The Philadelphia Story, 240–1 n.47
Picasso, Pablo, 137, 143, 146
'Pictograph' series 139
Pierce, Elijah, 152

pink flamingoes, 251 n.66
Pinky, 128–29
Pippin, Horace, 152, 155–6, 168
The Pittsburgh Courier, 46, 48, 54–5, 57, 76
Platoon, 215
plastic, 183
PM, 8, 46–7, 56
The Pride of the Marines, 117
Poitier, Sydney, 107
Pollock, Jackson, 137, 138–9, 143–4, 243–4
   n.10
Pool Parlour, 148
Pope Paul VI, 21
Porter, Cole, 101–3, 105
Porter, James, 147, 152
Porter, Katherine Anne, 35
Post, Emily, 191, 251 n.71
Powell, Bud, 92
Powell, Congressman Adam Clayton, 68
Pozo, Chano, 92
precisionism, 136
Prelude to War, 124
Pride of the Marines, 129
Priestley, J. B., 70
Production Code, 119, 133
Progressive Party, 16
propaganda, 170–3
Pyle, Ernie, 59, 211, 235 n.96

Rabi, I. I., 19
race riots, 12–13, 182, 204, 250 n.51
racism, 179, 181–3, 189, 228–9 n.42, 239–40
   n.22
   in film, 119, 128–9
Radar, 165
Rafferty, Keith, 221, 222
Rafferty, Pierce, 221, 222
Rains, Claude, 118
Rand, Ayn, 39, 121, 122
Randolph, A. Philip, 12
Rankin, Allen, 152
Ransom, John Crowe, 35
rationing, 175–8
Rawlings, Marjorie Kinnan, 45
Read, Herbert, 143
Reader's Digest, 46, 48, 49, 50
Reagan, Ronald, 121, 122, 223
Rebecca, 126
Red Channels, 123
The Red Pony, 95
Red Ryder, 80, 165
Reinhardt, Ad, 139–40
Reston, James, 56, 230 n.71

Rich, Buddy, 82
Riddle, Nelson, 88
A Rising Wind, 13
Rivera, Diego, 146
Robards, Jr, Jason, 108
The Robber Bridegroom 44
Robbins, Jerome, 96, 100
Robin, Leo, 100
Robinson, Edward G., 123, 132
Robinson, Jackie, 201
Rochester (aka Eddie Anderson), 77, 78–9
Rockwell, Norman, 135, 144–5, 149, 154,
    156–60, 161, 171, 207
Rodeo, 95
Rodgers, Richard, 97, 100, 101–2, 104, 112
Rodman, Selden, 156
Rogers, Ginger, 120, 121, 122
Rogers, Leila, 121, 122
Rogers, Roy, 94, 165
The Romance of Helen Trent, 79
Romberg, Sigmund, 102
Rome, Harold, 104
Rooney, Andy, 208–10
Roosevelt, Eleanor, 49, 65, 106
Roosevelt, Franklin Delano (FDR), 5, 9, 10,
    16, 33, 47, 48, 52, 55, 66, 69, 103, 114,
    136, 158, 185, 211
Roosevelt (FDR) Memorial, 221, 223, 225
Rope, 127
Rosenberg, Ethel, 222
Rosenberg, Harold, 137
Rosenberg, Julius, 222
Rosenthal, Joe, 218, 220
Rosie the Riveter, 173, 231 n.96
Rossen, Robert, 121–2, 123
Rothko, Mark, 136, 139, 140
Rubin, Jerry, 123
Russell, Harold, 128
Russell, Jane, 90
Russell, Rosalind, 240–1 n.47
Rushing, Jimmy, 87

Saarinen, Eero, 188, 196, 197
Saboteur, 126, 127
Sahara, 118
The Sands of Iwo Jima, 118
Saroyan, William, 38
Sartre, Jean Paul, 6–7, 142
The Saturday Evening Post, 46, 49, 50, 59,
    156–7, 159, 160, 161
The Saturday Review, 21, 53–4
Savage, Augusta, 147
Saving Private Ryan, 202, 215, 216

Schaeffer, Mead, 161
Schindler's List, 202
Schomburg Center/Library, 107, 147
Schulberg, Bud, 122
Schultz, Sigrid, 59
Schuyler, George, 57
Scott, Adrian, 122
Scott, Howard, 161–2
screwball comedy, 240–1 n.47
Scruggs, Earl, 93
Seamstress, 148
Seduction of the Innocent, 166
Seeger, Pete, 95
See Here, Private Hargrove (1942), 45
segregation
    armed forces, 12, 13, 48, 118, 119, 146, 148,
        228–9 n.42
    in music, 86–7, 90–2
    on stage 104
    in film, 119, 125
self-taught artists, 135
Sengstacke, John, 54–5
Sennett, Max, 239 n.4
Sergeant York, 117
service flags, 179
Sevareid, Eric, 64, 70
The Seven Lively Arts, 103
The Shadow, 80
Shadow of a Doubt, 126
Shahn, Ben, 136, 146, 159
Shannon, Charles, 153
Sharecroppers, 146
Shaw, Artie, 82, 84–5, 86–7, 88
Shaw, Irwin, 37
Sheean, Vincent, 70
Sherrod, Robert, 235 n.96
Sherwood, Robert E., 103
Shirer, William, 64, 65
Shore, Dinah, 89, 90
Shuster, Joe, 162, 163
Siebel, Frederick, 172
Siegel, Jerry, 162, 163
silk stockings, 173
Silkwood, 223
Silly Putty, 191, 252 n.76
Silver Bedhead, 142
Silvers, Phil, 100
Simms, Hilda, 107
Since You Went Away, 117, 120
Skelton, Red, 74
The Skin of Our Teeth, 108
Slaughterhouse Five, 203
Sledge, E. B., 211, 254 n.38

Slim Gaillard Quartette, 238 n.91
Slinky, 191, 252 n.76
Smith, Betty, 45
Smith, Kate, 89
SNAFU (situation normal: all fouled up), 202, 204, 226
social problem films, 127–30
social realism, 136
Something for the Boys, 102
Song of Russia, 122
So Proudly We Hail, 121
Sorry, Wrong Number, 80
South Pacific, 104–5
Southern Agrarians, 35
southern literature, 33, 35, 41–5
Soviet Union, 15, 17–18, 20, 21, 25–8, 222, 223
Spanish Civil War, 64, 145
Spellbound, 126
Spielberg, Steven, 202, 210, 215, 216
Spillane, Mickey, 37, 38
Spock, Benjamin, 250 n.55
Stage Door Canteen, 98–9, 123
Stalin, Josef, 15, 16, 172, 185, 227–8 n.22
Stanislavsky, Konstantin, 110
Stanwyck, Barbara, 132–3, 240–1 n.47
Staples, Roebuck 'Pops', 93
Star and Garter, 100
Stars and Stripes, 208–9
Stewart, James, 124
St. Louis Woman, 104
Steinbeck, John, 39–40, 113
Stieglitz, Alfred, 148
Stimson, Henry L. 18
Stone, I. F., 47, 56–7, 59
Stone, Oliver, 215
Stormy Weather, 125
Strange Fruit, 106
The Stranger, 115
Strayhorn, Billy
streamform, 187
The Street, 39–40, 232 n.16
A Streetcar Named Desire, 110
Street Scene, 99
Strictly a Sharpshooter, 160
Stuart, Jessie, 45
Sturges, Preston, 117, 240–1 n.47
Still Clyfford, 139–40
Styne, Jule, 100
Sub-Mariner, 164
suburban conformity, 28, 131, 189
Suddenly Last Summer, 110
Sullavan, Margaret, 121

Summer and Smoke, 110
Sunset Boulevard, 241 n.54
Superman, 162, 163–4
Superman (character), 80, 168
surrealism, 136, 138
Suspense, 80
Suspicion, 126
Swing, Raymond Gram, 66–7
synthetic materials, 169, 191, 194–6

Tanguy, Yves, 143
Taps for Private Tussie, 45
Taylor, Robert, 121, 122
T. B. Harlem, 136
Teague, Walter Dorwin, 186, 187
television, 65, 72, 191
Teller, Edward, 19
Temple, Shirley, 120
Tender Comrade, 120, 122
Terkel, Studs, 207–8, 215, 226
Terry, Clark, 87
Terry, Sonny, 95
Testament, 223
Thatcher, Margaret, 223
They Were Expendable (memoir), 45
    (film), 121
The Thin Red Line, 204, 216
The Third Man, 115
The 39 Steps, 130
Thirty Seconds over Tokyo, 118, 119
This Damn Tree Leaks, 45
This is the Army, 100, 103
Til the End of Time, 128
Thomas, Congressman John Parnell, 68, 122
Thomas, Lowell, 66, 67, 70
Thompson, Dorothy, 59, 65, 66
306 studio, 146, 147
The Thunderstorm, 154
Time, 46, 50, 51, 161
Tobey, Mark, 137
Tombstones, 148
Tom Sawyer series, 160
Tony Awards, 99
Tooker, George, 144
Touch of Evil, 115
Traylor, Bill, 144, 152, 153–4
Tregaskis, Richard, 45, 118
A Tree Grows in Brooklyn (1942), 45
Trinity Test at Alamagordo, New Mexico, 19
Truman Doctrine, 25–26
Truman, Harry S., 12, 16–17, 18, 21, 25–6, 47, 55, 66, 154, 181, 201

Trumbo, Dalton, 122
TV dinners, 169, 191, 192
Tupper, Earl J., 188, 195–6
Tupperware, 176, 188, 195–6
Turk, Jerry, 255 n.42
Turner, Joe, 237 n.49

Ultimate Paintings, 140
Underground to Palestine, 56–7
Understanding Fiction, 35
United Nations Organization, 22, 52
Up Front, 45
Up in Central Park, 102

Vann, Robert L., 48, 55, 76
Van Vechten, Carl, 99
Vaughn, Sara, 89
Vera Vague (aka Barbara Jo Allen), 90
Veteran's History Project, 226
V/Victory campaign, 170, 173, 175
victory gardens, 175, 179, 182
Victory Vase, 156
Vietnam War, 61, 89, 202, 203–4, 214–15
Vonnegut, Kurt, 203

WAACS (Women's Army Auxiliary Corps),
    174, 249 n.16
'The Vagabonds', 77
Waldorf Statement, 123
Walker, Robert, 117, 121
Wallace, Henry, 16, 54van der Rohe, Mies,
    140–2, 196
Warner, Jack, 121, 122
Warren, Robert Penn, 35, 41–3, 233 n.28
The War, (memoir, Willis, ed.), 211
    (documentary, Burns, dir.), 226
The War that Refreshes: The Four Delicious
    Freedoms, 159
Wartime, 202, 204, 206–7, 211, 214
Watch on the Rhine, 106
Waters, Ethel, 45, 103, 104, 125
Waters, Muddy, 92
WAVES (Women Accepted for Volunteer
    Emergency Services), 174
Wayne, John, 118, 165
Webb, Chick, 82, 86
Webb, Jack, 77–8
Weegee (aka Arthur Feller), 47
Weill, Kurt, 99, 102, 104
Welles, Orson, 103, 114–16, 123, 133
Welty, Eudora, 35, 44
A Well-Wrought Urn, 35

Wertham, Fredric, 166, 167
We Wore Jump Boots and Baggy Pants, 204,
    205–6
Whalen, Grover, 185
Where's Charley?, 100
'White Christmas', 88
White, Walter, 13, 15, 17
White, William L., 45
Wilder, Billy, 131, 241 n.54
Wilder, Thornton, 108
Williams, Cootie, 85, 86
Williams, Hank, 93
Williams, Tennessee, 100, 109–10, 112
Williamson, Sonny Boy, 92
Willie Gillis series 158
Willis, Clint, 211, 254 n.38, 254–5 n.40
Willkie, Wendell, 16, 22, 45, 48, 54
Wilson, Dooley, 103, 125
Wilson, Ed, 145
Wilson, Teddy, 86
Winchell, Walter, 55, 66, 67, 68–9, 70
Wise, Brownie, 196
With the Old Breed at Peleliu and Okinawa,
    211, 254 n.38
The Wizard of Oz, 103
Wollstonecraft, Mary, 30
Woman series, 138
Wonder Woman, 165
Wood, Maxine, 106
Woodruff, Hale, 146, 147
World Trade Center bombings, 1–2
World War II Memorial, 225
WPA (Works Progress Administration), 136,
    147
Wright, Frank Lloyd, 140
Wright, Mary, 190, 196
Wright, Richard, 37, 38, 40–41
Wright, Russel, 32, 187, 188, 189–91, 196
Wyeth, Andrew, 144, 145, 146, 149–50, 245
    n.49
Wyeth, N. C., 150
Wyler, William, 127–8
Wylie, Philip, 29, 30

Yordan, Philip, 107
You Bet Your Life, 73
You'll Never Get Rich, 117, 125
The Young Lions, 37–8
Young, Loretta, 115
Your Hit Parade, 81

zoot-suit riots, 13, 250 n.51